The Wisdom and Foolishness of God

The Wisdom and Foolishness of God

First Corinthians 1–2 in Theological Exploration

Christophe Chalamet and
Hans-Christoph Askani, editors

Fortress Press
Minneapolis

THE WISDOM AND FOOLISHNESS OF GOD

First Corinthians 1–2 in Theological Exploration

Cover image: Albrecht Dürer, Christ Nailed to the Cross, c. 1509-10. Woodcut. Rosenwald Collection.

Cover design: Tory Herman

Library of Congress Cataloging-in-Publication Data

Print ISBN: 978-1-4514-9020-6

eBook ISBN: 978-1-5064-0151-5

The paper used in this publication meets the minimum requirements of American National Standard for Information Sciences — Permanence of Paper for Printed Library Materials, ANSI Z329.48-1984.

Manufactured in the U.S.A.

This book was produced using Pressbooks.com, and PDF rendering was done by PrinceXML.

Contents

Abbreviations   ix

Introduction   xi
Christophe Chalamet and Hans-Christoph Askani

1. Crucifixion as Wisdom: Exploring the Ideology of a Disreputable Social Movement   *1*
John M. G. Barclay

2. The Weakness of God: A Radical Theology of the Cross   *21*
John D. Caputo

3. On a Road Not Taken: Iterations of an Alexandrian Paul   *67*
Kellen Plaxco

4. Maximus the Confessor on the Foolishness of God and the Play of the Word   *89*
Andrew Louth

5. Paul's Refusal of Wisdom in Aquinas's *Commentary on 1 Corinthians*: Notes on Philosophy in the *Summa of Theology*   *101*
Adam Eitel

6. Election and Providence in the Theology of   119
    Thomas Aquinas: Reading the *Summa* in Light of
    His Commentary of 1 Corinthians 1–2
    Michael T. Dempsey

7. Luther's *Theologica Paradoxa* in Erasmus and   139
    Cusanus
    Günter Bader

8. The Cross of Wisdom: Ambiguities in Turning   167
    Down Apologetics (Paul, Anselm, Barth)
    Anthony Feneuil

9. The Wisdom in God's Foolishness: Karl Barth's   183
    Exegesis of 1 Corinthians 1–2
    Andrew R. Hay

10. The Word of the Cross in the Conflict of   201
    Interpretive Power: On the Genealogy of
    Theology Deriving from the Spirit of Pauline
    Rhetoric
    Philipp Stoellger

11. On Justification and Beyond—An Attempt   239
    Matthias D. Wüthrich

12. The Foolishness and Wisdom of All God's Ways: 261
    The Case of Creation
    Ex Nihilo
    Kathryn Tanner

13. Witnessing to the Cross, Forgetting Human Sin: 289
    A Systematic-Theological Inquiry in the "Word
    of the Cross" (1 Cor. 1:18)
    Henning Theissen

14. The Cross of Christ and God's Power   307
    Marc Vial

15. God's Weakness and Power 325
    Christophe Chalamet

16. The Paradox of Faith 341
    Hans–Christoph Askani

17. "To Know Nothing Except Jesus Christ, and 359
    Him Crucified": Supralapsarian Christology and a
    Theology of the Cross
    Edwin Chr. van Driel

    Contributors 383
    Index of Names 387

Abbreviations

AWA	Archiv zur Weimar Ausgabe
BCG	Buchreihe der Cusanus-Gesellschaft
BGPhMA.NF	Beiträge zur Geschichte der Philosophie (und Theologie) des Mittelalters. Neue Folge.
BHTh	Beiträge zur historischen Theologie
BoA	*Luthers Werk in Auswahl* (Bonn)
BThSt	Biblisch-theologische Studien
BZNW	Beihefte zur *Zeitschrift für die neutestamentliche Wissenschaft*
CD	Karl Barth, *Church Dogmatics*
EKK	Evangelisch-katholischer Kommentar
ETR	*Études théologiques et religieuses*
EvTh	*Evangelische Theologie*
GS	*Gesammelte Studien*
HBS	History of Biblical Studies
HNT	Handbuch zum Neuen Testament
HSCL	Harvard Studies in Comparative Literature
HUTh	Hermeneutische Untersuchungen zur Theologie
IJST	*International Journal of Systematic Theology*
JBL	*Journal of Biblical Literature*
JR	*Journal of Religion*

JSNT	*Journal for the Study of the New Testament*
KD	Karl Barth, *Kirchliche Dogmatik*
KKTS	Konfessionskundliche und kontroverstheologische Studien
LW	*Luther's Works*
LW.NS	*Luther's Works*, New Series
PG	*Patrologia graeca*
PL	*Patrologia latina*
RGG	*Religion in Geschichte und Gegenwart*
SC	Sources chrétiennes
TCL	Textes cunéiformes. Musée du Louvre
ThBT	Theologische Bibliothek Töpelmann
ThLZ	*Theologische Literaturzeitung*
TRE	*Theologische Realenzyklopädie*
VerFor	*Verkündigung und Forschung*
WA	*Luthers Werke: Kritische Gesamtausgabe* [*Schriften*] (Weimar Ausgabe)
WABr	*Luthers Werke: Kritische Gesamtausgabe: Briefwechsel*
WATr	*Luthers Werke: Kritische Gesamtausgabe: Tischreden*
WUNT	Wissenschaftliche Untersuchungen zum Neuen Testament

Introduction

Christophe Chalamet and Hans-Christoph Askani

"It would be very unfortunate for us if, because of distraction or cowardice, we no longer heard the three most fateful expressions which will determine the future of Christianity even more than they determined its past: Logos of the Cross—God's foolishness—God's Power." –Stanislas Breton[1]

"Claiming to be wise, they became fools."–Rom. 1:22

The present volume gathers most of the papers presented at an international theological conference held May 23–25, 2013, at the University of Geneva and organized by the *Faculté de théologie protestante* and the *Institut romand de systématique et d'éthique* (IRSE) of that University. The conference's main purposes were to examine the first two chapters of Paul's First Epistle to the Corinthians, (aspects of) the reception of these chapters in the history of theology, and, in a constructive approach, their potential meaning today. The fact that two systematic theologians (the co-editors of this book) and a historian of early Christianity (Enrico Norelli) were the main

---

1. Stanislas Breton, *Unicité et monothéisme* (Paris: Cerf, 1981), 156.

organizers of the conference probably has something to do with the fact that the last two purposes (the history of interpretation and the constructive engagement with Paul's text) overshadowed the first (the actual exegesis of the text), despite the contribution of John M. G. Barclay, one of the most distinguished scholars of Paul today, as a keynote speaker. But the conference signaled something very clearly, namely that one is never finished thinking about "the word of the cross" and the foolishness and power of God's ways as manifested, "crucially" according to the Christian faith, in Jesus of Nazareth's passion and death. What does it mean that, according to Christianity, the one who is confessed to be God's emissary, God's own Son, suffered such an atrocious end, a "death by torture" which is the fate of blasphemers according to Deut. 21:23 ("anyone hung on a tree is under God's curse,"), a verse of course well known to Paul and the earliest communities ("Christ bought us freedom from the curse of the law by coming under the curse for our sake; for scripture says, 'Cursed is everyone who who hangs on a tree'," Gal. 3:13)?

Right from the beginning of what would eventually become known as "Christianity"—that is, a religious movement distinct from Judaism—the disciples of the crucified Galilean named Jesus had to wrestle with that massive, shocking event. In the history of reception of Paul's text, one encounters moments when its shock value was acknowledged and even magnified—the name of Martin Luther immediately comes to mind, but Friedrich Nietzsche's call for a "transvaluation of all values," as well as certain passages in his works, in the midst of his deeply adversarial position with regard to Paul, certainly owe much to Paul's text as well.[2] We, on the other hand,

---

2. "Obtuse to all Christian terminology, modern people can no longer relate to the hideous superlative found by an ancient taste in the paradoxical formula 'god on the cross.' Nowhere to date has there been such a bold inversion or anything quite as horrible, questioning, and questionable as this formula. It promised a revaluation of all the values of antiquity." Friedrich Nietzsche, *Beyond Good and Evil: Prelude to a Philosophy of the Future*, ed. Rolf-Peter Horstmann

are now so accustomed to commemorating and celebrating Jesus' crucifixion, and have seen so many deep or superficial artistic depictions of it (including pendants and earrings), that the shock is incomparably smaller, indeed, almost nonexistent. Similarly, in various periods of Christian history, the "edge" or the "radicality" of Paul's text was somewhat smoothened, as claims about divine power in connection with imperial politics overshadowed Paul's dialectics of weakness and power—but where and when, and how exactly, did that happen? We better leave the answer open at this point, noting, however, that radical interpretations of the "word of the cross" coexisted simultaneously with marginalizations of it. In many respects, the various interpretive options in the history of (especially Western) Christian theology reflected, and had an impact on, diverging decisions with regard to theistic notions of divine omnipotence and majesty. The Eastern tradition, for its part, has at times read 1 Corinthians 1–2 through its apophatic lens—that is, through its acute sense that human language is utterly unable to grasp who God is in God's very being (see Andrew Louth's contribution to the volume, ch. 4), not just because of the inadequacy of human words and language, but also and above all because of who God is.

The question Paul's text raises does not simply concern the figure of Jesus, confessed as the crucified Christ, but also the community, where few "were wise by human standards," few "were powerful, … of noble birth." God "chose what is low and despised in the world, things that are not, to reduce to nothing things that are" (1 Cor. 1:26b, 28). The two keynote lectures of the conference, with which the present volume opens, both address what Paul calls τὰ μὴ ὄντα ("things that are not," 1 Cor. 1:28), in exegetical-sociological-

---

and Judith Norman (Cambridge: Cambridge University Press, 2002), 44. Anders Nygren adds: "Nietzsche can well be described as the modern exponent of Paul's statement in 1 Cor. 1.23." *Agape and Eros* (London: SPCK, 1953), 202n2. See also Jean-Luc Marion, *Dieu sans l'être* (Paris: Presses universitaires de France, 2013), 135.

theological perspectives (see John Barclay's contribution, "Crucifixion as Wisdom: Exploring the Ideology of a Disreputable Social Movement") as well as in philosophical-theological perspectives (John D. Caputo, on "The Weakness of God: A Radical Theology of the Cross"). These two distinguished scholars signal the importance of Paul's opening sections in 1 Corinthians for our understanding of earliest Christianity and of Paul's "message of the cross," not just as an idea or a thought but also as a physical and social phenomenon (Barclay), and for further reflection about divine power and weakness, where weakness and power are not simply two successive moments (the cross followed by Easter Sunday) in which the resurrection reverses divine weakness in a Hollywood-like final triumph or, worse even, revenge (Caputo). Whether contemporary theologians, not to mention biblical exegetes, can embrace Caputo's "weakness-trip"[3] remains to be seen. His challenge to Christian theology and Christian proclamation, however, must be heard.

In "On a Road Not Taken: Iterations of an Alexandrian Paul," Kellen Plaxco examines Clement, Origen, and Didymus the Blind's interpretations of 1 Corinthians 1–2, wondering why the Alexandrian school is so different from the Western, and especially the modern and late-modern, emphasis on the opposition between worldly wisdom and the word of the cross. The beginning section of 1 Corinthians barely appears, for instance, in Didymus's writings. In the process of his study, Plaxco uncovers some of the diverging interpretations of "Wisdom" in these thinkers, showing how Origen relates it exclusively to the Son, whereas Didymus links it to the Son *and* the Spirit.

Andrew Louth, an eminent scholar of the Eastern theological tradition, studies the interpretation of 1 Corinthians 1–2 in three

---

3. Philipp Stoellger's expression, in the discussion that ensued following Caputo's paper; see below, 60–61.

of its greatest thinkers: John Chrysostom, Maximus the Confessor, and Pseudo-Dionysius. The results, as with Plaxco's contribution, confirm how different the Eastern tradition of scriptural interpretation often has been from the Western one. Whereas Chrysostom underlines the link between what appears as divine foolishness and the incarnation, in Dionysius the themes of divine foolishness and wisdom are embedded in a broader interpretation that combines cataphatic and apophatic moments: playing foolishness against wisdom contributes to the strategy of pointing out the alterity and transcendence of divine wisdom. In his *Ambigua*, Maximus the Confessor combines these two interpretive strands before suggesting that divine foolishness can be understood in terms of a divine "play with the Word": God's Word dwells among human beings, expressing puzzling parables and stories.

Turning to medieval Scholastic theology, more precisely to Thomas Aquinas, and painting a different picture than is commonly known, Adam Eitel suggests we use caution when we conceive of the great Scholastic thinker as a "philosopher" or as a "philosophical theologian." Such characterizations are closer to Pope Leo XIII's vision of Aquinas than to Aquinas's own perception of himself and his works. Studying closely Aquinas's commentary on 1 Corinthians 1–2, Eitel shows the rather limited role of human wisdom may play, according to the Scholastic theologian, in doctrinal reflection. The *Summa theologiae*'s first pages ("Prologue" and first question) and his commentary on 1 Corinthians converge in showing that inadequate use of philosophical resources risks "emptying the cross" or rendering it void (1 Cor. 1:17). Also focusing on Thomas Aquinas as biblical scholar, and making similar points, Michael Dempsey focuses on the theme of divine sovereignty and government over and in the world (divine providence), as well as the question of the objects, in creation, of God's election: Who does God elect? In Dempsey's reading of Aquinas, and with an emphasis on the great Scholastic thinker as a mendicant theologian, it is the *"abjectus* or the destitute that stands as the end of God's election in Jesus Christ" (125). Human wisdom thus finds itself radically challenged and undermined, as God's government of the world "subvert[s] human arrogance and the domination of the powerful over the powerless" (136).

In his contribution, Günter Bader examines the "epidemic of paradoxes" that characterizes the Renaissance and Luther's theology, comparing and contrasting Erasmus's and Cusanus's uses of paradoxes. Erasmus was notoriously adverse to paradoxes, but that doesn't mean paradoxes are absent from his works. Several types of paradoxes may be identified: the "rhetorical paradox," which is indirect, implicit, nameless, its explicit version having been banished from discourse. The "rhetorical paradox" comprises a "first-degree" paradox, which upends everything and, as a result, reveals the wisdom of the fool. The "second-degree" paradox arises when a "second level of speaking comes through," saying "the exact opposite of what has been said, effectively canceling it" (151). The logical paradox, especially prized by Cusanus as a mathematician-logician, seeks to respect the law of non-contradiction, for the sake of the scientificity of the philosophical discourse. Finally, something which may be called the "theological paradox" is at hand when another voice and another language is—and *must* be—heard, as may be the case in the occurrence of *prosopopeia*. In his dense and learned contribution, Günter Bader uncovers instances of these various paradoxes in the writings of Erasmus and Cusanus.

Recalling Anselm's interpretation of the "fool" (*insipiens*), Anthony Feneuil delves into the ambiguities of the decision, still frequent in many quarters of modern theology, to reject apologetics. In what name do we reject apologetics? In the name of a sort of fideism, which postulates that the theme of theology lies beyond what can be demonstrated by reason, or in the name of skepticism? Taking a closer look at Anselm's supposed "proof" of God's existence, and following Karl Barth's interpretation, Feneuil argues that the true *insipiens* is the one who, convinced of the possibility of proving God's existence, thereby reveals the foolishness of his or her own "wisdom." And yet, Anselm wrote a proof in order to show the *insipiens*'s foolishness. Feneuil concludes that "it is just as foolish to deny apologetics in an absolute manner as it is to engage in apologetics on purely rational ground, through a bracketing of faith," and that the *insipiens*, who is a biblical and, indeed, a faith character, is not simply the "other," for the theologian is always already exposed to unbelief (176–77).

How did one of the great theologians of the twentieth century, namely Karl Barth, interpret 1 Corinthians 1–2? Andrew Hay seeks to answer that question by focusing on Barth's commentary of Paul's epistle, published in 1924, which Rudolf Bultmann warmly, if not uncritically, recommended. Placing this commentary in the context of Barth's works in those years (lectures on the Reformed confessions, the first full cycle of lectures on the main *loci* of systematic theology), Hay shows how 1 Corinthians 1–2 confirmed Barth in his rejection of natural theology and his attempt to think theologically ἀπὸ τοῦ θεοῦ (literally, "from God").

In "The Word of the Cross in the Conflict of Interpretive Power: On the Genealogy of Theology Deriving From the Spirit of Pauline Rhetoric," Philip Stoellger develops a complex and fruitful reflection on how a powerful word (*Wortmacht*) may become distorted into a word of power (*Machtwort*), and how Paul's first chapters in 1 Corinthians reveal a deep-seated conflict over the interpretation of the gospel. Paul was not immune to the desire to legitimize his interpretation of the gospel through recourse not just to rhetorical and interpretive power, but to his God-given authority as apostle of

Jesus Christ. That is unfortunate, for "whoever has something to say wishes also to have the say but should not wish to have it, because by so doing that person undermines what she has to say" (234).

What about Paul's doctrine of justification by faith, which is certainly not present at the forefront in the Corinthian correspondence? Shifting from the "word of the cross" to modern transformations and reductions of "justification" and the contemporary lack of relevance of that key Protestant doctrine, Matthias D. Wüthrich reflects, using Martin Walser's book on justification as a springboard, on the place and meaning of "justification by faith" in Christian soteriological discourses, advocating that theology move "beyond" justification so as to recover the breadth of the scriptural witness and attempt to reconnect it with our modern world.

In another significant shift, away from the central *locus* of reconciliation to the doctrine of creation, Kathryn Tanner explores the ways in which Christian theology sought (and seeks) to make sense both of God's transcendence and of God's involvement in the world, "raiding" and twisting categories it finds in many different fields of discourses, repudiating "all ordinary canons of sense making" (264). The doctrine of creation *ex nihilo* is the Christian attempt to express God's radical otherness and involvement simultaneously, beyond emanationist or pantheist interpretations of creation.

Drawing on Paul Ricoeur as well as on philosophical and theological reflections on the notions of "witness," "word," and "symbol," Henning Theissen distinguishes "the cross" from "the word of the cross." Whereas the cross itself is "soteriologically mute" (Ingolf U. Dalferth), the word of the cross is at the beginning of soteriological discourses in Christian theology; the christological word of the cross grounds the apostolic word of the cross. The word of the cross, as wisdom of the cross, "teaches those who bear witness to it new understandings of God's wisdom and makes them forget the old ones" (302). What that means, in relation to God's grace and freedom, is that God's freedom, far from signifying "unlimited sovereignty," means in fact God's readiness to repent and to show mercy.

But it is not just divine "freedom" that finds itself recalibrated by the word of the cross. The same goes for divine power, as Marc Vial shows. Divine omnipotence needs to be thought about, not just in relation to the presence of evil in our world, not just in connection with theodicy, as is often the case (Vial mentions the example of Hans Jonas), but also and above all in relation with the event of the cross. Then theologians will learn to think about divine power without reducing it to a "capacity to intervene in history in order to change its course" (309). Following Eberhard Jüngel, Vial suggests we consider the notion of omnipotence not in an abstract way but as a predicate with a specific subject: God, whose Son is the crucified and the risen one.

Along similar lines, Christophe Chalamet explores some of the ways in which Calvin interprets 1 Corinthians 1–2, particularly Paul's boldest claims concerning divine power and weakness, as well as divine wisdom and foolishness. Are there Docetic tendencies in Calvin's interpretation, and more broadly in his Christology, as some have suggested? Was Calvin, as a theologian focused on divine majesty and glory, "deaf" to Luther's *theologia crucis*? An affirmative answer to that question does not seem warranted.

Hans-Christoph Askani seeks to retrieve the radicality of Paul's assertions in the first chapters of 1 Corinthians, in critical conversation with several translations and commentaries of Paul's text. Where many are intent on finding a resolution of Paul's paradoxes and a harmonious conclusion to his conflicting claims about human wisdom and divine foolishness, Askani, pondering the reversal of human through God's altogether different logic, aims to show that such reconciliations are too hasty. The text bothers and disturbs us, because something comes to expression in the text that Paul himself was unable to control or master.

Last, but not least, Edwin Chr. van Driel raises the question of the compatibility between his own supralapsarian Christology, whereby the event of the incarnation is not simply a response to sin ("plan B") but, rather, is part of God's overall plan, and what he calls "cross theologies." In several ways, supralapsarian Christology can be seen as an ally of some of the theologies of the cross, for both approaches seek to interpret the cross not as conditioned by sin, but within a broader narrative of God's unconditional, gracious, and prevenient relation to the world. But a supralapsarian approach contests what theologians of the cross at times seek to defend, namely that forgiveness follows from an acknowledgment of sin, that despair is the first step toward being reconciled with God, and it also contests J. Louis Martyn's apocalyptic interpretation of Paul's theology, an interpretation which presupposes that the incarnation is contingent upon sin.

* * *

Throughout the book, the abbreviations generally follow Siegfried M. Schwertner, *Abkürzungsverzeichnis*, 2nd ed., *Theologische Realenzyklopädie* (Berlin: W. de Gruyter, 1994).

The editors of the present volume, who, along with Enrico Norelli, were the main organizers of the conference, wish to thank the following people for their assistance during the conference and in the preparation of this book: Brigitte Dugué and Sabine Tschannen, both of the Faculté de théologie (University of Geneva), Vjollca Ahmeti, Andreas Dettwiler, Lorraine Dubuis, Anthony Feneuil, Christine

Hahn, Mathias Hassenfratz (who also helped prepare the index), Mariel Mazzocco, Matthieu Mégevand, and Janique Perrin.

Crucifixion as Wisdom: Exploring the Ideology of a Disreputable Social Movement

John M. G. Barclay

The title of this volume—*The Wisdom and the Foolishness of God*—is drawn from the paradoxical maxim that Paul enunciates in 1 Cor. 1:25: "for the foolishness of God is wiser than human wisdom, and the weakness of God is stronger than human strength" (translations from the New Testament my own). Paul's arresting expression borders on blasphemy: to speak of the foolishness and the weakness of God is to contradict standard assumptions about the divine, assumptions necessary to maintain God's status as God. The way Paul's maxim has reverberated down the centuries, spawning one form of radical theology after another, is one of the central threads of this volume.[1] In this essay I aim to place this expression in the *literary* context of the opening chapters of 1 Corinthians, and in the *historical* context of the Greco-Roman world. I will focus on the way Paul associates this wisdom/folly polarity with the *crucifixion* of Jesus, and on the multiple ironic effects of this association. In particular, I will argue that we should hear "wisdom" and "folly" not merely in intellectual terms, as rationality or illogic, but as umbrella labels for the presence or absence of "civilized" values. Paul's declarations about the "folly" of the crucifixion correspond, I will suggest, to the social experience of the early Christians, a disreputable movement whose subversive stance toward Greco-Roman culture was founded on, and given deep ideological support by, the Pauline message of "Christ crucified."

Wisdom, Foolishness and Webs of Association in 1 Corinthians 1–4

Paul's statement that "the foolishness of God is wiser than human wisdom" (1 Cor. 1:25) forms the conclusion to his description of the content of his preaching: "we preach Christ crucified, a stumbling block to Jews and folly to Gentiles, but to those who are called, both Jews and Greeks, Christ the power of God and the wisdom of God" (1:23-24). For Paul the foolishness of God is evidenced very specifically in an *event*, the event that formed the core of his "good news": the crucifixion of Jesus. What is folly to Gentiles but wisdom to those who are called is not in this context an abstract doctrine about God, nor a general analysis of divine activity in the world, but a highly particular event which is also the highly particular source of salvation: it is "the word of the cross" which is "folly to those

---

1. The essays show, however, that it has not always been read as culturally subversive. For reflection from the Lutheran perspective, see Vitor Westhelle, *The Scandalous God: The Use and Abuse of the Cross* (Minneapolis: Fortress Press, 2006).

who are perishing, but to us who are being saved it is the power of God" (1:18; cf. 2:1-2, 6-8). As these citations make clear, running alongside the polarity of wisdom and folly is another polarity, one of power and weakness: folly is closely associated with weakness, wisdom is linked to power. The two polarities are entwined, and they are shortly joined by a third, a contrast between the noble and the ignoble, or the honorable and the shameful. These latter terms appear alongside wise/foolish and powerful/weak as descriptors of the people who receive and embody the message of Christ crucified, both in 1:26-28 (regarding the Corinthian believers) and in 4:10 (regarding Paul). Thus, in the verses that immediately follow our paradoxical maxim (1:25), Paul urges the Corinthians to consider their own "calling": "not many of you were wise in human terms, not many were powerful, not many were of noble birth" (1:26). God chose what is foolish in the world, what is weak, what is ignoble or despicable, even the nothings or nobodies (1:27-28). This expansion and elaboration of categories alerts us to the fact that all these terms have *social* connotations: wisdom, power, and honor are overlapping characteristics that reach their acme among the elite, whose education, influence, and status give them the authority and the means to shape social norms.

The "wisdom," which is the target of Paul's ironic critique, is associated with a variety of representatives. At one point these are labeled "Greeks" ("Jews seek signs, and Greeks seek wisdom," 1:22), but "Greeks" seem practically interchangeable with the Gentiles (or "nations," ἔθνη), to whom the message of Christ crucified is folly (1:23). But in the majority of cases wisdom is associated in even more general terms with "the world" (ὁ κόσμος) or "this age" (ὁ αἰὼν οὗτος): "Has not God rendered foolish the wisdom of the world?" (1:20; cf. 1:21; 3:20); "Where is the wise man, where is the scribe, where is the dialectical debater of this age?" (1:20; cf. 2:6, 8). As has

3

often been noted, such denigrating references to "the world" or "this age" are characteristic of apocalyptic, with its dualistic configurations and its totalizing tendency to negative depictions of the world.[2] Paul regularly uses such language (cf. Gal. 1:4), but here its reference is primarily to the *people* who make up "the world": the wisdom of "this world" is the wisdom of "human beings" (ἄνθρωποι, 1:25), whose tendency to celebrate themselves is part of Paul's target throughout (1:29; 3:19). Thus, even if wisdom can be associated particularly with "Greeks," it is not confined to them. What is at stake is something endemic to humanity.

There is a similar breadth to the connotations of the term *wisdom*.[3] At times it is closely linked with speech (1:17; 2:1-5), but it hardly limited to the spoken realm of culture. Wisdom is also a form of perception or an epistemological stance: "by the wisdom of God, the world did not know God through wisdom" (1:21; cf. 2:6-10). It is also associated with canons of evaluation. The wisdom that Paul speaks among the mature (2:6) is able to evaluate (ἀνακρίνομαι) all things by the Spirit (2:15); it was in their misperception and erroneous evaluation that "the rulers of this age" crucified the one who was actually "the Lord of glory" (2:8). Criteria for evaluation and celebration are, in fact, the presenting issue that evokes this whole discussion of wisdom and folly. Disputes within the Corinthian church have evolved around the differential evaluation of various leaders (1:10-17), an issue to which Paul keeps returning (3:1-4, 18-23), especially in relation to himself and Apollos (3:4—4:6).[4] If the antidote to these disputes is not to "boast in human beings" (3:21),

---

2. E.g., Alexandra R. Brown, *The Cross and Human Transformation: Paul's Apocalyptic Word in 1 Corinthians* (Minneapolis: Fortress Press, 1995).

3. For discussion, see Duane Litfin, *St Paul's Theology of Proclamation: 1 Corinthians 1-4 and Graeco-Roman Rhetoric* (Cambridge: Cambridge University Press, 1994).

4. For the background to these party groupings, see L. L. Welborn, "On the Discord in Corinth: 1 Corinthians 1-4 and Ancient Politics," *JBL* 106 (1987): 85–111.

and if that is made possible only by abandoning "the wisdom of this world" (3:18-20), it is clear that this "wisdom" entails a matrix of normative judgments concerning value or worth which Paul sees as still operative, and destructive, in the Corinthian church.

The rhetorical force of these chapters lies in the fact that they do not just *contrast* two forms of wisdom, God's wisdom and the wisdom of the world; they announce a divine intention to *overturn or destroy* the wisdom that is not God's own. Citing and adapting Isaiah 29, Paul declares early on God's aggressive intent: "I will *destroy* the wisdom of the wise, and the discernment of the discerning I will *thwart*" (1:19).[5] "Has not God *rendered foolish* the wisdom of the world?" (1:20). The wisdom of the cross is not just an alternative wisdom but an anti-wisdom, refuting or subverting what would normally be taken for granted. When he draws out the correlation of this message with the status of its recipients, Paul insists that God's election does not simply bypass the wise and powerful: it shames them by an act that confounds the normal ranking of status or honor (1:27-28). According to the third and climactic colon of this statement, "God has chosen what is ignoble in the world, and despicable, what is non-existent, *in order that he might render inoperative what exists*, so that no one should boast before God" (1:28-29).[6] The theme recurs elsewhere (e.g., 3:18-20), notably in connection with scriptural citations. To align oneself with the message of Christ crucified is not just to sidestep the wisdom framework of the world, but to disturb its claims and to confront its hegemony: "if anyone thinks he is wise in this age, *let him become a fool,* in order that he may be wise" (3:18).

---

5. Paul appears to have adapted the Greek version of this text, so that the last verb reads not "hide" but "thwart": the negative divine intent is thereby strengthened.

6. The verb καταργέω means to render inactive or inoperative (cf. 2:6; 15:24), not necessarily to destroy.

The Cross as Weakness and Foolishness

As a death penalty, crucifixion was designed to cause the maximum degradation of the body and the psyche over the longest possible period of time.[7] In the Roman era it was used freely and frequently in the execution of slaves, to the extent that it was known simply as the "slave punishment" (*servile supplicium*; e.g., Tacitus, *Hist.* 4.11). Slaves, who had no legal rights, could be put to death in any way one wanted, but the special semiotics of crucifixion—the ironic elevation of the tortured victim in the public gaze—provided a perfect deterrent to slaves who were liable to be seen as insubordinate or "uppity." The Romans also used crucifixion extensively for anyone, free or slave, who was perceived to challenge their authority in the provinces: as an instrument of torture and terror it was regularly used to quell revolts. Ever conscious of the "body language" of different forms of capital punishment, the Romans used crucifixion to inflict the greatest possible dehumanization.[8] Victims were brutally flogged, verbally abused, and psychologically humiliated; they were stripped naked, pinned to wood in various positions, and then hoisted high in a publicly visible spot; they were left to a long and excruciatingly slow death with the gradual loss of bodily control, until they died by suffocation; their corpses were then normally left for some time on the cross to be eaten by vultures, and thus denied the final moment of dignity, a burial by family or friends.

It is easy to see why Paul would consider "Christ crucified" the epitome of weakness. Victims were deliberately rendered powerless, as a punishment for usurping the power of their owners or political

---

7. The classic work remains Martin Hengel, *Crucifixion* (London: SCM Press, 1977).
8. On the body language used in punishments, see Maud W. Gleason, "Mutilated Messengers: Body Language in Josephus," in Simon Goldhill, ed., *Being Greek Under Rome: Cultural Identity, the Second Sophistic and the Development of Empire* (Cambridge: Cambridge University Press, 2001), 50–85.

masters: they were pinned to wood, unable to cover their nakedness, and taunted in their helplessness. Josephus talks of Roman soldiers nailing their victims up in various positions "by way of jest" (*War* 5.451), and recounts a case when the victims were required to watch their wives and children being slaughtered before their eyes, powerless to come to their defense (*War* 1.97-98; *Ant.* 13.380-83). In a world where physical integrity and strength were essential components of honor, it is hard to imagine any more exposed form of humiliating weakness: the crucified victim is as vulnerable and powerless as it is possible to imagine a living human individual to be.

It is less easy to see why Paul should also associate the crucified Christ with the motif of "folly" (μωρία). It has been common to interpret this at the intellectual level and to speak of the senselessness of imagining that divine salvation could be effected through so gruesome a death and so powerless a victim: the cross is folly inasmuch as it makes no sense within the rational structures of ancient theology.[9] However, recent research by Larry Welborn has opened up a new and more convincing approach.[10] In a detailed investigation of the figure of the fool (μωρός in Greek, *stultus* in Latin), especially as depicted in ancient mimes (the popular entertainment of the ancient world), Welborn has clarified the ancient associations of the terms *fool* and *folly*. The "fool" is the object of ridicule and contempt in at least four interconnected respects. Physically, the fool is depicted as deformed and grotesque: with a bald head, squinting eyes, a large nose, or a humped back, the fool is quintessentially ugly. This is just the sort of person one subjects to physical and verbal abuse, and the mime-actor who plays the "fool" on stage can expect to be beaten with canes, punched, buffeted about the

---

9. So Justin, *Apol.* 1.13.4, who takes the folly to mean μανία, that is, a form of madness.
10. L. L. Welborn, *Paul, the Fool of Christ. A Study of 1 Corinthians 1-4 in the Comic-Philosophic Tradition* (London: T&T Clark, 2005).

head, shaved, and spat upon—all signs of the disdain and derision that mark their victims' inferior status. Intellectually, the "fool" is of course uneducated and stupid, what Americans might call "dumb": his speech is expected to be confused, uncontrolled, and amusingly self-contradictory, his thought processes slow, befuddled, and witless. This mental weakness accompanies obvious psychological or moral incapacities: superstitious and moody, the fool is by turns anxious and rash, fatuous in his self-inflated opinion, and prone to vulgar, obscene, and sacrilegious speech. Finally, all this is accompanied by, and symbolic of, a low social and economic status: the fool is poor, ill-clad, a vagabond and parasite, on a level with pimps, prostitutes, and thieves, the kind of human "scum" too low on the social scale to be noticed by the elite, or, if noticed, useful only as the epitome of everything that is opposite to the sophistication which culture and civilization are designed to create.

Viewed from this angle, the wisdom/folly polarity in Paul's discourse embraces not just the spectrum of intellectual capacity or rationality, nor just eloquent or stumbling speech, but the whole composite polarity between the values of "civilization" and its vulgar, worthless opposite. The σοφός is the sophisticated person, endowed with the very opposite of the deficiencies of the fool. The term σοφία evokes not just intellectual training, investment in knowledge and rhetoric, and the confident control of speech and thought that were the essence of Greek παιδεία. It also evokes the equally significant acquisition of bodily control and beauty, the poise, gait, and physical toning that marked the superior classes, their inviolability from physical punishment and from the degrading blows that characterize inferior people and slaves. The whole point of education and its associated "wisdom" is to attain balance and control—physically, emotionally, and morally—so that, in distinction from the fool, the sophisticated individual has his emotions well under control, is refined in tastes, maintains a respectable demeanor, and is, as far as possible, both socially and financially independent. The σοφός is the καλοκἀγαθός, the beautiful/noble and good, with a mix of physical, moral, and social virtues as intertwined characteristics of culture. Not everyone pursued wisdom to the degree or in the ways that the philosophical schools argued were its ultimate forms, but it could be generally agreed that the purpose of wisdom was the development and perfection of the human self. It is wisdom that elevates the human above the bestial and the mean, to rise as far as possible toward the divine, of which the human has, by nature, a share.

We can now appreciate why Paul would associate crucifixion not only with weakness but also with folly. The crucified victim is the degraded human, the subhuman, an object of ridicule and contempt at the moment when he is ejected from the company of humans. Physically tortured and deformed, he is stripped of every last remnant of human dignity, debased to a condition in which all rational speech and thought are rendered impossible, and all emotions and bodily functions out of control. If the Romans, like the Greeks, enjoyed images of the barbarian "other" being killed in battle, humiliated by divinely favored victors, they also loved their entertainments in which criminals, whose life was unworthy of living, were put to death in exquisitely choreographed forms.[11] Crucifixion was, Josephus says, the most "pitiable" of deaths (*War* 7.202), but it was rare for anyone actually to pity the victims, because by being pinned on the cross they had crossed the line from humanity to scum: unless there were strong reasons still to identify with them, they had simply become disposable to the human race. Cicero talks of the "horror" which the very thought of crucifixion raises among Roman citizens, meaning not that they are horrified that so cruel a punishment should

---

11. Carlin A. Barton, *The Sorrows of the Ancient Romans: The Gladiator and the Monster* (Princeton: Princeton University Press, 1993).

be inflicted on others, but that they shiver at the unthinkable thought that that could ever be them (*Pro Rabirio* 16). There are, indeed, very rare moments when such a horror takes place, and Cicero makes much of the notorious case of Gavius, a Roman citizen who was convicted of treason and crucified by Verres, the governor of Sicily (Cicero, *In Verrem* 5.165-70). Verres presumably thought that Gavius had forfeited his rights and that he deserved exactly what he got. From Cicero's point of view, that a man with the rights and dignities of Roman citizenship should be submitted to the utter degradation of crucifixion was an outrage: that Gavius should hang there, "suffering the worst extreme of the tortures inflicted upon slaves," was an assault on all the values of decency by which Roman civilization was preserved.

To hail Jesus the crucified as the Christ, the Son of God, was even more an outrage. If he was executed as a criminal by legitimate authorities, he was rightly degraded to the rank of human trash, and could not possibly be honored, still less associated with the divine. If he *was* properly to be honored as divine, then one of two conclusions had to be drawn. *Either* his death was the most monstrous miscarriage of justice—though, for the Gospel writers, one for which Rome was not entirely to blame—*or* the whole system of values that made crucifixion a symbol and enactment of abject worthlessness was itself completely worthless, mistaken to the core. Paul takes the latter course. He makes no attempt to exonerate the executioners of Jesus, nor to pass off his crucifixion as a temporary error in the otherwise sound practice of Roman justice. At the same time, he does not finger Rome as a peculiarly corrupt or oppressive empire. The "rulers of this age" who are here said to have crucified Jesus (2:6, 8) are given no ethnic characterization: what matters about them is that they belong to "this age" and as such are being rendered inoperative and outdated by a new reality given in Christ (2:6).[12] They simply did not grasp what was going on, and the extent of their ignorance, of the bankruptcy of their norms, is that they crucified the one who is in fact, as Paul puts it, "the Lord of glory" (2:8). Jesus is Lord (κύριος), not slave, and the Lord of glory or honor (δόξα), not a piece of human scum. If the crucifixion of a Roman citizen is an outrage, for which Cicero wants Verres humiliated and exiled, the crucifixion of the Lord of glory by "the rulers of this age" is the clearest possible indication that this age understands nothing of the divine system of value. The crucifixion is not just a temporary aberration in an otherwise well-functioning system: it is the clearest possible proof that the norms which pass for "wisdom" are completely unable to grasp what God is doing in the world. To read the crucifixion with the eyes of Paul is like reading the systems of justice in the old American South with the eyes of Harper Lee (author of *To Kill a Mockingbird*):[13] it is to expose a whole system of evaluation, a matrix of norms and judgments that prides itself on its advanced state of civilization, as blind, corrupt, and barbaric, utterly worthless in its judgment of worth.

Paul emphasizes this clash of wisdoms in the strongest possible terms. The death of Christ is neither marginalized (in favor of the resurrection) nor euphemized (by not drawing attention to the instrument of death). To the contrary, "cross" and "crucifixion" are emphatically foregrounded, and Paul declares that "I decided to know nothing among you except Jesus Christ, and him *crucified*" (2:2). This is, he insists, folly and weakness: "the word of the cross is folly to those who are perishing" (1:18); "God has decided through the folly of what we preach to save those who believe" (1:21). In this first

---

12. For Paul's attitude to Rome in this regard, see my essay "Why the Roman Empire Was Insignificant to Paul," in J. M. G. Barclay, *Pauline Churches and Diaspora Jews* (Tübingen: Mohr Siebeck, 2011), 363–87.
13. Harper Lee, *To Kill a Mockingbird* (London: Heinemann, 1960).

rhetorical move it is crucial to *embrace* the standard evaluation of the cross. This is a "stumbling block to Jews and folly to Gentiles" (1:23); it does not match and cannot be made to match the normal scales of value. Then comes the second rhetorical move, the paradoxical inversion of terms: "the foolishness of God is wiser than human wisdom, and the weakness of God is stronger than human strength" (1:25). It is not the wisdom of God that is wiser, but the foolishness of God. This is not locating God's wisdom or strength on a scale extending *beyond* the human, as if the wisdom of God were continuous with, just considerably further along, the spectrum of human wisdom. Paul's jarring, paradoxical expression is meant to separate entirely the divine from the human scale of norms. If one may say that God is wise, it is only after knowing, through the crucifixion, that this is not on humanly definable terms; if Paul preaches wisdom among the mature (2:6), this can express nothing other than a cross-based "wisdom."[14]

It is important to see that the rhetorical inversions necessary for the paradoxical maxim of 1:25 do not require that divine and human wisdom be the opposite of one another in ontological terms. Paul is not saying that everything humanly weak is divinely strong, nor that everything humanly vulgar and uncivilized is directly representative of the wisdom of God. His aim is not to turn the human scale simply on its head, but to break the presumption of congruence that makes a human value system reflective or representative of the divine. As L. L. Welborn shows, there are partial parallels in antiquity in the life of Socrates and in the stories about Aesop.[15] Socrates's famed ugliness, social awkwardness, and "ignorance" were intended not to valorize the opposite of the commonsense norms but to call them

---

14. On 2:6-16 as an extension, not a contradiction, of 1:18ff., see L. L. Welborn, *Paul, the Fool of Christ*, 182–223.

15. Ibid., 167–73.

into question, to challenge the presumed correspondence between Athenian justice and the justice that is rightly so called. Similarly, Aesop, a slave who had no education and a stupid-looking face, turned out to be wiser than his Hellenic owners, but the story is told not to *invert* the standard hierarchy of Greek over barbarian, but to make one ask whether Greek was always and necessarily best. Paul likewise accords no ontological superiority to what humans consider foolish or weak: he simply opens the possibility that that is precisely where God might be active in wisdom and power. Through this epistemological challenge, the glue that fixes the divine hierarchy of values onto its human equivalent is dissolved: no extrapolation can be made from one to the other without passing through the acid bath of the cross. The Jews seek "signs" (1:22), but no human strength or human wisdom can act as a sign or iconic representation of the divine equivalent. Humans may be wise, strong, and noble, but no one can celebrate such accomplishments as symbols of the divine (1:26-31). This negativity induces not inversion but irony: the Christian stance is not to celebrate everything that is humanly weak, but to stand apart, at an ironic distance, from all that is normatively valued as a matter of pride. "Let no one deceive himself," says Paul (3:18): "if anyone seems to be wise in the terms of this age" ("seems"—δοκεῖ—being the standard vocabulary of irony in Paul; cf. Gal. 2:6, 9), "let him become a fool, that he may be wise." What is described here is a dislocation, a disruption, a deconstruction of the deep foundation of human norms: henceforth, everything that appears humanly valuable will have to be qualified with the ironic epithet *so-called*.

The Disreputable Community as the Embodiment of the Message

It is crucial for Paul that "the message of the cross" is not just words but actions, not just a verbal but a physical and social phenomenon. He recalls the conditions in which he first preached the gospel in Corinth: "When I came to you, brothers and sisters, I did not come proclaiming the mystery of God to you in lofty words of wisdom. For I decided to know nothing among you except Jesus Christ, and him crucified" (2:1-2). What he disowns here are "lofty words of wisdom" (ὑπεροχὴ λόγου ἢ σοφίας), more literally, "the superiority of speech or wisdom": the language reflects the hierarchical scale by which refinements of speech and culture mark superior social status. I had none of that, says Paul, but came among you "in weakness and in fear and in much trembling" (2:3)—tokens of physical and psychological vulnerability that betray a lack of sophistication and poise. For Paul it matters that the medium fits the message. The condition of the messenger matches the substance of what he proclaims: what he is announcing is not just a new way of looking at the world, but a new way of *being*.

It is equally important that the people drawn to this message, those who receive God's "calling," are of a condition and status commensurate with its countercultural content.

> Consider your call, brothers and sisters, not many of you were wise in human terms [κατὰ σάρκα], not many powerful, not many of noble ancestry. But God has chosen the foolish things of the world in order to shame the wise, God has chosen the weak things of the world, in order to shame the strong, and God has chosen the ignoble things of the world, and the despised—the nothings [τὰ μὴ ὄντα]—in order to render inoperative the things that exist [τὰ ὄντα], so that no one should take pride before God. (1:26-29)

This statement has been much pored over as evidence that there might be some—not many, but some—in the Corinthian church of high social status.[16] That might indeed have been the case (e.g., Erastus, Rom. 16:23), but Paul's emphasis is on the fact that the *majority* were not at all in this social bracket.[17] On the three overlapping scales of wisdom, power, and ancestry, the Corinthian church was largely made up of social nobodies. If these are the people God chose, God's criteria have nothing to do with the normal standards of worth in Greco-Roman society. These are people with no social or cultural capital, no networks of influence, and no natural or expensively acquired skills in the repertoire of civilized behavior. Paul does not shrug his shoulders and suggest that, despite these deficiencies, God has chosen this unprepossessing material, as if God's choice made up for their lack, and propelled them up the scale to join the elite. God's choice is not a substitute for a shortage of wisdom; it is a decisive argument against the pretentions of a "wisdom-so-called." God has shamed the so-called wise, and dishonored the so-called powerful: none of the standard criteria of honor apply, and all of the standard criteria of honor are scrambled, confused, and brought into crisis. Paul's language gets more and more extreme: God has chosen the despised things (ἐξουθενημένα)—a strong term for social contempt—indeed, the nothings. The old motif of *creatio ex nihilo* that fascinated and puzzled philosophers in antiquity Paul here turns into a radical social comment: those who count for nothing on the social scale of worth are precisely those whom God has counted for something. The divine and human scales of value do *not* correspond,

---

16. E.g., Gerd Theissen, *The Social Setting of Pauline Christianity: Essays on Corinth* (Philadelphia: Fortress Press, 1982).

17. For recent discussion on the social level of Paul's converts in Corinth, see Justin J. Meggitt, *Paul, Poverty, and Survival* (Edinburgh: T&T Clark, 1998); Steven J. Friesen, "Prospects for a Demography of the Pauline Mission: Corinth among the Churches," in Daniel N. Schowalter and S. J. Friesen, eds., *Urban Religion in Roman Corinth* (Cambridge: Harvard University Press, 2005), 351–70; Bruce W. Longenecker, *Remember the Poor: Paul, Poverty, and the Greco-Roman World* (Grand Rapids: Eerdmans, 2010).

and that lack of correspondence is designed to demolish human confidence in its own evaluation of worth—"so that no one should boast [καυχάομαι: take pride, celebrate, rest confident] before God" (1:29). Just as the message concerns someone—Christ—consigned to the waste heap of civilization, the community that gathers around it bears no resemblance to anyone's expectation of "the great and the good." The ironic gap opened up by the cross is socially embodied in the mismatch between the "so-called important" and the community of the called: without this embodiment, the gap would be invisible and could begin to close.

In 1 Corinthians 4 Paul returns to this cross-created irony one last time, on this occasion turning his fire on the church itself and extending his irony into full-scale sarcasm. Despite their lowly origins, it seems that the Corinthian Christians are deeply attracted to the status system of Corinthian society and have begun to evaluate themselves and their leaders by the criteria of eloquence, power, and display that permeated Greco-Roman culture. Relatively untroubled by the other, pagan, residents of Corinth, they have absorbed the competitive ethos of the system of honor and are falling into party groupings based on the attributes of various leaders (1:10-17; 3:1-4, 18-23; 4:6).[18] Paul attacks these presumptions at a deep level and in 4:6-13 launches a withering broadside against the church as a whole: "already you are filled, already you are rich, without us you reign—and would that you did reign so that we might reign with you" (4:8). He then presents, in contrast, the life experience of the apostles, an experience unmistakably shaped by the message of the cross: "We are fools on account of Christ, but you are sensible in Christ; we are weak, but you are strong; you are honored [ἔνδοξοι],

18. On the low social barriers between the Corinthian Christians and their nonbelieving environment, see J. M. G. Barclay, "Thessalonica and Corinth: Social Contrasts in Pauline Christianity," *JSNT* 47 (1992): 49–74 (reprinted in *Pauline Churches and Diaspora Jews*, 181–203).

but we are disreputable [ἄτιμοι]" (4:10). The third polarity brings out the social implications of the other two, and the following statements clarify what it means to be "disreputable" (4:11-13). "To the present time we are hungry and thirsty and poorly clothed"—the standard condition of the poor, whose life was constantly on the verge of malnutrition, and whose clothes were notoriously inadequate and torn; "we are buffeted"—the beatings that mark the inferiority of those subjected to physical abuse; "we are constantly on the move"—the instability and insecurity of the vagabond life; "we labor, working with our own hands"—the grubby manual labor on which the elite looked down with undisguised disdain; "when reviled, we bless; when harassed, we endure; when insulted, we speak kindly"—a life without honor, subject to continual derision and verbal abuse; "we have become like the refuse [περικαθάρματα] of the world, the scum [περίψημα] of all things"—the two "worst terms of abuse in the Greek language" (Martin P. Nilsson), used for beggars, parasites, no-hopers, anyone treated with extreme contempt. In this remarkable catalogue Paul sums up what it means to be at the bottom of the social heap—and insists that *that* is the authentic lifestyle of the apostle of Jesus Christ.

Paul's clash with the Corinthian church shows that it was not inevitable that to be a Christ believer entailed the lack or loss of social and cultural capital, or a challenge to the cultural status quo. It was possible to express the Christian message in words and in patterns of behavior that were well accommodated to the normal hierarchy of values, but to do so, Paul insisted, would be to lose altogether the force and meaning of the message of Christ crucified. His task was to preach the good news, but not "in the wisdom of words" (the poised and polished rhetoric of the educated orator), "lest the cross of Christ be rendered vacuous" (1:17). The verb he uses here (κενόω) means to empty, to hollow out, to remove all substance.

The message of Christ crucified may still be mouthed in conditions of frictionless accommodation with so-called civilized standards of honor, but it will cease to mean anything in such a context. A Christ crucified spoken to and for the elite, neatly corresponding with the standards of value that undergird the social status quo, is a vacuous gospel, all words and no substance. Here as elsewhere one sees why Christian communities, governed by the "foolishness" of the gospel, are of such significance in Paul's vision of the truth: without practice, experience, and social embodiment, the Christian message has no significant meaning, and is constantly in danger of canceling itself.

The Cross as the Symbol for the Social Misfit

To embrace the crucifixion as folly—as the denial and dislocation of the standard evaluations of worth—and then to re-label and acclaim it as *God*'s wisdom and *God*'s power makes perfect sense for those like Paul who are continually harassed, insulted, and derided. The deep homology between symbol and experience is what he expresses elsewhere when he speaks of being "crucified to the world and the world to me" (Gal. 6:14), again as a reason against boasting in human credentials (Gal. 6:13). It makes far less sense to speak of Christ crucified from a position of social power and respectability, or when the cross itself has become a symbol of power, or even an item of decoration and beauty.[19] Once it becomes itself the token of civilization, this divine foolishness is in danger of becoming all too reasonable and respectable; in such circumstances it loses not only its capacity to induce a visceral sense of horror but also its association with the scumbags, the wastrels, and the junk elements of society.

Things were quite different in the first century when crucifixion was still practiced and still associated with the degraded and the slave.

19. See Ernst Käsemann, "The Saving Significance of the Death of Jesus in Paul," in *Perspectives on Paul* (London: SCM Press, 1971), 32–59.

After the fire of Rome, Tacitus reports, and in order to suppress suspicions that Nero himself had started the blaze, the emperor

> fabricated scapegoats, and punished with every refinement the notoriously depraved (*per flagitia invisos*) Christians, as they were popularly called. Their originator, Christ, had been executed in Tiberius' reign by the governor of Judaea, Pontius Pilatus. But in spite of this temporary setback, the deadly superstition (*exitiabilis superstitio*) had broken out afresh, not only in Judea, where the mischief (*malum*) started, but even in Rome. All degraded and shameful practices (*atrocia aut pudenda*) collect and flourish in the capital. (Tacitus, *Annals* 15.44)

The passage reeks with Tacitus's elitist scorn of the lower social classes, and betrays a common Roman assumption (found also in Pliny) that the Christians were a degraded and disreputable superstition; just after this, Tacitus speaks of their "hatred of the human race" (*odium humani generis*), which (if the genitive is objective) probably reflects their social awkwardness, especially their refusal to participate in the normal religious practices of the Roman world. These are misfits and ne'er-do-wells, human effluent backed up from the sewer system of Roman civilization. By a process of arrests and torture-induced incriminations, Nero acquired enough suspects to give credibility to the notion of a concerted terrorist plot. As we would expect, their deaths were made the occasion for derisive contempt (*ludibria*): "dressed in wild animals' skins, they were torn to pieces by dogs, or crucified, or made into torches to be ignited after dark as substitutes for daylight." Bestialized, degraded, utilized as human fuel—it is no surprise to find crucifixion among the punishments meted out to these social nobodies and presumed criminals. This is the Roman system operating exactly as it should, though Tacitus, who was strongly critical of Nero, adds a comment that questions Nero's motives: "Despite their guilt as Christians and the ruthless punishment it deserved, the victims were pitied. For it was felt that they were being sacrificed to one man's brutality, rather than to the national interest (*utilitas publica*)." If these degrading deaths had been unambiguously in the national interest no questions would have been asked at all.

These punishments of the Roman Christians express a deep homology between the status of Christians, as misfit criminals at the bottom of the social pyramid, and the degrading forms of death they deserved. This is the same homology as the one we have found between crucifixion and weakness or folly: Jesus' crucifixion expresses a value judgment that ranks him as a laughably worthless specimen of the human race. The Romans could not have devised a better punishment for such people than crucifixion; and for the crucified Christians in Rome there could not have been a better form of identification with the originator of their so-called superstition, the crucified Christ. Tacitus asks about imperial egos and public utility, but he does not ask about where in this suppression of a disreputable social movement is *God*. From the Christian point of view, God does not reside either in the imperial will or in the national interests of Rome: God is present in the mangled and burned bodies of the Christian victims. The authorities have degraded and crucified the saints of God, just as they humiliated and crucified the Lord of glory. To read Tacitus's narrative from the perspective of the Christian victim is to place an explosive charge under the whole edifice of refined Roman sensibilities that undergirds Tacitus's configuration of Roman history and civilization. That is exactly what Paul does when he reads the crucifixion of Jesus as, in fact, the wisdom and the power of God. Only in his case what is subverted is not just the Roman nexus of so-called civilized values, but all that passes for wisdom and power in society as a whole.

2

———

The Weakness of God: A Radical Theology of the Cross

John D. Caputo

A *theologia crucis* radically conceived requires the crucifixion of the God of being on the cross of nonbeing, of the God of wisdom on the cross of foolishness, of the God of power on the cross of weakness (1 Cor. 1:20-25). Everything is demanded of theology, up to and including the most austere renunciation, the most shocking deprivation of its privileges, of its regal aspirations as the queen of the sciences, of its own special knowledge, revelations, and inspirations, requiring it to be poor and itinerant, naked and obedient, even unto death. Still more, the same thing is asked of God in the highest. Even what has been called the theology of the cross up to now, in whose debt this work clearly stands,[1] has preserved the transcendence of God, so that if God suffers it is because God is strong enough to take on suffering, to absorb suffering into the eminence and immensity, the mystery and abyss of the Godhead. But on the more radical view taken here the call that is called in and under the name (of) "God" calls for even more, demands we go still further, so that the cross touches upon the godhead of God on high, exposing what is called "God" in the great monotheisms to weakness and nonbeing. This crucifixion, this desertification of God, does not contradict the eminence or the power of this name; it is what *constitutes* it. God's power is constituted by powerlessness and God's eminence by being what is least and lowest among us. Otherwise—and this is the lever in my argument—the name of God is a power play, a strategic move made by theology on its adversaries, a play that turns God into a player in the game of power in the world, in which theology lays its cards on the table and makes it plain that the God of glory inevitably wins (*theologia gloriae*) and theology is all about winning.

In what follows I begin with exegesis but I do not end there. I pursue what we are given to think in 1 Corinthians 1–2 beyond what its author could have intended to say in order to stay on the tracks of a matter to be thought. I seek to probe the force of what Paul has captured in the explosive expression "the weakness of God" (τὸ ἀσθενὲς τοῦ θεοῦ) in order to construct, not a radical philosophy of St. Paul, as does Stanislas Breton,[2] but a radical theology of the cross. Such a radicalization continues what Luther started, the crucifixion of the theology of glory on the cross of weakness, nonbeing, and foolishness, which was first announced by Paul. In a radical theology we seek to follow the way of the cross to the end, depriving theology

1. My thanks to Christophe Chalamet whose contribution to the present collection makes this debt plain and has been helpful to me in preparing the revised version of this paper.
2. Stanislas Breton, *Saint Paul* (Paris: Presses Universitaires de France, 1988); idem, *A Radical Philosophy of Saint Paul*, trans. Joseph Ballan (New York: Columbia University Press, 2011).

of its glories and inscribing weakness and nonbeing in the depths of the Godhead. We pursue the foolishness of the λόγος of the cross to the point of an austere faith that, unadorned with the ornaments of religion and divested of the garments of doctrine, presses forward through death to new life, and through crucifixion to resurrection.

Method: 1 Corinthians 1:19—*destructio* (ἀπολῶ)

Clearly, such a proposal requires some explanation of its method, which I draw from Jacques Derrida, but not without recourse to both Martin Heidegger and Rudolf Bultmann. All three thinkers condense their work into a term of art that is semantically negative—*déconstruction, Destruktion, Entmythologisierung*—even while the point of their work is affirmative. In order to avoid giving that linguistic impression, I speak instead of a "hermeneutics" but a *radical* one. This qualification is meant to show that this hermeneutics does not lack the heart for the heartless operation of the cross each requires, for the dismantling signified by the negative prefix. Such a hermeneutics is from start to finish an operation of the heart (*cor inquietum*), from the necessary and always preliminary and always unfinished work of dealing hermeneutic death, to its culmination in a more fundamental affirmation of new life, an even higher operation of the heart. Hermeneutics thus construed follows in its own way along (μετά) the way (ὁδός) of the cross, in which death is followed by life, crucifixion by resurrection. The *theologia crucis* that follows represents a hermeneutic Good Friday, a theology both *of* the cross, of the Crucified, and a theology crucified, itself subjected to the cross, stripped naked, humbled, and divested of its power and prestige. The dying off in these methods is real and unremitting, but it is neither morbid nor nihilistic. It always serves the purpose of life, not death; of new life born of passing through death.

But following the λόγος of the cross proves to be a delicate operation, and this is (literally) crucial to the present argument. For it must avoid *compromising* the cross, turning the λόγος of cross into a "strategy" to bring down the strong, or an "economy," a good investment with long-term rewards. Such a λόγος would be cunning, not foolish, the death in question a merely Docetic death, and the theology in play a theology of glory traveling under the incognito of a theology of the cross. The death must be intrinsic to the life, and the weakness to the strength, not something that is finally laid aside or passed through on the way to glory.

What Heidegger calls *Destruktion* belongs to a work of "repetition" or "retrieval" (*Wiederholung*) that recalls what has fallen into oblivion. Retrieval requires hermeneutic violence or unbuilding (*Abbau*) in order to loosen what is to be restored from its sedimented condition. It makes contact with something going on *in* the history of metaphysics that metaphysics as such is unable to think. This does not mean razing metaphysics to the ground but breaking through to the ground of metaphysics as the treasure house of what is to be thought. "Overcoming [*überwinden*] metaphysics" releases something uncontainable *in* metaphysics.

Demythologizing follows an analogous rule. It is not the destruction of myth but its hermeneutics, the interpretation of the mythological schema so that we can understand what it means for our life today, when the mythological schema itself is obsolete. In the New Testament, not unlike a Greek tragedy or Shakespearean play, our lives are put on stage, inserted into a great cosmic drama with a divine *dramatis personae*, supernatural players acting in dramatic (mythic) time and space. God dwells on high, up in the seventh heaven, Satan down below, in the dark and forbidding recesses beneath the earth. On the earth in between, legions of angels from on high do combat with demons. The promise of new being, of life not death, is transcribed as a new "age," the coming time, brought about by the God come down to earth, who takes on our sins and washes them away with his blood sacrifice. In the "end time" the God will come in judgment, when in a great apocalyptic confrontation the enemies of the God are dashed to pieces, death is defeated, and we are taken up into the sky with the God. But of course, as history attests, death and destruction, suffering and evil, continue unabated; the end time does not come, two thousand years now and counting. The hurried command to prepare turns out to be a false alarm. There are no demons, but there are viruses and bacteria; no Garden of Eden, but there is evolutionary biology; no "heaven above" or "Hades below," but solar systems and galaxies in an ever-expanding universe that radically relativize "up" and "down." What is needed now is hermeneutic violence, which disengages the proclamation from the mythic time and space into which it has been transcribed. What *has* come is the time of demythologization, the age of interpretation.

What Heidegger calls destruction and Bultmann calls demythologization depends upon what Derrida calls the structure of the "trace," the ability of the signifier to function in the absence of what it signifies. As such the trace is "iterable," repeatable, able to be removed from its original context and to take on new life in a new context. Otherwise, signification would be tied to the immediate presence of the signified, communication would be bound hand and foot, and traditions would be unable to move beyond their inaugural moment. Indeed, if a trace is not repeatable, it cannot even be used the first time; it is not a trace, but a mute presence. Deconstruction is the general theory of the trace (γραμμή, grammatology), of its necessary contextuality and recontextualizability, which is what Derrida means by the "text" and why he says there is no signification outside the textuality of context and recontexualizability.

Without such "play"—recontextualizability—the trace would be deprived of a future, and the very *point* of deconstruction is this future. Its motive and desire is to embrace the risk of repetition, of the ambiance, ambiguity, and polyvalence of the trace, precisely in order to experience its *promise*, toward which in every case deconstruction is turned, just the way the λόγος of the cross is turned toward the promise of resurrection. It is fitting that the first word of deconstruction, "come," *viens, oui, oui,* the affirmation of the promise, of what is to come, which Derrida calls the "event," is the last word of the New Testament (Rev. 22:20). But what is to come is not to be confused with an *eschaton*, a "coming age" or future happening, which is what he calls the "future-present." The "to come" (*à venir*) is a not a coming era but a "weak messianic force"[3] that presses in upon the present construction in order to allow it to have a future, a promise never free from risk. Deconstruction is the affirmation of the incoming (*invention*) of the event, the reinvention of the event, again and again.

So in each case, we see the same λόγος—destruction is *re*trieval; demythologizing is *re*interpretation; deconstruction is *re*invention—which is the λόγος of the cross: crucifixion is *re*surrection. This is not a whimsical association but a matter of a rigorous philology. Derrida first uses the word *déconstruction* as a gloss of Heidegger's *Destruktion*. But Heidegger's use of *Destruktion* was itself inspired by Luther's account of the *theologia crucis* in the *Heidelberg Disputation*, where Luther demands the *destructio* of Scholastic metaphysics and of the *theologia gloriae* in order to recover the original experience of the New Testament (*destructio* is

---

3. Jacques Derrida, *Spectres de Marx: État de la dette, le travail du deuil, et la nouvelle Internationale* (Paris: Galilée, 1993), 55; ET, *Specters of Marx: The State of the Debt, the Work of Mourning, and the New International*, trans. Peggy Kamuf (New York: Routledge, 1994), 95.

*ref*ormation).[4] Luther in turn is rendering the Greek ἀπολῶ, which is the Septuagint translation of Isa. 29:14, which Paul is citing in 1 Cor. 1:19. The word *déconstruction*, which does not mean to abolish but to weaken the grip of sedimented presence in order to release the promise of the future, is not a passing French fashion; it is handed down to us from the ancients across (*trans latus*) five languages. The word does not distract us from the biblical text by a side glance to the philosophers; it is itself of biblical origin, transmitted to us down the corridors of the Hebrew Bible, the Septuagint, and the Latin Vulgate.

With the spirit and the letter of the word *déconstruction* in mind, let us read what Paul is saying in 1 Corinthians 1–2.

Τὰ μὴ ὄντα (1 Corinthians 1:28)

Paul tells us he did not meet Jesus in the flesh, which explains, at least in part, why references to what Jesus said and did are so rare in the letters. Nonetheless, in the first chapter of 1 Corinthians, I think he has distilled the very core of the Gospels, and in particular of what I prefer to call the "poetics" of the kingdom of God sayings. By a poetics I mean the constellation of metaphors and metonymies, parables and paradoxes, images and narratives that cumulatively evoke the lived experience of the kingdom, its form of life. The poetics of the kingdom is the topsy-turvy dynamic of these sayings, the reversals, the paradoxes, the shocking logic in virtue of which the last are first and the first are last, the lost are saved, the outside are inside and the inside are out. Indeed, in New Testament scholarship this logic or a-logic is one of the markers of sayings with an authentic tradition behind them. A poetics always requires an interpretation, a

4. There is hardly a better example of what Derrida means by textuality than this amazing story, which was first laid out by John Edward van Buren, *The Young Heidegger* (Bloomington: Indiana University Press, 1994), 159–68, where Heidegger's early interest in Luther's *theologia crucis* is documented in detail.

hermeneutics. I love the bold and audacious way in which Paul gets in the face of the Corinthian elite, while not sparing the feelings of the saints at Corinth, forcibly reminding them of the humbleness of their condition, about which Paul is absolutely frank, albeit in a spirit of brotherly love.[5] They are not well born, not well educated, not wise or powerful as the world knows wisdom and power. They are in fact low and despised and, to use John Dominic Crossan's marvelous English translation, they are "nuisances and nobodies" (τὰ μὴ ὄντα).[6]

No philosopher can fail to take appreciate the pointedness of τὰ μὴ ὄντα where Paul, who we have reason to believe has never read Heidegger, is not so much "overcoming metaphysics" as overwhelming it with irony and mocking. What he says is meant to shock the Corinthian elite by taking on one of the most revered words in their philosophical vocabulary, τὸ ὄν, while taking his stand—tauntingly, polemically, mockingly—with the opposite. Against all reason, all logic, all ontologic, all onto-theologic, he prefers nonbeing to being, being nothing to being itself. The dripping irony, the sarcasm, reminds one not of Heidegger's ponderous German, but the barbs and biting wit that Kierkegaard directed at Hegel. As we know, in common use the Greek word οὐσία, which the philosophers translate as "substance," as if the word dropped into their laps from the moon, refers to one's property, to earthly possessions, even to real estate, a usage that conducts a not-so-subtle transfer from what one owns to what one is, from having to being. The communication between the two senses, one high and the other common, shows up in modern English in expressions like a "man of substance" (and until recently that really did mean men) or the "powers that be," where the ontological order is enlisted

---

5. For more on the sociology of the Corinthians, see John Barclay's contribution in this volume.
6. John Dominic Crossan, *Jesus: A Revolutionary Biography* (San Francisco: HarperOne, 1994), 54–74.

in the service of the sociological order. Οὐσία meant having a big house, plentiful slaves, and beautiful garments, all the trappings of power, possessions, and prestige. Having becomes being; not having becomes not being. So Paul taunts the logic of being, power, and wisdom of the Corinthian elite and takes his stand with the logic of nonbeing, weakness, and foolishness, strategically reversing the logic of being with the λόγος of the cross, with its a-logic or poetics. He seeks to confound the stratification of the flourishing Greco-Roman city of Corinth that has worked its way into the community of saints[7] with the confounding logic of the cross that throws the ways of the "world" into confusion. I single out for particular attention the theme of weakness in these texts, treating weakness, as it were, as Paul's strongest point.

The Two Bodies of Jesus

The word *Christianity* literally means that Jesus is proclaimed the "anointed" one. Without being drawn into a debate about the high Christologies that were constructed in the early councils that made the anointed one into much more than that, it is enough for my purposes that we single out Jesus as the focal object or subject of anything we call Christianity. Had the Jesuits not already co-opted the word, I myself would have preferred the expression Jésus-ists, Jesuits. As such, Jesus is not just any man, not just a just man, and in particular not just a "great" man or a "genius," which Kierkegaard thought was paganism.[8] To see this I turn to Ernst Kantorowicz's

---

7. As Dale B. Martin, *The Corinthian Body* (New Haven: Yale University Press, 1995), 108–36, has shown, the saints were quarreling among themselves in a city that did not lack for Greek philosophers, who were evidently making light of their beliefs. In ch. 15, Paul felt called upon to buck up their flagging faith in the resurrection of the body by distinguishing between the corruptible body of earth and water, which Martin calls the "hyletic" body, from an incorruptible or "pneumatic" body (σῶμα πνευματικόν), composed of the elements of fire and air, hence a light, airy, fiery body. Even the Greek philosophers would grant that the celestial bodies were made of incorruptible matter.

well-known distinction between the two bodies of the king.[9] The king is not just this miserable, arthritic, gout-ridden fat fellow. He is his royal majesty, whose very presence commands our respect, before whom one bows and upon whom one would never dare to turn's one's back when leaving a room. The first body is mortal, but the second one lives and on, as when say, "The King is dead; long live the King."

In Christianity, there is a comparable distinction. The body of Jesus is not just this man from Nazareth, who had several brothers, who seems to have caused a stir in his hometown when he launched his mission, a man like everyone else who attended to his most basic bodily needs, and whatever else we can cull about this man largely lost in the fog of history. That body belongs to what the historians call the Jesus of history. Over and beyond that, the body of Jesus is what the author of Colossians calls the visible image, the "icon," of the invisible God (Col. 1:15), which belongs to what the historians call the Christ of faith. This distinction between his two bodies became what the theologians of the councils reworked into the distinction between the "human nature" and the "divine nature."[10]

If we say that an idol remains forever confined to the plane of visibility, while an icon gives us an insight or intuition of the invisible God, then to call Jesus an icon means that everything Christians know about God passes through the image they have of Jesus. This

---

8. Søren Kierkegaard, "The Difference Between a Genius and an Apostle," in *Kierkegaard's Writings*, vol. 24, *The Book on Adler*, trans. and ed. Howard and Edna Hong (Princeton: Princeton University Press, 1998), 173–88.

9. Ernst Kantorowicz, *The King's Two Bodies: A Study in Medieval Political Theology* (Princeton: Princeton University Press, 1957).

10. In freely citing a deutero-Pauline text like Colossians, I follow Breton, *A Radical Philosophy of Saint Paul*, 35, who is likewise following a thought, not an author. While these texts lack the identifiable authorship of Paul, they do not lack his broader reach or authority. Like Breton, I am not here engaged in exegetic-philological reconstruction of the "authentic" Paul, of a "signature," something better left to experts more prepared than I am, but in a work of repetition, of constructive theology, following a "thought." My concern is with something that his texts contain without being able to contain, what these texts promise and what they risk.

image is well known. Jesus plainly announces his mission as good news for the poor and the imprisoned, as a day of jubilee and of the forgiveness of debt. He tells us to greet hatred with love, not retribution; violence with peace, not war; those who do us harm with forgiveness, not retaliation. He says that the last shall be first and the first last. He scandalizes the well-born and the pious by his open commensality with sinners, mixing with prostitutes and tax collectors. When he is arrested, he tells Peter to put down his sword. He was not well-born, not wise as the world knows wisdom, not strong as the world knows strength. This image is beautifully captured by Dostoevsky. After listening silently to the Lord Cardinal Grand Inquisitor boast of his power, how he holds the life of Jesus in the palm of his hand, Jesus simply approaches him and gives him a kiss, which utterly disarms this powerful man. It is no less beautifully distilled in 1 Corinthians 1.

The Foolishness of the Cross

One way to appreciate the "foolishness" of the λόγος of the cross is to pose the hypothetical question, Could Jesus have come down from the cross had he so chosen? Could he with the merest blink of his eye have sent those powerful Roman soldiers crashing against the rocks, shattered the cross to splinters, and called down twelve legions of angels from heaven to rally to his defense? Or was he really nailed there, both hands and both feet, against his will, unable to escape an agonizing fate? How is the invisible God made visible here in all this terrible cruelty? In the classical view, the λόγος of the cross is found in a Jesus *willingly* suffering on the cross even while he possessed the power to destroy his enemies. That makes the crucifixion primarily an exercise in loving obedience, humility, and self-restraint, the willing suspension of divine power that could have been unleashed in all its fury. In the high Christology of Thomas

Aquinas, Jesus in his human nature was immediately joined to the beatific vision in his divine nature, so that for all the suffering his vulnerable human body endured, the divine nature remained invulnerable, hypostatically joined to and inseparable from the human nature, immune from suffering and untouched by death. That infinite resource, all its power and joy, was fully at his disposal, but Jesus declined to avail himself of it on the cross.

But if the logic of the icon is to be taken seriously, the lack of power cannot be merely apparent, behind which can be found a real and imperishable power, much greater than the perishable power of Rome and its soldiers, a long-term power that will make its enemies its footstools, eventually. The suffering of the man must touch upon the divine and reveal a suffering God. When the ancient church condemned "Patripassionism" it was simply giving in to the maxims of Greek metaphysics instead of embracing the scandal and the paradox of the New Testament. According to the logic of the two bodies of Jesus, the crucifixion does not depict a man whom we admire because he holds up calmly under persecution, who died with grace and dignity when he was put to death by the Romans who occupied his land. This scene, along with the rest of the picture that is drawn of Jesus in the Synoptic Gospels but never cited by Paul, functions on a second and iconic level, where it provides a depiction not of a φρόνιμος but of God. The Gospels are not a portrait of a just man who died bravely, obedient to the law to the end, like Socrates, say, but an iconic portrait of God, so that our gaze should be drawn from this crucified body to God.

My claim is that the mark of God in Christianity, the one that is drawn from the characteristic image of Jesus, is systematically found on the side of the "weak" features—of forgiveness, peace, nonviolence, poverty—not of the strong or "virile" features. If indeed *crux sola est nostra theologia*, then the human weakness must be an icon of the divine weakness, albeit in such a way that "God's weakness is stronger than human strength" (1 Cor. 1:25). The position struck in the councils and classical orthodoxy, that the human nature is weak while the divine nature is strong, *contradicts the logic of the icon.* Still, it is not a question of a one-sided absolutizing of weakness but of redeploying the distinction between strength and weakness along the lines of the iconic life of Jesus where weakness is a new and amazing divine name. The weakness of Jesus is also strong, but it is not strong as the world knows strength. The divinity he reveals does not abolish strength in favor of weakness *simpliciter* but redescribes a weakness stronger than what the world calls strength. On this accounting, Jesus is much more powerful than any purely worldly show of strength, by him or anyone else, in just the way that the majesty of the body of the king has nothing to do with whether he is a loathsome sight or cuts a regal figure.

From Metaphysical Theology to Radical Theology

Clearly, everything depends upon understanding this "stronger than" (ἰσχυρότερον) in such a way as not to compromise the λόγος of the cross by turning it into a disguised form of power, which reduces it to a strategy, a ruse, or an economy. In my view, the λόγος of the cross throws the classical concept of the omnipotence of God into question, which is where it departs from any orthodox understanding of the theology of the cross. To take a more radical view of the weakness of God in turn demands a more radical idea of God's strength, which becomes clear when we examine the two sources of the classical idea of omnipotence. First of all, omnipotence is rooted in a system of metaphysical distinctions—between eternity and time, being and becoming, actual and potential being—that go back to Plato and Aristotle. The irony could not be greater: this is the *very* tradition in which the Corinthian philosophers stand and that Paul is mocking. This God is a cluster of omni-perfections like omniscience and omnipotence, a super-being able to outwit and outpower any sublunary being down below. These metaphysical distinctions go hand in hand with classical political models of sovereignty and kingship, where the power of God serves both metaphysical and political purposes. Drawn from the very order of οὐσία that Paul is taunting, God is the supreme and sovereign power, the king of kings, in whose kingship his proxies down here on earth participate.[11] The sovereign power of God is a player in the power game of the world, in which God, the supreme omni-power that dwarfs every merely mundane power, is by definition guaranteed to win.

This is not to say that this can all be blamed on the Greeks and that it would be enough to "overcome metaphysics." This brings us to the second source, the authors of the God of the Bible, who, like the Greek philosophers, are also in love with power. The classical idea of "God almighty" is steeped not only in Greek metaphysics but in a mythic world in which the demonic powers of the world prove no match for the mighty power of God. So the Reformation project of *destructio*, of purging theology of Greek metaphysics by going back to the Bible, is at best a half step. Even if the New Testament knows nothing of the metaphysics of οὐσία, it trades in mythic power at every turn, including in the ministry of Jesus himself, who as seems likely exorcised demons and preached of the coming end time of the rule of God.[12] If the metaphysics needs overcoming, the New

11. God's sovereignty over the world provides the model of the sovereignty of the king over the nation, of the father over his family, of humanity over the (other) animals and the earth itself. Even in modernity, the sovereignty of God is what Derrida calls the "unavowed theologeme" behind the sovereign freedom of the autonomous individual, when the funds of sovereignty in the divine account are transferred to the liberal individual. God stands behind and supports a system of top-down binaries, all of which reflect his sovereign power—king/subject, master/slave, father/family, male/female, human/animal, humanity/earth. See Jacques Derrida, *Voyous: Deux essais sur la raison* (Paris: Galilée, 2003), 155; ET, *Rogues: Two Essays on Reason*, trans. Pascale-Anne Brault and Michael Naas (Stanford: Stanford University Press, 2005), 110.

Testament needs demythologizing. The whole thing needs a more radical *déconstruction,* a hermeneutic Good Friday in which theology is crucified on the cross of weakness—if it is to release the promise of life embedded in the New Testament.

A theology of the cross, pursued without compromise, requires a deconstruction of the metaphysics, the mythology, and the politics of power. Its watchword is the revolutionary texts of 1 Corinthians 1, where God systematically takes his stand with everyone on the *lower end* of these binary systems—with foolishness instead of wisdom, with nonbeing instead of being, with weakness instead of power. Unlike the militant mythic hero-gods of antiquity, Jesus forgives his enemies, takes his stand with the oppressed and imprisoned, the outsider, the lost sheep, and the like. The "divine order" that forms around Jesus is anarchic, unruly, topsy turvy, upside down, bottom up, in short, hier*an*archic, foolishness in the eyes of the world. When Jesus is called a king, that is a taunt, and when he speaks of God's kingdom, he immediately adds that it is not a kingdom as the world knows kings and kingdoms. In fact, it was the unbelievers who thought that if Jesus really were the Son of God, he should be able to come down from the cross. So they taunted him—as did Satan—let's see you save yourself. Let's see if your divine power is stronger than the Romans, which meant they measured strength by the strength of wood and nails. But such strength belongs to the order of myth and magic and it expects a Hollywood superhero with supernatural power to reduce his enemies to dust with the merest thought in his mind.

---

12. In dealing with the historical Jesus, we do well to keep our adverbs weak. "Likely," which is as strong a word as we can risk, also implies possibly not. On this matter John Dominic Crossan is famous for thinking not. He writes, "But, for myself, while the New Testament starts with the first coming of a nonviolent historical Jesus, it ends with the second coming of a violent theological Christ." John Dominic Crossan, "Response to Luke Timothy Johnson," in James K. Beilby and Paul Rhodes Eddy, eds., *The Historical Jesus: Five Views* (Downer's Grove, IL: IVP Academic, 2009), 187. Crossan blames the apocalyptic violence on the church while Jesus is innocent as a lamb among Christianizing wolves.

Jesus and the God of whom he is the icon have nothing to do with this idea of strength and nothing to do with such magic. Jesus really is nailed to that cross and his "weakness" on the cross is not a willing suspension of the infinite power at his disposal. The divinity in this iconic scene is found first and foremost in the forgiveness that rises up from the cross in majesty, which soars beyond the swords of the Roman soldiers for whom it is perfect foolishness, and resonates across the centuries: It belongs to another order of strength because it is embedded intrinsically in the weakness and as such is incomprehensible to the world. The weak force of forgiveness is foolishness to mythological, metaphysical, and political power. It is a power *without* power, a power of powerlessness that is in its own way greater than the power of the Roman army, greater than the mythic powers and principalities, and *greater than the metaphysics of omnipotence.* In forgiveness, the power of the God of myth and metaphysics is deconstructed, a word that provides a surprisingly felicitous, even exegetically precise gloss on 1 Cor. 1:19.

1 Corinthians 2: The Reversal

Now we must raise a question that poses a kind of test case of my thesis, one that requires the heart to take up the cross of a radical hermeneutic: What does Paul mean when he says that the weakness of God is stronger than human strength? Did Paul mean that God's strength—not the power of powerlessness, but unqualified divine power—would ultimately, in the long run, triumph in and over the world? Of that I think there is little doubt, and from that position, I say in a whisper, I must dissent. His views, like those of the author of John's Gospel, are framed in terms of a vast cosmic drama in which Paul thinks the powers of Satan are laid low by the blood sacrifice of Jesus. From that mythic violence, I must, as peacefully as possible, take my leave. For how far is such a view from Nietzsche's critique of *ressentiment*, from using weakness as a treacherous weapon to steal upon the strong and healthy and bring them down? My own view is that Paul did not believe in weakness strongly enough, and while he distrusted the power of the Greek elites and their philosophers of οὐσία he did so in the name of another, secret, opposing and stronger divine power. He entered the figure of weakness into a long-term economy of divine strength that was too much like the power of the world. For Paul, to invest in weakness here and now, where we see things darkly, is to reap the profits of true strength in the long run, when everything will be clear and all accounts will be settled.

1 Corinthians 1–2—now I take the two chapters together—turns upon the confrontation of two contradictory realms. In the first chapter, Paul opposes the realm of the world (αἰών, κόσμος), of the well-heeled elite, the powers that be, the best and the brightest, to the realm of God, of those who are nothing by the world's standards. But in the second chapter, this stratification is apocalyptically reversed to the advantage of the saints and catastrophically for the world. It turns out that the powers of this world are backed by the power of Satan, and the wisdom of this world by the powers of darkness, and they are doomed to perish. Perishing is perishing, and it matters little whether one perishes at the hands of an army of flesh and blood and steel or of legions of warrior angels; that is still perishing *as the world knows perishing*. Apocalyptic eschatology is divine violence, as bloody and lethal as any worldly power and indeed—given its divine provenance—even more so. The world is to be overthrown by the real wisdom and real power of God. I came to you in weakness, in fear and trembling, he says to the Corinthians, *but* this worldly weakness rests upon "the power of God" (1 Cor. 2:5). That is true, but by the power of God Paul means real worldly triumph, entitative-ontological victory, achieved by an apocalyptic reversal. With this

reversal, the radically revolutionary potential of the rhetoric of weakness in first chapter is compromised by the divine violence, the *apocalyptic eschatology* of the second chapter, in which the rhetoric of the weakness versus strength is revealed. By the power of God Paul does not mean the power of forgiveness, the power of the kiss, but *apocalyptic power* and the mythic strife with Satan and his minions. The radically revolutionary potential of the first chapter is compromised by the second chapter, in which Paul shows his hand. For the ones who are seasoned, mature, perfected in the long-term ways of God (τέλειοι, 1 Cor. 2:6), for those who know the secret hidden from the world, God is the one who has true wisdom and real power. As Dale Martin says, "Ultimately, what Paul wants to oppose to human power is not weakness but divine power (2:5)—that is, power belonging to the other realm."[13] The ones who have the πνεῦμα, who know the secret, know that God will come and establish his rule on earth, that the Evil One will be deprived of his power, while they will be given such gifts as eye has not seen, nor ear heard.

The mythic scene will be spectacular, with all the *magic* of a Hollywood film. Jesus will come down to earth on a cloud, the demons will be scattered, the dead will rise from their graves, and the powers of this world will perish! There will be a final reckoning when God will be all in all, when it will be clear just how unwise it was to reject the foolishness of the cross. The wise will live to regret it. Had they known, "they would never have crucified the Lord of glory" (2:8). The tables will be turned and the lowly Christians will have the glory (2:7). Even the crucified body of Jesus is now the icon of glory, not of weakness. Those who are not in the πνεῦμα will be judged; they will get their come-uppance. They will rue

---

13. Martin, *The Corinthian Body*, 62.

the day they mocked the (seeming) weakness Paul extols. The saints will ultimately have the upper hand—if they are patient; it won't be long. The film ends, the credits roll down the screen, the music is triumphal. God has vanquished his enemies. God's weakness is only apparent; his real power crushes their strength. The faithful leave the theatre certain and reassured that true power and wisdom are on their side. In the language of deconstruction, Paul is content with "reversal," with turning the tables on the powers that be. He leaves the place of real power—the power over life and death—still standing, while seeing to it that this place is occupied by God, not Satan. Paul does not move on to "displacement," to a radical disturbance of hierarchy, a radical hier-anarchy, in which strength and power are redescribed in terms the world will not understand. The world will understand the coming conflagration all too well. The world will rue the day it did not believe Paul.

Overcoming Metaphysics, Demythologizing the New Testament

Paul, I claim, does not finally offer the power of powerlessness, but a shrewder, more strategic power in which weakness gains the upper hand, eventually, in the long run. That is precisely the gesture exposed by a radical theology of the cross, precisely what is rejected, precisely the source of the trouble with theology, precisely the reason why theology inspires such widespread mistrust, scorn, and even *odium*.[14] In its place, I propose, we take up an uncompromised theology of the cross, in which power is genuinely crucified on the

---

14. I am happy to leave Rom. 13:1-3 to the interpretation of the exegetes. I wish them well. I pray that they may be given not only the seven gifts of the Holy Spirit, but two more—a holy hermeneutics and a devout deconstruction—so that the Spirit may help them find a way around what Paul appears to be saying, which reflects the authoritarian side of Paul and of theology that I am worried about. As I do not deny—in fact, deconstruction demands it—that Paul's text is polyvalent, a multiplex, and that one can read Paul against Paul, I oppose Rom. 13:1-3 by way of τὰ μὴ ὄντα of 1 Corinthians 1.

cross of powerlessness. This imposes a twofold requirement: first, to keep faith with the weak, ill-born, foolish, and powerless, and not to treat this solidarity as part of a long-term strategy, or to enter it into an economy, or to inscribe it in mythic war with the powers of darkness. Second, it requires a more radical subjection of God to the crucifixion of weakness and powerlessness, one that moves beyond the weakness of the saints at Corinth to the weakness of God on high, to follow through without compromise on what Paul so evocatively calls the "weakness of God."

First, a radical theology of the cross requires a systematic weakening of the top-down order of authority that Paul describes in Rom. 13:1-3, one more in keeping with the egalitarianism of Gal. 3:28 where Paul weakens the binary differences between male and female, master and slave, Gentile and Jew. If Jesus and the kingdom that is the centerpiece of his preaching constitute the icon by which any community is established, then it ought to reflect a systematic weakening of the authoritarian structures that Paul seeks to reinforce with the power of God in Romans as well as by the apocalyptic reversal in 1 Corinthians 2. We see this alternative, let us say, this other side of Paul, in contemporary progressive social movements that are marked by weakening the old aristocratic privilege of the few (the powers that be) over the many and the widespread dispersal, dissemination, and redistribution of the notion of rights among τὰ μὴ ὄντα, the ones who hitherto were nothings and nobodies. This issues in a decentering, decolonializing, democratizing movement in the ethical, social, and political order that weakens the supremacy of men and strengthens the dignity of women, that weakens the privilege of the "West" and builds up the "third world," which worries about "human" rights when they come at the cost of torturing animals to death for food, amusement, or trinkets, which weakens our domination over and respects the "rights" of the earth, which is something more than material for our domination. It issues in a view of human life that deprivileges οὐσία, the order of possessions, power, property, and prestige, and instead privileges a simplicity and poverty of life that is at odds with the rule of global capitalism and its politics.

To be sure, the point of such egalitarian movements is to empower the disempowered. I am calling for a new understanding of power, not claiming that power is an evil word. The point is to redistribute power so as to empower the dispossessed to lead lives of dignity and self-respect, empowered to provide a meaningful life for themselves and their own, but *not* in such a way that they simply trade places and become the new powers that be whose turn it is to oppress others. The uncompromised effect of the icon of weakness in 1 Corinthians 1 is to stand always and systematically on the side of τὰ μὴ ὄντα, of everything weak and marginalized, on the sound sociological principle that the nuisances and nobodies will always be with us. The iconic body of Jesus, is always the *ironic* "rule" of "the least among you" (Matt. 25:44). It means precisely the opposite of Rom. 13:1-3 and stands completely free of the apocalyptic reversal of powers of 1 Corinthians 2.

Second, the iconic body of Jesus and his kingdom extends beyond God's solidarity with the weak and the ill-born into the inner citadel of theology, into the very idea of God; beyond the crucifixion of the theology of power, it requires the crucifixion of the God of power. We ask the theologians to lead a more ascetic life, to take up the cross, and to allow both the myth and the metaphysics of the power of God to be crucified. Beyond a poverty of spirit on the part of the theologians, it implies a poverty of God in which omnipotence is demythologized and deconstructed. The weakness of God not only implies God's solidarity with τὰ μὴ ὄντα; it means that God is to be numbered among them (Emmanuel), not merely in what high

Christology calls the "human nature" of Jesus, but more radically in the divine nature, instead of immunizing the divine nature against weakness and suffering. That much is addressed by the *theologia crucis* from Luther to Moltmann and Barth.[15] But the logic of the icon invites us—provokes us—further, beyond a suffering God, beyond a God strong enough to suffer, to a genuinely weak God, to God rethought as a weak force, not a strong one. This involves a Golgotha in which God is divested not only of metaphysical omnipotence but also of an apocalyptic power that makes his enemies his footstools. God must always be found on the side of weak forces like forgiveness, not a strong force like triumphing over one's enemies—politically, metaphysically, or apocalyptically. Solidarity—God takes the side of τὰ μὴ ὄντα—is rooted in the very reality of God—God belongs to the order of τὰ μὴ ὄντα. The weakness of God goes all the way down; the sociological sense of τὰ μὴ ὄντα invades the ontological sense.

The power of God is a dangerous "power trip," a metaphysical or biblical fantasy, the law of whose construction is perfectly identified by Kant: it allows a concept to run unimpeded to completion free of empirical constraints. This leads to "divine command" theories of ethics, the absolutization of institutions like the Roman Church or of books like the Scriptures (fundamentalism), to conundrums about the power of God to square circles or change the past, and to all the confusion of "theodicy," trying to figure out why God does not stop

---

15. Chalamet gives an adroit and economic sketch of the history of the *theologia crucis* from Luther and Calvin to Moltmann, Jüngel, and Barth, according to which Calvin's God "appears" to suffer in the suffering of Jesus, while Barth wants to inscribe the suffering of Jesus in the very being of God, which is a project much closer to mine. But I have nothing to do with Barth's unrelenting valorization of the absolute transcendence of God. Metaphysics needs to be overcome, but the Bible needs to be demythologized. The challenges this poses, as Chalamet rightly points out, is not to turn weakness into an absolute, not to hold God captive to weakness, completely and binarily opposed to power, but precisely to understand the power of weakness, the weak force, or power of powerlessness, without entering weakness into a long-term game of power in which weakness finally triumphs and shows itself in all its glory as the true power.

tsunamis before they happen, prevent cancer before it starts, or see to it that cruel tyrants are never born in the first place. It is complicit with obscene visions of God cruelly dashing his enemies to pieces. Worst of all, it culminates in the obscenity of all obscenities, the pathological fantasy of the eternal suffering of the damned in the face of which an unforgiving God, like a deranged and outraged tyrant, his arms folded and his face fixed forever against those who have offended his glory, eternally refuses to relent, an exquisitely perfect contradiction of the parable of the prodigal son and of the preaching of Jesus on forgiveness. Christians take a perverse satisfaction in reflecting on the cruelty of a Roman crucifixion, the slow, torturous death and the awful humiliation. But Christian torturers outdo the Romans. They dream of a still more unimaginable torment, an omni-torture, an infinitely worse pain, far more excruciating than the cross itself, and most cruelly of all—the art of torture lies in prolonging pain—the impossibility of death. This is suffering *ad infinitum*, forever and ever, in comparison with which Roman cruelty is but a trifle that mercifully ends after just a few hours. All this, as Nietzsche says, in the name of love! Nietzsche called this the "stroke of genius of Christianity." "Can you believe it?" he asks.[16]

The Call: How God is God in Radical Theology

In a radical theology of the cross, the theologians are asked to live an ascetic life and take up their cross by giving up the God of power, not just for Lent but forever, to make a sacrifice of Lord of Hosts and King of Kings, to renounce their long and illicit love affair with power. But if the power of God is a powerless power,

---

16. Friedrich Nietzsche, *On the Genealogy of Morals,* trans. Walter Kaufmann (New York: Viking, 1969), Essay Two, Sections 22–23. These texts are glossed in Jacques Derrida, "*Donner la mort,*" in *L'Éthique du don: Jacques Derrida et la pensée du don* (Paris: Métailié-Transition, 1992), 106–7; ET, *The Gift of Death,* trans. David Wills (Chicago: University of Chicago Press, 1995), 114–15.

if both metaphysical and mythic power have been crucified, if the "dominion" signified by the kingdom of God is *always* ironic, then, the theologians will protest, is not the result some kind nihilism of weakness, death, and defeat, a kind of theological masochism, a story that ends on Good Friday? What is left? How is God still God? What will they have left to offer the faithful or, as Kierkegaard might have quipped, how will they will able to earn a living? After all, their livelihood depends upon the power of religion, the "triumph of religion": the priests soothe hearts (*d'apaiser les coeurs*), as Jacques Lacan once said, and they are "absolutely fabulous" at it![17]

This brings us back to the question of method with which we began. For Heidegger, overcoming metaphysics, its destruction, means a retrieval of metaphysics, which thinks a "call" (*Ruf*) or "claim" (*Anspruch*) of Being that metaphysics contains but cannot itself think. For Bultmann, a demythologization is a reinterpretation of what having first been proclaimed (*kerygma*) in mythic terms is now proclaimed in such a way that its claim can be heard today. For Derrida, a deconstruction is a destabilization of the present order, of the order of presence, in order to remain open to the promise, to the coming of the unforeseeable event, which calls upon us like a stranger knocking on our door in the night requiring our response. In each case—the claim, the proclamation, the promise—we have to do with a "call" that is always calling and always being recalled, a call ever ancient and ever new, to which we are called upon to respond. *That call—and here we come to the crux of this* theologia crucis—*is what is meant by "God."* A radical theology of the cross has to do with the call that is harbored in and by the name (of) "God." The name (of) "God" is the name of the event that is being called, in the middle voice, in

17. Jacques Lacan, *Le Triomphe de la Religion précédé de Discours aux Catholiques* (Paris: Seuil, 2005), 79–80; ET, *The Triumph of Religion Preceded by Discourse to Catholics*, trans. Bruce Fink (Cambridge: Polity Press, 2013), 64.

what we call (in response to this event) "God," an event that is being promised, ever soft and weak, ever insistent and incessant.

So, like Nietzsche, who was dreaming a new species of philosophers, I am dreaming of a new species of radical theologians of the cross, theologians to come, theologians of the weakness of God, theologians of the life that rises from the crucifixion of the God of being, omnipotence, and omniscience on the cross of nonbeing, weakness, and foolishness. In radical theology, God is indeed the alpha and the omega, the beginning and the end, but God is not something absolute in the order of being. God is neither a highest being (classical theology), nor the Being of beings (Hegel, Tillich), nor even beyond-being (ὑπερούσιος) (mystical theology); God is neither eternal being (Augustine) nor becoming (process theology). God's being-first is not a matter of being a First Being in the order of being but, rather, of something "unconditional" in the order of a call or solicitation. God is not a great being but a suggestive voice; not a powerhouse of force but an insistent solicitation; not a mighty conqueror but a spectral spirit; not a show of "overwhelming force," the dream of every Pentagon official, but an invitation. God is indeed the name of something first and last, not in the ontological order, but in the "hauntological" order. God is a spirit, a holy and insistent specter. God is not a locatable or identifiable entity, neither a material being up in the sky nor an immaterial one outside space and time. God is not located on some planet we have yet to discover, nor in some kind immaterial sphere that can be reached only by the vehicles manufactured in the plants of metaphysics. God is not coming on the day of the Apocalypse to scatter our enemies and open the graves. God is the weak force of a spirit, a spectral visitation, a solicitation difficult to discern.

God does not belong to the order of being, presence, essence, substance, entity, or actuality. God does not exist; God insists. God does not subsist; God calls. God is not an absolute being but an unconditional call. But God is not a being calling. *Then exactly who or what is calling?* A similar issue was vexing Paul and it provided the occasion of his letter to the church at Corinth (1 Corinthians 10–17). There is a parallel problem in radical theology, where it is the call that calls. This Heideggerianism sounds to all the world like an evasive and empty tautology, but it is in fact a salutary warning against hypostatization, ontologization, mythologization. In just the way "it is raining" does not mean there is an "it" which "rains," Heidegger means that in the structure of the authentic call there is no caller who does the calling; rather, the call is getting itself called, getting itself insinuated, in the midst of a cacophony of voices, where the identity of the caller is beyond determination and must be self-authenticating.[18] In the authentic call, the authority of the caller must be crucified and the call left to hang unprotected and vulnerable. The only authenticity the call can invoke is the authenticity of the response, by means of which the call accumulates mundane reality, substance, force, strength, prestige, authority. The call calls in or under the name of God—but also under other names, which is why not everyone who is in the spirit signs on to what is called in Christian Latin "religion."

The caller of the call, the name of the caller of the call, what is finally being called for, who or what we call upon—all this is crucified, stripped away, forever secreted from the world. For the world exists but the call insists; the world is visible, but the call is invisible; the world is overt, but the call is secret. This inability to identify the caller of the call belongs *constitutively* to the authentic call; it is not a temporary dark glass that will become clear later. I hasten

18. Martin Heidegger, *Sein und Zeit*, 15th ed. (Tübingen: Niemeyer, 1979), §56-57, 272–80; ET, *Being and Time*, trans. John Macquarrie and Edward Robinson (New York: Harper & Row, 1962), 317–25.

to add that in trying to deprive the call of an identifiable caller, I am not trying to invalidate it but to maximize responsibility. I identify its authenticity by crucifying everything of worldly glory and authority that can attach itself to it. By throwing the call back on itself it is forced to be self-authenticating. The only thing that can make the call authentic is the call itself; the only thing we know about the authenticity of the call is the authenticity of the response. By their fruits you shall know them. The authenticity of the response to the call is not diminished by the crucifixion of nonknowing to which it is subjected; it is constituted by it. It is the crucifixion that gives life.

From the moment the call comes in glory, the call begins to be annulled. From the moment we identify the caller of the call, from the moment the call rests upon the identifiable authority of an authoritative entitative caller—so that we can say, this is God, this is Nature, this is the Law, this is Jesus—the authenticity of the call begins to be annulled and becomes a matter of following the orders of an assured, powerful, prestigious, identifiable, or even intimidating voice (like the God who bullies Job). True responsibility, which means the responsibility we assume for the call, devolves into a commanded response. God is not an agent who does things like calling. From the moment we attribute agency to God, we are back in mythology, metaphysics, and theodicy. The name of God is instead the name of something that is getting itself named and called in and under this name, something in whose name agents are mobilized. "Mobilized" is strong talk, a militant metaphor—but the force so mobilized is not being attributed to God but to us; it is a human attribute, not a divine one.

God is the insistence for which we are to supply existence, where we are the ones that belong to the order of existence, being, presence, and actuality.[19] God is an inexistent solicitation, to which we are to be the existential response. God insists; we exist. We are responsible for the existence of God, for the material reality of God in the world, called upon to fill up what is lacking in the body of God, to cite again the author of the letter to the Colossians. We cannot be separated from God and God cannot be separated from us, but the difference between God and us cannot be closed; it is a distance that is never crossed between an unconditional solicitation, on the one side, and the conditional responses made by us, on the other side. God is the question to which we should be the answer; God is the problem to which we should be resolution. But we are always giving finite answers to an infinite question, making finite responses to an infinite demand. So by "unconditional" I do not mean an ideal that runs to completion, which is a fundamental operation common to both metaphysics and mythologization. The unconditional is not an ideal but an ordeal, an injunction, and a "hope against hope" (Rom. 4:18) in the open-endedness of the future.

The unconditional insistence of a call means that it is inextinguishable yet also weak. In 1 Corinthians 1 the call is clearly audible as the unconditional solicitation or appeal that issues from, that hovers over and inhabits, the body of the crucified Jesus. The spirit of the God of Jesus rises from the cross like a specter that haunts and solicits us. The call is issued in and under the body of the crucified Jesus and is expressed in the paradoxical, paralogical, and foolish logic of the cross, which is a scandal to the order of power and being. The singling out of weakness is unconditional: not weakness as part of long-term strategy that requires biding our time, but the unconditional embrace of the order of τὰ μὴ ὄντα.

But a call is itself a weak force, not a strong one. Calls may be ignored, misunderstood, unanswered, manipulated, refused, and defied. In such cases the call as such, the call as call, has no army it

---

19. For a fuller elaboration of this point, I beg leave to refer to my *The Insistence of God: A Theology of Perhaps* (Bloomington: Indiana University Press, 2013).

may call upon; it has no physical or metaphysical force with which it may enforce what it calls for. The law has a police to enforce it, and worldly kings have armies, but the force of the call is weak and naked and without recourse, left to plead its own case, to speak for itself. The call is not enforced by an *Über*-being who will see to it that we will rue the day we ignored his (sic!) will. It is left to hang on the cross, abandoned by its God. *Eli, Eli.*

We in turn are the ones called upon, the *ek-klesia*, the recipients of the call, the ones who are addressed and laid claim to (1 Cor. 1:24), the ones who answer the call and as such we are called upon to be strong. We are called upon to be the *Antwort* to God's *Wort*, to make strong what is still weak in God, giving existence to God's insistence. To put the classical language of metaphysics to a strictly phenomenological use, I would say that the essence of God lies in God's insistence, while God's existence is *our* responsibility.[20] God belongs to the order of unconditional insistence, not infinite existence; to an order that is not existential but vocative, evocative, provocative, while we, on the other hand, belong to the order of existence, of the vocational, of responsibility, of the ones who are called—like an apostle.

---

20. What I mean is found in a radical theology of the Trinity, where the Father and the Son empty out without remainder into the Spirit, who in turn empties out into the people of God, the *populus Dei*, who give strength to God's weakness, existence to God's insistence. It is found in Bonhoeffer's religionless Christianity, in which we are asked to be "mature" (τέλειοι), and to understand that God is not a superbeing who will come down from heaven to rescue us in distress; in Kierkegaard, where the name of God is taken to be a *deed*, something to be enacted existentially; in Meister Eckhart's interpretation of the story of Mary and Martha where Mary savors the insistence of God, but Martha understands that it is our responsibility to see that God exists; in Walter Benjamin's idea of the Messiah, where we are the messianic age, the ones called upon to remedy the injustice done to the dead. In each case, the name of God is an insistence that, lacking a response, would dissipate and be forgotten in a night of oblivion and inexistence.

Neither Paul nor Apollos nor Cephas (1 Corinthians 1:12): Demythologizing the Call

The immediate occasion of 1 Corinthians is Paul's effort to quell the quarrels that have broken out among various factions of the saints, some of whom are loyal to Paul, others to Apollos or Cephas. As I mentioned above, I see in this question of Corinthian factionalism a parallel problem of special importance to a radical theology of the cross, one whose terms I want now to spell out by returning to Bultmann.

It would be a mistake to think that I have, by a circuitous route through deconstruction, simply gone back to Bultmann. Unlike Heidegger, I am not trying to go back to the early Greeks, and unlike Luther and Bultmann, I am not going back to the Bible. Both "overcoming metaphysics" and "demythologizing the Bible" are, I think, too narrow and too monological when it comes to the λόγος of the cross. I am trying to make my way back, cautiously and with fear and trembling, to the event, to the call—with all the help I can get from overcoming metaphysics, demythologizing the Bible, the deconstruction of presence, and whatever other help is offered me, whatever its source. But the call I have in mind has been stripped of worldly adornment, robbed of its historical authority and prestige, crowned with the thorns of unidentifiability, humiliated, and made to take up its cross. So I subscribe completely to Bultmann's notion of relieving the "call" of its mythological context in the New Testament and recontextualizing it in such a way that the call can be heard by what he described—back in the middle of the twentieth century—as "modern man," an expression I would hasten to update on his behalf with "*post*modern men *and women*" (as I am sure he would also have done today), in all their complexity and multiplicity. I wholeheartedly subscribe as well as to his crowning of supernaturalism with the thorns of skepticism. The historical record of supernatural interventions in nature or history on behalf of the good since the advent of Christianity, not to mention the history of the good example given by Christians being guided by the light of supernatural revelation, is so bad one wonders why Christian theologians keep bringing it up.

My difference with Bultmann—and my difference with Paul—lies in the meaning of the "call" and the "event," which Bultmann like Paul has contracted to *the* kerygma, that is, *the* historical proclamation by Paul and the early church of Jesus as *the* one, the *One*, as *the* saving light unto the nations, *the* revelation of God to humanity. I certainly agree that that is what we mean by "Christianity," a project in which I involve myself by pursuing the motif of the iconic weakness of Jesus. But if that is the way to identify Christianity, it is not the mark of the call or the event, not as such, which is unidentifiable, desert-like, and austere. The identifying feature of the call as such, as we have seen above, is that it is precisely unidentifiable, that it is precisely impossible to call out the caller of the call, to locate the provenance and future of the call, which would be its domestication and ruin. The call is neither Paul's nor Apollos's nor Cephas's nor that of *any* identifiable agent, including the New Testament *kerygma*. That means that we are always and everywhere driven by a desire beyond desire, called by a future we cannot foresee while trying to recall something immemorial. So the *one* thing we do know about the "event" is that there is no such thing as *the* event, *the* call, no such thing as *the* response to a call whose "defining" trait is that it gives us no rest. There is no such thing or person who can be said to be *the* icon of *the* invisible god, no such thing as *the* kerygma, or even of "religion," in the singular, *"la" religion*. There are always and everywhere many calls, many historical revelations, many gods and many alternatives to God and the gods (not to mention many planets, solar systems, galaxies, more dimensions than three, and, we are now being told, many universes, and who knows how many forms of life).

So my complaint with Bultmann is not the orthodox one, that he has gutted Christian doctrine—I think by demystifying it he has gone a long way toward revivifying it—but the more radical one, that he not quite managed to lift himself off the ground of myth. The event is not what happens, but what is going on *in* what happens. The event is not to be identified with Aeschylus or Shakespeare, Athens or Jerusalem, the Christ or Buddha, democracy or the universal declaration of human rights, God or reason, art or politics. The world is a bit wider than that. As factually situated historical beings we must always and necessarily nominate the event, but the event, ever weak and modest, always declines the nomination. The event is what is going on *in* these happenings, what is being called and recalled there, what is being promised and desired there, with a desire beyond desire. *The very structure of the mythic operation is to conflate the event with an entity, to reduce the insistence of the event to a concrete existent*, to confuse the name or the desire for this or that with the structurally restless movement of that desire beyond desire which keeps the future open and subjects the past to ever-changing meanings. The watchword of deconstruction, its first, last, and constant word, its constant prayer, is "come," *viens, oui, oui*. Given our historical facticity or situatedness, the event is never found, never experienced, except *in* this or that tradition, time or place, given text or person, but the call itself has not the wherewithal to lay down its head. The final crucifixion of the call is to confess that it is never reducible to this or that. While it has an "identity" (we can name and locate it), this or that thing or text or tradition is never identifiable with itself, never self-identical. It is always at odds with itself and suggestive of a polyphony, a cacophony of voices within, a palimpsest of calls and memories too interwoven to untangle. That is paradigmatically true of our own lives, which is captured so beautifully by Augustine's *quaestio mihi magna factus sum*.

We might say that what I am calling radical theology of the cross is *more* than demythologization, more radical than that, that it goes further than Bultmann and regards *the kerygma* as itself one more myth in need of demythologizing. That would be true enough. But I would prefer to say that it is *less* than demythologizing, much weaker, not nearly as audacious or strong enough to identify the call, to speak the name of *the kerygma*, *the* call, *the* event. Demythologization is too strong, too glorious for a *theologia crucis*.

On the Road to Damascus

Nothing illustrates this point about the poverty of the call better than Paul himself. Everything about Paul speaks of the call. He is an apostle, a man sent off (ἀπο στέλλειν) on an expedition around the known world in response to a call heard by no one else in the world, especially not by the church back in Jerusalem. His life is the effect of an address of traumatic proportions, a solicitation that broke into his life and turned him around. But what is this call—actually, specifically, really, ontically, ontologically? Luke repeats the story three times in Acts (9:1-9; 22:6; 26:12-18)—he is overtaken by a voice and a blinding light on the road to Damascus—and Paul himself tells it to the Galatians (1:11-17), where it is a revelation of the risen Jesus, no mention of lights or voices or the road to Damascus. For one of the most famous visual elements, the unhorsing, we owe the artists who visualized it for us, Tintoretto and other Renaissance painters. So it is impossible to settle on exactly what actually happened, what did or did not take place in the entitative order, which entirely lacked a worldly or mundane witness. If there were a video camera at the scene, we are not sure whether it would record a man in quiet prayer or a man on a horse struck by a light that his companions could not see although they could hear the voice. All this confusion suggests something amiss in this line of inquiry, something that invites us to suspend or prescind from such empirical-entitative considerations. What we know is that a call was called and heard, that there was above all, first and last, a call, an *unconditional* call, which changed everything in Paul's life. Was there a physical voice that would have been recorded by a microphone? A visible being in the sky that would have been recorded on a camera? An invisible inaudible supernatural being issuing the call? That is all foolishness, an uncomprehending literalization of an event, the hypostasization of an appellation, the ontologizing of a solicitation. The call is an insistence whose *only existence in the world is found in the response to the call*, in the life of Paul, whose traces have been preserved best of all in seven surviving short letters. What we know is that the call insists, while Paul exists. What we have, what has appeared in the world is Paul, not the call. Paul is visible; the call is invisible, inaudible. The only reality the call possesses is Paul. The only existence the call enjoys is found in the response, which is the life of Paul thereafter, and then the afterlife of Paul in the community, in the *Wirkungsgeschichte* of Paul, which a lot of people think is pretty much what we mean by "Christianity."

But if it is a gross literalization to ask whether Paul heard something with his physical ears or saw something with his physical eyes, is it not still fair to ask who or what was calling Paul? Was it not Jesus of Nazareth, as Paul said? Not in any ordinary sense, since Jesus had been crucified some years earlier. Then might it have been some event buried deep in his unconscious—say, the stoning of Stephen or some unexpected encounter with members of the

Jesus movement—that resurfaced later in the form of this call? Might he have caught a fleeting glimpse of Jesus one day, inadvertently, and been forever incapable of forgetting that moment which finally revisited him? Was it remorse? Was it a dream? Was Paul suddenly visited by something in the memory of Jesus to which the followers of "the way" gave testimony that unexpectedly touched his heart and in turn brought about his abrupt change of heart? Was this moment preceded by a long reflection or was it really just a sudden turnabout? Was it a mystical vision of the risen Jesus, and was that a hallucination? We cannot say; we only know what Paul says, which describes a "revelation," which is a phenomenological event, not an ontological one, to which he gives an explanation, which is a hermeneutic one.

Now what interests me still more is that not only can *we* not say what took place in the ontological or entitative order, but Paul cannot say, either. I do not only mean that he cannot, by definition, say what is going on in his unconscious, or that he was left speechless by an overpowering mystical experience. On the contrary, we could fill many libraries many times over with the speeches of the people who have had experiences that left them speechless. I mean, rather, that what he does say is entirely enmeshed, woven (*textere*) within the imagery, the vocabulary, and the messianic hopes of the Judaism he inherited and the world in which he lived. On this point, his calling is like other callings belonging to other people in other times and other places, which are no less dramatic and transforming, but are entirely woven or enmeshed in other terms, in which the name of Jesus is completely unknown. We can even imagine, counterfactually, that were Paul to be found in another time and place, speaking another language and inheriting another tradition, having read other books and been taught by other masters, whatever happened to him that day, if it were just one day, would have been put quite differently. (In just the way that we can ask, if we take Augustine at his word, what would Augustine have done had the book that lay by chance on the table when he heard the children playing *tolle, lege* had been Ovid's *Metamorphoses* and not Paul's letter to the Romans conveniently translated into Latin?) Calls are events that are embedded virtually in networks of texts and messages, angelic or otherwise, events that circulate about us and solicit us in a nascent state and which, occasionally, reach a point of explosive intensity in intense personalities and explosive agents like Paul or Augustine or the Buddha under the Bodhi tree. The occasion of the call, which results in something exceptional, may "for all the world" be something simple and unexceptional and ontologically unimpressive—children at play, or a man at prayer—when suddenly something rushes in upon him, something insistent which issues in a surge in existence.

Given such occlusion, Paul wisely makes everything depend on faith. But here I would distinguish faith (*foi*) from belief (*croyance*), a *foi* that underlies but simultaneously destabilizes any given *croyance*, a *fides* that founds and unfounds a *credo*.[21] Beliefs have grounds, but faith is a groundless ground. A creedal belief belongs to the world. It is directed toward some identifiable being or actual entity, in this world or up in some other world, toward a being past, present, or to come. It participates in the glory of the world, the prestige of powerful propositions and the creeds of famous councils, of famous orthodoxies that persecute infamous heresies. Beliefs concern beings, propositions, arguments, institutions; beliefs are part and parcel of the glory of the world, of politics and religion; they are mundane

---

21. Jacques Derrida, "Foi et savoir: Les deux sources de la 'religion' aux limites de la simple raison," in Jacques Derrida and Gianni Vattimo, eds., *Religion* (Paris: Editions du Seuil, 1996), no. 11, p. 16; ET, "Faith and Knowledge: The Two Sources of 'Religion' at the Limits of Reason Alone," trans. Samuel Weber, in Gil Anidjar, ed., *Acts of Religion* (New York and London: Routledge, 2002), no. 11, p. 47.

actualities, and they are capable of spilling a great deal of blood. But faith has to do with inexistence, with a poor and worldless and unidentifiable insistence, with a solicitation by something, I know not what, which calls upon me with a spectral presence, by which I am visited, unexpectedly, like a knock on the door in the middle of night, which acquires body, substance, existence, and mundane reality only in my response. Faith cannot be contracted to stable and identifiable positions and propositions. Faith has to do with an open-ended promise of something, I know not what. I am not trying to simply oppose faith and belief but to describe the dynamics of their intertwining or interweaving, in virtue of which faith haunts belief, disturbs, and ungrounds it, exposing its contingency, while belief gives faith worldliness, mundane reality, existence. Faith insists; beliefs exist.

I also hasten to add that I am not saying all calls are the same, that there is some universal a priori self-same truth in all calls, that all "religions" are the same, that all the "mystics" have the same message. I am not turning deconstruction into the historically naïve universalism of the old comparative religion. On the contrary, I started out by underlining the specific and distinctive, revolutionary, and radical reconception of God in 1 Corinthians 1, the "special revelation," which picks up the (literally) crucial point in the iconic glimpse we catch of God in the figure of Jesus. I am saying neither that this experience, this revelation, is invalid nor that every revelation is the same. I am trying to identify the self-validating, self-authenticating element in Paul. There is something special in Paul, and in the special something that was getting itself said and called in 1 Corinthians 1, something that was circulating in the complex network of meanings (the phenomenological "world") in which Paul lived, something solicited and called for, in whatever happened to Paul.

Conclusion

In a radical theology of the cross, the call that is harbored in the name (of) "God" is stripped of all worldly glory; its power and prestige are mocked and humiliated; and it is forced back on itself, on its nakedness, unworldliness, lack of being, and abandonment by God. The call is reduced to an inspiring spirit or a haunting specter, a voice ever soft and low, of unknown provenance, *sans papiers*, without assurances or guarantees, risky and uncertain. Its only credentials are the call itself, the call that it makes, a call that could not be more foreign or more foolish to the world—to greet one's enemies with love, the offender with forgiveness, to say "come" to the coming of the unforeseeable, which is always dangerous. Its only authority is the authority without authority of a call divested of an author; its only worldly reality is the response, the history of the responses made in and under its name.

But the λόγος of the cross is not a recipe for impotence and nihilism. On the contrary, it is the very tissue of hope in life, a λόγος of the most profound *faith* in life. This faith does not come decked out in the glory of creedal confessions, robed in grand and well-adorned doctrines, wearing the breastplate of religion, supported by the power of inerrant books and infallible institutions. It is a pure faith, insecure and exposed, uncertain and unprotected, a crucified faith without faith that calls for what is to come, calling for something coming, recalling something from time immemorial. This faith is naked; this nakedness is faith. This faith is in the future, in the spectral possibility of being otherwise, in life as it is transmitted across the time of our own lives and the time of the generations, in more life, which is the meaning of resurrection—precisely in accord with the λόγος of the cross and the weakness that is stronger than the world.

Discussion Following John D. Caputo's Keynote Lecture[22]

Anthony Feneuil: Overall I am in agreement with your proposal, but there is something that perplexes me. I think there is something paradoxical in your proposal, both on the epistemological and the political levels, since it seems to me that the idea of an all-powerful God has been used in the history of theology and philosophy to limit the power of human thought. And so I wonder whether the idea of the weakness of God would not leave us with an all-powerful human thought. When you combine the onto-theological critique in Paul with the idea of the weakness of God, there is something paradoxical, and the same applies on the political level: when you call for a new theology which would be radical and poor, but at the same time you give theologians the responsibility of making God exist, it seems to me that there is something paradoxical.

John Caputo: The first point is this: I agree with you that Paul should have drawn a different conclusion when he spoke about the absolute power and authority of God, when he argued that no one has genuine authority except God. Instead of an order or chain of command, he should have simply said that it relativizes human power, and therefore all human power is constructed, historically constructed, and thus it is deconstructible, and intrinsically so, because nobody has real authority except God. That means this is a case of *ignoratio elenchi*—he drew the wrong conclusion. But then we're stuck with this omnipotent God and we get all these problems of theodicy, all the difficulties that ensue from an absolute authority, the absolute power of God.

Second, I am not transferring (in a Feuerbachian move) God's

---

22. This is not a word-for-word transcript of the discussion; some details have been revised here and there, for stylistic reasons as well as for the sake of clarity.

qualities to human beings. I am not saying that human beings are omnipotent or powerful. I am saying they are very fragile, very weak, and they are called to be strong. What happens in the name of God is a solicitation that calls us out and summons us, and calls us to do the best we can and to be as strong as we can. It doesn't endow us with any omnipotence. We don't become superheroes.

Michel Grandjean: Thank you for your thought-provoking paper. With your proposal and your christological, or even Jesusological, concentration, is there still a space for a trinitarian theology, or is the door completely shut to it?

John Caputo: Christianity is christocentric. The very idea of Christianity is christocentric. But I do want to rethink the Spirit and the Trinity in terms of an absolute emptying of the Father and the Son into the Spirit, and an absolute emptying or kenosis of the Spirit into the people, into the *populus Dei.* Vatican II said the church is not the hierarchy but the *populus Dei* (and that's the first thing Pope John Paul II went after). There is a theology of the Trinity in which the Spirit, recalling Joachim of Fiore, finally becomes the people of God. And so, yes, this would involve a radical theology of the Trinity.

Philipp Stoellger: I am ready to follow you in your (how should I call it?) weakness-trip, but could you give us some further clarification on what happens to the two expressions of "power" and "weakness" if there is such a thing as the "power of weakness" or the "power of powerlessness." It's an oxymoron, of course, and I am not sure whether weakness, love, or forgiveness are infected by the old use of power. Just one small additional remark: I would resist using a strong theory of icon, following Jean-Luc Marion, to buttress your idea of the symbolic body of Christ. There I would look for another theory to avoid such a strong cataphatic theory of icon. But my main question is: What happens when the two, that is, power and weakness, are meeting?

John Caputo: Well, this is actually the first time I have used or had Jean-Luc Marion on my side. I normally give him a hard time, mostly because of his ultramontane Catholicism. So you think that my use of weakness, my treatment of forgiveness tends to infect it with power in the strong sense. I actually am trying not to do that; I am trying to do the opposite. I want to say that the ethical-religious majesty of forgiveness is mad by the standards of what the world calls power, because it is a weak force or a power of powerlessness. We can see this in the political sphere in nonviolent activity, in nonviolent protest—not passive resistance, because it's not passive, it's very active, but it's nonviolent, and it's very dangerous; it's a good way to get killed. And so nonviolent protest, walking into the teeth of danger and speaking the truth to power, παρρησία, is what I mean by "power of powerlessness." We do not arrive at the scene packing a gun; we are only wearing the truth.

Andrew Hay: Thank you very much for your paper. Coming from a "strong" position, I would like a little clarification on a few terms that you used. You used the expression "divine summons," for instance. What do you make of the fact that Paul, in 1 Corinthians 2, does use the expression "Lord of glory," and he does that obviously in retrospect from the fact that the divine missions play out: there is a resurrection, there is an ascension, there is the coming of the Spirit. What do you make of that final movement?

John Caputo: I take Paul in the second chapter to be walking back what he says in the first chapter, or: I take him to be pulling the trigger of the rhetorical structure he has set up in the first chapter. I

61

think that he should stay with the power of powerlessness, he should stay with the weakness of God, stay with τὰ μὴ ὄντα, and not pull that trigger, not turn God into the Lord of glory, unless you mean by that the majesty of hospitality, of forgiveness, of nonretaliation: the Lord of glory in *that* sense. Because you can't simply excommunicate words, you can't say you're never going to use the word *power* or the word *glory*, you can only recontextualize them. So I would recontextualize words like "glory" in the sense of "the glory of saying to my executioner: 'you are forgiven.'" That would be δόξα, for me. But, you see, I don't think Paul is just doing that. I think Paul has an apocalyptic vision, and those people who disagree with him are going to perish, they're going to burn. And the authors of the canonical Gospels have Jesus say the same thing.

John Barclay: Thank you very much for such an interesting paper. It seems to me you are willing to reuse the language of power in a certain sense. You talk about "strengthening the dignity of women," "building up the third world," and that is exactly what one wants, is it not, politically? To the people who are up to their neck in debts, paying thousands of percents in debt, unable to feed their children, you don't say, "Just forgive the people who are actually absolutely ripping you off," you say: "Work with people who can call these people to account." You need to empower the powerless, and it seems to me that to a point you are willing to reuse that language, in other words to a point you seem to be going to a full reversal, where all we want is a God who has absolutely no power, but then you don't finish there because you want a different kind of power. And it seems to me: I would give a reading of Paul as doing exactly that, if he reuses the language of "power," as he explicitly does when he says that "the weakness of God is *stronger* than human strength"—the text which, as you say, is absolutely crucial for this discussion—then why is it not the power precisely of ἀγάπη? After all, that's where 1 Corinthians 13 finishes, with "faith, hope, and love," these things abide eschatologically, and the greatest of these is ἀγάπη, and it seems to me that that is the power with which Jesus will rule the universe.

John Caputo: I don't think Paul settles simply with that. I think he should, but I don't think it stops there, I think he has a vision of an apocalyptic climax to the world in which those who reject this word will regret it. He doesn't stop with love, love is without why (*"ohne warum"*); ἀγάπη is without retaliation, without recrimination, and without a system of rewards and punishments; it is an expenditure without return. Paul has an economy, he has a calculus, he has a story, he has built a cosmic drama that goes from Adam to Jesus, and Jesus redeems us with his crucifixion, and Paul has that straight from God—and he tolerates no dissent. He has that straight from Jesus himself. Sometimes he tells something on the basis of the Scriptures, telling us to do this or that, sometimes he says: "I have this from the Lord," period. And if you don't sign on, you'll wish you did. He says that. They will regret it. They crucified the Lord of glory. They will perish. He doesn't stop with love. Love is entered into an economy.

Adam Eitel: Just as an immediate response to what you just said: Can you say more about why love is incompatible with punishment? I am not sure how you are conceiving what you just said. You seem to be suggesting that there is this agapic love which you want to attribute to God, but it's incompatible with Paul's claim that those who don't acknowledge God will be sorry. Where is the incompatibility?

John Caputo: The sense in which they will be and should be sorry is the sense in which they demean themselves, they degrade themselves,

63

they make themselves complicit with cruelty and ugliness. If that's all that is meant, then I agree. But I don't think that's all that Paul meant. He meant: the time is short, get on board with what I am telling you, or you're going to be sorry because you're going to fry. Let me make a more general point. In case you missed it: I am saying something highly unorthodox. I don't think the name of God is the name of an entity who does things, and who rewards and punishes. I think the name of God is the name of—to put it in Derrida's terms—the possibility of the impossible, or—to put it in St. Augustine's terms—it's the name of our *cor inquietum*, that is, of the restlessness of the heart which dreams, with prayers and tears, of the coming of something inconceivable, unimaginable, that eyes have not seen nor ears heard. There are a number of ways to embody, incarnate, and actualize that kind of aspiration of the heart. What we today call, in Christian Latin, "religion" is one of them, but it is only one of them. It happens in a lot of ways. So, to fully explain this we would need to examine what Derrida calls an "event." I think the name of God is the name of an event, where the event of all events is the possibility of the impossible. The name of God is systematically associated with the possibility of the impossible in the Scriptures, and even in common parlance. So, I am not interested in God. I am not interested in the name of God. I am interested in the event which is harbored by the name of God, by what is going on in that event. For me, it is mythologizing to turn an event into an entity. Something is getting itself said and done in a tradition that organizes itself around the name of God and of Jesus. What I am interested in is what is going on *in* that tradition.

Denis Müller: Thank you, John, for your theological boldness. You are a philosopher who challenges us with real theological questions. We may agree or disagree with you, we do wish to continue the conversation. Many things come up in our minds as we listen to you. Personally, hearing you I was thinking about Melanchthon and his claim about how the *beneficia* matter, and so the event, and not how Christ's two natures relate. At the same time, I would like to read Nietzsche with you, and as a theologian I would perhaps be more Nietzschean than you, for Nietzsche probably preferred 1 Corinthians 2, and its emphasis on strength and force, compared to 1 Corinthians 1, which centers on weakness in a way that sidesteps creativity and strength. But that conversation will be for another time. We are grateful for your contribution. Thank you!

3

———

On a Road Not Taken: Iterations of an Alexandrian Paul

Kellen Plaxco

Late-modern questions and concerns lead Paul's readers to suppose that Paul's opposition of "wisdom" to "folly" is the lens for focusing Paul's meaning.[1] Just so, the best reading of Paul's First Letter to the Corinthians is the reading that best interprets that opposition's dissonance as the center of Paul's thought.[2] It is not as though Paul

1. Research for this essay was conducted with the support of a Fulbright Belgium Student Research Grant. I am grateful to the Belgian Fulbright Commission and the Lectio Centre at Katholieke Universiteit Leuven, under whose generous auspices I was able to work at leisure during the 2012–13 academic year. My thanks to Christophe Chalamet for his invitation to attend the conference in Geneva where I read a version of this essay. I would also like to thank Michel Barnes, Adam Eitel, and Drew Harmon for helpful comments on earlier drafts. All shortcomings remain my own.
2. A number of issues philosophical and hermeneutical divide Paul's late-modern interpreters. One

does not oppose cruciform folly to worldly wisdom. Any exegete must acknowledge Paul's playful polarities of wisdom and folly, power and weakness, and so on. But it is not a foregone conclusion that this opposition forms the core of Paul's theology in 1 Corinthians or elsewhere. (It is even less a foregone conclusion that such a Pauline theology should form the heart of Christian doctrine itself—but that is another matter.) Late-modern readers often belie concerns neither neatly nor simply "Pauline" as they elevate Paul's opposition of "wisdom" to "folly" to a position of utmost importance for getting Paul right and understanding his meaning on the whole.

We do not find the same kinds of anxieties animating Alexandrian exegetes. Or, at least, not the same kinds of anxieties *to the same degree*. It is not as though one cannot find remarks in the Greek

---

point of wide agreement, explicit or implicit, is that the opposition of "wisdom" to "folly" in chs. 1–2 lies at the heart of Paul's letter. So the way to succeed or fail at interpreting the Paul of 1 Corinthians is to get these chapters right. Two clear examples, each from different exegetical and philosophical perspectives, are John Barclay and John Caputo. Barclay argues that "wisdom" and "folly" are not to be viewed, by Paul's lights, "merely in intellectual terms, as rationality or illogic, but as umbrella labels for the presence or absence of 'civilized' values" (Barclay, above, 2). Yet, in spite of Barclay's compelling exegetical transposition of a familiar theme (rationality opposed to absurdity) into the key of social marginalization (those without power subverting those who have it), the fundamental opposition between "wisdom" and "folly" remains the overarching lens for his interpretation of Paul: "The wisdom of the cross is not just an alternative wisdom but an anti-wisdom, refuting or subverting what would normally be taken for granted" (above, 5). Barclay does not argue explicitly that chs. 1–2 form the core of 1 Corinthians, but it is safe to infer from his presentation that he presumes their centrality to Paul's gospel. Barclay does not go so far as Caputo, who argues that Paul's *Christianity* should preach the "power of weakness" all the way down, even to the point of denying God's existence. "God does not exist; God *insists*," Caputo claims (above, 45). Paul's opposition of the "power of powerlessness" to "the things that are" drives Caputo to this position. The hermeneutical centrality of Paul's opposition of "foolishness" to "wisdom" extends to other influential New Testament interpreters, such as J. Louis Martyn, who presumes a radicalized version of the opposition in his "apocalyptic" reading of Paul. Martyn argues not only that "wisdom" is opposed to "foolishness" for Paul, but also that the "word of the cross" "obliterates" any prior human reasoning that might have been developed prior to its advent: "[Paul] denies that . . . the gospel of the crucified Christ . . . is subject to human evaluation, whether that of the Gentiles or that of the Jews (1 Cor. 1:22-24). And in this denial Paul obliterates in one stoke the thought that the gospel is subject to criteria of perception that have been developed apart from the gospel!" J. Louis Martyn, "John and Paul on the Subject of Gospel and Scripture," in *Theological Issues in the Letters of Paul* (Edinburgh: T&T Clark, 1997), 220.

fathers about the "weakness of God" in discussions about divine impassibility. However, the extent to which early Greek readers of 1 Corinthians were exercised by Paul's alleged "opposition" of cruciform folly to worldly wisdom is much less evident than it is in modern commentary on the same biblical material.[3] When Clement, Origen, and Didymus comment on 1 Corinthians 1–2, they make little of what some see as Paul's fundamental "opposition" of worldly wisdom to cruciform folly.

We might explain the apparent silence as an accident of history. The polemical context, perhaps, did not lend itself to reflection on this aspect of Paul's letter to the Corinthians. Or it could have been that opposing pagan to Christian wisdom was not well suited to the purposes of the Alexandrians, who never shied from plundering the spoils of the Egyptians.[4] Yet, in the final analysis, one gets the sense that the Alexandrians never felt obliged to account for such an opposition in the first place. At the very most, as Andrew Louth has noticed in the case of Maximos the Confessor, although God's foolish "play" with human beings is important, "it seems to be a stage that may well be necessary, but only because of human weakness and sin."[5] The Alexandrian Paul preaches a cross that only *seems* to be foolish but is ultimately prudent.

Alexandrian exegesis of 1 Corinthians implicitly questions late-modern anxieties about Paul's hyperbolic rhetoric. The following account of Origen's and Didymus's theological exegesis is not intended to challenge those who take Paul to have been motivated by or committed to a fundamental opposition of "wisdom" to "folly."

3. For more on the topic of divine impassibility in patristic thought, see Paul Gavrilyuk, *The Suffering of the Impassible God: The Dialectics of Patristic Thought* (Oxford: Oxford University Press, 2004).
4. Origen famously followed the spirit of Clement's *Protrepticus* with his statement about plundering the spoils of Egypt.
5. Andrew Louth, below, 97–98.

Rather, I place alongside such late-modern accounts a reading of 1 Cor. 1:24 that finds in Paul an ultimate wisdom. Nevertheless, it is a "wisdom" that inscribes the "folly of the cross" within God's very being—the Trinity. For these readers, as well as their Paul, the cross that appeared "foolish" to the Gentiles was indeed God's power and wisdom.[6] Christ, the eternal Son of God was and remains the power and wisdom of God. The Alexandrians' attempt to inscribe that "foolishness" within divine nature was their way of ensuring that Christian doctrine would always teach the powerful message of God's self-donation and love, which in turn is inscribed on the soul that believes in this God who gives without ceasing to give—and without ceasing to be God. Origen was responsible for using this Pauline verse to show that the Father could never be without this "foolish" Wisdom. Didymus, for his part, ensured that God's self-donation should come to be sealed in the soul. Taken together, these theologians secured such important doctrinal *desiderata* without recourse to a fundamental opposition of the cross to wisdom.[7] Origen and Didymus thus mark out a path not often taken in late-modern readings of 1 Corinthians 1–2.

This essay sketches the function of "power" and "wisdom" in the trinitarian theologies of Origen and Didymus. My historical-theological account is as follows. Origen identifies the Son as God's Wisdom and Power. However, he does not succeed in linking the Holy Spirit to Wisdom's creative activities. This failure undermines his own anti-monarchian protestations that the Holy Spirit is more than mere divine activity. Following my account of Origen's

---

6. Not God's "ruse," as Caputo insinuates, but God's Wisdom.

7. I reiterate that I do not take issue with modern readings that underline that Paul opposes "wisdom" to "folly," but with the fact that modern readers fail to take seriously the possibility that Paul's opposition is a rhetorical device, and so only depicts an apparent opposition. That possibility seems to have been more plausible to Paul's ancient readers than to his late-modern exegetes.

doctrine, I will provide a new account of Didymus's revision of the tradition he inherited from Origen.[8] Didymus would stay true to Origen's tendency to see in the Son an "image" of the invisible Father, the Father's Wisdom hypostasized. On the other hand, he provides the Holy Spirit with a more clearly articulated divine office: the Holy Spirit is the divine, creative power that creates Christ's body in Mary, and the Holy Spirit is the untutored Wisdom that teaches the Son. Didymus also excludes the possibility that the Holy Spirit is "divine" in a way comparable to the angels or sanctified human souls. The Holy Spirit, for Didymus, is unequivocally God.[9] Didymus's adjustments stay within the bounds of Origen's established identification of the Word with Wisdom, but they mitigate Origen's implied *reduction* of divine "power" to the Son, and introduce the possibility that the Holy Spirit, too, is a "power" that proceeds from a "power."

Origen

We begin with an account of Origen's reading of the Power and Wisdom of God.[10] "Power" and "Wisdom" were technical

---

8. I will not here rehearse what little is known of Didymus's life. A brief but useful introduction may be found in Andrew Louth, "The Fourth-Century Alexandrians: Athanasius and Didymus," in Frances Young, Lewis Ayres, and Andrew Louth, eds., *The Cambridge History of Early Christian Literature* (Cambridge: Cambridge University Press, 2004), 275–82. The account of Didymus in this paper is limited to the theology of Didymus's *On the Holy Spirit*. French readers will be familiar with the *Sources Chrétiennes* edition and translation of the work—already the translation of Jerome's original, Latin translation; see *Traité du Saint-Esprit*, ed. Louis Doutreleau, SC 386 (Paris: Cerf, 1992). English readers may make use of a recent English translation, by Mark DelCogliano, Andrew Radde-Gallwitz, and Lewis Ayres, *Works on the Spirit: Athanasius and Didymus* (Crestwood, NY: St. Vladimir's Seminary Press, 2011). In what follows, I abbreviate *On the Holy Spirit* as *Spir.* for *de Spiritu Sancto*, followed by the paragraph numbers in Doutreleau's edition, also used by the English translation.

9. See esp. *Spir.* 83, 130, and 224, for Didymus's explicit professions of the Spirit's divinity.

10. The following background sketch of Origen's theology is not intended to break new ground. The account of Origen's Wisdom Christology is a compressed form of the account found in ch. 3 of Michel René Barnes, *The Power of God: Δυναμις in Gregory of Nyssa* (Washington, DC: Catholic University of America Press, 2001). The description of Origen's pneumatology owes

theological terms and were invoked by Origen within the context of a tradition that knew them as such.[11] In 1 Cor. 1:24, Paul brings these terms together and says that Christ is both God's "Power" and God's "Wisdom." Origen invokes the verse at two points in *On First Principles* in trinitarian contexts: 1.2.1 and 1.2.9. In 1.2.1, Origen links Paul's statement that Christ is the "Power and Wisdom of God" to the "Wisdom" who speaks in Prov. 8:22. From this identification Origen proceeds to the conclusion that "the only-begotten Son of God is God's wisdom hypostatically existing."[12] Based on this conclusion,

---

much to the narrative related in Michel Barnes, "The Beginning and End of Early Christian Pneumatology," *Augustinian Studies* 39 (2008): 169–86. My presentation of Didymus's theology of the Holy Spirit, on the other hand, *does* introduce an original synthesis of Didymus's trinitarian contributions. I take as my point of departure the excellent introduction to a new English translation of the text of *On the Holy Spirit* in DelCogliano, Radde-Gallwitz, and Ayres, "General Introduction," *Works on the Spirit*, 11–50. The appendix to Anthony Briggman, *St. Irenaeus and the Theology of the Holy Spirit* (Oxford: Oxford University Press, 2012), contains a related discussion of Origen's pneumatology as compared with that of Irenaeus.

11. If modern accounts of Paul's claim that Christ is the "power and wisdom of God" often focus on Paul's opposition of the "folly of the cross" to the "wisdom of the world," Paul's earliest readers tended to focus on the presence of the terms "wisdom" and "power" in 1 Cor. 1:24 as distinctive names or titles for Christ. The term "power" (δύναμις) could connote for them a heavenly "Power" or force, an angelic "power." Given a philosophical *milieu*, "power" could also convey the sense of a given entity's capacity to reproduce itself or its nature. Those not familiar with early Christian literature may not recognize such senses of "power" that early readers recognized. Many will remember Simon "the Magician," that infamous magnet of early heresies. He is first mentioned in Acts, and, in Acts 8:10, his full title is a foil to Paul's title for Christ in 1 Corinthians. Simon is identified as "the Power of God called 'Great.'" Origen would turn this passage against Celsus by arguing that the Christians had found Christ to be "the great Power of God." (The connection to Simon Magus in the context of early Christian speculation about "the powers" is made [first?] by Jules Lebreton, *Histoire du dogme de la Trinité. Des origines au concile de Nicée*, vol. 1: *Les origines* [Paris: Beauchesne, 1927], 551; more recently, Jarl Fossum has drawn scholarly attention to Simon's "name" in *The Name of God and the Angel of the Lord: Samaritan and Jewish Concepts of Intermediation and the Origin of Gnosticism*, Wissenschaftliche Untersuchungen zum Neuen Testament [Tübingen: Mohr Siebeck, 1985], 162–75.) For non-Christian medical and philosophical background for "power" in early Christian theology, see esp. Barnes, *The Power of God*. Those interested in Jewish literature may consult Alan F. Segal, *Two Powers in Heaven: Early Rabbinic Reports about Christianity and Gnosticism* (Leiden: Brill, 2002); Jarl Fossum, *The Name of God*; and David Winston, *Logos and Mystical Theology in Philo of Alexandria* (Cincinnati: Hebrew Union Press, 1985). Much older but still useful notes can be found in Lebreton, 1:198–209 (on Philo), and 1:548–51 (on Greek and early Christian literature generally).

12. *Unigenitum filium dei sapientiam eius esse substantialiter subsistem*; 1.2.2.

Origen constructs a doctrine of eternal generation of the Son. In this section of *On First Principles*, then, 1 Cor. 1:24 serves as part of the scriptural foundation of Origen's Wisdom Christology. The title "Wisdom" is primary, and what is said of it in reference to Christ may be transferred to any other titles of Christ that Scripture discloses (1.2.4).

In *On First Principles* 1.2.9, Origen turns to the Wisdom of Solomon 7:25-26, and asks: "What is the meaning of that passage which we find written in the Wisdom of Solomon, who speaks of wisdom as follows: 'She is a breath of the power of God and a pure effluence (that is, emanation) of the glory of the Almighty and the brightness of the eternal light and an unspotted mirror of the working or power of God and an image of his goodness.'"

Origen notes that Solomon provides five definitions (*definiens*) of God "and from each of them in turn he indicates a certain characteristic belonging to God's Wisdom." The five "definitions"—which really amount to titles—are "power," "glory," "eternal light," "working," and "goodness." But Wisdom is a "breath" of God's "power." Origen suggests that

> the breath, then, or if I may so call it, the strength of all this power, so great and so immense, comes to have a subsistence of its own; and although it proceeds from the power itself as will proceeding from mind, yet nevertheless the will of God comes itself to be a Power of God. There comes into existence, therefore, another power, subsisting in its own proper nature, a kind of breath, as the passage of Scripture calls it, of the first and unbegotten power of God, drawing from this source whatever existence it has; and there is no time when it did not exist.[13]

Next Origen concludes that, "in regard to the apostle's saying that

---

13. The clarification regarding the question as to whether the "power" ever "began" may not be original to Origen. For more on the use of "power" as a psychological faculty in this passage, see Barnes, *The Power of God*, 115–18. The following paragraph in my account is a compressed version of Barnes's reading of this text.

'Christ is the power of God', this power must be called not merely a breath of the power of God but a power proceeding from the power." First Corinthians 1:24 identifies Christ with God the Father's "power" in the following sense. There are two divine powers, one unbegotten and one begotten. In Origen's reading, Paul here speaks of the power of the first, unbegotten "power." The Son is "a power proceeding from the power."[14] Since Wisdom 7:25 refers to Wisdom (= the Son) as a *breath* of God's power, one might suppose that the Son is merely a "breath"—something that comes into existence and dissipates. But Origen, in opposition to monarchian theology, wants to establish that the only-begotten Son does not come and go, is not a mere "breath" of the power of God. The Son, rather, "comes to have a subsistence of its own," and this independent subsistence is named by Paul "Christ, the Power of God." When Origen states that the Son is "a power proceeding from a power," he is using 1 Cor. 1:24 to save Wisdom 7:25 from monarchian purposes, which would have in God only a single existent to the exclusion of the Son's independent divine existence.

But how should "a power proceeding from a power" be interpreted? Does it mean that the second "power" is *of the same nature* as the first? Or does it imply a hierarchical or participatory scheme, in which the second power is subordinated to the first? Michel Barnes draws together texts from Origen's *Dialogue with Heraclides*, *On First Principles*, and *Commentary on John* to show that Origen's use of "power" took on three distinct senses across his writings, none of which is reducible to any of the others.[15] Because of the dates of these works, it is impossible to ascertain a development in any particular

---

14. As Barnes notes, the psychological analogy (Son as will proceeding from Mind) has developed into something else. The primary sense of "power" that governs Origen's statement that "a power proceeds from the power" is ontological. In this sense, a power-as-cause reproduces itself or its nature.

15. See ibid., ch. 3.

direction.[16] The *Dialogue* evinces a theory of "one power," in which the Father and the Son are two Gods who share the same "power," and "power" is identified strictly with neither the Father nor the Son. In *On First Principles* an *X from X* power causality is put forward, but its sense is ambiguous—it could be equivocal or univocal. (This is the ambiguity I have already indicated.) In the *Commentary* another conception of "power" emerges in which "power" is not intrinsic to God, but stands alongside a list of divine attributes that are "not God simply, but something else."[17] In this case, the Son is subordinate to the Father, and the Holy Spirit is a "thing made" through the Son.

Origen, along with Tertullian, marks the end of early Christian "high" pneumatology.[18] Earlier Jewish and Christian tradition had associated the divine title of "Wisdom" with the Holy Spirit. This association paved the way for "high" pneumatology in some early Christian theologies.[19] Origen's identification of "Wisdom" with the Son *instead of the Holy Spirit* removes exegetical support for the Holy Spirit's role in creation. As Anthony Briggman suggests, "the identification of the Son as Wisdom secures the Son's divinity by establishing his everlasting presence with the Father, his eternality."[20] As noted already, 1 Cor. 1:24 links "wisdom" to "power" and allows Origen to argue that the Son is not merely a "breath" of Wisdom, but a "power proceeding from a power." Andrew Radde-Gallwitz calls

---

16. Ibid., 124n78.
17. Ibid., 123.
18. Barnes, "The Beginning and End."
19. Most importantly, Irenaeus. See Briggman, *St. Irenaeus.*
20. Ibid., 206. See also Robert Grant, "The Book of Wisdom at Alexandria," *Studia Patristica* 7 (1966): 462–72; William R. Schoedel, "Jewish Wisdom and the Formation of the Christian Ascetic," in Robert Wilken, ed., *Aspects of Wisdom in Judaism and Early Christianity* (Notre Dame, IN: Notre Dame University Press, 1975), 169–99; A. H. B. Logan, "Origen and Alexandrian Wisdom Christology," in R. P. C. Hanson and Henri Crouzel, eds., *Origeniana Tertia* (Rome: Edizioni dell'Ateneo, 1985), 123–29; and William Horbury, "The Christian Use and the Jewish Origins of the Wisdom of Solomon," in John Day, et al., eds., *Wisdom in Ancient Israel: Essays in Honour of J. A. Emerton* (Cambridge: Cambridge University Press, 1995), 182–98.

our attention to Origen's engagements with monarchian theology regarding the Holy Spirit.[21] Radde-Gallwitz argues for the authenticity of a fragment (Fragment 37) of Origen's lost *Commentary on John.* There Origen advances an argument to the effect that the Holy Spirit is a substance, and so a divine agent, not a divine activity. On the other hand, Origen's high Christology, according to Briggman, comes at the cost of his pneumatology.[22]

Origen taught a doctrine of the Trinity governed by a taxonomy of the persons one over the other, such that the Holy Spirit, Son, and Father are arranged in a *taxis,* or ordering, with the Father as supreme. The consequences of Origen's *taxis* are more debatable, depending on how one gauges the model's place within Origen's thought as a whole and the extent to which that model influenced various fourth-century figures.[23] Less controversial is the fact that Origen bequeathed to the fourth century a potentially problematic trinitarian scheme.[24] On the christological side, the hierarchical

21. See Andrew Radde-Gallwitz, "The Holy Spirit as Agent, not Activity: Origen's Argument with Modalism and Its Afterlife in Didymus, Eunomius, and Gregory of Nazianzus," *Vigilae Christianae* 65 (2011): 227–48.

22. Briggman, *St. Irenaeus,* 209: "Origen's identification of the Son as Wisdom provides structure and content for his Christology, but it leaves his pneumatology ill-defined and deficient when compared to that of Irenaeus. Origen lost a significant way to speak of the Holy Spirit's creative activity, eternality, and divinity. He does not tender an adequate replacement for the logic he has rejected."

23. The question of sources intervening between Origen and Didymus, and the extent to which Didymus drew directly upon Origen's writings, is important, but I will not take up the matter here. For more on Origen's legacy in the fourth century, see, chronologically, Rowan Williams, *Arius: Heresy and Tradition* (London: Darton, Longman and Todd, 1987), 131–57; Barnes, *The Power of God,* 111–24; Lewis Ayres, *Nicaea and Its Legacy* (Oxford: Oxford University Press, 2004), 20–30, with attendant bibliography; and Barnes, "The Beginning and End": 180–86. Williams's statements regarding ambiguities in Origen's uses of participation are intriguing (see Williams, *Arius,* 142–43). However, I would suggest that, where Williams sees an Origen whose mind has changed in exegetical fragments on the Psalms and the Apocalypse, he is actually seeing Didymus's hand or its influence. For more on this topic and related issues, see my forthcoming paper, "Participation and Trinity in Origen and Didymus the Blind," in *Origeniana Undecima,* ed. Anders-Christian Jacobsen (Leuven: Peeters Press, Forthcoming).

24. I am *not* saying that Origen's taxological ordering was, or is, necessarily problematic. I only mean to highlight the ambiguity of Origen's reflections. I adopt the position of Ayres, *Nicaea,* 25–26: "the question that Origen's usage [of *hypostases*] stimulates is: 'if the three are truly three

structure could be used for anti-Nicene subordinationist purposes—in spite of the doctrine of eternal generation implied by Origen's God-and-his-Wisdom model (*On First Principles* 1.2.1). In regard to pneumatology, Origen's doctrine of the Trinity is even more ambiguous. Indeed, the underdetermined aspects of his pneumatology were vulnerable to angelomorphic pneumatology.[25] His argument in the *Commentary on John* that the Holy Spirit is a substance leaves open the possibility that the Holy Spirit is a rational, incorporeal substance—an angel. If one reads his ontological "positioning" of the Holy Spirit as subordination to the Son and the Father, the Holy Spirit's identification with the "powers of heaven," the angels, is tempting. It was angelomorphic pneumatology that Athanasius and Didymus would find themselves opposing in late fourth-century Alexandria.

A tension at the heart of Origen's trinitarian writings remained for his fourth-century heirs. Origen's exegesis of 1 Cor. 1:24 was widely influential in the trinitarian debates over the divinity of the Son.[26] The result of Origen's influence was an elevation of the Son to divine status, even if the nature of that divine status remained contested. The use of Wisdom 7:25 fell away as it became associated with the favorite Arian proof text of Prov. 8:22.[27] Origen supplanted the Jewish-Christian underwriting of "high" pneumatology that had identified the Holy Spirit as an agent of creation. In his struggle to correct tendencies toward Spirit-Monarchianism *and* "hyper-pneumatology," Origen identified the Son *instead of* the Holy Spirit

in distinct existence, by what mode of participation or action are they together?' His answer is not clear: difficult and often incompatible fragments are scattered throughout his corpus . . ." (Ayres, 21). Whether one should characterize Origen's Trinity as "subordinationist" is a thorny matter, whose resolution I do not need here to attempt.

25. An important work on this topic in Alexandrian theology is Bogdan Bocur, *Angelomorphic Pneumatology: Clement of Alexandria and Other Early Christian Witnesses* (Boston: Brill, 2009).

26. Barnes, *The Power of God*, 111.

27. Ibid., 112.

with Wisdom. Origen thus bequeathed an ambiguous theology of the Trinity to the fourth century: he defined the Father, Son, and the Holy Spirit as the "three," but also left underdetermined taxological tendencies in thinking about the three.

Didymus the Blind

Didymus the Blind's *On the Holy Spirit* clarifies some of the ambiguities of Origen's account of the Holy Spirit. Here, I draw attention to three of his advances of Origen's trinitarian model[28] and will focus on how Paul's trinitarian terms, "Power" and "Wisdom," take on new functions in Didymus's account of the Trinity.[29] But I

---

28. The following analysis and comparison takes as a point of departure, though does not strictly rely upon, Alasdair Heron, "The Holy Spirit in Origen and Didymus the Blind: A Shift in Perspective From the Third to the Fourth Century," in Adolf Martin, ed., *Kerygma und Logos* Ritter (Göttingen: Vandenhoeck & Ruprecht, 1979), 298–310.

29. Though I limit what follows to Didymus's remarks in *On the Holy Spirit*, a quick glance at *Biblia Patristica*, vol. 7, reveals a few pages worth of references to passages from 1 Corinthians. Among those references, however, the "folly of the cross" is not a matter of great concern to Didymus. 1 Cor. 1:23, for example, is never cited in Didymus's extant writings. Though further investigation into Didymus's exegetical writings may show otherwise, it would be surprising to find Didymus dwelling on the "folly of the cross" in 1 Corinthians 1–2. In keeping with Alexandrian tradition, he tends to fix upon Paul's use of "power" and "wisdom" as christological titles, as well as Paul's reference to the "power of the Spirit." Didymus uses Paul's opposition of folly to wisdom to show that the "wisdom of the world" is in darkness when it is compared to Christian wisdom (see *Kommentar zur Ecclesiastes*, Papyrologische Texte und Abhandlungen, vol. 16, ed. J. Kramer and B. Krebber (Bonn: Rudolf Habelt Verlag, 1972), 208, line 23, with a strained "reference," according to the *Biblia Patristica*, to 1 Cor. 1:20). But this is not the same as reading Paul's opposition as an "exhortation to folly." See his *Commentary on Zechariah*, for example (trans. Robert Hill [Washington, D.C.: Catholic University of America Press, 2006], 291). Having identified the "wicked horses" of Zech. 12:4 with those who teach "the wisdom of this age and its rulers," Didymus claims that "God does not strike [them] with the intention of their never existing any longer, but for them to understand what they are saying and asserting, since they have lost their wisdom and forfeited their intelligence." The "shock" of God's striking the "wicked horses" only serves to bring their riders to their senses, not to destroy what little sense they have had all along. Scholarship has viewed Didymus's Christology as bearing anti-"Apollinarian" marks, and so, as not given to unduly divinizing Christ to the point that he has no human mind. Yet Didymus is not given to a Christology that focuses solely upon the human Jesus, or only upon the crucified Christ. He explicitly rejects such a position as short-sighted, since Paul knew "only Christ crucified" (1 Cor. 2:2) among the perfect, but among those who were "outside," who refused to proceed to the higher understanding of Christ as God's "invisible image," to which Paul proceeds in 2 Cor. 5:16 (see *Didymos der Blinde: Psalmenkommentar Teil III: Kommentar zu Psalm 29–34*, Papyrologische

will not stop at the use of these terms: I will provide a synopsis of what I consider to be a distinctive feature of Didymus's trinitarian doctrine in *On the Holy Spirit*. First, whereas Origen associates God's eternal, hypostatic Wisdom only with the Son, Didymus associates the Holy Spirit's activities with the activities of Christ, the "Power" and "Wisdom" of God, without reducing the Holy Spirit to the Son. In doing so, Didymus characterizes the Holy Spirit as the Creator and agent in moral transformation in a way only befitting of God: the Holy Spirit creates Christ's body and teaches the Wisdom that Christ is without having learned wisdom from Christ. Finally, and joining these two points, Didymus establishes a moral psychology that is trinitarian in the following sense. The imprinting of Christ's virtue on the soul is the result of the Trinity's activity. None of the divine persons operates separately when God inscribes virtue in the soul: the Son, as Wisdom, is the image of the Father "sealed" in the soul by the Holy Spirit.

The Holy Spirit as Creative Power

Didymus associates the Holy Spirit with God's creative power. He draws our attention to another passage in 1 Corinthians that refers to the "power of God."[30] In 1 Corinthians 2:4, Paul says "And my word and my preaching are not with persuasive words of human

Texte und Abhandlungen, vol. 8, ed. Michael Gronewald [Bonn: Rudolf Habelt Verlag, 1969], 90, lines 4–12). Adolphe Gesché's pioneering study of Didymus's Christology only reports a few instances of verses from 1 Corinthians 1–2, and these do not pick up on what moderns see in Paul as a discourse about the "folly of the cross" (see A. Gesché, *La christologie du 'Commentaire sur les Psaumes' découvert à Toura* [Gembloux: Duculot, 1962], 71, 305, 318, and 343). Rich Bishop's fine study of Didymus's commentary on Psalm 21 demonstrates Didymus's ingenious use of Stoic moral psychology to resolve the riddle of Christ's real humanity and his sinlessness. Christ only experienced *propatheia*, not passion, and so was tempted in a way that allowed him to be fully human and still sinless (see Richard Bishop III, "*Affectus hominis: The Human Psychology of Christ according to Ambrose of Milan in Fourth-Century Context*," PhD diss., University of Virginia, 2009, 79–115).

30. The Latin *virtus* appears more than thirty-five times in *On the Holy Spirit*, bearing at least the following three distinct senses: (1) virtue; (2) angelic power; (3) divine power.

wisdom but with the demonstration of the Holy Spirit and the power of God."[31] After this, Didymus glosses the "power" of 1 Corinthians 2:4 as "Christ the Lord," and then quickly redirects our attention to two passages in which Scripture speaks of the "power" of the Holy Spirit.[32] In the next paragraph (145), Didymus invokes Psalms 103 and 130 to identify the Holy Spirit as "Creator." By associating 1 Cor. 2:4, Acts 1:8, and Luke 1:35 with "the creating power of the Most High," Didymus distinguishes the "power of the Holy Spirit" from the angelic powers.[33] And, if the Holy Spirit is to be identified with God's "creating power," Didymus can show that the Holy Spirit plays an essential role in creation—specifically, in the creation of the body of the Son. Didymus concludes this section by invoking his earlier arguments for the consubstantiality of the Trinity (in the lead-up to

31. This English, which renders Jerome's Latin translation of Didymus' quotation of the verse, is offered by Mark DelCogliano, Andrew Radde-Gallwitz, and Lewis Ayres, trans., *Athanasius and Didymus. Works on the Spirit*, 188; see Didymus, *Spir.* 143.

32. This passage (§144) is complicated. The English reads: "It is true that we cannot interpret the *power* which is equal to the Spirit as another besides Christ the Lord." The Latin is *aequalem uero Spiritui uirtutem non possumus aliam praeter Christum Dominum interpretari*—phrasing that echoes Didymus's statement to similar effect in §86. Here Didymus is referring back to Paul's reference to "the Spirit and the power of God," which, curiously, is implied to mean a power *equal to* the Spirit. Didymus goes on to explain his statement with recourse to Acts 1:8 and Luke 1:35, two traditional "power" texts. In the Acts passage, Jesus tells his disciples that they "will receive the power of the Holy Spirit when he comes upon you." This is not the standard text of that biblical text. For, in turning to the critical text of the New Testament we find "but you will receive power when the Holy Spirit has come upon you" (ἀλλὰ λήμψεσθε δύναμιν ἐπελθόντος τοῦ ἁγίου πνεύματος ἐφ' ὑμᾶς). The difference is subtle but potentially important. Didymus's version of the biblical text allows him to distinguish between the "power *of* the Holy Spirit" and "the Holy Spirit." As the translators note, "in the standard text it is 'the Holy Spirit' who comes upon the disciples. Here, it is 'the power of the Holy Spirit' which does" (translation, 188n121). On the other hand, Didymus interprets Luke 1:35 as meaning that "when the Holy Spirit came upon the virgin Mary, the creating power of the Most High fashioned the body of Christ." In both cases, then, Didymus distinguishes between the "creating power of the Most High" or the "power of the Holy Spirit," on the one hand, and the Holy Spirit as such, on the other. But there seems to be some confusion, and Didymus does not appear to be using the distinction that appears in a technical way. For, in the case of the disciples, the *Power* comes upon them, but in the case of Mary, *the Holy Spirit* comes upon her. And yet in both cases the Holy Spirit is associated with the "power of God." The most likely conclusion is that Didymus is not here invoking a technical distinction between the "power of the Holy Spirit" and "the Holy Spirit."

33. At §23.4 and §58.3, Didymus distinguishes an "angelic power," see also §30.

§81): "'the Holy Spirit's activity is the same as that of the Father and the Son,' and 'a single substance is implied by the same activity, and, vice versa, … [T]hose who are ὁμοούσια [the same in substance] do not have an activity that is diverse.'"

The Holy Spirit as Wisdom That Teaches Christ without Having Learned Him

Didymus maintains Origen's association of Christ with God's Wisdom in a number of places in *On the Holy Spirit*. He refers to 1 Cor 1:24 only twice (§§17 and 92). In both cases, the verse is used to identify Christ with Wisdom. In §86, he reasons that what the apostles "are taught by the Spirit is wisdom, which we cannot understand as anything other than the Son."[34] He then turns to characterize the Holy Spirit as the "Spirit *of Wisdom*" and so the Spirit *of Christ*. Later (§§118–119), Didymus reads Wisdom 9:16-18 as sending the Son and the Holy Spirit. The verse says: "Who has come to know your will, unless you have given Wisdom and sent your Holy Spirit from on high?"[35] Didymus glosses "Wisdom [of God]" as "Only-Begotten Son" so that this passage may be taken to refer to the sending of the Spirit *and the Son*. Didymus is careful to respect what had become, thanks to Origen, a strong tradition in Alexandria of associating the Son with the Father's eternal Wisdom.

However, Didymus moves beyond Origen's identification of the Son with Wisdom. He extends the association of God's wisdom to the Father and the Holy Spirit as well. For Didymus, the Holy Spirit is the divine "teacher" who makes wise but is not made wise, who teaches without having learned.[36] In §§91–95, Didymus offers an

---

34. *Si ergo Spiritus Patris in apostolis loquitur, docens eos quid debeant respondere, et quae docentur a Spiritu sapientia est, quam non possumus aliam praeter Filium intellegere …*
35. DelCogliano, Radde-Gallwitz, and Ayres, trans., *Works on the Spirit*, 181.
36. *Spir.* 140–43.

expanded argument that the Holy Spirit should be characterized in terms of divine Wisdom. God the Father, who is Wisdom, both *generates* Wisdom and *makes others wise*. Presumably, we are to associate the Father's eternal production of Wisdom with the Son, and the Father's "making-wise" with the Holy Spirit. The operative assumption is that Scripture often speaks of an impartation of divine Wisdom to creatures, so there must be a divine agent who produces wisdom in created entities. The Holy Spirit is that agent of instruction and implementation of the divine Wisdom.[37] However, Didymus is careful to exclude the possibility that the Holy Spirit teaches us like humans teach one another—as having first learned a tradition handed on.[38] "But he will not teach as an instructor or teacher of a discipline which has been learned from another. For this method pertains to those who learn wisdom and the other arts by means of study and diligence. Rather, as he himself is the art, the teaching, the wisdom, and the Spirit of Truth, he invisibly imparts knowledge of divine things to the mind."[39] Didymus thus argues that the Holy Spirit *just is* the very Wisdom that the Son is. The Spirit both teaches Wisdom, that is, Christ, and *is* the Wisdom he teaches.

---

37. See *Spir.* 91: "God is called *Only-Wise* not by receiving wisdom from another. Nor is he named wise through participation in someone else's wisdom. If in fact many are called wise, it is due not to their own nature but to their communion with wisdom. But God is called *Only-Wise* not because he is made wise by participation in another's wisdom or from some other source, but because he generates wisdom and makes others wise. This wisdom is our Lord Jesus Christ. For Christ is *the power of God and the Wisdom of God*. The Holy Spirit is also called the Spirit of Wisdom, since in the old books it is recorded that *Joshua the son of Nun was filled* by the Lord *with the Spirit of Wisdom*."

38. This is a form of the doctrine of the "undiminished giver," which plays a central, unitive role in Didymus's thought. For more on this, see Lewis Ayres, "The Holy Spirit as the 'Undiminished Giver': Didymus the Blind's *De spiritu sancto* and the Development of Nicene Pneumatology," in D. Vincent Twomey and Janet E. Rutherford, ed., *The Holy Spirit in the Fathers of the Church* (Portland: Four Courts Press, 2010), 57–72.

39. *Spir.* 141.

A Trinitarian Moral Psychology

Didymus describes the actions of the Son and the Holy Spirit in a way that binds their actions to one another, which in turn demonstrates their unity of nature. In several places, Didymus characterizes the action of one person in terms that imply and entail the divine action of the other. Didymus announces a doctrine of inseparable *possession*.[40] To possess the Son, Didymus says, is to possess the Holy Spirit, and vice versa. It was not only the Word that came to the prophets, but also the Holy Spirit, "since he too is possessed inseparably with the only-begotten Son of God."[41] Didymus also extends this logic to the "possession" of the Father: "he who receives the Son receives the Father, and the Son with the Father makes his home in those who are worthy of his presence."[42]

Didymus also argues that "whenever anyone receives the grace of the Holy Spirit, he has it as a gift from God the Father and our Lord Jesus Christ."[43] Here Didymus is even more explicit that this is a doctrine of divine activity (*operatio*) according to which each member of the Trinity plays an essential part: "The fact that there is a single grace of the Father and the Son perfected by the activity of the Holy Spirit demonstrates that the Trinity is of one substance." The underlying logic is that there is a single action of donation by God, begun by the Father, continued in the Son, and "perfected" or "completed" by the Holy Spirit. The singleness of this activity

---

40. Didymus introduces the doctrine in §9 and returns to it in §125. The reason Didymus argues this way is not only to prove the Spirit's divinity, but also to counteract the doctrine that the Spirit of the Prophets and the Spirit of the Apostles are not one and the same Spirit. This argument may be the sign of an anti-Manichaean polemic in Didymus's theology. See Byard Bennett, "The Origin of Evil: Didymus the Blind's *Contra Manichaeos* and Its Debt to Origen's Theology and Exegesis," PhD diss., University of Toronto, 1997.

41. . . . *quia et inseparabiliter possidetur cum Vnigenito Filio Dei* (*Spir.* 9). Notice that Didymus makes sure elsewhere that the Son and the Spirit remain irreducible—on which, see below in my paragraph on "Spirit-Christology."

42. *Spir.* 125.

43. *Spir.* 76.

demonstrates that "the Trinity is of one substance," that the Trinity is single.[44] This is a form of an argument from the inseparability of a trinitarian operation for the singularity of the divine substance that is the Trinity.

Didymus does not only argue that the three persons are "of the same substance." He also describes the activities of the Son and the Holy Spirit in such a way that their work in sanctification is the same work. The Son is the Father's image, and the Holy Spirit is that image's "seal." Didymus fuses his conception of the production of virtue in the soul with the divine actions of the Son and the Holy Spirit, and the indwelling of the Trinity. The result is what I would like to call a "trinitarian moral psychology." "The gifts of the virtues," Didymus argues, "always imply the Holy Spirit, in such a way that he who has him is considered to be filled with the gifts of God" (§41). In *On the Holy Spirit* §20, Didymus connects the model he invokes here to Eph. 1:13-14 and Origen's identification of the Son with the Father's image. Didymus adds a twist by characterizing the Holy Spirit as the seal by means of which the "image" of Christ is imprinted on the soul. Didymus explains that "just as someone, who takes up a practice and a virtue, receives into his mind, as it were, a seal and an image of the knowledge which he takes up, so too the one who is made a sharer in the Holy Spirit becomes, through communion in him, simultaneously spiritual and holy."[45] The Holy Spirit is the "seal" of the Father's "image," or the Son, in the virtuous soul.[46]

44. As is often the case, Didymus does not make the logic that underlies this argument explicit. It seems to be that entities that display unified activities must themselves be unified. Or, to put the position inversely, unified activities do not arise from plural entities.

45. Here especially the utility of the doctrine of the "undiminished giver" should not be missed. There is one gift of sanctification, one trinitarian act of giving, and so, Didymus reasons, one "undiminished giver" that is the Trinity.

46. Though Didymus does not stress it here, elsewhere (e.g., in the *Commentary on the Psalms*) Didymus emphasizes that Christ is the *invisible* image of the *invisible* God. Christ's "invisibility" is construed, then, as his divinity, whereas his "flesh" or his being-as-a-man is what the apostles saw, his visibility. See Michael Gronewald, ed., *Didymos der Blinde: Psalmenkommentar Teil III:*

Didymus argues that we can presume the presence of the Spirit when Paul speaks of the presence of the Son: "When he said: 'But if Christ is in you, although your body is dead because of sin,' in no way does he mean that the body is a slave to vices and wantonness." In other words, even though Paul only *said* that "Christ is in you," Paul does *not* fail to assert the presence of the Spirit, which produces the gifts of the Spirit and the life of virtue. In responding to faulty exegesis of Rom. 8:10a, Didymus assigns idiomatic roles to the Son and the Holy Spirit in the generation of virtue. The Son generates virtue in the soul by his presence, and the Holy Spirit by its presence. The Son is present when "those who have made their own bodies dead [to sin]." The "Spirit of life" is present when those same souls "do righteous works," either by correcting "deadly vices" or by believing in Jesus Christ and living accordingly. Together, then, the Son and the Holy Spirit generate, respectively, the death of vice and the life of virtue in the soul. Neither the Son nor the Holy Spirit is separable from the other in this divine act of the production of psychological virtue.

The heart of Didymus's argument along these lines comes in *On the Holy Spirit* §§184–191. Didymus ties the action of the Holy Spirit to the action of the Son, on the grounds that the Holy Spirit is the Spirit *of* the Son.[47] Didymus uses Rom. 8:9b ("But if anyone does not have the Spirit of Christ, he does not belong to Christ") to reach this conclusion.[48] In Rom. 8:10a, Paul says, "But if *Christ* is in you." He does not say, "But if the Spirit of Christ" is in you. This, Didymus argues, "demonstrates most clearly that the Holy Spirit is inseparable from Christ because wherever the Holy Spirit is, there also is Christ,

---

Kommentar zu Psalm 29-34, Papyrologische Texte und Abhandlungen Band 8 (Bonn: Rudolf Habelt Verlag, 1969), 90, lines 4-12.

47. He also does this at §111.

48. DelCogliano, Radde-Gallwitz, Ayres, trans., *Works on the Spirit*, 200; Didymus, *Spir.* 189.

and from wherever the Spirit of Christ departs, Christ also withdraws from that place" (§188). In the next paragraph, Didymus argues from another angle. After quoting Rom. 8:9b again, he says, "If anyone were to assume the contrary of this conditional proposition, he could say: 'If anyone belongs to Christ such that Christ is in him, then the Spirit of Christ is in him.'" Didymus goes one step further, however, and uses this verse to show the inseparability of the Holy Spirit, not only with respect to the Son, but also the Father: "This same logic can also be deployed likewise in the case of God the Father." Didymus simply replaces the word "Christ" with the word "God" in Rom. 8:9b so that it reads, "If anyone does not have the Spirit of *God*, he does not belong to *God*." This statement is then transformed into a contrapositive, leaving us with, "If anyone belongs to God, then the Spirit of God is in him." This, Didymus says, makes sense of 1 Cor. 3:16 and 1 John 3:24/4:13, verses that speak of the indwelling of the Holy Spirit and God's dwelling in people when God gives them God's Spirit. Finally, Didymus concludes that "all these passages demonstrate that the substance of the Trinity is inseparable and indivisible" (§191).

Conclusion

Paul's elevation of "power" and "wisdom" to the level of christological titles constituted an important scriptural point of departure for the trinitarian theologies of Origen and Didymus. In the end, Didymus produced a pneumatology whose expression, in comparison to Origen's, was evolved in terms of ontological specificity. I noted the ambiguity of Origen's use of the *X from X* formula in his statement that the Son is a "power that proceeds from a power." That statement could be taken equivocally or univocally. The various ways in which Origen's remarks imply it should be understood do not all neatly agree. Didymus, on the other hand, rules out the possibility that the divine power of the Holy Spirit is only an equivocal *X from X* formulation. The Holy Spirit is unequivocally God. In Didymus's formulation, the Holy Spirit is identified fully with God's "power and wisdom."

Each in their own ways, these Alexandrians took a road not taken in much late-modern exegesis of Paul. One wonders whether, "ages and ages hence," Origen and Didymus would have sighed that the road less traveled turned out to make all the difference.[49] Untroubled by Paul's juxtapositions of wisdom and folly, Origen and Didymus contributed to a developing tradition in which the beautiful "folly of the cross" would be inscribed forever as the height of wisdom—both in God the Trinity and in the soul who worships the Trinity as God.[50]

---

49. With all apologies to Robert Frost.

50. In his article "Basil of Caesarea, Didymus the Blind, and the Anti-Pneumatomachian Exegesis of Amos 4:13 and John 1:3," *Journal of Theological Studies* 61, no. 2 (2010): 644–58, Mark DelCogliano has argued that Didymus's arguments in *On the Holy Spirit* were useful for Basil's early direct engagements with Eunomius's pneumatology. More work is necessary to uncover other connections between Didymus and the later figures such as Gregory of Nyssa and Gregory of Nazianzus. Nazianzen, for his part, could speak of the Holy Spirit as "participated, not participating," and "filling, not filled," as though the proof for those terms were a settled matter (in both *Orations* 41.9 and 31.29, in 380). It may turn out that what scholars have tended to see as a vaguely "Origenian" influence upon Basil and Gregory of Nazianzus was actually Didymus filtering the great Alexandrian's trinitarian legacy to Cappadocia. Nazianzen's recent champion, Christopher Beeley, reads him as having drawn directly from Origen in all the right ways. (For a critique of the novelty of Nazianzus on this point, see Andrew Radde-Gallwitz's engaging review of Christopher Beeley, *Gregory of Nazianzus on the Trinity and the Knowledge of God* [Oxford: Oxford University Press, 2008], in *Conversations in Religion and Theology* 8, no. 2 [2010]: 177.) The possibility remains that a line runs from Didymus to Basil, and then possibly to Gregory, who wrote much later than either Basil or Didymus on the question of the Holy Spirit. To posit such a trajectory would be speculative at the moment. In any event we should keep in mind the potential presence of Didymus when we see "Origen" alleged by scholarship on late-fourth-century doctrine.

4

———

Maximus the Confessor on the Foolishness of God and the Play of the Word

Andrew Louth

I have to begin by confessing that when asked to present something on St. Maximus the Confessor, I chose the title because I was very familiar with one passage in St. Maximus that relates the theme of the foolishness of God to the play of Wisdom, or strictly the Word—because I had included the passage in the works I had translated in a book on the Confessor—and rather imagined that I would find several parallel passages, if I looked, and could build up something on that basis.[1] It didn't quite work out like that: Maximus quite rarely refers to the passages about the foolishness of God, and

1. Andrew Louth, *Maximus the Confessor* (London: Routledge, 1996), 163–68.

what is more, he finds nothing startling about these passages, so often enough he mentions them without comment. So I started to explore a little more widely, and found, as I have frequently in the past, that the tradition of scriptural interpretation in the Greek fathers—especially, perhaps, of the apostle Paul—really has quite different presuppositions from what is taken for granted in the tradition of scriptural interpretation in the West. When we think about the foolishness of God, we think—don't we?—about how the ministry of Jesus, and especially its human ending on the cross, seems to be the story of failure. If the resurrection turns the tide, it seems to do this by snatching some kind of future for the mission of the Lord from the very jaws of failure. The early Christian community was, as John Barclay has put it, in his keynote lecture, "a disreputable social movement": not at all a propitious beginning for the Christian church.[2] Paul seems to be reflecting on this in the passage where we read: "not many of you were wise according to the flesh, not many powerful, not many of noble birth" (1 Cor. 1:26, my trans.)—precisely, a marginal and maybe disreputable group. God's way with humankind, as seen in the incarnation and death and resurrection of Christ, seems hazardous, folly by any human standards—more likely to fail than achieve success. This leads us into reflection on the nature of Christian discipleship today that lays emphasis on the marginality of such discipleship and slogans such as "Priority for the Poor!"

I don't, however, find much of this in the fathers. St. John Chrysostom is a good place to start: his homilies on the Pauline epistles are easily accessible, and they were highly valued by Byzantine Christians. He gives, I think, a good idea of how these texts were read in late antiquity and later in the Greek-speaking East. The passage I've just quoted—1 Cor. 1:26, "not many wise . . ."—

2. See above, ch. 1.

attracts two ways of commentary. First of all, "not many": yes, indeed, but there were those who were wise among the Christian contemporaries of Paul—Chrysostom mentions a proconsul, presumably Sergios Paulos of Acts 13, the Areopagite (in Chrysostom's time the *Corpus* ascribed to him had not been written) and Apollos.[3] His second line of comment is that, nevertheless, the fact that there were not many of these highly educated Christians was to demonstrate that the success of the Christian gospel was not the result of human endeavor, but simply of the power of God himself, which is surely Paul's point (1 Cor. 2:5).[4]

I want to stay with St. John Chrysostom for a little, and mention a few features of his reflection on the theme of the foolishness of God. The first point may be obvious, but it needs to be noted: Chrysostom sees the foolishness of God as manifest in the Lord's death on the cross, and his submitting to be reviled and abused. He relates this directly to the portrayal of the incarnation in Phil. 2:5–11. After drawing out a bit what is meant by saying that the word of the cross is folly to the Greeks—mostly in terms of their using wisdom to turn aside the power manifest in the cross, so that they "rail against it and take offence at the saving remedies"—he continues:

> What do you read, man? Christ became a slave for you, taking the form of a slave, and was crucified and rose up; therefore it is right to worship the one who rose up, and be amazed at his love for human kind, because what no father, or friend, or son did for you, the master has worked all these things for you, an enemy opposed to him. It is then right to be amazed at him for these things; do you call folly something full of such wisdom?[5]

Chrysostom then seeks to show how none of what we confess as

---

3. John Chrysostom, *In hom. 5 ad I Corinthios*, in *Interpretatio omnium epistolarum Paulinarum*, ed. Frederick Field (Oxford: Academiae Typus, 1847), 2:45.

4. *In hom. 4 passim* (Field, 31–44).

5. *In hom. 4* (Field, 32).

Christians could have been demonstrated by the so-called wisdom of the philosophers; instead, it relies on faith:

> For to believe in one who was dead and buried, and to be assured that this is the same as rose up and is seated on high, this does not need wisdom, or reasoning, but faith. Therefore the apostles proceeded not by wisdom, but by faith, and they became wiser and more exalted than those who only have a wisdom from outside (τῶν ἔξω σοφῶν) . . .[6]

It is faith that the apostles have, not some wisdom superior to the Greeks:

> God is well-pleased to save through the folly of preaching, not that it is really folly, but it seems so. For what is greater is not that they introduce another such wisdom, greater than that, but rather one that seems to be folly, and thus it prevails. For Plato is cast out, not by some other wiser philosopher, but through an unlearned fisherman. For so the worse has become greater, and the victory more radiant.[7]

The preaching of the cross, the gospel of Christianity, is not some improved philosophy, better than what the Greeks have; it is faith in God and God's power, and it is this that seems to be folly to those who are perishing. It is folly because humans can't understand it, not because it is a way through defeat and failure: far from it, it is a victory more radiant.

Before moving to Maximus, I want to pursue another digression, this time by looking at the one whom Maximus thought to be the Areopagite, mentioned by Chrysostom as one of the wise among the early adherents of Christianity, for he introduces another way of understanding God's "foolishness." The Dionysian treatise, *Divine Names*, is concerned with the attribution to God of various names:

---

6. *In hom.* 4 (Field, 35).
7. *In hom.* 4 (Field, 35–36).

"good," "being," "life," "wise," and so on, ending with "one." Chapter 7 treats of the ascription of wisdom:

> And this the truly divine man, the common sun of us and leader, conceived supernaturally when he said, "the foolishness of God is wiser than men," meaning, not only that every human thought is a sort of error compared with the stability and permanence of the divine and most perfect thoughts, but also that it is customary among the theologians to deny negative terms of God, but in an opposite sense. So the oracles say that the all-radiant light is "unseen," and the many-hymned and many-named ineffable and without name, and the one who is present to all and found from all incomprehensible and past finding out. In this same way, the divine apostle is now said to hymn as God's foolishness what appears to be contradictory and absurd in it, so as to lead us up to the truth, which is ineffable and before any reason.[8]

And a little later on Dionysius says, "Praising, in a transcendent way, the foolish wisdom that is beyond reason and intelligence, let us say that it is the cause of all intellect and reason and all wisdom and understanding."[9] The ascription of "foolishness" to God is being subsumed under Dionysius's doctrine of apophatic and kataphatic theology, that is, the theologies of denial and affirmation, according to which every attribute can be ascribed to God, as the cause of all, but must even more fundamentally be denied of God, who is beyond all—what Dionysius calls attribution in a transcendent sense—for in denying that God is good, wise, and so on, we are not saying that God lacks these attributes, but that God transcends any human conception of them. To call God foolish is to deny wisdom to God in a transcendent sense: as the source of wisdom, God is beyond wisdom. This is clearly a long way from what the apostle meant by the "foolishness of God," which clearly applies in some way to God's

---

8. Dionysius the Areopagite, *In divinis nominibus* 7,1, in *Corpus Dionysiacum*, ed. Beate Suchla (Berlin: W. de Gruyter, 1990), 1:193, 10–194, 6.
9. Ibid., 1:194, 16–18.

saving the world through the incarnation and the cross. Nevertheless, we need to note it now, because it is part of the theological legacy that Maximus inherited.

Maximus gives more than passing consideration of what the apostle Paul meant by the foolishness of God in the last of his first set of *Ambigua*, "problems" or "difficulties" (normally cited as *Amb.* 71). There are two sets of these difficulties, the first addressed to a bishop John of Kyzikos, who would have been Maximus's bishop when he was at the monastery of St. George on the Erdek peninsula in the mid-620s, the second to a certain Thomas, probably a monk, maybe from Constantinople. Most of them concern difficult passages from St. Gregory the Theologian, or Gregory of Nazianzus, as does this difficulty, which is unique, however, in being a couple of lines from one of his poems, rather than from his homilies. In the poem, Gregory says, "The high Word of God plays in every kind of form, mixing, as he wills, with this world here and there" (another reading would say "dividing the world"). Maximus immediately relates this to the psalm where it says that "abyss calls to abyss in the noise of your cataracts" (Ps. 41 [42]:8, LXX); this, he comments, "perhaps [τυχὸν, Maximus is often quite tentative in his resolution of the difficulties] shows that every contemplative mind, because of its invisible nature and the depth and multitude of its thoughts, is to be compared to an abyss, since it passes beyond the ordered array of the phenomena and comes to the place of intelligible reality."[10] As the phrase, "the noise of the cataracts," shows, this takes place in this world, "in which was accomplished the great and dreadful mystery in the flesh of the divine descent to the human level of God the Word."[11] It is this mystery, the Confessor continues, that the divine apostle called the "foolishness of God and weakness, because I think of its transcendent wisdom

10. Maximus the Confessor, *Amb.* 71 (PG 91:1408D; trans. Louth).
11. *Amb.* 71 (1409A).

and power."[12] What we can see Maximus doing is to relate the kind of meaning of the passage in 1 Corinthians we have found in St. John Chrysostom with the interpretation of divine foolishness we have found in Dionysius: divine foolishness is wisdom that transcends human capacity, manifest in the mystery of the incarnation of the Word of God. (The Dionysian interpretation is explicitly noted by Maximus: "for the transcendent attributes of the divine, spoken of by us in a contrary sense as privations, fall a long way short of their true meaning."[13]) What the apostle called "foolishness," the Theologian, Gregory, calls "play." So, concludes Maximus, "the mystery of the divine Incarnation is called the foolishness and weakness of God according to the holy Apostle Paul, and God's play according to the wonderful and great teacher Gregory, since it oversteps in a way that transcends being every order and harmony of all nature and power and energy."[14] Maximus has introduced yet another point: words like foolishness, weakness, and play are appropriate, not just because the incarnation escapes the human mind's conceptual capacity, but for a more fundamental ontological reason, for the incarnation breaches the structures of the universe—the "play" of the Word of God cannot be confined to the ontological structures of the created order, for the Word created that order and transcends it. Nonetheless, the incarnation, or, rather, the love of God for humankind in the incarnation, needs to be grasped in some way by the human intellect, for such knowledge, such assimilation of like to like, is the purpose of the incarnation in which "the Word of God became man, so that man might become God," to quote the famous passage from St. Athanasius.[15] The deeper meaning of "abyss calling to abyss" is to

12. *Amb.* 71 (1409B).
13. *Amb.* 71 (1409C).
14. *Amb.* 71 (1409CD).
15. Athanasius, *On the Incarnation* 54, ed. John Behr (Crestwood, NY: St. Vladimir's Seminary Press, 2011), 166.

be found in "the mind that reaches after knowledge and calls upon wisdom, and thus discerns a tiny reflection of the mysteries of the divine and ineffable descent among us."[16]

Quite often, in these *ambigua* or difficulties, Maximus offers not just one solution, but several, intimating by this, I think, that human ways of understanding God's purposes can never be definitive. So here: after the first explanation, he offers three more (they are called θεωρίαι, "contemplations," or, maybe, "insights"). The second, almost as long as the first, focuses on the notion of the Word "playing." He finds other scriptural passages and passages from Gregory the Theologian and Dionysius the Areopagite that suggest that the play of the Word is, as we might say, transgressive, passing across fixed boundaries, and so relating things that are customarily kept apart. The passage from the Areopagite speaks of the cause of all, "in his wonderful and good love for all things, through the excess of his loving goodness, is carried outside himself . . . so enchanted is he in goodness and love and longing," and mentions "an ecstatic and transcendent power which is yet inseparable from Himself."[17] This is usually interpreted by the fathers, as by Maximus here, of the leaping of the Word of God into the world at the incarnation (cf. Wisd. of Sol. 18:14-15), though Dionysius may have meant creation itself. Maximus's interpretation of this passage serves to link Dionysius's understanding of God's foolishness with the incarnation. Maximus then goes on to illustrate the notion of play from the way in which parents and teachers adapt themselves to the level of their children or students, often by a kind of play, and suggests that God, both by leading us through created things and historical events, is playing with us, and getting us to grasp what is beyond our present capacity.

---

16. *Amb.* 71 (1412A).
17. Dionysius, *In divinis nominibus* 4,13 (ed. Suchla, 159,9–11.12), quoted by Maximus, *Amb.* 71 (1413AB).

So, "foolishness," "play," and "enchanting ... being carried outside himself" are different ways of thinking of God's movement toward us in love. Two further brief "contemplations" compare play to the flux of material things; the Word in play leading us, as it were, through flux to "that which really is and can never be shaken."[18] The last contemplation suggests that life itself is a kind of play, as we dance, as it were, toward the stillness of eternity. He quotes from Gregory of Nazianzus's funeral sermon for his brother, Caesarius:

> Such is our life, brothers, the passing life of living beings: a sort of play upon the earth. As those that have not been, we come into being, and having come into being we are dissolved. We are a dream that does not last, a passing phantom, the flight of a bird that is gone, a ship passing through the sea and leaving no trace, dust, vapor, the morning dew, a flower that blooms for a time and is gone, "man, his days are like grass, like the grass of the field, he flourishes," as the divine David says as he reflects on our weakness.[19]

Coming from Durham, I am reminded of the story Bede tells in his *Church History* of human life being like the flight of a sparrow through a hall in winter.[20]

There is something both profound and also unsettling about Maximus's seeing the foolishness of God in terms of the play of the Word. What is profound will lead us into the consideration of a fundamental theme in the Confessor, with which I will conclude this paper. But the unsettling? Even though Maximus is thinking of a transcendent foolishness, it seems to me that in his comparison of it with play, he is thinking of something that is merely a transient stage. Play is important (we shall see more of that later), but it seems to be a stage that may well be necessary, but only because of human

---

18. *Amb.* 71 (1416B).
19. Gregory of Nazianzus, *Hom.* 7,19 (PG 35:777).
20. Bede, *Historia Ecclesiastica* 2,13, ed. Bertram Colgrave and R. A. B. Mynors (Oxford: Clarendon Press, 1969), 184.

weakness and sin. There seems to be nothing intrinsic in the role of play: the parents and teachers who are playing are not really playing, just pretending to for pedagogic purposes. I don't pick up anything of the sense of the intrinsic significance of play we find in studies of play such as Johan Huizinga's *Homo Ludens* or Hugo Rahner's *Man at Play*.[21] The "play of Wisdom" that I originally had in my title is not there in Maximus. Nor should I have thought it might be: he would not have known of Jerome's inspired translation of Prov. 8:31, speaking of Wisdom, *ludens in orbe terrarum*.

The theme of the Word of God playing among human beings, coming down to their/our level, expressing the deepest mysteries in riddling ways that we can make something of: that is a recurrent theme in the writings of St. Maximus. A good example can be found in the second of his *Centuries on Theology and the Incarnate Dispensation*, a treatise summarizing in groups of a hundred chapters his various theological insights. There we read:

> The Word of God is said to be flesh not only when he is incarnate, but in another sense as well. When God the Word is contemplated with single vision as he is in the beginning with the God and Father, he possesses the clear and naked types of the truth concerning all things, but does not contain parables and puzzles, or stories needing allegories. When he dwells among human beings who are unable to make contact with the naked intellect through naked concepts, he selects from things that are familiar to them, combining together a variety of stories, puzzles, parables, and dark sayings, and in this way becomes flesh. In its first encounter, our intellect does not engage with the naked Word, but with the Word made flesh, that is, through a variety of sayings. Although he is the Word by nature, in appearance he is flesh, so that the many appear to behold the flesh and not the Word, even though he is, in truth, the Word. The meaning of the Scriptures is not what appears

---

21. Johan Huizinga, *Homo Ludens: A Study of the Play-Element in Culture*, trans. R. F. C. Hull (after Huizinga's own translation) (London: Temple Smith, 1970); Hugo Rahner, *Man at Play*, trans. Brian Battershaw and Edward Quinn (New York: Herder & Herder, 1967).

to the many, but is other. For the Word becomes flesh in each of the recorded sayings.[22]

This theme works its way through Maximus's theology. Understanding God's revelation in Scripture, nature, through the living presence of the Word in the church is an encounter in which God meets us at our level, accommodating Godself to our foolishness, and drawing us up to the contemplation of God's glory.

22. Maximus the Confessor, *Capitum theologicorum et œconomicorum Centuria* 2:60 (PG 90:1153B–1156A).

5

Paul's Refusal of Wisdom in Aquinas's *Commentary on 1 Corinthians*: Notes on Philosophy in the *Summa of Theology*

Adam Eitel

Thomas Aquinas wrote on conventional topics in conventional genres in medieval faculties of theology. Well over half of his corpus comprises commentaries on Scripture, a commentary on Peter Lombard's *Sentences*, and two pedagogically motivated revisions of its topics known as the *Summa Against the Gentiles* and the *Summa of Theology* (hereafter *Summa*).[1] Much else in his corpus consists

1. Angelus Walz, "De genuino titulo Summae theologiae," *Angelicum* 18 (1941): 142–51, suggests that the *Summa*'s received title may not be Thomas's. For a survey of the circumstances and pedagogical motivations of the *Summa*, see Leonard E. Boyle, *The Setting of the Summa Theologiae of Saint Thomas* (Toronto: Pontifical Institute of Mediaeval Studies, 1982); and idem,

in disputed questions on theological topics, sermons and liturgical works, and commentaries on books by Boethius and Dionysius.[2] Thomas also exposited many of the Aristotelian texts that were available in the thirteenth-century Latin West.[3] Can he for that reason be called a "philosopher"?[4] Modern answers to this question too often forget that *philosophus* was a pejorative term in thirteenth-century Parisian schools.[5] Its connotation can be surmised, if only in part, from Thomas himself. Take the case of the *Commentary on the Gospel of John,* where Thomas adverts to the danger of philosophical teaching: "the wisdom of no philosopher has been so great that it could keep human beings from error; the philosophers have rather led many into error."[6] And again, in the *Commentary on 1 Corinthians,*

"The Setting of the *Summa Theologiae* of St. Thomas—Revisited," in Stephen J. Pope, ed., *The Ethics of Aquinas* (Washington, DC: Georgetown University Press, 2002), 1–16. See also Mark D. Jordan, *Rewritten Theology: Aquinas after His Readers* (Oxford: Blackwell, 2006), 116–53.

2. Jean-Pierre Torrell, *Saint Thomas Aquinas* (Washington, DC: Catholic University of America Press, 1996), 330–61, contains an annotated catalogue and proposed chronology of Thomas's corpus.

3. The scholarly consensus concerning the literal motive of Thomas's expositions of Aristotle dates to the mid-nineteenth century. A generous selection of the relevant bibliography can be found in Jordan, *Rewritten Theology,* 68n26.

4. See Joseph Owens, "Aquinas as Aristotelian Commentator," in *St. Thomas Aquinas (1274–1974): Commemorative Studies* (Toronto: Pontifical Institute of Medieval Studies, 1974), 1:213–38; R.-A. Gauthier, *Introduction. Somme contre les gentils* (Paris: Éditions universitaires, 1993); idem, "St. Thomas et l'éthique à Nicomaque," in Thomas Aquinas, *Opera omnia* (Rome: Leonine Comm., 1971), 48:xxiv–xxv; Mark D. Jordan, *The Alleged Aristotelianism of Thomas Aquinas* (Toronto: Pontifical Institute of Medieval Studies, 1992). One does not have to endorse Owen's and Gauthier's view that the Aristotelian commentaries are "theological works" to disagree with recent attempts to instate them as works of philosophy. Here I must especially dissent from James C. Doig's recent claim that Thomas's *Sententia libri Ethicorum* represents his own "correct vision of moral philosophy" (Doig, *Aquinas's Philosophical Commentary on the 'Ethics': A Historical Perspective* [Dodrecht: Kluwer Academic, 200], xvii). For a clear-sighted critique of Doig, see Denis J. Bradley, "Aquinas's Philosophical Commentary on the 'Ethics'," *The Review of Metaphysics* 57, no. 2 (2003): 402–3. For a discussion of the ambiguities attending the few works in which Thomas seems to not write as a theologian (e.g., *On Kingship, On the Unity of the Intellect, On the Eternity of the World, On Being and Essence*), see Mark D. Jordan, "Theology and Philosophy," in Norman Kretzmann and Eleonore Stump, eds., *The Cambridge Companion to Aquinas* (Cambridge: Cambridge University Press, 1993), 232–51; and idem, *Rewritten Theology,* 155.

5. See Marie-Dominique Chenu, "Les 'philosophes' dans la philosophie chrétienne médiévale," *Revue des sciences philosophiques et théologiques* 26 (1937): 27–40.

he identifies "philosophers" with the "the rulers of this world, insofar as they fancy themselves as rulers of men in teaching. Of these," he continues, "it says in Isaiah 19, 'The princes of Zoan are utterly foolish; the wise counselors of Pharaoh give stupid counsel.' From these rulers all human philosophy has come."[7] It should not surprise that Thomas refused to call himself or any other Christian a "philosopher."[8] Why, then, are contemporary readers so tempted by the prospect of finding a philosophy "in" the *Summa*?

One reason follows from the originating circumstances of modern Thomism. At least since Pope Leo XIII's encyclical *Aeterni Patris*, the *Summa* has been looked to as a tool for re-securing authority. Leo traced the church's loss of political and social power to a congeries of sixteenth-century philosophical errors. He contended that those errors could only be undone by a new philosophy—one that could be separated, albeit subordinated, to ecclesial teaching. Here lies the aegis of "Thomistic philosophy."[9]

6. Thomas Aquinas, *Lectura super Ioannem.* 6.1. All references to Thomas's works cited herein are from Busa, *Opera omnia: Sancti Thomae Aquinatis Opera omnia*, ed. Robert Busa (Stuttgart-Bad Canstatt: Fromman-Holzboog, 1980), available online at http://www.corpusthomisticum.org.

7. *Expos. Pauli, I ad Cor.* 1.3, following Bar. 3:16-19. See also *De Trin.* 3,3; 6,4; *Contra gent.* 3,48, nn. 14-15.

8. Following Gauthier, Jordan dispatches an apparent exception in *Expos. Pery* 1,6 para. 4, where Thomas attributes the term *philosophus* to a one Johannes Grammaticus—an Aristotelian commentator known to Thomas only by second-hand. The text involves an instance of textual corruption, and, in any case, Thomas could not have known that Johannes was a believer. See Jordan, *Rewritten Theology*, 63n12, as well as Gauthier's remarks in Leonine *Opera omnia: Opera omnia iussu impensaque Leonis XIII. P. M. edita*, ed. by members of Leonine Commission (Rome: 1989), vol. 1*/1 (1989).

9. Wayne J. Hankey, "Pope Leo's Purposes and St Thomas's Platonism," in *S. Tommaso nella storia del pensiero: Atti dell VIII Congresso Tomistico Internationale*, vol. 8 and Studi Tomistici 17 (Vatican City: Libreria Editrice Vaticana, 1982), 39–43; See also James Hennesey, "Leo XIII's Thomistic Revival: A Political and Philosophical Event," in *The Journal of Religion* 58 (1978): 185–97. Recent efforts to find a discreet philosophy or philosophical theology "in" the *Summa* and in Thomas's works more generally are amply available. See, for example, Leo J. Elders, *The Philosophical Theology of St Thomas Aquinas* (Leiden: Brill, 1990); Scott MacDonald, "Ultimate Ends in Practical Reasoning: Aquinas's Aristotelian Moral Psychology and Anscombe's Fallacy," *The Philosophical Review* 100, no. 1 (1991): 31–66; Paul O'Grady, "Philosophical Theology and Analytical Philosophy in Aquinas," in Rik van Nieuwenhove and Joseph Wawrykow, eds., *The*

Of course, there is a more obvious reason that Thomas's readers ask about the place of philosophy in the *Summa*: Thomas alludes to, appropriates, and explicitly cites ancient philosophic authorities. Chief among them are Aristotelian authorities, but there are others, too: Plato, Cicero, ancient philosophical schools, and many others besides figure prominently in Thomas's dialectical exegesis. But precisely how does he use philosophic authorities? The question cannot be answered until we have relearned to ask it well. In what follows, then, I am not so much looking for an answer but the proper form of a question. To this end I will explore Thomas's conception of philosophy in the forms of Christian teaching he inherits. First, I turn to Thomas's interpretation of just one of the Pauline epistles in which he finds "nearly the whole of theological teaching."[10] Specifically, I take up the epitome of Christian pedagogy that Thomas finds in Paul's refusals of wisdom in 1 Corinthians 1–2. Then, second, I ask to what extent Thomas finds the same pedagogical principles at work in his ancient Christian authorities. In closing, I begin to show how his efforts to trace this Pauline pattern might illuminate his use of philosophy in the *Summa*.

Human Wisdom in the Commentary on 1 Corinthians

In his *Commentary on 1 Corinthians*, Thomas specifies Paul's teaching with respect to its (1) author, (2) its "subject matter" (*materia*), and (3) its "manner of teaching" (*modus docendi*). Paul's wisdom is "from God in a special way—*viz.*, by revelation."[11] Then, too, it is chiefly *about* God, since the *principium* of Paul's subject matter is nothing

---

Theology of Thomas Aquinas (Notre Dame: University of Notre Dame Press, 2005), 416–41; Craig Paterson and Matthew S. Pugh, *Analytical Thomism: Traditions in Dialogue* (Burlington, VT: Ashgate, 2006); Eleonore Stump, *Aquinas* (London: Routledge, 2003).

10. *Expos. Pauli: in Rom, pr.*
11. *Expos. Pauli, I ad Cor.* 2,1.

but Christ—the very wisdom of God who died: "the chief element in the teaching of the Christian faith is salvation effected by the cross of Christ; hence in 1 Cor. 2:2 Paul says, 'For I decided to know nothing among you except Jesus Christ and him crucified.'"[12] Finally, Paul exhorts the Corinthians to hold fast to the manner of teaching that comports with this cruciform teaching. Paul's own "manner of explanation" (*modum enarrandi*) makes use of only those things that serve "the demonstration of Christ's power."[13]

Thomas is especially struck by Paul's pedagogy—his manner of teaching—not least because he takes it to be the same pedagogy proposed by "the first teachers of the faith."[14] Paul's is an apostolic pedagogy. So it is not just one among several pedagogies available to the teacher of Christian wisdom. For Thomas, it is, rather, *the* pedagogy of Christian teaching.[15] The limits and procedures of this apostolic pedagogy, Thomas thinks, can be inferred from Paul's several refusals of wisdom.[16] Paul refuses to teach "in eloquent wisdom" (*in sapientia verbi*) and "in loftiness of speech or wisdom" (*in sublimitate sermonis aut sapientiae*); he purges his teaching of "persuasive words of human wisdom" (*verbis persuasibilibus humanae sapientiae*) and of every sort of "wisdom of this age" (*sapientia huius saeculi*).[17] So says Paul. But precisely what does he mean? What do his refusals exclude?

First, Paul refuses "elegant philosophical teachings" (*ornatu philosophiae doctrinis*) and the "teachings of philosophers" (*doctrinis philosophorum*)—and not just the teachings of some philosophers, but

---

12. Ibid., 1,3: ". . . principale autem in doctrina fidei Christianae est salus per crucem Christi facta. Unde, cap. II, 2, dicit non iudicavi me scire aliquid inter vos, nisi Iesum Christum et hunc crucifixum."
13. Ibid., 2,1 and 2,3.
14. Ibid., 1,4 and 2,1.
15. Ibid., 2,1.
16. Ibid., 1,3.
17. Ibid., 1,3 and 2,1.

rather of "all human philosophy."[18] Then, second, he rejects philosophic pedagogies or manners of teaching. Here we must be more specific. Philosophers' "manner of argument" (*modum ratiocinandi*) proceeds through "certain subtle paths"; they moreover urge assent by "ordering speech in order to persuade."[19] Paul, on the other hand, refuses all efforts to "prove" (*probare*) his claims with "words drawn from human wisdom."[20] Nor does he employ "rhetorical persuasions" (*rhetoricis persuasionibus*)—say, "obscure discourses" (*alti sermones*) and "empty arguments" (*vanis rationibus*) that produce useless speech.[21]

But what grounds Paul's refusals? On what basis does he forswear philosophic manners of teaching? Thomas notes that Christ first chose men who lacked "carnal and earthly wisdom" (*carnali sapientia et terrena*)—ignorant fisherman and peasants who could *not* have made use of philosophical teaching or rhetorical persuasion. Not so Paul. Here is a man of noble birth who was educated in "worldly wisdom" (*sapientia mundana*).[22] Here is a "golden vessel" spilling over with "brilliant wisdom" (*fulgorem sapientiae*).[23] Thomas thus contends that Paul's refusals cannot be motivated by uncritical adherence to custom.[24] Rather, they must follow from Paul's own considered judgment—a judgment that Thomas finds expressed *in nuce* in Paul's contention that to preach in eloquent wisdom would be to empty the cross of its power (1 Cor. 1:17). For Thomas, the point discloses a pedagogical maxim endorsed by philosophers themselves:

. . . it should be noted that even in philosophical teachings the same

18. Ibid., 1,3.
19. Ibid., 2,1.
20. Ibid., 2,1 and 2,3.
21. Ibid., 1,3 and 2,1.
22. Ibid., 1,4, following Rom. 6.
23. *Expos. Pauli: in Rom, pr.*
24. *Expos. Pauli, I ad Cor.* 1,4.

method does not suit every teaching. Hence the forms of discourse must fit the subject matter, as it says in *Ethics* 1. Now a particular method of teaching is especially unsuited to the subject matter, when that method refutes the chief element in that subject matter—for example, when in purely intellectual matters a teacher wishes to use metaphorical demonstrations which do not go beyond the imagination of things and leave the hearer stranded in images, as Boethius says in *On the Trinity.*[25]

A teacher knows that the method of teaching must suit the subject matter if it is to be learned. Take the case of the *Nicomachean Ethics.* Thomas notes that Aristotle's "method of manifesting truth" (*modus manifestandi vertitatem*) in the *Ethics* differs from the one found in the *Metaphysics.*[26] For the subject of moral philosophy, human action, is too variable to be analyzed according to the methods of first philosophy.[27] The same lesson applies *mutatis mutandis* to Paul's refusal to teach *in sapientia verbi*: to adopt the methods of teaching found in any of the philosophical disciplines would be to refute the very *principium* of what he must preach: "Now someone who depends chiefly on eloquent wisdom in his teaching, in this respect renders the cross of Christ void. Therefore, to teach in eloquent wisdom is a method unsuited to the Christian faith."[28]

Thomas's point cannot be well understood without knowing

---

25. ". . . considerandum est, quod etiam in philosophicis doctrinis non est idem modus conveniens cuilibet doctrinae. Unde sermones secundum materiam sunt accipiendi, ut dicitur in primo Ethicorum. Tunc autem maxime modus aliquis docendi est materiae incongruus, quando per talem modum destruitur id quod est principale in materia illa, puta si quis in rebus intellectualibus velit metaphoricis demonstrationibus uti, quae non transcendunt res imaginatas, ad quas non oportet intelligentem adduci, ut Boetius ostendit in libro de Trinitate." Ibid., 1,3.

26. *Sent. Ethic.* 1,3. n. 1.

27. Ibid., 1,3.

28. *Expos. Pauli, I ad Cor.* 1,3. "Principale autem in doctrina fidei Christianae est salus per crucem Christi facta. Unde, cap. II, 2, dicit non iudicavi me scire aliquid inter vos, nisi Iesum Christum et hunc crucifixum. Qui autem principaliter innititur in docendo sapientiam verbi, quantum in se est, evacuat crucem Christi. Ergo docere in sapientia verbi non est modus conveniens fidei Christianae. Hoc est ergo quod dicit ut non evacuetur crux Christi, id est, ne si in sapientia verbi praedicare voluero, tollatur fides de virtute crucis Christi. Gal. V, 11: ergo evacuatum est scandalum crucis. Ps. CXXXVI, v. 7: qui dicunt, exinanite usque ad fundamentum in ea."

precisely what he thinks (and thinks that Paul thinks) philosophical manners of teaching demand. He elaborates the point in terms of judgments, rules, and powers of soul. Philosophers oblige themselves "to judge every teaching proposed to them according to the rule of human wisdom."[29] In broad outline, that rule stipulates that claims to knowledge—say, about God or about human virtue—must be judged by the likes of "philosophical reasons, all of which are received in accordance with the powers of sense."[30] Philosophical methods of teaching thus admit only what can be known about God and human virtue "within the range of human senses."[31] What, then, can "the philosophers of this age" (*saeculi philosophi*) know? They can at least know some things about God "through the creatures he has made."[32] Nor is the practical wisdom of philosophers to be counted as mere folly.[33] For "men, no matter how evil, cannot be totally deprived of God's gifts," just as God's gifts in them cannot be "absolutely destroyed."[34] Such knowledge is not nothing. Yet it only "seems to touch the surface" (*superficie tenus videntur esse*) of the true wisdom of God.[35]

Nevertheless, Paul's teaching contains something "that cannot be grasped by one who depends solely on knowledge gained through the senses." His gospel proposes truths about God and human virtue that exceed the grasp of human reason.[36] Indeed, it contains something that the wisdom of this world takes to be *impossible*:

---

29. Ibid., 1,3.
30. Ibid., 2,3.
31. Ibid., 2,2.
32. Ibid., 1,3.
33. Ibid., 1,3. Indeed, Thomas's estimation of pagan virtue may be far more capacious than contemporary interpreters have allowed. See David J. Decosimo, *Ethics as a Work of Charity: Thomas Aquinas on Pagan Virtue* (Palo Alto: Stanford University Press, 2014).
34. Ibid., 1,3.
35. Ibid., 2,2.
36. Ibid., 2,3.

... if the teaching of the faith is proposed through eloquent wisdom, the cross of Christ is made void, because ... the preaching of the cross of Christ contains something which seems impossible according to human wisdom—for example, that God should die or that Omnipotence should suffer at the hands of violent men. It moreover contains something that seems contrary to the practical wisdom of this world—for example, that a person not avoid shame when he can, and other things of this sort.[37]

It seemed against the nature of human wisdom (*contra rationem humanae sapientiae*) that God should die and that a just and wise man should voluntarily expose himself to a very shameful death.[38]

Has God not made—that is to say, has he not demonstrated—the foolishness of the wisdom of this world by achieving what is considered impossible—*namely*, that a dead man rise, and other things of this sort.[39]

Paul proclaims that Christ the very wisdom of God has died. He implies that Omnipotence has suffered. He announces that Christ has risen. Such claims contravene the theological and metaphysical limits of what "the rule of human wisdom" can admit. Nor can that rule countenance Paul's claim that Christ—a wise and just man—would voluntarily expose himself to shame, powerlessness, and death. This is why Paul refuses philosophy. This is why he purges his preaching of lofty and persuasive speech. The *modus docendi* by which philosophers know what they teach and teach what they know is incompatible with the *principia* of his gospel. Paul, then, does not try to prove anything because he cannot. For to capitulate to philosophical argument would require him to endorse a manner of teaching that cannot suffer what he must say.

37. Ibid., 1,3.
38. Ibid.
39. Ibid.

The Place of Philosophy in Ancient Christian *Auctoritates*

Thomas's judgment of Paul's pedagogy is decisive: it is, he thinks, the proper method of Christian teaching insofar as it (1) suits the subject matter of the Christian faith and, thus, (2) excludes certain forms of philosophic argument and rhetorical persuasion. In enacting this judgment does Thomas not judge himself? Does he not advert to philosophical authorities in order to persuade? And what of Thomas's ancient Christian authorities who, as Jerome says, "have filled their books with elegant teachings of philosophy and the sciences"?[40]

Elsewhere, Thomas admires Ambrose's and Hilary's commitment to "just one manner of teaching (*modum*)—namely, from the authority (*per auctoritates*) [of Scripture]." Each set down the doctrine of the Trinity by arguing from Scripture. Still, Jerome's point is well taken. Many of Thomas's authorities *have* filled their books with philosophical teaching. "Boethius," for example, "chose to proceed according to the other mode of explanation—namely, according to reasoned arguments (*per rationes*), presupposing what had been concluded by others on the grounds of authority." Whereas Ambrose and Hilary appeal to the authority of Scripture, Boethius "investigates by reason" (*ratione investigabit*).[41] Does Boethius not contradict Paul?

There is a deeper problem still: What of Thomas's ancient Christian authorities who seem to have endorsed philosophical doctrines? What of Augustine, who "followed Plato as far as the Catholic faith would allow"?[42] What of the "obscure style" of Dionysius—Paul's own convert—who so often speaks in "the manner of the Platonists" that his books can scarcely be understood?[43] Thomas acknowledges the disparity between Paul and his other ancient

40. *Expos. Pauli, I ad Cor.* 1,3.
41. *Super De Trin. prol.*
42. *De spir. creat.* 10, *ad 8.*
43. *Super De div. nom. proem.* See also *De spir. creat.* 8, *ad 10.*

authorities. Yet he insists that disparity is more apparent than real. I refer again to the *Commentary on 1 Corinthians*:

> The answer is that it is one thing to teach in eloquent wisdom, however you take it, and another to use eloquent wisdom in teaching. A person teaches in eloquent wisdom when he takes eloquent wisdom as the main source of his teaching, so that he admits only those things which contain eloquent wisdom and rejects others which do not have eloquent wisdom: and this is destructive of faith. On the other hand, one uses eloquent wisdom who builds on the foundation of the true faith, such that if he finds any truths in the teachings of the philosophers, he makes them obedient to the faith.[44]

The apparent conflict among Thomas's ancient Christian authorities occasions a distinction that, he thinks, is already implicit in Paul: it is one thing "to teach *in* eloquent wisdom" (*docere in sapientia verbi*) and quite another "to *use* eloquent wisdom in teaching" (*uti sapientia verbi in docendo*)—and Paul, says Thomas, only rules out the former. So while Thomas and his ancient Christian authorities have *used* philosophy and rhetoric, they have *not* taught *in* eloquent wisdom. That is to say: they have not subjugated the scope and content of Christian faith to the procedural and material commitments of philosophical teaching. Quite the contrary. With a string of Augustinian citations, Thomas explains that the subjugation has run the other way: "Hence Augustine says in *On Christian Doctrine* 2 that if philosophers have uttered things suited to our faith, they should not be feared but reclaimed from them as from a wrongful owner for our use."[45] *If* a Christian finds any truth in the teaching of the

44. "Dicendum est ergo quod aliud est docere in sapientia verbi quocumque modo intelligatur, et aliud uti sapientia verbi in docendo. Ille in sapientia verbi docet qui sapientiam verbi accipit pro principali radice suae doctrinae, ita scilicet quod ea solum approbet, quae verbi sapientiam continent: reprobet autem ea quae sapientiam verbi non habent, et hoc fidei est corruptivum. Utitur autem sapientia verbi, qui suppositis verae fidei fundamentis, si qua vera in doctrinis philosophorum inveniat, in obsequium fidei assumit." *Expos. Pauli, I ad Cor.* 1,3.
45. "Unde Augustinus dicit in secundo de doctrina Christiana, quod si qua philosophi dixerunt

philosophers—and the implication is that he may not—then he not only can but *must* subjugate those truths to the faith as a general who usurps a rebel army. And again: "in *On Christian Doctrine* 4 he says, 'Since the skill of eloquence has great power to persuade for what is base or for what is right, why not acquire it in order to make war for truth …?"[46] *If* a Christian finds rhetorical devices somehow suited to Christian teaching—and again, he or she may not—he or she should reclaim them as a judge returns stolen goods to their rightful owner. As if to demonstrate the distinction Thomas seals the point with these arresting images: if Thomas and his authorities have used philosophy and rhetoric, they have usurped and disciplined them in obedience to the Christian faith. Thomas takes it that Paul himself does nothing less.

The Limits of Philosophy: Convergences between the *Summa*'s Prologue and the Commentary on 1 Corinthians

One way to ask whether and how Thomas inherits these pedagogical commitments would be to explore the degree to which they implicitly govern his use of philosophic authorities.[47] A more direct route into the problem is through the first Question of the *Summa*: there, Thomas specifies the work's intention and manner of teaching, paying specific attention to the role of philosophic authority in *sacra*

---

fidei nostrae accommoda, non solum formidanda non sunt, sed ab eis tamquam ab iniustis possessoribus in usum nostrum vindicanda." Ibid., 1.3.

46. "Et in IV de doctrina Christiana dicit: cum posita sit in medio facultas eloquii, quae ad persuadendum seu prava seu recta valent pluribus, cur non bonorum studio comparetur ut militet veritati, si eam mali in usum iniquitatis et erroris usurpant." Ibid.

47. For exemplary approaches of this sort, see G. B. M. Wilhelmus Valkenberg, *Words of the Living God: Place and Function of Holy Scripture in the Theology of St. Thomas Aquinas* (Leuven: Peeters, 2000); and Jordan, *Rewritten Theology*, esp. 18–32, 60–89, and 116–35.

doctrina.[48] Yet, to grasp Thomas's position we must first look to the *Summa*'s prologue.

> Because the doctor of catholic truth should teach not only the proficient but also instruct beginners—according to the apostle in 1 Corinthians 3, 'As unto little ones in Christ, I gave you milk to drink, not meat'—we propose our intention in this work, which is to treat whatever belongs to the Christian religion in such a way that is well suited for the instruction of beginners.[49]

Although Thomas claims to write for beginners, modern readers tend to doubt that he means what he says. Then, too, they seem to forget Thomas's description of the beginners for whom he writes: Thomas's beginners are, like Paul's beginners in Corinth, *parvulis in Christo*—"little ones in Christ." The allusion precedes a crucial if not familiar cluster of pedagogical exclusions:

> We have considered that newcomers to this teaching have many times been hampered by various things written, in part because of the multiplication of useless questions, articles, and arguments; in part because those things that are necessary for them to know are not passed on according to the order of the discipline, but rather as the exposition of a book might require, or as disputation might occasion; partly, too, because frequent repetition generated weariness and confusion in the minds or souls of the readers. Eager to avoid these and other such faults, we shall try, with trust in divine help, to set down whatever is included in this sacred teaching as briefly and clearly as the matter itself permits.[50]

---

48. *ST* I,1 *pr.* "Et ut intentio nostra sub aliquibus certis limitibus comprehendatur, necessarium est primo investigare de ipsa sacra doctrina, qualis sit, et ad quae se extendat."

49. "Quia Catholicae veritatis doctor non solum provectos debet instruere, sed ad eum pertinet etiam incipientes erudire, secundum illud apostoli I ad Corinth. III, tanquam parvulis in Christo, lac vobis potum dedi, non escam; propositum nostrae intentionis in hoc opere est, ea quae ad Christianam religionem pertinent, eo modo tradere, secundum quod congruit ad eruditionem incipientium." *ST*, pr.

50. "Consideravimus namque huius doctrinae novitios, in his quae a diversis conscripta sunt, plurimum impediri, partim quidem propter multiplicationem inutilium quaestionum, articulorum et argumentorum; partim etiam quia ea quae sunt necessaria talibus ad sciendum, non traduntur secundum ordinem disciplinae, sed secundum quod requirebat librorum expositio, vel secundum quod se praebebat occasio disputandi; partim quidem quia eorundem

First, Thomas proposes to avoid the multiplication of useless arguments that might generate weariness and confusion in the souls of readers. Second, he vows to proceed as briefly and clearly as the *materia* of his teaching will allow.[51] I hesitate to say that these exclusions recall Paul's refusal of vain arguments, if only because the date of the *Commentary on 1 Corinthians* relative to the *Summa* eludes scholarly consensus.[52] Does the prologue's invocation of Paul's pedagogical authority suggest that we could?

I have fewer doubts about the Pauline echoes in Thomas's elaboration of the limits of philosophy in *Summa* I,1. How interesting that Thomas distinguishes *sacra doctrina* from the philosophical disciplines by specifying its (1) author, (2) subject matter, and (3) manner of teaching? We have seen this procedure before. It is well to note that Thomas brackets each distinction by citing Pauline Scripture? Rather than belabor the obvious, let me begin to close by sketching these distinctions in a way that lets connections speak for themselves.

First, Thomas distinguishes *sacra doctrina* from the "philosophical disciplines" (*philosophicas disciplinas*) with respect to their authorship and subject matter: "On the contrary, 2 Tim 3:16 says, 'All scripture, inspired of God, is profitable to teach, to reprove, to correct, to instruct in justice.' But divinely inspired Scripture does not belong to the philosophical disciplines, which have been built up by human reason. Therefore, it is useful that, besides the philosophical disciplines, there should be another science that is divinely inspired."[53]

---

frequens repetitio et fastidium et confusionem generabat in animis auditorum. Haec igitur et alia huiusmodi evitare studentes, tentabimus, cum confidentia divini auxilii, ea quae ad sacram doctrinam pertinent, breviter ac dilucide prosequi, secundum quod materia patietur." *ST*, pr.

51. *ST*, pr.

52. See Torrell, *Saint Thomas Aquinas*, 1:340. Cf. James A. Weisheipl, *Friar Thomas d'Aquino: His Life, Thought, and Work* (Washington, DC: Catholic University of America Press, 1983), 372–73.

53. "Sed contra est quod dicitur II ad Tim. III, omnis Scriptura divinitus inspirata utilis est ad

Thomas goes on to show that sciences may be distinguished according to "the diverse means by which knowledge is introduced."[54] Because each of the philosophical disciplines has been built by human reason, the *theologia* of philosophers extends no further than what can be known about God by "the light of natural reason." Their *materia* thus comprises what only a few have discovered after a long time and with much error.[55] In contrast, *sacra doctrina* is both about God and from God: it regards "truth about God" that "exceeds the grasp of human reason"—truth that God has revealed to bring about "the entire salvation of humanity."[56] *Sacra doctrina,* then, is not one among several other philosophical disciplines. Its *theologia* is something altogether different from that of philosophers.[57] *Sacra doctrina* is something distinct from philosophy. That is the point of Thomas's first distinction.

The second further specifies Thomas's manner of teaching in the *Summa*: he intends to treat the subject matter of *sacra doctrina* dialectically by arguing both "from authority" (*ex auctoritate*) and "from reason" (*ex ratione*).[58] Yet he does so in the same manner as Paul: ". . . Titus 1:9 says this about a bishop: 'He must embrace that faithful word which is according to doctrine, that he may be able to exhort in sound doctrine and to convince the gainsayers.'"[59] If *sacra doctrina* should argue as Paul does—if it is to exhort and convince—it nevertheless must not try to prove its *principia*: "*sacra*

---

docendum, ad arguendum, ad corripiendum, ad erudiendum ad iustitiam. Scriptura autem divinitus inspirata non pertinet ad philosophicas disciplinas, quae sunt secundum rationem humanam inventae. Utile igitur est, praeter philosophicas disciplinas, esse aliam scientiam divinitus inspiratam." *Summa theol.* I,1,1 *sed contra.*

54. *ST* I,1,1 *ad* 3.
55. *ST* I,1,1, *co.* and *ad* 3.
56. *ST* I,1,1.
57. *ST* I,1,1, *ad* 2.
58. *ST* I,1,8, *arg.* 2.
59. *ST* I,1,8, *sed contra.*

doctrina does not argue in order to prove its first principles, which are articles of the faith, but rather proceeds from its principles in order to show something else—just as the Apostle does in 1 Corinthians 15."[60] Nor, then, should a theologian seek to prove the articles of faith to those who altogether deny divine revelation: "if our adversary believes nothing that has been divinely revealed, then there is no longer any way of proving the articles of the faith by arguments (*per rationes*)—but only of answering his objections against the faith—if he has any."[61]

For Thomas, then, *sacra doctrina* differs from philosophy, since it teaches truths about God that are revealed by God and not by human reason, and since it does not argue in proof of its principles. Still, Thomas contends that a theologian *can* make *use* of human reason and philosophy whenever doing so proves useful. Here again he secures the point by invoking the authority of Paul:

> Nevertheless, *sacra doctrina* uses human reason as well—not, to be sure, in order to prove the faith, since this would destroy the merit of faith—but rather to clarify certain other things that are treated within this teaching. . . . This is also why *sacra doctrina* uses the authority of philosophers in those places where the philosophers have been able to know the truth through natural reason—just as Paul in Acts 17:28 Paul cites Aratos, saying 'As one of your own poets said: "For we are also His offspring."'[62]

The passage comprises a cluster of increasingly narrow circumscriptions: yes, *sacra doctrina* can use arguments from reason—yes, even human reason—but only "to make more manifest other things treated in this teaching."[63] Yes, *sacra doctrina* can make use of philosophical authorities, but only "in those places where

60. *ST* I,1,8.
61. Ibid.
62. *ST* I,1,8 *ad* 2.
63. *ST* I,1,8 *arg* 2, *co.*, and *ad* 2.

philosophers were able to know the truth."[64] Which is to say that it cannot use it everywhere. Thomas draws narrower lines still when he specifies how little arguments from philosophical authority can achieve: "*sacra doctrina* only uses such authorities as probable and extrinsic arguments. But it properly uses the authority of the canonical Scriptures when arguing from necessity."[65] So yes, *sacra doctrina* can advance arguments by appealing to philosophical authorities, but only when those arguments regard matters that are inessential to the Christian faith. No philosopher has uttered a truth necessary for *sacra doctrina* that cannot already be found in Scripture.

After all this, we may wonder what can be left for philosophy in a *summa* of theology to do. Thomas does make use of philosophical teachings and texts. But in doing so he judges them—"condemning as false" any claim that contradicts the revealed truth he knows more firmly by faith.[66] He appropriates philosophical teachings and texts only to disband them, restricting them to topics that could just as well be discarded or ignored. So there is philosophy in the *Summa*. Notice, though, just *how* it is there. The *Summa* is not so much a storehouse for philosophical doctrines as a school of reform. This, too, hails from Paul, who drives "into bondage every understanding in obedience to Christ."[67]

---

64. *ST* I,1,8 *ad* 2.
65. Ibid.
66. *ST* I,1,6, *ad* 2, following 2 Corinthians 10.
67. *ST* I,1,8.

6

―――

Election and Providence in the Theology of Thomas Aquinas: Reading the *Summa* in Light of His Commentary of 1 Corinthians 1–2

Michael T. Dempsey

If we wish to understand Thomas as a Dominican friar and biblical theologian, we must move beyond conventional portraits of him as the perennial philosopher and see how Thomas's great *Summa* attempts to build a new theological science that is grounded in Scripture and expressed with the aid of natural reason. As Thomas himself says with Paul in 2 Cor. 10:5, all thought and understanding is to be taken captive in obedience to Christ in his battle of spiritual warfare against the powers and principalities of this world.

One of the best places to witness Thomas in this light is in his scriptural commentaries, especially on 1 Corinthians 1–2. Here, the true wisdom and power of God in Christ is revealed on the cross that convicts the world of its pride and arrogance and stands in solidarity with the poor and lowly. Since Thomas is known for his careful and precise use of language, it should not be surprising to find that the wisdom or *ratio* of God in Christ in 1 Corinthians finds parallel expression in the *Summa Theologiae* in Thomas's discussion of theology as wisdom and in his doctrine of providence as the rational ordering (*ratio ordinis*) of all things in Christ. For close readers of the text, reading Thomas's *Summa Theologiae* is like going into a great medieval cathedral of thought in which each room is decorated with insights from a variety of different sources that match the patterns and tapestries from other rooms, such that one can learn a lot about the whole from concentrating on one or two small parts.

This paper will offer an analysis of his commentary on 1 Corinthians 1–2 in order to consider how the wisdom and power of the cross in 1 Corinthians is expressed in Thomas's understanding of theology and divine providence. Indeed, the very structure of the *Summa* itself follows the pattern laid out in 1 Corinthians, as does his doctrine of providence and divine government. As we shall see, providence is not simply about the sovereign rule of God in and through the natural contingencies of human freedom, but is, rather, the specific ordering of human action according to the wisdom or *ratio* of God in Christ.

Deus Elegit Abjectos: Thomas's Commentary on 1 Corinthians 1–2

One of the most striking features of Thomas's biblical commentaries is the way he uses Scripture to comment on Scripture, so that a single passage is illuminated by the whole biblical testimony. In the commentary on 1 Corinthians, Thomas begins by noting that Paul's name in Latin, *Paulus*, which means "little one," is a mark of true humility. As such, he is called by the will of God to the highest rank in the church: an apostle, according to 1 Sam. 15:17: "Though you are little in your own eyes, are you not the head of the tribes of Israel?" and Matt. 11:25 (which Thomas quotes repeatedly in this section): "Thou hast hidden these things from the wise and prudent and revealed them to the little ones" (Vulgate).[1] In characteristic mendicant fashion, Thomas sees the election of Paul as representative of the biblical pattern of election and humility where Paul, who is the least of the apostles, is lifted up to the greatest dignity in the church: to preach the gospel. The basis of this model is the incarnation itself, in which the overflowing love of God is poured out into the world according to 2 Cor. 8:9: "For your sakes he became poor, so that by his poverty you might become rich."

The pattern of election and humility is evident throughout the commentary. In his discussion of the nature of Christian teaching, for instance, Thomas argues that since the central element of Christian doctrine is salvation through the cross of Christ, the means of communicating that message must be consistent with the message itself. That is to say, the language of Christian preaching and teaching must also eschew exalted rhetoric and adopt a simple, humble language so that the cross of Christ not be emptied of its power, for the lofty words of human eloquence, as seen in the rhetorical heights of pagan antiquity, would seem to justify human arrogance and undermine the virtue of humility. It would also subject the teaching of faith to the ridicule of secular and vain reasoning, as Thomas explains:[2]

---

1. Thomas Aquinas, *In Omnes S. Pauli Apostoli Epistolas, Super Primam Epistolam St. Pauli ad Corinthios* (Taurini: Marietti, 1820), I,1 (ch. 1, lecture 1), 221.

if the teachings of faith are presented in eloquent wisdom . . . they appear foolish to them that are perishing, i.e., to unbelievers, who consider themselves wise according to the world, for the preaching of the cross of Christ contains something which to worldly wisdom seems impossible, for example, that God should die or that Omnipotence should suffer at the hands of violent men [or] that a person not avoid shame when he can, and other things . . . [which] are matters which seem contrary to the prudence of this world.[3]

Yet, to those of the faith, the power of the cross is evident in the fact that through it, Thomas states, "God has overcome the devil and the world and has given sinners power over themselves when together with Christ they die to their vices and concupiscence."[4] Such wisdom only appears foolish to those who have their hearts set on *vana doctrina* ("the vain teachings of the world") and not *sana doctrina* of the gospel, the saving, healthy teaching of God which condemns the arrogance and greed that prevent us from seeing the true wisdom and power of God on the cross.

For Thomas, the humility and lowliness of the cross functions to subvert human arrogance and vanity, as well to undermine the quest for power and domination over others. This is what it means for the cross to "destroy the wisdom of the wise and the prudence of the prudent." It destroys the "earthly, sensual, and diabolical" wisdom that people have "invented for themselves,"[5] which considers that

---

2. Yet this does not mean that all eloquence or philosophy is to be avoided, but only when it becomes the main focus of the doctrine that seeks to elevate the speaker instead of the subject matter. Here, one cannot help but notice the influence of Augustine's *De doctrina christiana*, for even Augustine, Thomas notes, accepts secular reasoning when it proves useful for preaching the gospel. This is the "ore of divine providence" that is found throughout creation but must first be taken captive in obedience to Christ. See Saint Augustine, *Teaching Christianity*, trans. Edmund Hill (New York: New City Press, 1996), 160. On his part, Thomas also accepts natural reason when perfected by grace to minster to the needs of charity (see *ST* I.1.8, citing 2 Cor. 10:5), so that philosophical thinking helps to clarify biblical revelation insofar it leads to a greater love of God and neighbor.

3. *Super Primam Epistolam St. Pauli ad Corinthios*, 1,3:229.

4. Ibid.

5. Ibid.

one's happiness is found in the things of creation instead of in the Creator. Moreover, it destroys the prudence of those who "cling to the goods of this world" and look out only after themselves. This is precisely why the wisdom and power of God are not recognized by the powers of the world, Thomas notes, such as the philosophers and nobility, because they judge things according to worldly reason and self-interest, but not according to the love of God which, though complete in itself, is poured out for others. Although there may be traces of this wisdom in creation, the true wisdom of the cross is not self-evident on account of the vanity of the human heart that is easily seduced by worldly power, glory, and comforts. For this reason, theology must be grounded in revelation and not natural reason, which must be taken over and converted before it can be applied to the teaching of faith.[6]

However, if the wisdom of this teaching transcends what the carnal mind is capable of grasping, who, then, Thomas asks, can understand it? It is not the Jews, for they demand a sign. Nor is it the Gentiles, for they judge things according to human wisdom. It is, rather, those who are given the Spirit of God, who are called by the power and wisdom of Christ to see that God, who is wisdom and power himself, is made manifest through the foolishness of the cross.

In characteristic mendicant fashion and in close coordination with his metaphysics of divine being, Thomas follows Paul to show how

---

6. In *ST* I.1.1 Thomas cites two passages that are repeatedly quoted throughout this section and show the link in his thought between *sacra doctrina* and the wisdom of God in 1 Corinthians. The first is Isa. 64:4, also cited by Paul in 1 Cor. 2:9: "the eye hath not seen, O God, nor the heart of man conceived, what things Thou has prepared for those that wait for Thee." The second is Sir. 3:25: "Many things are shown to you above the understanding of man." Both are significant not only because they refer to the transcendence of God that does not fall, as he says, "within the range of human senses," but also because the wisdom and power of God in Christ makes no sense according to worldly reason. Thus, revelation is necessary for this teaching that has "no part of philosophical science" (*ST* I.1.1) "built up" by reason. Interestingly, Thomas repeats this point *three times* (!) in the first article of the *Summa* (*ST* I.1.1), which indicates just how important it is for Thomas to ground theology in revelation and not philosophical learning corrupted by sin and self-interest.

God's election of the little ones in Christ undermines the wisdom of the world. By choosing the weak and powerless, Thomas writes, such as peasants and plebeians, God shames the strong and points out the "defect" of worldly power according to Isa. 2:17: "The haughtiness of man shall be humbled, and the pride of men shall be brought low" (RSV). By electing those of lowly and ignoble birth, God "excludes the excellence of race or class" and puts down the "grand opinion" that people have of nobility, according to Isa. 23:9: "The Lord of hosts has purposed it, to defile the pride of all glory, to dishonor all the honored of the earth" (RSV). God even elects the *abjectus*, the rejected, in order that none will boast of themselves, according to Jer. 9:23: "Let not the wise man glory in wisdom, the mighty man glory in his might, and let not the rich man glory in his riches."[7] For in electing the rejected, the powerless, and the despised, God corrects the exalted opinion people have of worldly power so that they know that they are saved by God and not worldly excellence.

Clearly, for Thomas, there are important pastoral and political implications of this teaching. Yet it is not the case that God rejects the greatness of the world as such. Thomas does not share the radical *contemptus mundi* of St. Francis. Indeed, he acknowledges that that worldly excellence also comes from God and ought to be recognized as such. Rather, the goodness of God is evident in the way God draws the great of this world *by means of the lowly* in order to give the lowly a great honor and to serve the proud and mighty by bringing them down from their heights. With Augustine and the early church, Thomas agrees, contraries are cured by contraries, by which he means that the sins of one are corrected by the virtues of another, just as the pride of some is corrected by the exaltation of the lowly.[8]

---

7. *Super Primam Epistolam St. Pauli ad Corinthios*, I,4, 232–33.

But Thomas also goes beyond Augustine when he repeatedly makes use of the word *abjectus*, the rejected, given the meaning of that term in the Middle Ages. According to one medieval historian, there was a descending scale of destitution and social ostracism among the poor at that time. There was "the weakness of the little man, the *impotens* [who] is close to the vulgarity of the peasant (the *ignobilis, vilis*, and even *vilissimus*)," but at the bottom, the most repulsive pauper was the *abjectus*, who was "dirty, dressed in rags, foul smelling, and covered in sores."[9] By applying this term to the elect, Thomas stands with Dominic, Francis, and Jesus himself. It is not simply the peasant and plebes who are among the elect, while "*non multi nobiles*" are. It is, rather, especially the *abjectus* or the destitute that stands as the end of God's election in Jesus Christ for the purpose of bringing down the proud and exalting those whom the world regards as insignificant.

Here, the folly of the cross undermines the so-called wisdom of those who would value human life according to money, power, or social status. Because the teachings of Christ are a hidden, secret wisdom that makes no sense to worldly people, Thomas insists that this teaching is *contrarium sapientiae, contrarium potentiae*, and *contrarium nobilitate*. Even as Thomas accepts his medieval worldview that God orders things according to a social hierarchy, while acknowledging that greater gifts are the result of God's greater love (*ST* I.20.3), his interpretation of how that hierarchy ought to function follows the wisdom and power of the cross by giving the greatest gift of all, namely, election, to those who are the very least. Hierarchy thus remains intact but only insofar as those who enjoy

8. *Super Primam Epistolam St. Pauli ad II Corinthios*, X,1, 486. See Augustine, *Teaching Christianity*, 111, which also makes use of 1 Corinthians 1 to cure the sin of pride.
9. Michel Mollat, *The Poor in the Middle Ages: An Essay in Social History*, trans. Arthur Goldhammer (New Haven: Yale University Press, 1986), 3.

positions of power and privilege are called, humbled, and enabled by God to follow Christ by serving the hated and despised as nothing less than Christ himself (cf. Matt. 25:40).

Sacra Doctrina and the Wisdom of God

The wisdom of Christ in the election of the rejected finds a similar iteration in Thomas's understanding of theology in the *Summa*. In the *Prologue* of his great work, Thomas begins:

> Because the Master of Catholic Truth ought not only to teach the proficient, but especially to instruct beginners (according to the Apostle: "As unto Little Ones in Christ, I gave you milk to drink not meat"—1 Cor. 3:1, 2), we propose in this book to treat of whatever belongs to the Christian Religion, in such a way as may tend to the instruction of beginners.

As Marie-Dominique Chenu tells us, such dedications were common among the mendicants at that time: "All of the new apostles, from Robert of Abrissells (died 1117) to Francis of Assisi, addressed their wonderful message to the little people of the shops and cellars . . . to the unfortunate ones with neither fire nor shelter, to the serfs bound to the soil."[10] While many have pondered whether Thomas's "little ones" refers to university students or the *fratres communes* of the Dominican Order, Thomas's commentary on 1 Corinthians explains that the beginners are those whose lives are marked by jealousy and strife and have their minds still set on the things of the world. They need basic teaching in morals and justice and not the advanced meat of mystical teaching.[11]

Thomas's sensitivity to the needs of the little ones is evident

---

10. Marie-Dominique Chenu, *Nature, Man, and Society in the Twelfth Century: Essays on New Theological Perspectives in the Latin West*, trans. Jerome Taylor and Lester Little (Toronto: University of Toronto Press, 1997), 242.
11. *Super Primam Epistolam St. Pauli ad Corinthios*, III,1, 244.

throughout his understanding of theology as *sacra doctrina* as well. He argues for a science of revelation "because the truth about God such as reason could discover, would only be known by a few, and that after a long time, and with the admixture of many errors" (*ST* I.1.1). Since most people have neither the time nor capacity to ponder the being of God or the way to salvation, God has revealed it in Jesus Christ so that "even the little ones might contemplate and love someone who, so to speak, would be like them."[12] In the *Summa Contra Gentiles*, he adds that what is most wonderful about Christian revelation is that "there is inspiration given to human minds, so that simple and untutored persons, filled with the Holy Spirit, come to possess instantaneously the highest wisdom and readiest eloquence."[13] Thomas even argues for the use of metaphors in Scripture on the same grounds, so that "even the simple who are unable by themselves to grasp intellectual things may be able to understand it" (*ST* I.1.9).

Perhaps the most poignant expression is found in his understanding of theology as wisdom. Since the task of the wise person is to order, arrange, and judge all things according to the highest wisdom, which is Christ (a task that parallels God's providential ordering), the person who is wise in this science must order, arrange, and judge all things according to Christ in 2 Cor. 10:4–5: "destroying the councils and every height (*superbia*) that exalteth itself against the knowledge of God" (*ST* I.1.6).

But who, specifically, is to be condemned in Paul's battle of spiritual warfare against the powers and principalities of the world? In his commentary, Thomas explicitly names tyrants and political oppressors, the devils and philosophers, whose arrogance and social

---

12. Jean-Pierre Torrell, *Saint Thomas Aquinas*, vol. 2: *Spiritual Master*, trans. Robert Royal (Washington, DC: Catholic University of America Press, 2012), 109–10n24, quoting *De rationibus fidei*, c. 5, n. 976.

13. Thomas Aquinas, *Summa contra gentiles*, trans. A. C. Pegis (Notre Dame, IN: University of Notre Dame Press, 1975), I.6.1.

status lead them to exalt themselves above others and build themselves up with their own knowledge and power. Against them Thomas cites Isa. 5:21: "woe to you who are wise in your own eyes." The teaching of Christ thus exalts the poor and lowly while bringing down those who consider themselves wise in worldly wisdom or the law and abuse their political power according to Ps. 149:8: "binding kings in shackles and nobility in fetters of iron."[14]

For Thomas, then, the wisdom of God in Christ consists in the just ordering and judging of things according to the pattern set out in 1 Corinthians. This explains Thomas's harsh denunciations in the Prologue against those who write books for themselves or the occasion of an argument, as well as his meticulous ordering of the *Summa* according to the needs of the learner (*ordinem disciplinae*). Although examples of this wisdom abound throughout his work,[15] the clearest comes from his doctrine of divine providence, which explains not just *that* God works in and through secondary causes, but specifically *how* those secondary causes are wisely ordered for the common good.

Divine Providence and the *Ratio Ordinis Rerum*

Thomas's doctrine of divine providence is treated after his discussion of God's knowledge and will and thus belongs to the eternal being and action of God. Defined as the *ratio ordinis rerum ad finem,* providence is the work of God's wisdom and will in the ordering of all things to God as their final end. This ordering is the work of the whole Trinity, which is understood by appropriation according to the essential attributes of the power, wisdom, and love of the Father, Son, and Holy Spirit. Yet the *ratio* of this ordering refers to

---

14. *Super Primam Epistolam St. Pauli ad II Corinthios*, X,1, 485.
15. For example, see *ST* I.96.4; I.106.4; I.108.5; II–II.31.2–3; II–II.47.10; II–II.185.1.

the wisdom of Christ as the basic exemplar according to which all things are made and directed to their end.

Thomas first considers that providence is evident from the created goodness of things in terms of their substance and in being ordered to an end, which can be can be traced back to God as the first cause and final end. Although providence is an article of faith, understood by those who take counsel in God through prayer, it may also be discerned from the good in the being and action of things. Since this goodness comes from God, God must have an idea of this goodness in the divine mind, for the reason (*ratio*) or exemplar must preexist in God from all eternity. And this *ratio* (which is Christ) is providence.

Thomas then offers an analogy from sensory experience that compares providence to the way an individual orders her life toward her own best end, or the way a king directs others for the good of the kingdom. In this latter way, Thomas holds, we may understand the providence of God, that is, not in terms of individual self-interest, but in the way superiors direct their subordinates for the common good. The biblical basis comes from Matt. 24:45: "a faithful and wise servant whom his lord hath appointed over the affairs of his family."

Here we reach a point of great importance, for this ordering can be understood according to a general metaphysic derived from natural reason but not necessarily according to the wisdom revealed in Christ, which as we saw in Paul is not available to the corrupt and carnal heart. One twentieth-century neo-Thomist, John P. Rock, epitomizes the problem with this approach when he writes that "In man the lower parts are ordained to the higher, the vegetative and the sensitive to the intellectual, so in the universe all material creation is ordained to man—*to serve his bodily needs.*"[16] While this may be true in the biological realm, where lower forms of life are contained in and

---

16. John P. Rock, "Divine Providence in St. Thomas Aquinas," in F. J. Adelmann, ed., *The Quest for the Absolute* (The Hague: Martinus Nijhoff, 1966), 67–103 (emphasis added).

are necessary for higher forms, this is not the case in the social and ecclesiastical hierarchies, where higher orders are to minister to their subordinates. Just as mastership does not subject others to slavery, but for the common good (*ST* I.96.4), so, too, does providence govern subordinates for the well-being of all. To understand what this *ratio ordinis* means we must consult Thomas's scriptural commentaries to see how he understands this passage.

Matthew 24:45 occurs in the context of Jesus' parable on the final judgment, as he warns his disciples to be careful for they do not know when the master will return. They are to remain vigilant in looking after the affairs of the Lord's family, which Thomas understands to be the church, specifically, to "give food in due season." This refers not only to spiritual nourishment of sacraments, preaching, and their good example, but also and more importantly in cases of extreme need (*ST* II-II.188.6) to temporal assistance as well. In Thomas's collection of patristic authorities, the *Catena aurea*, as well as in his own commentary, Thomas comments at length how servants in the church are responsible for feeding Christ's sheep, by which he means feeding the poor. Unfortunately, Thomas does not quote the entire passage and so its precise meaning "to give food in due season" is not clear.

In the *Catena aurea*, Thomas recalls Hilary's claim that this passage offers a "general exhortation to all in common to unwearied vigilance," but especially to the bishops, who are to be "faithful in dispensing the revenues of the Church ... [not to] devour . . . that which belongs to widows" but to "remember the poor" and be "prudent [in] understanding the cases of them that are in need, whence they come to be, what has been the education and what are the necessities of each."[17] Although all Christians are called to

---

17. Thomas Aquinas, *Catena aurea: St. Matthew Volume I*, trans. J. H. Cardinal Newman (London: St. Austin's Press, 1999), 838–39. I have discussed this in "Providence, Distributive Justice,

distribute their wealth to the poor, it explicitly names the bishops of the church, which Thomas takes to be the principle servants of the poor, for he quotes the same passage in his question on the bishops (*ST* II-II.185.1) and on prudence (*ST* II-II.47.10). "As the Lord repeats to Peter three times" (John 21:15-17), Thomas states, "in order to stress its importance: 'Feed, feed, feed, my sheep.' Feed them by word, feed them by example, and feed them temporal assistance."[18] Unfortunately, as Thomas laments, there are many who "look after their own interests [Phil. 2:21], [but few who look] after those of Jesus Christ."[19]

> For rare indeed is such a faithful servant serving his Master for his Master's sake, feeding Christ's sheep not for his own [profit] but for the love of Christ, skilled to discern the abilities, the life, and the manner of those put under him, whom the Lord sets over, that is, who is called by God, and has not thrust himself in.[20]

After explaining the literal sense of giving food to those in need, Thomas then discusses the anagogical sense of eternal rewards and punishments. For those who give to the needy, especially those to teach others in justice, they will be "set over all his possessions" in eternal life. According to Dan. 12:3, "those who teach will be as the splendor of the firmament, and those who enlighten many in justice, as the stars for ever and ever" (Vulgate). However, for those in positions of power and authority who serve their own interests, setting an "evil example" to the flock, they will receive the maximum punishment according to Mic. 3:9-10: "Hear this, you heads of the house of Jacob and rulers of the house of Israel, who abhor justice

and Divine Government in the Theology of Thomas Aquinas: Some Implications for Ecclesial Practice," in *New Blackfriars* 90 (2009): 265–84.

18. Thomas Aquinas, *In Matthaeum evangelistam expositio XXIV*, 226, in *Opera Omnia*, vol. 10 (Parma: Fiaccadori, 1852-1873; Taurini: Marietti, 1820).

19. *In Matthaeum evangelistam expositio*, XXIV, 227.

20. *Catena aurea: St. Matthew*, 838.

and pervert all equity, who build Zion with blood and Jerusalem with wrong" (RSV). Elders in the church must not rule in this way, Thomas warns, according to Ezek. 34:2: "Woe to the shepherds who feed themselves!" (Vulgate). The shepherds should not serve with force or harshness which will only scatter the sheep in disunity, but according to 1 Pet. 5:2: "Tend the flock that is your charge, not by constraint but willingly, not for shameful gain but eagerly, not as domineering over those in your charge, but being examples to the flock."[21]

Therefore, to understand how Thomas's rational arguments explain biblical revelation, we must consider the goodness of creation that shows forth the divine providence in light of the scriptural commentaries. It is not simply goodness in general that testifies to the providence of God, but the specific goodness in the church when superiors are faithful to Christ by taking wise and prudent care of the spiritual and material needs of the poor. Here, everything depends upon understanding providence biblically and not in terms of an abstract philosophy or apologetics that replaces the providence of God with an ideology of unjust domination. Instead, according to Thomas's commentaries, the providence of God condemns such illicit interpretations as contrary to the faith. Providence, therefore, is not simply the reason things happen according to the divine order of hierarchical domination, but is the active ordering of things in their being and action to serve those beneath them in the social and ecclesial hierarchy. As the operation of God's power, wisdom, and love in human being and action, the providence of God extends to all creatures through individuals who participate in the primary, exemplary, and final causality of God by extending their resources to those in need.

21. *In Matthaeum evangelistam expositio*, XXIV, 226.

Divine Government and Human Agency

If providence is located in Thomas's doctrine of God, his theology of divine government is situated in his doctrine of creation in order to stress that human beings are the primary executors of God's providential care. For Thomas, human beings participate in the triune missions by preserving other creatures in their goodness and moving them to be a cause of goodness for others. "Every creature participates in the divine goodness, so as to diffuse the good it possesses to others. . . . So the more an agent is established in the share of the divine goodness, so much the more does it strive to transmit its perfections to others as far as possible" (*ST* I.106.4). Thus, while all creatures share in the divine goodness, the purpose of this participation is to extend those gifts to others. This is the "morality of divinization" whereby creatures participate in God by serving others, so that one comes to partake more in the divine nature by sharing the blessings one receives from God with others. As Thomas explains: "The ordering of the universe, as a result of the outpouring of God's goodness [requires that] superior creatures have that not only by which they are good in themselves, but especially that by which they are the cause of goodness for other things which participate at the greatest remove [*in extremis*] from God's goodness."[22] Hence, for Thomas, our participation in God actually increases in the degree to which we extend ourselves to those in need. And, therefore, we must conclude that since God is the very essence of goodness and since "[the] highest degree of goodness in any practical order, design, or knowledge ... consists in knowing the individuals acted upon, as the best physician is not the one who can only give his attention to general principles, but who can consider the least details ... we must

---

22. Thomas Aquinas, *Providence and Predestination: Truth, Questions 5 and 6*, trans. R. W. Mulligan (Chicago: Henry Regnery, 1961), 59.

say that God has the design of government of all things, *even of the very least*" (*ST* I.103.6, emphasis added).

This government is perfect not only in terms of its knowledge of particular details, but especially in that it "will be so much the better *in the degree the things governed are brought to perfection*" (*ST* I.103.6). Hence, for Thomas, the perfection of the divine government consists in leading those creatures that are the lowliest to their own perfection by becoming a cause of goodness in others. While the divine government is mediated by those better established in the divine goodness, the aim and goal is to share the abundance of God's blessings with those *in extremis* in order to lift them up and to empower them to care for others. The perfection of the universe itself is thus fulfilled through human service of the least. The social implications of this teaching are thus immediately clear:

> The perfection of divine providence requires that the excess of certain things over others be reduced to a suitable order. Now this is done when one makes available some good for those who have less, from the abundance of those who have more. So since the perfection of the universe requires that certain things participate in the divine goodness more than others . . . the perfection of divine providence demands that the execution of the divine rule be accomplished by those that participate more in divine goodness. (*SCG* III.77.5)

Clearly, for Thomas, the whole trajectory of God's government is geared for the good of all, but especially to those at the very bottom, that they may be empowered to attain their own perfection by receiving and sharing the wealth of God with those who are needful. But this government is also for the good of those creatures at the top or middle of the social hierarchy insofar as they are directed to the good of others. Indeed, following the tradition of Gregory the Great, Thomas notes that the highest creatures in the ecclesial hierarchy, such as bishops, have the responsibility to follow the self-giving of the poor Christ by undertaking any hardship and even sacrificing their lives for the needs of the poor.[23] Although Thomas does not hold with his Franciscan counterparts that poverty itself is a mark of perfection or that bishops are required to give up their personal possessions, he nonetheless insists that the mark of spiritual perfection comes from the greater love of God and neighbor which can be judged by the intensity with which one is willing to give up, suffer, and sacrifice oneself for others. But it is always and primarily the greater love of God that enables this most radical and Christ-like form of human providence.

Divine providence and government, therefore, operate according to the same *ratio* of God in Jesus Christ that we observed in his commentary on 1 Corinthians. Although Thomas unquestionably accepts the traditional form of ecclesial hierarchy, his thought nonetheless understands that human beings are perfected by the *perichoretic* indwelling of grace that moves them to love God and divest themselves of worldly attachment in order to lift up the poor and lowly as especially loved by God. Indeed, while hierarchy would appear to be essential for the distribution of ecclesial resources, insofar as a diversity of goods is necessary for the well-being of the whole, one can see in Thomas's thought how the eschatological goal of the divine self-giving would support the *Aufhebung* of hierarchy itself, in which the continual divestment of resources for the poor would strive toward a new heaven and new earth (Rev. 21:1).

It is important to acknowledge that such radical form of human providence is possible only through the love of God. With this the disciples will accomplish even greater works than Christ himself, according to John 14:12: "the works that I do, he shall do, and

---

23. Thomas Aquinas, *The Perfection of the Spiritual Life*, translated as *The Religious State* by John Procter (Westminster, MD: Newman Press, 1950), 81–82, 89–90, 93, and 94. See also Dempsey, "Providence, Distributive Justice, and Divine Government."

greater works than these shall he do" (*ST* I.105.8). And what could be greater, Thomas asks, than giving the power to work miracles to others for the justification of the unrighteous? (*ST* III.43.4). This is even greater than the creation of the world. For the world will one day cease to exist, but the justification of the unrighteous shall endure forever. Moreover, these works are even greater than the works of Christ not simply because they are in greater number, but precisely because they are accomplished by Christ through others *less than he*. In this way even simple and illiterate fishermen are chosen and given a great responsibility in God's work of salvation. Even Jesus could not convert the young rich man, Thomas notes, but Peter and others had brought many more to the faith so that there was not a needy person among them and distribution was made to each as they had need (Acts 4:33).[24]

Conclusion

This essay has offered an alternative interpretation of the theology of Thomas Aquinas as a mendicant Dominican friar and Master of the Sacred Page for contemporary theology. As we have seen, 1 Corinthians is not peripheral to his thought but, rather, central if we appreciate how the wisdom of the cross functions to subvert human arrogance and the domination of the powerful over the powerless while calling the church to live up to the full meaning of discipleship. When read in the light of Scripture, Thomas's doctrine of providence offers a clear vision for how the *ratio* of God in Jesus Christ is to be made manifest in creation and how ecclesial practice ought to reflect this in its preaching and pastoral care. Providence is not simply the reason things happen, as if all things were predetermined by a static

---

24. See *Evangelium Joannis* XIV,3, in *Opera Omnia*, 550.

divine plan. It is, rather, the dynamic working of God in shaping creation in the image of Christ in secondary causes.

For Thomas, the providence of God does not take the form of an ecclesial triumphalism but, rather, follows the teachings of Christ to correct those in the church and society whose values and practices are corrupted by the world and fall short of the gospel. Thomas's thought thus provides an essential resource for understanding the doctrine of providence today. Although we need not accept his neo-Platonic metaphysics of participation and Aristotelian causality, we can see how Thomas makes use of such concepts to explain analogically how God works in all things for the good by sharing God's abundance through others for those in scarcity.

Moreover, since providence is universal, it must include all creatures *everywhere*, including non-Christian and nonhuman life as well. Since all things have been created according to *ratio* of God in Christ to partake in the essential goodness of God in their own agency, we can see the providence of God everywhere creatures use their resources to preserve and improve the lives of others. This includes, of course, the appropriation of secular reasoning as well, which can be useful for advancing the gospel. Indeed, the more we are able to use our resources to provide for others in the manner of Christ, especially those who appear least and farthest from God, the greater our likeness and participation in God will be; but the less we strive to extend God's care for others and serve only our narrow self-interests, the more we shall exacerbate existing conflicts and continue to threaten creation with chaos and disorder. The providence of God thus continues to order and arrange things according to the wisdom of Christ, as demonstrated throughout this essay. It is my hope that other scholars will revisit the thought of Thomas Aquinas as biblical theologian and mendicant friar in order to see what new contributions the Angelic Doctor has yet to make toward this end.

7

Luther's *Theologica Paradoxa* in Erasmus and Cusanus

Günter Bader

Wisdom and foolishness intertwined—the theology of the cross—and consequently speeches in the form of *theologica paradoxa*, of paradoxical theology: these are all widely known as characteristics of Reformation theology, especially of the Lutheran style. Indeed, it was Luther who furnished this connection and put it under the rubric of *theologica paradoxa*. But why look for *theologica paradoxa* in Erasmus and Cusanus if this rubric is distinctive to Luther? Despite the somewhat strange juxtaposition of these two authors with Luther, it is likely that neither of them would have put their work under a

Lutheran heading. Therefore, this discussion does not depend upon our previous knowledge of Luther, Erasmus, and Cusanus.

So let's start again. Wisdom and foolishness intertwined—the theology of the cross *as* word of the cross—a clash of topics that in general is considered characteristic of Pauline theology. Nowhere else does Paul reflect on the gospel as the word of the cross as in his letters to the Corinthians. That is why, according to many, the singularity of Pauline theology and the singularity of Lutheran theology belong on the same line. But it is also true that in the letters to the Corinthians, as in no other letters, Paul gets caught up in the pull of the Socratic tradition.

Two observations will pave the way for us to connect Erasmus and Cusanus to Luther's *theologica paradoxa*. The first we will call "Pauline Platonism," the second "Reformational Renaissance."

Pauline Platonism

It is obvious how liberally Paul makes use of the Socratic tradition in 2 Corinthians. One can see that the final chapters (10–13) have been influenced by Plato's *Apology of Socrates*. These chapters are in fact the apology of Paul. The connection is explicitly, although ironically, carried out through ἀπολογούμεθα (2 Cor. 12:19). Additionally, a glance at the Stoic-Cynic Socratic tradition[1] shows Paul offering an ironic fool's speech that begins with ἀφροσύνη (2 Cor. 11:1) and ends with γέγονα ἄφρων (2 Cor. 12:11). Both apology and foolishness originate in the world of Greek wisdom, although only in terms of their rhetorical *forms*, as suggested by Hans Dieter Betz. The *content*, however, the word of the cross, is defined otherwise at the outset of 1 Corinthians, in which Paul declares the wisdom of the world

---

1. Klaus Döring, *Exemplum Socratis: Studien zur Sokratesnachwirkung in der kynisch-stoischen Popularphilosophie der frühen Kaiserzeit und im frühen Christentum*, Hermes / Einzelschriften, 42. Wiesbaden: Steiner, 1979.

as foolishness before God.[2] Through the distinction between form and content, Betz wants to uncover a "not-only/but-also" situation. Salvation in the cross of Christ works "not [only] as 'overcoming' the 'only human,' but [also] as its 'humanization.'"[3] But looking at 1 Corinthians 1–4 in the same way, you will find not only foolishness again, with μωρία ["folly"] used instead of ἀφροσύνη ["foolishness"], but also the Platonic *Apology*.[4] I would be so bold as to list at least twenty passages in Plato's *Apology* that have parallels in 1 Corinthians 1–4.[5] So Paul takes up the very Greek wisdom that he denies. Or to

2. Hermann von Lips, *Weisheitliche Traditionen im Neuen Testament*, WMANT 64 (Neukirchen-Vluyn: Neukirchener, 1990), 320–23. The sharp contradictory opposition of σοφία and μωρία is to be found only in 1 Cor. 1:21, the opposition of σοφία and μωρία only in 1 Cor. 1:27. The opposition is reduced when crossed by another in the manner of a quadruple. In that way σοφία/μωρία (1 Cor. 1:18; 2:5) is being crossed by δύναμις/[ἀσθένεια]. So far, the terms are unambiguous. Ambiguous iridescence begins when wisdom and foolishness diverge into divine and human perspectives. Then in each term itself a panoply opens up, which extends from the contrary to the contradictory. On one side μωρία (1 Cor. 1:18, 23; 2:14) appears as folly of the world, on the other side it mutates into folly of God (1 Cor. 1:21, 25; 3:19), which sounds preposterous and *risqué*. And, on the one hand, σοφία (1 Cor. 1:20; 2:6; 3:19) is to be taken as worldly or as human in 1 Cor. 2:5 and 2:13, but both times as wisdom of the wise (1 Cor. 1:19); on the other hand, it appears as God's wisdom (1 Cor. 1:21, 24, 30; 2:7). If the identity of the terms is thus being paralyzed, then in principle each of them can designate the opposite as soon as it enters the divine perspective from the human one and vice versa. That happens in 1 Cor. 1:20, where wisdom becomes foolishness, or the other way around: comparative in 1 Cor. 1:25 and absolute in 3:18. The peak is hit with 1 Cor. 3:19: ἡ σοφία . . . μωρία . . . ἐστιν; it cannot be topped.

3. Hans Dieter Betz, *Der Apostel Paulus und die sokratische Tradition: Eine exegetische Untersuchung zu seiner 'Apologie' 2 Korinther 10–13*, BHTh 45 (Tübingen: Mohr, 1972), 140. For Paul, apology is important "because he does not only defend himself with recourse to his Christology, but likewise with a certain tradition of Hellenistic Culture: 'socratic humanism'" (55); see as well 66–67, 88–89, 138–39, 146: "not only, but also"; 147: "not only, but more over"; 148: "not only, but to the same extent." His end is the juxtaposition of Pauline theological content and Socratic humanistic form; that is, the origin of the "and" in the title and headline of ch. 4.

4. Even if μωρία is absent in the *Apology*, σοφία in either negative or affirmative use is sufficient to indicate the opposite. Likewise, we miss the direct opposition of human and divine wisdom; instead, human wisdom is being ironized and confronted with greater wisdom (20d.e). Thus a hyperbolic move evolves, which is supported by the fact that Socrates is not directly the speaker of wisdom. He is only the witness of another speaker, Chairemon, who is himself only a witness of the Delphic Oracle, who is yet a witness of a completely different speaker: of the God himself, Apollo (20e–21b) (cf. n. 44). Thus figures of conversion are established, in which human knowing appears only as a mock of knowing and not-knowing (21c–23c), vice versa not-knowing as knowing (20dff.), that is, conscious of serving the God (23c, 30a). If you put both paradoxical structures of Paul and Plato on top of each other like blueprints, the compliance lets show what that is: Pauline Platonism.

put it in another way: the word of the *cross* denies what it sets up as the *word* of the cross.[6] This paradoxical fact is what I try to indicate by Pauline Platonism. It means: even if you follow Betz regarding the distinction between form and content, the theological content, which is the word of the cross, proves against all odds to have been influenced by Plato.

Reformational Renaissance

The first anomaly is followed by a second one. In the *Heidelberg Disputation*, in connection with concurrent writings, Luther arrives at his theological identity. Through these writings, in phrases like *theologia crucis* ("theology of the cross"),[7] *stultificari in Christo*

---

5. 1 Cor. 1:25 σοφώτερον→*Apol.* 21ac, 22d.; 1 Cor. 2:2 τι εἰδέναι→*Apol.* 21d, 22a.; 1 Cor. 2:4 πειθός→*Apol.* 17a.; 1 Cor. 2:5 σοφία ἀνθρώπων→*Apol.* 20de, 23a.; 1 Cor. 2:6-8 σοφία→*Apol.* 20dff., 23ac.; 1 Cor. 2:7 ἀποκεκρυμμένη→*Apol.* 22e.; 1 Cor. 2:13 ἀνθρωπίνη σοφία→*Apol.* 20d, 23a.; 1 Cor. 3:18 δοκεῖ→*Apol.* 21cde, 22ab, 29a, 36d, 41e.; 1 Cor. 4:4 σύνοιδα→*Apol.* 21b, 22c.

6. Samuel Vollenweider, "Weisheit am Kreuzweg: Zum theologischen Programm von 1 Kor 1 und 2," in *Kreuzestheologie im Neuen Testament*, ed. Andreas Dettwiler and Jean Zumstein, WUNT 151 (Tübingen: Mohr, 2002), 43–58, is perfectly right in assuming that Paul in 1 Corinthians offers a reflection on "the condition of possibility of theology." With Kant's phrase, "thoughts without content are void, intuitions without perceptions are blind" (*Critique of Pure Reason*, B 75), *theologia crucis* leads into the dialectic "the cross without theology is mute, but theology without the cross is deaf" (43). But what could appear as an impression of an oxymoron turns quickly into the challenge of an imposition. Paradox could "result in an extensively negative, apophatic way of talking. God then is completely different to the extent that you can talk of him only in the mode of paradoxes" (49). Paul does not stop there. "God is *differently* different. The Gospel pushes beyond sheer paradoxes" (49). Word of the cross does not "simply aim the different, paradoxical being of God" (50). It should, rather, "disambiguate the iridescent figure of Sophia" (53). But despite the concern that the "mode of mere paradoxy" could end in sterility, paradox does not want to go away: "The most confusing feature of the logos of the cross is probably its own self-sublation he [Paul] continuously brings forward; otherwise the 'cross of Christ' would be emptied (1:17b)" (58). What now: self-sublation or disambiguating?

7. Martin Luther, *Heidelberg Disputation* (1518), WA 1:354,17-28; 361,31–363,37; Bonner Ausgabe [hereafter: BoA] 5:379,1-12; 388,5–390,21. *Philosophical Theses from the Heidelberg Disputation*, WA 59:405-426; ET, in *Career of the Reformer I*, ed. Harold J. Grimm and Helmut T. Lehmann, *Luther's Works*, vol. 31 (Philadelphia: Fortress Press, 1957), 40,19–41,24; 52,19–55,24; *Philosophical Theses*, forthcoming LW, New Series 2. *Asterisci Lutheri adversus Obeliscos Eckii* (1518), WA 1:290,34–291,12. Marginal note referring to Heb. 12:11 (1518), WA

("becoming foolish in Christ"),[8] and the knowledge that *omnia praeter Christum scire sit nihil scire* ("to know anything besides Christ is to know nothing"),[9] the Socratic-Pauline[10] background clearly shines through. But why does Luther choose to express himself in the form of *theologica paradoxa*? It is only mentioned in the introduction of the theological theses.[11] Is it then, in the philosophical theses, a matter of *philosophica paradoxa*?

According to Cicero, paradoxes are eye-popping sentences that deviate from general opinion.[12] The conventional *propositiones* and *conclusiones* of Scholastic arguments mutate into *paradoxa* in the climate of the Renaissance. Under the name of Martinus Eleutherius, Luther prefers and plays with this. To the masses, paradoxes may appear to be *cacodoxa*, bad thoughts, but to those in the know they are *calo–* and *eudoxa*, marvelously good thoughts, and Luther himself even appreciates them as *aristo–* and *orthodoxa*, as higher or proper thoughts. This is the orthodoxy of paradox or, if you will allow, of

---

57/3:79,16–80,14. *Resolution on the Theses on Indulgences* no. 58 (1518), WA 1:613,21–614,37. *Operationes in psalmos* (1519–21), Ps. 5:12 (WA 5:176,32f./AWA 2, 319,3); Ps. 6:11 (WA 5:217,2f./AWA 2, 389,15f.); Ps. 9,8 (WA 5:300,1/AWA 2, 531,24); Ps. 15,2 (WA 5:445,36ff.; 446,3ff.). *Assertio omnium articulorum* (1520), WA 7:148,29; ET, *Defense and Explanation of All the Articles*, in *Career of the Reformer II*, ed. George W. Forell and Helmut T. Lehmann, *Luther's Works*, vol. 32 (Philadelphia: Fortress Press, 1958), 93. Later on: *Kommentar zu den Stufenpsalmen* (1532/33), WA 40/3:193,6f.; ET, *Commentary on the Psalms of Degrees*, forthcoming in LW.NS 3. Hubertus Blaumeiser, *Martin Luthers Kreuzestheologie: Schlüssel zu seiner Deutung von Mensch und Wirklichkeit. Eine Untersuchung anhand der Operationes in Psalmos, 1519–1521*, KKTS 60 (Paderborn: Bonifatius, 1995); Michael Korthaus, *Kreuzestheologie: Geschichte und Gehalt eines Programmbegriffs in der evangelischen Theologie*, BHTh 142 (Tübingen: Mohr, 2007).

8. Luther, WA 1:355,3; BoA 5:379,23; LW 31:41,29.
9. Luther, WA 59:409,14f.; BoA 5:403,16f.; forthcoming in LW.NS 2.
10. 1 Cor. 1:19→BoA 5:388,24f.; 1 Cor. 1:20→BoA 5:389,32.; 1 Cor. 1:21→BoA 5:388,20ff.; 1 Cor. 1:25→BoA 5:388,15f.; 1 Cor. 1:30→BoA 5:391,4; 403,13.; 1 Cor. 1:31→BoA 5:400,12.; 1 Cor. 3:18→BoA 5:379,22f; 403,7f.; 1 Cor. 3:20→BoA 5:399,29f.; 1 Cor. 4:10→BoA 5:379,23.25.
11. WA 1:353,11; BoA 5:377,20.
12. Cicero, *Parad. stoicor., prooem.* 4 (ed. Orelli 4/1:394): "*quia sunt admirabilia contraque opinionem omnium, ab ipsis etiam* παράδοξα *appellantur.*"

paradoxy.[13] To put it another way: a typical theme of the Renaissance was orthodoxy in the only possible form of paradoxy.[14]

What is crucial is that the theses are not only wrapped in paradoxes, they actually *are* paradoxes.[15] As is generally known, post-Scholastic anti-Aristotelism objects to the Aristotelian principle of noncontradiction and its claim for the absence of paradoxy. The antitheses from Plato's *Parmenides* are in the air,[16] and the philosophical theses of Luther amount to one slogan: "Plato!"[17] It is not an exclusive characteristic of the Reformation to place the paradox into the center of its sentences; it shares this characteristic with the Renaissance. Rosalie L. Colie has very strikingly described the epoch of the Renaissance as *paradoxia epidemica*.[18] From the point of view of the Renaissance, Luther's *theologica paradoxa* evoke the sense of *déjà vu*. As with the letters to the Corinthians, the formation

---

13. Paradoxy is hereby introduced and will be used throughout the text. Luther, Letter 38 to Scheurl (May 6, 1517), WABr 1:94,15-26: Karlstadt's theses referring to venerating relics are paradoxical for normal readers, "*eudoxa et calodoxa*" for those who know, "*aristodoxa*" for Luther. Letter 45 to Lang (Sept. 4, 1517), WABr 1,103,7: his theses against Scholastic theology may seem to be "*paradoxa, cacodoxa*" to some, however, for Luther "*non nisi orthodoxa*." Letter 46 to Scheurl (Sept. 11, 1517), WABr 1,106,36: the same theses as "*prorsus paradoxae*" in the eyes of many "κακιστοdoxae." Letter 52 to Lang (Nov. 11, 1517), WABr 1,121,4: 95: theses as "*paradoxa*." Letter 55 to Spalatin (Dec. 20, 1517), WABr 1,129,6: thesis 35 of the "Disputation against Scholastic Theology" as "*paradoxa*." The Heidelberg theses (April 26, 1518), WA 1:353,11; BoA 5:377,20; LW 31:39): "*Theologica paradoxa*." Martin Bucer's report on the disputatio: παράδοξα, WA 9:161,31, et al.

14. Ralph Venning, *Orthodox paradoxes, theoreticall and experimentall* (London: J. Rothwell and Hanna Allen, 1647, 1652).

15. Partly in the way one single thesis contains the paradox, as we can see in thesis 1, which is the only one dealing with *lex*: the law, by doing what it is supposed to do, works against its very aim. Partly in the way, as in theses 3–6, two following pairs of sentences express the paradox, or the way pairs of sentences are connected to one pair of sentences again and thus build a paradox of second degree.

16. Raymond Klibansky, "Plato's Parmenides in the Middle Ages and the Renaissance," in *Medieval and Renaissance Studies 1* (Millwood, NY: Kraus, 1984 [1943]), 281–330.

17. Theodor Dieter, *Der junge Luther und Aristoteles: Eine historisch-systematische Untersuchung zum Verhältnis von Theologie und Philosophie*, ThBT 105 (Berlin: de Gruyter, 2001), 619.

18. Rosalie L. Colie, *Paradoxia epidemica: The Renaissance Tradition of Paradox* (Princeton: Princeton University Press, 1966). See also *Le paradoxe au temps de la Renaissance*, ed. Marie-Thérèse Jones-Davies (Paris: Touzot, 1982).

of a specific Pauline theology took place in the context of Platonism—similarly, the development of specific Reformation paradoxy took place in the context of the Renaissance.

We will now consult two paradoxologies of the Renaissance, Erasmus's *Laus stultitiae* and Cusanus's *De docta ignorantia* in order to examine their relationship to Luther's *theologica paradoxa*.

Erasmus and Rhetorical Paradox

Erasmus, even more so than Luther, moves within the tradition of Renaissance paradox.[19] Erasmus also adheres to the Socratic-Pauline line of thought, particularly the *Apology* and the letters to the Corinthians. And both are influential texts to the *Praise of Folly* (*Encomium moriae*), perhaps more than anywhere else.[20]

Signs of Paradoxy

There is no doubt: while Luther searches for paradox, Erasmus makes it clear that he avoids it. The fundamental tone of avoiding paradoxy, phobia about paradoxy, permeates not only his complete works,[21] but reaches deep down into the middle section of the *Encomium moriae*. As much as one can speculate about the structure of the *Encomium*,[22]

19. Archibald E. Malloch, "The techniques and function of the Renaissance paradox," *Studies in Philology* 53 (1956): 191–203; Sr. M. Geraldine [Thompson], "Erasmus and the Tradition of Paradox," *Studies in Philology* 61 (1964): 41–63; Colie, *Paradoxia epidemica*, 7,12,25, et al.; Jean Lebeau, "Le paradoxe chez Erasme, Luther et Sebastian Franck," in Jones-Davies, *Le paradoxe*, 143–53.

20. *Moriae encomium id est Stultitiae laus, Ausgewählte Schriften* [AS], ed. Wendelin Schmidt-Dengler, vol. 2 (Darmstadt: Wissenschaftliche Buchgesellschaft, 1975); *Opera omnia Desiderii Erasmi Roterodami* [ASD], ed. C. H. Miller, vol. IV/3 (Amsterdam: Elsevier, 1979). Luther takes note of the encomium, WA 4:567,35; WA 20:146,31; LW 15:126–27; WA 31/2:305,12.15; LW 17:57. WABr 1,369,63 alludes to the title: *moria theologorum*.

21. Erasmus, *Ratio seu comp. ver. theol.* (AS 3:480); *De libero arbitrio diatr.* (AS 4, 18, 30, 182, 188; vicinity to the liar's paradox, 192); exception *Enchir. milit. chr.* (AS 1, 268): positive employment. Otherwise Luther, *De servo arbitrio*, WA 18:630f, 634; LW 33:57-59;63–65.

22. Part 1 (AS 2:8–112/ASD IV/3:71–134): *laudes, encomium . . . meum ipsius* 10/72, l. 28f; part 2 (112–172/134–176): *satyra* 172/176, l. 857; part 3 (172–210/176–94): *laudum mearum . . . finis*

one thing is undisputed and confirmed by the author himself: the middle section is composed in a satirical style. All kinds of groups from society and science have to dance in front of us, and vials of wrath are poured on them: satire of the estates in order to dress down the pandemic foolishness from the viewpoint of wisdom.[23] It is only here that he speaks of paradox: paradox is a sign of the foolishness of the others, the theologians. Cicero's *Paradoxa Stoicorum*[24] are only weak precursors of the impious pedantries Scholastic theologians dare to come up with. Erasmus gives examples, and old editions of the text show the marginal note: *Paradoxa theologorum*.[25] While Luther relishes taking *theologica paradoxa* (theological paradoxes) to the extreme, Erasmus meets them with reluctance. In scolding theologians, he understands both theology and paradoxy as outcomes of foolishness and urges them to cease.

Up to this point we have only heard folly be reprimanded. But is it not the *praise* of folly that frames the satirical middle section? Through this framing, scolded folly returns unwittingly and involuntarily as praiseworthy folly that somehow has already been praised. Theology, in its Scholastic form, being nothing but an expression of foolishness and an object of reprimand in direct

---

176/178, l. 886; *laudes nostras fulciamus* 178/178, l. 905. Clarence H. Miller, "Some Medieval Elements and Structural Unity in Erasmus' *The Praise of Folly*," *Renaissance Quarterly* 27 (1974): 499–511; Wayne A. Rebhorn, "The Metamorphoses of Moria: Structure and Meaning in *The Praise of Folly*," *Publications of the Modern Language Association of America* 89 (1974): 463–76; Richard Sylvester, "The Problem of Unity in *The Praise of Folly*," *English Literary Renaissance* 6 (1976): 125–39; Zoja Pavlovskis, *The Praise of Folly: Structure and Irony* (Leiden: Brill, 1983).

23. *Enkom.*, AS 2, 172/ASD IV/3, 176, l. 856–57: *Verum non est huius instituti . . . , ne cui videar satyram texere, non encomium recitare.* To some it occurs that Erasmus here talks like Sebastian Brant or Martin Luther: Kaiser, *Praisers* (cf. n. 31, below), 86; others hear their usual Erasmus: Miller, "Some Medieval Elements," 505.

24. Cf. n. 12.

25. *Enkom.*, 132/148, l. 411: γνῶμαι παράδοξοι. Likewise, 182/180, l. 953: *rara et pretiosa*—Latin equivalents for παράδοξα—should be concealed from the multitude. On the contrary, 8/71, l. 9.15–16: *nova*—another equivalent—with which Stultitia boldly appears. Regarding Cusanus, cf. n. 73, below.

intention, returns again as an expression of foolishness now un–Scholastic, un–Aristotelian, Platonizing, and thus an object of praise in indirect intention.[26] The same applies to paradox. Explicitly denied, it returns from behind, implicitly, indirect but effective. Indirect signs of paradoxy are the most important ones. The rejected paradox had a name; the indirectly effective paradox, which is irrefutable in the *Praise of Folly*, remains nameless. It is the rhetorical paradox.

Rhetorical Paradox

From the very start, rhetoric stands under the banner of paradoxy. In the beginning of the *Apology*, Socrates the orator tries to reject the suspicion that he is in fact an orator, "εἶναι ῥήθωρ."[27] The art of concealing art[28] shows inevitably the fundamental paradox of rhetoric as art, whether it likes it or not.

In rhetoric, however, there are not only fundamental, but also regional, paradoxes. In the *genus demonstrativum*—that is, the epideictic rhetorical model—there is nothing paradoxical in the praise of the praiseworthy. That is why it is called ἔνδοξον, or esteemable. In comparison, the praise of a fly, a bald head, illness, or similar things, meaning the praise of that which is unworthy of praise, are typical cases of a παράδοξον, of paradoxical encomium.[29] The mild form of paradox occurs mostly occasionally; Erasmus uses it. In his

---

26. While Erasmus has *theologia/theologus* thirty times in that satirical-critical sense of his reprimand of theologians starting in 130/144, l. 381, there are only two occurrences that at least allude to an exceeding sense, if there is no irony involved (138/154, l. 483; 4/68, l. 23). Only *one* instance goes beyond the critique of theologians; cf. n. 51, below.

27. *Apol.* 17b; by contrast *Gorg.* 449a.

28. Paolo D'Angelo, *Ars est celare artem: Da Aristotele a Duchamp* (Macerata: Quodlibet, 2005).

29. Heinrich Lausberg, *Handbuch der literarischen Rhetorik*, 3d ed. (Stuttgart: Steiner 1990), 56–60; ET, *Handbook of Literary Rhetoric: A Foundation for Literary Study*, trans. from the 2d ed. (Münich, 1973), trans. Matthew Bliss, et al., ed. David E. Orton and R. Dean Anderson (Leiden: Brill, 1998); Martina Neumeyer, "Das Paradoxe," *Historisches Wörterbuch der Rhetorik* 6 (2003): 516–24.

writing, foolishness takes the place of baldness and illness. It was the late Middle Ages that made fools (natural and artificial ones, village idiots, and jesters) the objects of art in poetry, literature, theatre, and iconography.[30] Now, praise of foolishness in the manner of the paradoxical encomium subverts all spheres of life: top becomes bottom, right becomes wrong. Reversal of this kind may in a single case at first appear as a punctual deviation. But if it becomes the characteristic of the nature of things—"an upside-down world"—then suddenly what had been the deficit of the fool, when compared to the wise, becomes his gain. Only a fool can be on top of an upside-down world. Thus Erasmus gathers the elements of the medieval motif of the fool and sharpens them: the fool is the only wise man.[31] In this way he brought forward the type of the Renaissance fool.[32] The fool is the only one who may praise himself with impunity; that is why he is the fool. And he is the only one who uninhibitedly may refer to himself. Thus the paradoxical encomium, initially just a deviation from the normal, punctual paradox, is displaced to the extent that it has to be regarded as the only possible form of encomium—just like the fool was the only possible form of the wise. Such an ironic encomium realizes what I would like to designate as "first-degree paradox."

Without a doubt, a certain layer of the *Praise of Folly* is a paradoxical encomium. But at the same time irony overflows and makes its way out of the rhetorical classification as a metaphor that is equivalent in degree with its opposite. It is not content to oppose

---

30. Vinzenz Pfnür, "Das Verständnis von Narrheit und Torheit im Spätmittelalter. Zur Frage des Verhältnisses von christlichen und gesellschaftlichen Wertvorstellungen," in *Weisheit Gottes, Weisheit der Welt. Festschrift Joseph card. Ratzinger*, ed. Walter Baier, et al. (St. Ottilien: EOS Verlag Erzabtei, 1987) 2:795–814; Angelika Gross, *'La Folie': Wahnsinn und Narrheit im spätmittelalterlichen Text und Bild* (Heidelberg: Carl Winter, 1990).

31. Walter Kaiser, *Praisers of Folly: Erasmus, Rabelais, Shakespeare*, HSCL 25 (Cambridge: Harvard University Press, 1963), 10–12.

32. Ibid., 21.

a finitude with its opposite, and so on and so forth. That would be a bad infinity! Rather, it opens up its own infinity.[33] It does so only in the way of negation, and not only in the way of double negation. So far it has been enough to detect the *genitivus obiectivus* in the title of the *Praise of Folly*: ΕΓΚΩΜΙΟΝ ΜΩΡΙΑΣ. Yet infinity beyond the bad one rises as soon as one detects the *genitivus subiectivus* in the *genitivus obiectivus,* swinging with it and against it: ΜΩΡΙΑΣ ΕΓΚΩΜΙΟΝ, which was the title of the first editions. If one would like to depict the interplay of the two genitives, it would look like this: ΜΩΡΙΑΣ ΕΓΚΩΜΙΟΝ ΜΩΡΙΑΣ.[34] Thus infinite self-reference—περιαυτολογία, "self-praise"[35]—is opened up.

The Theological Paradox

If we had to struggle to wrest the rhetorical paradox from a paradox-phobic Erasmus, we will have to double our efforts with the theological paradox. Whenever an author, in his speaking, starts to put forward the speaking of another, and this other's speaking differs from the level on which the first author speaks, something theological comes into play in a wider sense. It could have been that the rubric,

---

33. Ernst H. Gombrich, *Kunst und Illusion: Zur Psychologie der bildlichen Darstellung*, 2d ed. (Stuttgart/Zürich: Phaidon, 1986), 261; ET, *Art and illusion: A Study in the Psychology of Pictorial Representation*, trans. Ernst H. Gombrich, 5th ed. (London: Phaidon, 1996), points to Saul Steinberg's graphic art; Patrick Hughes and George Brecht, *Die Scheinwelt des Paradoxes: Eine kommentierte Anthologie in Wort und Bild* (Braunschweig: Vieweg, 1978), 37, point to Maurits C. Escher's graphic "Drawing Hands"; ET, *Vicious Circles and Infinity: A Panoply of Paradoxes,* trans. Patrick Hughes and George Brecht (London: Jonathan Cape, 1976).
34. Kaiser, *Praisers*, 36: "Fools had spoken before this and foolishness had been praised; but never before had a fool praised foolishness. Erasmus' great originality, then, was to make Stultitia both the author and the subject of her encomium, to conceive of 'Moriae' as being simultaneously both objective and subjective genitive. Thus, 'The Praise of Folly' only translates half of the title: it might more accurately be rendered as 'Folly's Praise of Folly.'"
35. Plutarch, *De se ipsum citra invidiam laudando*, Moral. 539B. Laurent Pernot, "Periautologia. Problèmes et méthodes de l'éloge de soi-même dans la tradition éthique et rhétorique gréco-romaine," *Revue des études grecques* 111 (1998): 101–24; Antonio Pitta, "'Il discorso del pazzo' o periautologia immoderata? Analisi retorico-letteraria di 2 Cor. 11,1–12,18," *Biblica* 87 (2006): 498–510.

Stultitia loquitur ("foolishness expressing itself"), was only patched to the text, and thus should be easy to withdraw again. But as a text above the text, it conveys the message of all messages.[36] In itself, *prosopopoeia/fictio personae*, or "personification," is a mere technical process; its author is the same as the author of the nonpersonified text. Indeed, it is Erasmus who makes folly speak.[37] Now you may well show how the connection between rubric (or heading) and text reaches down from the exterior[38] into the substance of the text.[39] But what makes it compelling?

Of course, wondering whether Erasmus knew[40] of the fundamental paradox of rhetoric *Ars est celare artem* ("the art consists in hiding the art"),[41] or of Epimenides's master paradox, the liar's paradox,[42] is much too narrow. But certainly, the hinge between rubric (or heading) and text and thus the encomium's exposition are a matter

---

36. Kaiser, *Praisers*, 35: "The rubric, *Stultitia loquitur*, that stands at the head of the *Moriae encomium* announces what is the most important single fact about Erasmus' book."

37. *Enkom.*, 6/69, l. 64f.: *quam [sc. stultitiam] cum loquentem fecerimus, decoro personae seruiendum fuit. Opus epistolarum Desideri Erasmi Roterodami* [hereafter: EE], ed. Percy S. Allen and Helen M. Allen (Oxford: Clarendon, 1910), 2:544 (no 337): Erasmus gives the impression the *decus personae* should be withdrawn from the matter.

38. Here we can detect certain signs such as *meus Erasmus* ("my Erasmus"), instead of just Erasmus: *Enkom.*, 174/178, l. 867; 184/182, l. 974f. Or techniques of allegorization and personification such as this one: foolishness does not remain abstract, but appears as a female person: *stultitia* turns to *Stultitia*, and the dramatic appearance escalates into an epiphany: goddess foolishness, *Stultitia dea*: *Encom.*, 14/76, l. 90; 20/80, l. 137; 80/114, l. 817–18, reveals names, bynames, court, and genealogy: *Encom.*, 8–20/71, l. 5–80, l. 142.

39. Here we think of the structure of the whole text: part 2 of the encomium could be interpreted as Erasmus *loquitur*, but in parts 1 and 3 *Stultitia loquitur*.

40. See above, n. 29.

41. Titus 1:12; *Die Fragmente der Vorsokratiker. Griechisch und Deutsch*, ed. Hermann Diels and Walter Kranz (Berlin: Weidmann, 1951), 3 B 1.

42. *Adag.* 2,8,78 (ASD 2/4:198–200); Margaret Mann Phillips, *The 'Adages' of Erasmus. A Study with Translations* (Cambridge: Cambridge University Press, 1964), 80–81. Nietzsche's "duty to lie according to a fixed convention, to lie with the herd and in a manner binding upon everyone," converges with Erasmus's *Colloquium Pseudodochei et Philetymi* (ASD 1/3:320–24); Friedrich Nietzsche, "On Truth and Lie in an Extra-Moral Sense," trans. Daniel Breazeale, in *The Continental Aesthetics Reader*, ed. Clive Cazeaux (London: Routledge, 2000), 56; *Kritische Gesamtausgabe Werke*, ed. Giorgio Colli and Mazzino Montinari (Berlin-New York: W. de Gruyter, 1973), 3/2:375, 9–10.

of such fundamental paradoxes. The liar's paradox says, "I lie," and the paradox of the fool says, correspondingly, "I speak foolishly." Precisely that sentence forms the basis, implicitly, of the installation of the *Stultitia loquens*. If it could be limited to an object-linguistic sense, it would contain only a first-degree paradox, equal to the paradoxes of stoics and theologians. As with the praise of that which is unworthy of praise, it has to do only with the *expressed* that stands against endoxical (or honorable) employment. But in the expressed, *expressing* itself comes forward and reveals a metalinguistic level. First, it is presupposed that a predication of speaking foolishly is in the first-person singular, present tense; and, second, that the predicate explicitly or implicitly negates the act through which it is uttered. Both requirements are met by the paradox of folly. "I speak foolishly," in an object-linguistic sense, presupposes the metalinguistic "I do not speak foolishly." Erasmus personifies this level of speaking within speaking in the figure of *Stultitia loquens*, of foolishness expressing itself. And thus the second-degree paradox is present. It arises as soon as a second level of speaking comes through and across the first one, exactly in such a way that it says the exact opposite of what has been said, effectively canceling it. The moment a self who is speaking fulfills both conditions with its speech, it cannot help dividing into two speakers who contradict and withstand each other. And although they are imperatively two, they are always voiced through *one* speaker. It now becomes clear: as soon as Erasmus says, "I speak foolishly," he has already made foolishness speak. He cannot do otherwise; foolishness is already speaking.

The paradox is strictly differentiated from forms that often compete with it (such as antinomy, amphiboly, and antithesis), insofar as it evokes two sentences from one single sentence of one speaker and thus calls, cites, and presupposes a second speaker distinct from the first. This second speaker runs contrary to the first sentence and its speaker. The liar's paradox and the paradox of the fool meet these conditions. Hence, the paradox offers the single case that *prosopopeia* not only may or may not be, but *has* to be. Certainly, it is Erasmus who makes foolishness speak, and without him it would not speak at all. But no sooner than he does so, it happens that it speaks for itself. It talks with a second, opposing voice not contained in the first one. But if, along with the presumed second speaker, a language of another kind is heard, then *prosopopeia*, which was once only rhetorical, has become inevitable. To put it another way: it has become theological. For whenever in the speech of the first speaker a second speaker of a different kind is not only heard, but must be heard, something like theology is at hand.

In the first part of the *Praise of Folly*, the sentence of the fool cannot be found *tel quel*. Now it has always been remarkable that this very first part overflows with allusions and quotations of pagan antiquity, while biblical reminiscences abound in the third part, to the not-inconsiderable annoyance of the classical philologists. Correspondingly, in the first part, Plato's *Apology* represents the systematic center,[43] and along with it the report of how Socrates was able to perceive a metalinguistic meaning, a meaning opposed to the familiar, object-linguistic meaning, in the sentence "I know nothing." No less than a complex chain of messengers and even a Delphic oracle were necessary in order to hear the divine declaration from Apollo's mouth. Socrates was unable to communicate it to himself, although it is heralded nowhere else but in his own words.[44]

---

43. AS 2:12/ASD IV/3:74, l. 50f→*Apol.* 17bc.; 50/96, l. 478→*Apol.* 20d-21d.; 50/96, l. 479f→*Apol.* 20e, 27a, 30c.; 50/98, l. 481f→*Apol.* 23a.; 50/98, l. 482→*Apol.* 31c-32a.; 50/98, l. 485f→*Apol.* 21cd, 36b-d.; 104/130, l. 98ff→*Apol.* 21d.; 202/190, l. 171f.→*Apol.* 39. Cf. Kaiser, *Praisers*, 37, 137.

44. Apol. 20e-21a. The passage starts with οὐ γὰρ ἐμὸν ἐρῶ τὸν λόγον ὃν ἂν λέγω and as relay stations mentions the messenger Chairemon and the prophetess Pythia, who transmit the oracle of the god Apollo.

Socrates represents paradigmatically what I just said about *prosopopeia*, paradox, and the origin of theology—talking of God.

It has been feared that what was displayed in joy and jest in the first part of the *Praise of Folly* would have to find a sorrowful end through the pious solemnity of the third part. In fact, the contrary is true. The Socratic tradition is, as we already saw, also the Pauline tradition, and both come together in the tradition of paradox characteristic of the Renaissance. Just as the *Stultitia* establishes the relation to Plato's *Apology* in the first part, the third part overflows with references to the apology of Paul.[45] Is there a sign of irony and paradoxy more flippant than *quod loquor non loquor* ("it is not me who is speaking as I am speaking")? This is a quotation from Paul's speech as a fool.[46] This speech constitutes the systematic center of the third part of the encomium; only after this speech does the passage about wisdom and folly from 1 Corinthians follow.[47] Through a reversal in the sequence of the letters, the fool's speech in 2 Corinthians becomes the prologue of the *stultitia crucis* (the foolishness of the cross) in the first one.[48] To put it another way, theology of the cross is no wisdom speech; in fact, it requires foolishness as its speaking subject. This is also the place in Erasmus's text where we finally find direct proof of the foolish phrase "I speak foolishly." It is also a quotation from Paul and reads as follows: παραφρονῶν λαλῶ, *insipienter loquor*, "I speak foolishly."[49]

---

45. 2 Cor. 11:16→AS 2, 192/ASD IV/3, 186, l. 68; 2 Cor. 11:17→192/186, l. 68f.; 2 Cor. 11:19→192/186, l. 67; 2 Cor. 11:23→184ff/182, l. 970.978f.982.990f.993; 2 Cor. 12:2→130/146, l. 388; 2 Cor. 12:2f.→210/194, l. 262f.
46. 2 Cor. 11:17.
47. 1 Cor. 1:18→AS 2,194/ASD IV/3, 186, l. 76–77; EE n.337,497; 1 Cor. 1:19→194/186, l. 88–89; 1 Cor. 1:21→194/186, l. 86–87; 196/188 l. 110; EE n.337,497; 1 Cor. 1:24→196/188, l. 107–108; 1 Cor. 1:25→194/186, l. 74–75; EE n. 337,497; 1 Cor. 1:27→194/186, l. 86–87; 1 Cor. 2:9→208–209/193, l. 255–56; 1 Cor. 3:1→194/186, l. 90.; 1 Cor. 3:18→192–93/186, l. 71–72; 1 Cor. 4:10→192/186, l. 69.
48. *Enkom.*, 196/188, l. 110.
49. 2 Cor. 11:23→*enkom.*, 184–86/182. Cf.: *minus sapiens dico; enkom.: ut [minus] insipiens dico*; Erasmus, *Novum Testamentum 1516* (ASD VI/3:426) *desipiens loquor*. In the apology in 2 Corinthians Paul begins to signal the foolishness: *Utinam sustineretis modicum quid insipientiae*

153

Now the array is complete: Epimenides—"I lie"; Socrates—"I know nothing"; Paul and, subsequently, Erasmus—"I speak foolishly." One and the same paradox, one and the same paradoxical logic constitutes the backbone of the encomium from beginning to end. Only Paul's self-stultifying foolish phrase provides the rubric *Stultitia loquitur* with the right tone. Hitherto theology was just an object of mockery for *Stultitia*;[50] now a new window has opened. In continuance of the paradoxical line, theology overtakes *Stultitia*, insofar as *Stultitia* herself becomes a theologian.[51] But while she—*Stultitia*—even appropriates words of Holy Scripture through the fool's speech, she loses nothing of *stultitia*, but in fact gains *theologia*. Now it is clear: the starting rubric, *Stultitia loquitur*, is correctly understood when read as *Theologia loquitur*.[52] This is because it is theology that does not cease to move its adepts and *mystai* until they, in ecstasy that unites Platonic *Mania* and Pauline *Raptus* in a being-outside-the-body, see what no eye has seen and hear what no ear has heard.[53] Concerning the spark for transcendence, however, we have to keep in mind that, in Paul's meaning, his strength is broken by weakness.

---

meae (11:1), and repeats: *Iterum dico ne quis me putet insipientem, alioquin velut insipientem accipite me* (11:16), and leads the sequence of self-reflective recursions like *dico, loquor* (11:16f., 21, 23) into the adventure of self-praise: only the fool praises himself. Paul does so by comparing himself with his adversaries: *et ego* (11:17f., 21f., 29), and surpasses them: *plus ego* (11:23); now the fool's speech is at its end: *minus sapiens dico*.

50. See 177n27.

51. Only in the very last proof foolishness embraces theology; it calls itself a theologian, although a weak one, as weak as the wood of a fig tree: *mihi quoque plane συνίκῃ θεολόγῳ* (192/186, l. 65; cf. *Adag.* 1,7,85; ASD 2/2:212–14).

52. Johann Valentin Andreae, *Theologiae Encomium Jesu Nazareno Sacrum, 1618*; GS 7, ed. Frank Böhling (Stuttgart-Bad Cannstatt: Frommann-Holzboog, 1994), 266–307. Cf. also Günter Bader, *Lob der Theologie—Theologiæ encomium* (Rheinbach: CMZ, 2002).

53. *Enkom.*, 206–10/192–94; cf. 2 Cor. 12:2-3; Platon, *Phaidr.* 245b; 1 Cor. 2:9. See as well Marjorie O'Rourke Boyle, *Christening Pagan Mysteries: Erasmus in Pursuit of Wisdom* (Toronto: University of Toronto, 1981), 27–61.

Cusanus and Logical Paradox

Treaties on the Renaissance paradox rarely miss out on taking Cusanus's point of view into account: *coincidentia oppositorum*, the coincidence of opposites, is a theme with which later paradoxologies would continue to work.[54] But neither Erasmus[55] nor Luther[56] imply that they share that point of view. So how can we connect Cusanus with Erasmus and Luther? The points of view leading us so far can still be applied. This would mean to look out for traces of *apologia*, be it Platonic or Pauline, and for the magic word *paradox*, which Luther employed with relish and which Erasmus could not eliminate despite his reluctance. Unfortunately, Cusanus's texts remain remarkably silent in both regards. As far as I know, one searches in vain for the word *paradox*, and he is notoriously demure in the use of classical texts. And if we now call out for *theologia crucis*, under whose banner we started off, moving on to Cusanus risks dispersion into the incomprehensible.[57] And yet. . . .

---

54. Kaiser, *Praisers*, 9sq.,22,24; Colie, *Paradoxia*, 22, 27, 458, 460; Verena Olejniczak Lobsien, *Skeptische Phantasie: Eine andere Geschichte der frühneuzeitlichen Literatur* (Münich: W. Fink, 1999), 49–51.

55. So far we could find only one explicit mention in Erasmus *Apol. ad Fabr. Stapul.* (1517), ASD IX/3:178, l. 2300, which deals with the contentious question whether the soul of Christ experienced suffering during the descent into hell. For the rest see Stephan Meier-Oeser, *Die Präsenz des Vergessenen: Zur Rezeption des Nicolaus Cusanus vom 15. bis zum 18. Jahrhundert*, BCG 10 (Münster: Aschendorff, 1989), 89–90.

56. Luther mentions Cusanus's issues only marginally: WA 2:303,3.5: Conc. Cath. 2:34; WA 30/2:205,7: Cribatio Alcorani; WA 31/1:516,37f. (forthcoming in LW.NS 2). Regarding Ps. 16(15):10 whether Christ descended into hell *secundum substantiam* or *secundum efficatiam*: Johann Faber Stapulensis, *Quincuplex psalterium* (Paris: ex calcotypa Henrici Stephani officina, 1513, new ed. Geneva: Droz, 1979), fol. A.iij; WATr 5, 685,5–6: squaring the circle. Meier-Oeser, *Die Präsenz des Vergessenen*, 85–94. See also Erwin Metzke, "Nicolaus von Cues und Martin Luther," in *Coincidentia oppositorum: Gesammelte Studien zur Philosophiegeschichte* (Witten-Ruhr: Luther-Verlag, 1961), 205–40; Volker Leppin, '*Cusa ist hie auch ein Lutheraner*'? *Theologie und Reform bei Nikolaus von Kues. Eine evangelische Annäherung*, TCL 15 (Trier: Paulinus-Verlag, 2009).

57. Walter Andreas Euler, "Does Nicholas Cusanus Have a Theology of the Cross?," *JR* 80 (2000): 405–20.

Signs of Paradoxy

When we turn toward the first main work, *De docta ignorantia*, and other texts such as the contemporary *Sermones* or the subsequent *Apologia doctae ignorantiae*, what has just been said fully applies to them. And yet we can detect some signs of paradoxy. The titles themselves can count as such. The expression *docta ignorantia* makes the Platonic-Pauline tradition ubiquitous, and Socrates is present in the text right from the start.[58] With *Apologia doctae ignorantiae*, the Platonic matrix becomes immediately tangible.[59] Regarding the Pauline apology, we do not find the brilliant reinterpretation Erasmus offered, but nevertheless allusions and quotations from both epistles to the Corinthians can occasionally be found.[60]

While the beginning of *De docta ignorantia* stands under the banner of Socrates, the end stands under the banner of Paul. The initial *mysteria intellectualia* ("the intellectual mysteries"),[61] *mysteria cognitionis divinae* ("the mysteries of divine knowledge"),[62] mutate into *mysteria fidei* ("the mysteries of faith") during the course of the work;[63] *docta ignorantia* and *fides* are in danger of becoming

---

58. *Doct. ign.* I,1 (h 1, 6,10f/w 1, 196): . . . *ut Socrati visum sit se nihil scire, nisi quod ignoraret*→Platon, *Apol.* 23b, followed by Salomon→Prov. 1:8 and Job→Job 28:20-21. Two further mentions fall back to the niveau of Scholastic teachings. With *h* we refer to the Heidelberg academy-edition, Leipzig-Hamburg, 1932ff. ["Heidelberger Akademieausgabe"], with *w* to the edition by Leo Gabriel (Vienna, 1964–1967).

59. *Apol. doct. ign.* (h 2, 2,9ff./w 1, 522)→Platon, *Apol.* 23b; in Cusanus's version lightened by his own hand; h 2, 31,11/w 1, 580: *libellum Platonis De apologia Socratis*→Platon, *Apol.* 23b.

60. Referring to 1 Corinthians 1–4 and 2 Corinthians 10–13 in the *Docta-ignorantia* texts: 1 Cor. 2:2→*Doct. ign.* 3,11 (h 1, 153,6/w 1, 494); 1 Cor. 2:4→*Apol. doct. ign.* (h 2, 4,17f/w 1, 526); 1 Cor. 2:14→*Doct. ign.* 3,6 (h 1, 136,12/w 1, 458); *Apol. doct. ign.* (h 2, 16,12ff/w 1, 552); 2 Cor. 11:13→*Apol. doct. ign.* (h 2, 5,8.13/w 1, 528); 2 Cor. 11:3→*Doct. ign.* 3,11 (h 1, 153,27/w 1, 496); 3,12 (h 1, 163,3/w 1, 514); 2 Cor. 12:1f→*Apol. doct. ign.* (h 2, 14,18/w 1, 548); 2 Cor. 12:2→*Doct. ign.* 3,11 (h 1, 152,29f/w 1, 494); 2 Cor. 12:2-4→*Apol. doct. ign.* (h 2, 5,24-26/w 1, 528). No text from 1 Corinthians 1–4 and 2 Corinthians 10–13 is ever the basis for the *Sermones*.

61. *Doct. ign.* 1,2 (h 1, 8,11/w 1, 200).

62. *Doct. ign.* 1,24 (h 1, 51,21/w 1, 286).

63. *Doct. ign.* 3,11 (h 1, 151,25/w 1, 492).

indistinct.[64] The reader is overcome by the same concern as the reader of the *Praise of Folly*: what begins buoyantly ends drearily. Indeed, what has concluded in Book 1 of *De docta ignorantia* with the impossibility of naming the divine name, amounts to naming the name of Jesus in Book 3, in perfect accordance with the characteristic style of some *Sermones* written around the same time.[65] The end of *De docta ignorantia* does not call Socrates, but Paul, to witness the knowing of not-knowing, which is probably the most direct reference to the Corinthian texts.[66] Even if the term *paradox* is absent, it should be noted: the title *docta ignorantia*, the gateway to the text, is the clearest sign that the text is pregnant with paradoxy.[67] Wherein: *ignorantia*, which is closely focused on knowledge, takes the place of Erasmus's multidimensional *Stultitia*.

The Logical Paradox

Why speak of a "logical paradox"? Paradoxes belong to Sophism; Aristotle pursues the strategy of weakening paradoxes.[68] At the most, they may be assigned to rhetoric, which is Sophism, insofar as it appears to be permissible.[69] Subject-related (*sachbezogene*) science, unlike language-related (*sprachbezogene*) science, seeks to avoid

64. *Fides*, initially mentioned in *Doct. ign.* 3,6 (h 1, 138,8/w 1, 462), becomes relevant in 3,11.

65. *Serm.* 19, 11-14 (h 16, 311-313), 20 (317); *Serm.* 22, 31-41 (h 16, 351-56); *Serm.* 23, 36-42 (h 16, 377–80); *Serm.* 24, 47-49 (h 16, 431–33); *Serm.* 48, 24-31 (h 17, 210–12).

66. *Doct. ign.* 3,11 (h 1, 152f./w 1, 494): *per quam [fidem] in simplicitate rapimur, ut supra omnem rationem et intelligentiam in tertio caelo* [2 Cor. 12:2] *simplicissimae intellectualitatis ipsum in corpore incorporaliter, quia in spiritu, et in mundo non mundialiter, sed caelestialiter contemplemur incomprehensibiliter, ut et hoc videatur, ipsum scilicet comprehendi non posse propter excellentiae suae immensitatem. Et haec est illa docta ignorantia, per quam ipse beatissimus Paulus ascendens vidit se Christum, quem aliquando solum scivit* [1 Cor. 2:2], *tunc ignorare, quando ad ipsum altius elevabatur.* Ulli Roth, *Suchende Vernunft: Der Glaubensbegriff des Nicolaus Cusanus*, BGPhMA.NF 55 (Münster: Aschendorff, 2000), 119–21, 164–66.

67. *Die Scheinwelt des Paradoxes*, ed. Hughes and Brecht, 115, has "Cusa, N., Of Learned Ignorance. London 1954" in the literature regarding the philosophical paradox.

68. Aristotle, *Soph.* el. 172b31-35; 175b28-38.

69. Aristotle, *Rhet.* 1412a26f.

paradoxy. Aristotle enforces the distinction between rhetorical and logical paradoxes; more precisely, he excludes logical paradoxes. It is science as long as the principle of noncontradiction is maintained.[70] This separation does not affect Erasmus. He starts out with the rhetorical paradox, which he conveys into its first degree of power through the paradigm of *paradox encomium* ("the praise of paradox")[71] and then into its second degree of power through the *prosopopeia* (the personification) of foolishness. Thereby he intimates that he does not want to leave the field of Aristotelian science to the usual anti-Scholasticism, but sees ways and means to retrieve the logical paradox by way of the rhetorical paradox. As a rhetorician, Erasmus writes *in intentione obliqua*, indirectly. But Cusanus, as a mathematical logician, is anxious to eliminate obliquity from his texts, except for exclamations, but they sound completely standardized.[72] He begins, according to the *intentio recta*, with the logical paradox. His Socratic/Platonic/Platonistic-inspired anti-Aristotelism leaves the paradox-free zone of science to *ratio*, "the intellect." Yet here he orchestrates those contradictions, using mathematical, geometrical, and, not least, linguistic models which are conversely reinforced by being avoided, until it becomes evident to the intellect that the logical paradox offers a knowledge of paradoxicality (*Wissen von Paradoxalität*), which trumps the rhetorical paradox with regard to clarity.

Shockingly, Cusanus intended to use paradoxicality as his title, which is surprising enough in itself.[73] *Docta ignorantia* has a long

---

70. Aristotle, *Met.* 3,3.6f. The ontological version of the principle of noncontradiction (1005b17ff.: the first and firmest of all axioms) leads directly to the logical version (1011b16); it serves excluding paradoxical sentences from the realm of science (1012a18).

71. Ps.-Aristotle, *Rhet. ad Alex.* 1430b1ff.: distinction of *endoxon* und *paradoxon*; expanded by Menander of Laodicea through the distinction of *adoxon* and *amphidoxon*, cf. Neumeyer, "Das Paradoxe," 517.

72. See the book conclusions: *Doct. ign.* 1,26; 2,13; 3,10; 3,12 (2 Cor. 11:31); *Apol. doct. ign.* In the continuous text: 3,11 (h 1, 153,27/w 1, 496; 2 Cor. 11:31).

73. *Doct. ign., Epist. ded.* (h 1, 1,12/w 1, 192): *novitas tituli*. Furthermore *Doct. ign., Epist. ded.* (h

history;[74] its usage is diverse and blurred. It could be a matter of informed, and more and more informed, ignorance, and it would be best to end that miserable condition; or of partial knowledge and partial ignorance, and thus of a mixture of both. As a non-rhetorician, Cusanus does not forget to take into account flaws of language: language does not bear a relation to the matter that would not imply an even greater disproportion.[75] So already on the level of language the *regula doctae ignorantiae*, the rule of learned ignorance, takes effect, saying that there is no relation between finitude and infinitude whatsoever.[76] Indeed, even as an expression, *docta ignorantia* is not altogether congenial. Two different stems of a word are employed. Thus the impression is conveyed, against the *regula*, that two different things need to be related to each other. *One thing* actually happens, however, which is excessively different in itself, that is to say, not only different but contrary, and not only contrary but contradictory. The rigor of contradiction is weakened by the use of two stems of a word. It is weakened even more when *sacra ignorantia* takes the place of *docta*.[77] In German and English we have the means to express the opposite meaning by using one root: knowing of not-knowing (*Wissen des Nicht-Wissens*). Already *un*knowing would be too mild; it would convey privation instead of negation. Yet, as a knowing of not-knowing, the *docta ignorantia* can be precisely

---

1, 2,4f/w 1, 192): *Rara quidem, et si monstra sint, nos movere solent.* Justly one detects pathos of novelty and Renaissance: Kurt Flasch, *Nikolaus von Kues: Geschichte einer Entwicklung: Vorlesungen zur Einführung in seine Philosophie* (Frankfurt/M.: Klostermann, 1998), 46–47, 77, 88, and 119. Beyond the well-trodden ways of the many/*multi* it is all about rare things/*rara* and things never heard/*prius inaudita: Doct. ign., Epist. auct.* (h 1, 163,17/w 1, 516); 2,11 (h 1, 99,15/w 1, 388).

74. Johannes Uebinger, *Der Begriff der docta ignorantia in seiner geschichtlichen Entwicklung*, in *Archiv für Geschichte der Philosophie* 8 (1895): 1–32, 206–40; Gerda von Bredow, "Docta ignorantia," in *Historisches Wörterbuch der Philosophie* 2 (1972): 273–74.

75. *Doct. ign.* 1,2 (h 1, 8,9-17/w 1, 200).

76. See 193n81.

77. E.g. *Doct. ign.* 1,17 (h 1, 35,2f/w 1, 252); 1,26 (h 1, 54,19/w 1, 292); 2,2 (h 1, 65,13/w 1, 322).

understood. One and the same thing is set and negated by her. Following the account of Cusanus's *docta ignorantia* is the first-case, of falling-into-one, of coincidence.[78] And as such it is placed at the beginning of the work so that from Book 1 with the name of God, via Book 2 with the names of the universe, it finally leads to the name of Jesus in Book 3.

The Theological Paradox

The moment the logical paradox takes effect, it reveals itself as theological. Admittedly, knowledge exists in the finite province of more or less, of progresses on the way, of proportionality from ease to difficulty. But the greatest knowledge, *docta ignorantia*, is all about demolishing proportion and opening up infinitude as infinitude.[79] The *regula docta ignorantia* says that there is no proportion between finitude and infinitude,[80] it denotes the endlessness of the infinite within the finitude of definition, or, which is the same: the definition implodes. If knowing of not-knowing is the model-case of coincidence, then the opposition of maximum and minimum follows close upon its heels; the greatest knowledge falls into one with the least (that is, with not-knowing).[81] Within this frame, Book 1, being distinct from the cosmology and Christology of Books 2 and 3, elaborates theology more specifically. It asks for the *name* of the greatest.[82] And with the answer to that question, a second question is posed, asking for the *word* of the greatest. While the matter of the name ends with Book 1, the matter of the word carries through

78. *Doct. ign.*, *Epist. auct.* (h 1, 163,7–11/w 1, 516).
79. *Doct. ign.* 1,1 (h 1, 6,1/w 1, 194): *infinitum ut infinitum.*
80. *Doct. ign.* 1,3 (h 1, 8,20f./w 1, 200): *infiniti ad finitum proportionem non esse.* Later on Cusanus often designated that sentence of incommensurability *regula*; e.g., *De ven. sap.* 26 (h 12, 79,1–3/ w 1, 124).
81. *Doct. ign.* 1,4.
82. Structure of *Doct ign.* 1: 1,5: *De unitate*; 1,6: *De necessitate*; 1,7–10: *De triunitate*; 1:11–23: Mathematic-geometrical treatise (outline 1,12); 1,24–26: theology of the name of God.

until the end of Book 3. This challenges us to read *De docta ignorantia* starting with the end, instead of the beginning as is usually done.

Whoever asks for the *name* of the greatest also asks for the smallest; the *nomen maximi* is itself a *minimum*, albeit one that coincides with the *maximum*. In its endless disproportion it is only possible as *innominabiliter nominabile* ("nameable in an unnameable way").[83] In a process that was fundamental in the search for *theologia prisca*—that is, the original or ancient theology—in the Renaissance, by referring to the Jewish name of God, Cusanus makes it clear: precisely insofar as the *tetragrammaton*, in its endless minimizing of speech and Scripture, loses the proportionality to the world, it is capable of being the name of that which has lost its proportionality to the world in the way of infinite maximizing.[84] The introduction of the tetragrammatic name at the end of Book 1 is a direct consequence of *docta ignorantia* from the start, and *De theologia negativa*, the final chapter, has to become a chapter *De infinitate Dei*, that is, on divine infinitude.[85] As a sign of

---

83. *Doct. ign.* 1,5 (h 1, 11,26/w 1, 206). Taking up the name-subject 1,5 (h 1, 11,15ff.; 12,11-3/w 1, 206f.); continuing 1,6 (h 1, 14,13ff./w 1, 212); 1,18 (h 1, 36,27-37,7); closing it 1,24-26 (h 1, 48,3ff./w 1, 278ff.).

84. *Doct. ign.* 1,24-26, prepared in the sermones since *Serm.* 1 and effective beyond *Doct. ign.* Rudolf Haubst, "Zu den für die kritische Edition der Cusanus-Predigten noch offenen Datierungsproblemen," in *Mitteilungen und Forschungsbeiträge der Cusanus-Gesellschaft* 17 (1986), 83n93, lists the following adaptions of the *nomen Tetragrammaton*: Serm. 1,3,16-24 (1430; h 16,5): *ineffabile, inconceptibile, semel in anno voce profertur, vocatur Jehova'*; cf. 7,16; 8,15; 12,17.19; *Serm.* 20,7,1-21 (1440; h 16, 305): '*Jehova', non legunt hoc Judaei nomen nisi semel [anno], ineffabile, nec est nomen, nec pars orationis*; cf. 3,4 'Jehova'; *De doct. ign.* 1,24 (1440; h 1, 48,17f): *ipsum proprium nomen, ineffabile*; *De doct. ign.* 1,24 (1440; h 1, 51,24f.): *ioth he vau he, proprium et ineffabile*; *Serm.* 23, 35,8-10 (1441; h 16, 377): *non est translatum, Joth, He, Vau, He*; *Serm.* 24,48,2-6 (1441; h 16, 431f.): *ineffabile, complicatio omnis expressibilis significativae vocis*; *Serm.* 48,11,1-10 (1445; h 17, 205): *unum nomen supra regionem intellectualem, scilicet 'Jehova'*; *Serm.* 48,29,1-19 (1445; h 17, 211): *ineffabile, Jehova est collectio vocalium in unitate, Ioth, He, Vau, He, i, e, o/v, a, Jehova' non est nisi vocalitas omnis, ineffabile, omnem vocalitatem in se complicat*; *De Gen.* 4,168,1-5 (1447; h 4, 120): *ineffabile, Iehova, complicatio omnis vocalitatis, fons omnis effabilis verbi quasi ineffabilis in omni verbo effabili ut causa resplendet*; *De Gen.* 5,176,5-9 (1447; h 4, 214): *ineffabile, Iehova, omnis vocalitatis complicatio, sine quibus vocalibus nullum verbum potest esse vocale*; Repercussion in Erasmus, *Enkom.*, 142/158, l. 521: *Tetragrammaton*; 150f/164, l. 11ff.: name of Jesus. Werner L. Gundersheimer, "Erasmus, Humanism, and the Christian Cabala," *Journal of the Warburg and Courtauld Institutes* 26, nos. 1-2 (1963): 38–52.

paradoxy, *docta ignorantia* brings the maximum, namely knowing, to coincide with the minimum, namely not-knowing, just as the aim and the end of Book 1 bring the absolute maximum, God himself, to coincide with the absolute minimum, that is, God's name. In analogy to the sentence he has already introduced, *"minimum est maximum"* ("the smallest is the greatest"), Cusanus accomplishes this by daring to assert *"[quod] nomen Dei sit Deus"* ("[that] the name of God is God"),[86] although "is" is not a statement of identity but must be understood as the coincidence of infinite opposition. If the name of God, considered thusly, is the purpose of *docta ignorantia*, then it shares her paradoxical structure. The initial paradox proves to be controlled by the final paradox. The latter is: the name of God is what God names.[87] It goes beyond the opposition of *theologia affirmativa* and *negativa*, under whose rule the end of Book 1 still finds itself.

We talk of a theological paradox, because if you look at the name of God starting from the end of the text, it proves to be the paradox that has stimulated and incited the desire for the *docta ignorantia* right from the start. And in the same sense it shows from the end of Book 3, and thus from the end of the complete work, that the name of Jesus was the beginning of the whole journey, or at least should have been such a beginning according to the guiding intention.[88] In spite of all the late medieval pious concentration on the name of Jesus shared by *De docta ignorantia* and the *Sermones*, Cusanus in *De docta ignorantia* avoids the excursion into the Christian Kabbalah, which seeks to explain the name of Jesus as an utterance of the

85. *Doct. ign.*, 1,26; asset of negative theology 1,18 (h 1, 35,10; 37,6f/w 1, 252, 256).
86. *Doct. ign.* 1,24 (h 1, 49,21f./w 1, 282).
87. Peter J. Casarella, "His Name is Jesus: Negative Theology and Christology in Two Writings of Nicholas of Cusa from 1440," in *Nicholas of Cusa on Christ and the Church: Essays in Memory of Chandler McCuskey Brooks for the American Cusanus Society*, ed. Gerald Christianson and Thomas M. Izbicki (Leiden: Brill, 1996), 281–307. Casarella speaks of a "coincidence of naming and being" (286).
88. Casarella, *ibid.*, 290: "Book Three is the foundation of the entire system."

unutterable name. Instead, he pursues the christological title *Word*, which plays a prominent role among the designations of Jesus, a role almost equal to the *name*. Going with the prologue of John, he begins in John 1:1 with the second person of the Trinity, and via the cosmological function of the Word (John 1:3) he reaches its christological function in John 1:14, in conformity with the three parts of *De docta ignorantia*: theology,[89] cosmology,[90] Christology.[91] The specific contribution of Cusanus is the application of the *regula doctae ignorantiae*. If the rule comes into play according to which every definition of a word on the level of *ratio* is exposed to a much stronger infinition (*Infinition*) on the level of *intellectus*, then it entails that the traditional distinctions of inner and outer word, *verbum increatum* and *creatum*, *verbum mentis* and *vocis*, are sent into a tailspin. These two aspects do not relate like inside and outside, well arranged by proportionality, but in the spoken word/*verbum*, in the spoken words/*verba*, speaking itself, the word itself/*ipsum verbum* becomes effective.[92] It relates to spoken speech like speaking itself. Or like the speech of speech, language of language,[93] yet expressing not a relation of the relation, but, rather, one of nonrelation. Thus Cusanus gets to the point where he repeats the main claim of the theology of the name, "*nomen Dei [est] Deus*," as the main claim of the theology of the word, "*verbum Dei [est] Deus*."[94] Here, too, it remains that "it" is not to be understood as an expression of identity, but of the coincidence of endless opposition. The paradox of the name is

---

89. *Doct. ign.* 1,24.

90. *Doct. ign.* 2,7 and 2,9.

91. *Doct. ign.* 3,3–5 and 3,11.

92. *Doct. ign.* 2,9 (h 1, 96,5/w 1, 382): *in [v]erbo ipsum Verbum.*

93. *Doct. ign.* 2,9 (h 1, 94,11-19/w 1, 378): to *docta ignorantia* the *verbum in divinis* appears as *forma formarum et veritas veritatum.*

94. Serm. 24,47,5 (1441) (h 16, 431): *Dicit Johannes in Apocalypsi* [19,13], *quod 'nomen eius' est 'Verbum Dei', scilicet Christi. Unde cum Verbum Dei sit Deus—'Deus' autem 'erat verbum'* [Joh. 1:1]—*tunc nomen Dei est Verbum Dei.*

not conveyed in such a way to the paradox of the word. What is said is being said not for its own sake, but in order to make saying itself audible—and yet, if it is proclaimed *in* what is said, it is not exhausted *through* what is said. The endless transcending that takes place in and through the word does not happen as a metaphorical transfer, but as a metonymical *transumptio* (or *metalepsis*).[95] The ways in which Cusanus's sparse pronouncements on incarnation theology may relate to his even more sparse pronouncements on the theology of the cross would deserve an examination of their own.[96]

Conclusion

Two points provoke further thought. On the level of historical theology, what readers of Cusanus and Erasmus, but also of Luther, should pay close attention to is apparent. And on the systematic level it is clear that even the most engrained oppositions cannot have the final word, although awkward sentences arise in doing so.

Without doubt, Erasmus and Cusanus belong in the context of Luther's *theologica paradoxa*. The paradox of the cross, the paradox of foolishness, and that of not-knowing come together to form a single historical or factual context. Conversely, the young Luther, the Luther of the *theologica paradoxa*, who is nonconfessional, nonexistential, nonpositivist,[97] belongs in the context of Renaissance

95. Stephan Meier-Oeser, "Nikolaus von Kues (1401–1464)," in *Klassiker der Sprachphilosophie von Platon bis Noam Chomsky*, ed. Tilman Borsche (Münich: Beck, 1996), 106–7; Johannes Hoff, "Die sich selbst zurücknehmende Inszenierung von Reden und Schweigen," in *Religion und Rhetorik (Religionswissenschaft heute 4)*, ed. Holt Meyer and Dirk Uffelmann (Stuttgart: W. Kohlhammer, 2007), 222–36; J. Hoff, *Kontingenz, Berührung, Überschreitung. Zur philosophischen Propädeutik christlicher Mystik nach Nikolaus von Kues* (Freiburg-i.-Br.: Alber, 2007).

96. Incarnation: *Doct. ign.* 3,4–5; cross: *Doct. ign.* 3,6, "*Mysterium mortis Iesu Christi*," in the course of Book 3 argues not only cosmologically, but for the first time soteriologically as well. As *ineffabile crucis mysterium nostrae redemptionis*. Cusanus writes down (h 1, 139,1-4/w 1, 464): *Coincidunt enim minima maximis, ut maxima humiliatio cum exaltatione, turpissima mors virtuosi cum gloriosa vita, et ita in ceteris, ut omnia ista nobis Christi vita, passio atque crucifixio manifestant.*

97. "Nonpositivist" in the "revelatory-positivism" sense of the term.

theology and its knowledge of paradox. So if they all, Cusanus, Erasmus, and Luther, are theologians found in the vicinity of *paradoxia epidemica*, then we have to take care that Luther is not singled out by so-called theological reasons.

Theology of the cross is not a *ceterum censeo* of theology in opposition to the supposedly "high speculation" of paradoxology. When already high speculation touches nothing but reality itself, how much more will it touch the cross.

Translated from German by Johanna Breidenbach and Rosalyn Avent

8

The Cross of Wisdom: Ambiguities in Turning Down Apologetics (Paul, Anselm, Barth)

Anthony Feneuil

There is more than one fool in the Bible, and I would like to start with another fool than Paul's, but whose legacy in the history of theology (and philosophy) has been equally significant. I want to talk about the fool from Psalms 14 and 53, who dares to say in his heart: "There is no God." How is the foolishness of this fool (*nabal*), called in Latin *insipiens*, and in Greek ἄφρων, related to the foolishness of God (μωρία, in Latin *stultitia*) in Paul's epistle? It would certainly be interesting to compare philologically μωρία and ἄφρων, and to determine what version of the psalm Paul could have been reading, in order to guess whether he intended to distinguish the two kinds of foolishness. Unfortunately, I would be unable to do this, so I will stick to the concepts. Is it possible to articulate those two kinds of foolishness? The foolishness of the atheist and the foolishness of God?

One should at least notice their association in a major theological treatise: Anselm's *Proslogion*. At the end of chapter 3, devoted to show that it is "impossible for God not to be," Anselm goes on to ask: "Why then did 'the Fool said in his heart, there is no God' . . . when it is so evident to any rational mind that You of all things exist to the highest degree? Why indeed, unless because he was stupid and a fool [*stultus et insipiens*]?"[1] Anselm's gesture of identifying the *stultus* and the *insipiens* could be considered anti-Paulinian. To say the least, it gives a very modest interpretation of the distinction between divine and human wisdoms. The foolishness of the *insipiens* indeed seems to equate the weakness of his understanding with the fact that he did not realize that one cannot logically deny God's existence. Hence, the necessity to address him rationally in order to convince him of his own foolishness. Human foolishness is but a lesser divine wisdom, a wisdom of the same kind. And the foolishness of God is a folly only to an imperfect human wisdom. Therefore, the proper theological task would be to improve human wisdom, in order to grant it access to the wisdom of God.

Today, who would defend such a reading of Paul? Apologetics is not very popular among theologians anymore. Only a few of them would assert that unbelief is merely irrational. Arguments for the existence of God are, rather, studied for the sake of history. Hence, the theological mainstream would probably tend to interpret more radically the distinction between the two kinds of wisdom, as a distinction between two incommensurable realms. The wisdom

1. Anselm of Canterbury, *The Major Works*, ed. Brian Davies and G. R. Evans (Oxford: Oxford University Press, 1998), 88.

of God would not only seem foolish to a fake human wisdom, but would actually be a folly to *any* human wisdom as such. And the foolishness of human wisdom would not be the result of any weakness of understanding, but would name more truly *this* wisdom. With this kind of reading, one could then appeal to Paul in order to turn down any apologetic attempt as misleading. Why would someone use natural reason to know God and convince the fools, if natural reason is, as such, a folly contrary to divine wisdom?

I will not engage directly the question of whether this reading of Paul is correct. I would like to stress only its great ambiguity. This ambiguity is made clear by the fact that this antiapologetic reading of Paul often appears in apologetic contexts, as a last barricade for faith against rational strikes. It is the case, for instance, in William Alston's 1991 book *Perceiving God: The Epistemology of Religious Experience*, where the author aims at defending the rationality of cognitive claims based on what he calls perceptions of God. At some point, he investigates psychological theories that, roughly, pretend to reduce those kinds of perceptions to pathological hallucinations, in particular psychoanalysis. After having stressed internal weaknesses in Freud's theories, he finally engages in a surprising argument:

> But for the sake of argument let's take Freud seriously and see what follows. . . . Why suppose that this is not the mechanism God uses to reveal Himself to our experience? Because it seems very odd that God would choose such a means? But much of what happens in the world seems to us to be not the sort of things the Christian God would choose. Hence the problem of evil, and hence the paradoxicality of the cross (to the Jews a stumbling block and to the Greeks foolishness).[2]

So here is a strong advocate of apologetics who, when facing what could be an overwhelming counterargument, were it based on solid

2. William Alston, *Perceiving God: The Epistemology of Religious Experience* (Ithaca: Cornell University Press, 1993), 233.

grounds, eventually appeals to Paul and the "paradoxicality of the cross" in order to defend himself. It is as if the apologist could always, even with a bad hand, play a last joker or, rather, put a gun on the table and declare the end of all usual rules in the name of the superior rationality for which he is advocating and that is ungraspable by purely human minds. This strategy is not a new one. Here is what Blaise Pascal wrote in what was meant to be an apology of Christianity: "Who then will condemn Christians for being unable to give rational grounds for their belief, professing as they do a religion for which they cannot give rational grounds? They declare that it is a folly, *stultitiam*, in expounding it to the world, and then you complain that they do not prove it. If they did prove it they would not be keeping their word. It is by being without proof that they show they are not without sense."[3]

To be sure, those are not Pascal's final words on the topic. Even though he often insists on the irrational *origin* of many Christian dogmas, he also stresses how rationally powerful they are to explain the human condition.[4]. To find the denial of apologetics as a truly final kind of apologetics, without any compromise with rationality, one has to look at Montaigne:

> . . . they think we give them very fair play in putting them into the liberty of combatting our religion with weapons merely human, whom, in her majesty, full of authority and command, they durst not attack. The means that I shall use, and that I think most proper to subdue this frenzy, is to crush and spurn under foot pride and human arrogance; to make them sensible of the inanity, vanity, and vileness of man; to

3. Blaise Pascal, *Pensées*, trans. A. J. Krailsheimer (London: Penguin Books, 1995), 122 (no. 418/ 233, "the wager").

4. See ibid., 219 (no. 695/445): "Original sin is folly in the eyes of men, but it is put forward as such. You should therefore not reproach me for the unreasonable. But this folly is wiser than all men's wisdom, *it is wiser than men*. For without it, what are we to say man is? His whole state depends on this imperceptible point. How could he have become aware of it through his reason, seeing that it is something contrary to reason and that his reason, far from discovering it by its own methods, draws away when presented with it?"

wrest the wretched arms of their reason out of their hands; to make them bow down and bite the ground under the authority and reverence of the Divine Majesty. 'Tis to that alone that knowledge and wisdom appertain . . .'[5]

Montaigne then paraphrases Paul to summarize his thesis: "our wisdom is but folly in the sight of God." One could have said as well, on Karl Barth's humorous tone: "God is everything, man is nothing, and thou art a madman."[6] It is in Montaigne indeed that the ambiguity of this apologetic/antiapologetic use of Paul's epistle is altogether uncovered. Although it appears as an assumption of God's foolishness, it may only be one more *mondaine philosophie*. Montaigne's commitment to Christianity is a highly problematic question among scholars. The question is to determine whether his fideism is only a disguised atheism or the true expression of his irrational commitment to Christianity. This question is more than an anecdotal one. It shows that there is a structural analogy, and even a complete reversibility, between fideism and skepticism. And this reversibility does not mean that fideism should always be considered as a religious form of *rational* criticism: either a final religious attempt to resist the progress of rationalism, or the first intrusion of rationalism inside the religious sphere, a concealed atheism. Quentin Meillassoux has shown that fideism could be understood the other way around, as skepticism's truth. Not, then, as a religious form of a general process of rationalization but, rather, as the first figure of a shift *within rationality itself*, a shift toward what Meillassoux calls the "*religionizing* [*enreligement*] of reason,"[7] which he identifies as a

5. Michel de Montaigne, *The Essays of Montaigne*, trans. Charles Cotton (London: Reeves and Turner, 1877), 150–51.
6. Karl Barth, *Church Dogmatics* I/2, trans. G. T. Thomson and Harold Knight (Edinburgh: T&T Clark, 1956), 259.
7. Quentin Meillassoux, *After Finitude: An Essay on the Necessity of Contingency*, trans. R. Brassier (London: Continuum, 2008), 47.

distinctive feature of modern (and postmodern) thought: "Once the absolute has become unthinkable, even atheism, which also targets God's inexistence in the manner of an absolute, is reduced to a mere belief, and hence to a religion, albeit of the nihilist kind. Faith is pitched against faith, since what determines our fundamental choices cannot be rationally proved."[8]

The modern tendency to deny reason's ability to grasp the absolute would entail an a priori justification of any belief, *insofar as it does not pretend to be rationally justified.* Therefore, it is no longer the folly of God which is wiser than human wisdom, but any folly as such. It is likely that today one would probably find it more reasonable to declare oneself an atheist (or a Christian, or an Hindu) on the ground of one's cultural environment or intimate conviction, and to ask for tolerance, than to try to demonstrate that no God exists, or that Hinduism is true. According to Meillassoux, this situation has very concrete consequences: ". . . if nothing absolute is thinkable, there is no reason why the worst forms of violence could not claim to have been sanctioned by a transcendence that is only accessible to the elect few."[9]

So what? Paul, the founder of universalism, according to Alain Badiou (because the foolishness of what he proclaims shows that the universality of a belief depends more on the way it is believed than on its rational content), could also be, and for the exact same reason, the model for contemporary fanaticism?[10] Would his word of the cross

---

8. Ibid., 46.
9. Ibid., 47.
10. Badiou's reading of Paul prevents any "terrorist" interpretation of that kind. As a matter of fact, Badiou—who wrote a preface for Meillassoux's book—makes strong assertions against relativism, and claims that he has overcome this aspect of postmodernity. According to him, no folly is as such a true proposition, but only insofar as it demands a new kind of subjectivity and, in this regard, becomes universal. Nevertheless, one could easily argue that his reading of Paul is exemplary of what Meillassoux is trying to point at, namely the fact that piety in regard to belief (one's attitude toward one's beliefs, in this case the fact that one is willing to become an *absolute* subject, a "subject without identity" serving the event one is proclaiming) is more important

express, rather than Christian revelation, the wisdom of the world itself?

Whatever the answer may be, the question itself shows that any appeal to the foolishness of God in order to disqualify apologetics is somewhat suspicious. It looks like what Karl Barth calls "tax-collector pharisaism,"[11] that is, a reversed pride, the overly self-confident claim of one's own weakness, grounded on the belief that one can reach salvation by oneself—not by fulfilling the commands of the law (as a Pharisee), but by *not* fulfilling them (as the tax collector). Does this entail that we Christians should just give up on claiming for ourselves the foolishness of God and engage in natural theology? Should we build new arguments for the existence of God and improve the old ones? This seems to be what Meillassoux calls us to, from his materialist point of view: to choose Anselm (and Descartes) rather than Paul (and Kant, and Derrida).

Before that, it may be wise to look further into what Anselm actually does—we might find something quite different than in Descartes, and not so foreign to Paul. Otherwise, would Barth, a notably Paulinian theologian whose refusal of natural theology is famous, have written a whole volume on Anselm, one that he himself considered one of his most significant books? He may have seen

for its truth than its intrinsic rationality (objectivity). In one of his articles ("History and Event in Alain Badiou," trans. T. Nail, *Parrhesia* 12 [2011]: 1–11), Meillassoux acknowledges the religious (eschatological) dimension of Badiou's thought. The whole question is to determine if Meillassoux is right in thinking that the modern antirealist trend of thought bears in itself irrationality and a potential communitarian violence, or if there is something as an immanent rationality of this trend of thought, immanent to piety, so to speak, able to replace the first-hand irrationality of the content and to prevent relativism without negating the subjective aspect of all knowledge altogether. This second position seems closer to what Badiou holds. Paul precisely allows him to show how extreme "piety" (in Meillassoux's vocabulary) entails an attempt to universalize its content and, therefore, something like a regulation of the "faith against faith" violence.

11. Karl Barth, *Church Dogmatics* IV/1, trans. G. W. Bromiley (London: T&T Clark, 1956), 617, and already *The Epistle to the Romans*, trans. Edwyn C. Hoskyns (London: Oxford University Press, 1968), 109.

in Anselm a way to escape the ambiguities of too sharp a denial of apologetics, *without* giving up Paul's summon against worldly wisdom.

According to Barth, Anselm's proof is not natural theology. Anselm never places himself on the—supposedly common to the believer and the unbeliever—ground of natural reason. The definition of God Anselm gives at the beginning of the *Proslogion* is not, says Barth, a definition in the strict sense of the term but, rather, a confession of faith. It does not define the nature of God but acknowledges a divine command, actually the first of the Ten Commandments ("You shall have no other gods before me"): "We believe that You are something than which nothing greater can be thought."[12] It is not about the abstract essence of God, but about the relation of lordliness between the revealed God and God's creatures. Anselm does not place himself on the fool's ground, he does not think on the same level. And the proof does not primarily prove the existence of God but, rather, the fact that, on the ground of this lordliness relationship that God initiated, it is not even possible for us to imagine, even as a mere hypothesis, the inexistence of God. The mere hypothesis of the nonexistence does not fit God. In that respect as well, God is very different from any other object of the world (very different from a hundred-euro note, for instance). Therefore, Anselm's proof is not an ontological proof, that is, a proof that would go from God's essence in thought to God's actual existence. It is not a proof in which human thought is above God, in which human thought decides about God's existence. It is the other way around: the proof aims at showing, from the revealed name of God, that human thought cannot establish itself as a spectator above God. The proof shows that human thought, in relation to God, is unescapably limited.

12. Anselm of Canterbury, *The Major Works*, 87.

Therefore, one could say that, in a sense, the proof aims precisely at negating the possibility of any natural theology, understood as a human attempt to escape the relation of obedience to God, and to establish oneself in the position of being able to make judgments about God's existence, just as about the existence of any object. It is a proof that declares our wisdom as a folly before God. Hence, the *insipiens*, in Barth's reading of Anselm—that is, the one who does not understand the proof—is not only the one who *denies* the existence of God, but also the one who tries to *establish* this existence on purely rational grounds. Who, then, is the *insipiens*? He is Descartes, not less than Kant, because when Descartes attempts to ground the certainty of God's existence exclusively on human reason, he believes that he can consider God as a thought object similar to others, whose existence can always be put into bracket. Insofar, he is an *insipiens*: he believes that one can talk about God as about a thing or an absent person, using a third-person discourse, whereas one cannot talk about God without talking *to* God. Consequently, there is no fundamental difference between Anselm's *insipiens* and Paul's fool: both refer to those who do not acknowledge the foolishness of their own wisdom, but neither Anselm's *incipiens* nor Paul's fool refer to the one who cannot reason well, for any contingent cause.

But at the same time, and this is just as important, Anselm is actually stating a *proof* aimed at convincing the *insipiens*. In other words, the fact that natural theology is impossible and that, theologically speaking, the initiative belongs to no one but God, before whom human creatures have only to listen and pray, is revealed through the mask of that fact's opposite. But it is actually very sound: if only God can limit our arguments about God—if, in other words, it is the foolishness *of God*, and of God only, that is actually wiser than human beings—then reason alone cannot discover

175

its own limits. Therefore, when human thought does discover its own boundaries—for instance, at the occasion of a *Critique of Pure Reason*—far from actually pointing to its own limits, it overcomes them again:[13] "God is hidden, not because of the relativity of all human knowledge, but because he is the living God who reveals himself as he is, the triune God, inexhaustibly living, immutably the subject, from himself and not from us. It is not a much too skeptical philosophy that makes him the hidden God."[14]

Theologically, it is thus necessary that the boundaries of human reason appear through a *proof*, in which human reason seems to overcome itself—and actually overcomes itself, as long as God does not himself bind it. It is necessary, in order for human foolishness to be revealed in the greatest human wisdom ("Has not God made foolish the wisdom of the world?"; 1 Cor. 1:20). That is why Barth asserts that between theological truth and theological error, between the boastful philosophical folly and the humble theological wisdom, there is nothing but "the merest hair's breadth."[15] The merest hair's breadth, that is to say, no difference at all, *from the human point of view*. In other words, the true limitation of reason, the only limitation that is not a self-limitation, cannot reveal itself but through the features of an unbounded reason—Hegel's reason rather than Kant's.[16]

Therefore, it is just as foolish to deny apologetics in an absolute

---

13. This is probably the core of Hegel's critique of Kant's notion of "*Grenze*" in the first book of the *Science of Logic*, ch. 2, section B.1: "*Grenze*." The bound cannot appear as such but from the outside.

14. Karl Barth, *The Göttingen Dogmatics: Instruction in the Christian Religion*, trans. G. W. Bromiley (Grand Rapids: Eerdmans, 1991), 1:135.

15. Karl Barth, *Anselm: Fides Quaerens Intellectum*, trans. I. W. Robertson (New York: Meridian Books, 1962), 70.

16. A very good insight into the closeness of Barth's notion of reason to Hegel's, in its relation to the concept of boundaries and to Anselm's proof, is given by Sigurd Bark in his doctoral dissertation, "Seeking Out the Enemy on His Own Ground: Problems and Proof in Dialectical Theology," PhD diss., Princeton Theological Seminary, 2013.

manner as it is to engage in apologetics on purely rational ground, through a bracketing of faith.

1. It is foolish to deny apologetics, that is, the full rationality of faith, because one could only do that by denying God the privilege to limit human reason. Any human denial of the apologetics project could not be but the erection of *human* foolishness where *divine* foolishness should be. One could only do that by rejecting revelation as such, as the foolishness *of God*. Human rationality would probably be overcome if the kingdom of God were a present reality, but it is not. Until it is, we cannot give up rationality. We have to bear rationality as our cross, so to speak. Hence, there is no way, as a theologian, to reject the arguments of the fool (of the materialist thinker, the atheist, and the like) on the ground that faith is irreducible to reason. The theologian has to answer those arguments. She cannot live in a separate sphere, outside the intellectual and philosophical life. She has to engage into contemporary intellectual debates.

2. This apologetic dimension of theology does not contradict its revealed nature. Quite the opposite: it is only through faith that rationality can become our cross. We can go further: the *insipiens* herself is a faith character. She is a character that prevents the believer from reducing the gap between faith and anything given. She is then a character that forces faith to relentlessly refine itself. She is a theological insider. That is precisely why the *insipiens* is not, in Anselm, an empirical character (someone Anselm might have met), even less a political character (the contemporaneity of Anselm to the crusades, stressed by Franz Overbeck, is misleading). The *insipiens* is a *biblical* character. The *insipiens* reminds us that the foolishness of God is not *our* foolishness but the foolishness of the cross, that is, the foolishness

of the God who unveils Godself through God's own veiling, and so God's foolishness is nothing which the historical church could possess or which could be used to end the conversation with the world and within the church itself as it struggles to make its own proclamation clearer. In that sense, apologetics is *fides quaerens intellectum*, faith seeking intelligence, and not a theological incursion into enemy territory (as if the enemy was not always already inside theology).

Consequently, Barth's turning down of apologetics is very different from any postmodern attitude of withdrawal into one's own beliefs. It is true that, ultimately, there is no difference in Barth between apologetics and dogmatics ("the best apologetics is good dogmatics"). True also that dogmatics cannot be but *church* dogmatics, and that the theologian cannot talk but from the church and to the church. But that does not mean that it withdraws inside the sacristy. On the contrary, this means that the theologian is always already exposed to unbelief, because she is herself, as a human being, fundamentally an unbeliever. She is turned toward the inside, but the doors and the windows are wide open. The *insipiens* is a faith character, she comes from faith itself, and for this reason the theologian has to listen to her. Without the patronizing attitude of the one who knows better and whose only uncertainty is about the choice of pedagogical means to impose her own conviction, but with the consciousness of having no decisive vantage point and the hope that adverse arguments will allow her to better understand herself, "Thinking, albeit differently from him, the believer time and time again finds himself in human solidarity with the *insipiens*, whose objection serves to remind the believer of his own task, and he cannot refuse to make his answer."[17]

Would I dare to go further into exegesis, I would say that this

17. Barth, *Anselm: Fides Quaerens Intellectum*, 106.

conception of apologetics as a dialogue with the *insipiens*, not in a spirit of defense or conquest, but as theology's proper task toward itself, is a somewhat Paulinian conception. The question of foolishness comes back later in the epistle, when Paul talks about this mysterious "speaking in a tongue" (1 Cor. 14:22-23). Paul does grant this phenomenon spiritual value, but the way in which he tries to regulate its use is meaningful. On the one hand, he claims that this "speaking in a tongue," of which we know at least that it is not directly understandable, is a sign that should be directed toward the outside. This means the vanity of any apologetic attempt, as long as it is conceived as what Barth calls parliamentary apologetics,[18] in which the theologian is seen as leaving her chair to get down on the battlefield with a white flag in order to discuss peace with the unbeliever and never putting her own position into question. But on the other hand, Paul urges one not to speak in tongues during the assemblies of believers, where one should, rather, tell prophecies, that is, speak in an intelligible way. It is quite difficult to see precisely what this means, and how it fits the Corinthian context of the time. But the interesting thing for us is the justification Paul gives to this assertion: unbelievers that would join those assemblies (where Christians would be speaking in a tongue) would "think you are mad" (1 Cor. 14:23), and that could prevent them from converting to the faith. This is to say, the μωρία, the foolishness of God, cannot be merely identified with human irrationality. This also means that the unbeliever, as the outsider *inside* the church (it is only when the unbeliever is among the believers that Paul recommends speaking rationally rather than irrationally), is somewhat the witness of the difference between those two kinds of irrationality. The unbeliever summons the church from the inside and reminds it that it has no choice but to be part of the

---

18. Karl Barth, *Die Theologie Schleiermachers: Vorlesung Göttingen, Wintersemester 1923/1924*, ed. D. Ritschl (Zürich: TVZ, 1978), 438.

wisdom of the world, and that it cannot escape this wisdom without trying to escape the foolishness *of God*.

Ultimately, the *insipiens* reminds the church of its own unbelief, and she prevents it from boasting in its own foolishness. The *insipiens* warns the church that what it believes to be the foolishness of God might be a human, all-too-human, madness, a wisdom of the second order. The *insipiens* calls the church, from within, to rationality, and insofar she is the reason to do theology. We have to answer her, but at the same time we cannot, as theologians, answer her but from the standpoint of faith, that is, from a standpoint where we cannot stand. And there lies the foolishness of the church of Christ: it is not its last wall against the strikes of the *insipiens*, but the risk it takes out of solidarity with the unbelievers, its openness to the wisdoms of the world, *as an act of faith*. The foolishness of God is not the *sacrificium intellectus*—this would be too easy. It might be, so to speak, the sacrifice of the *sacrificium intellectus* or, even better, the renouncing of the sacrifice, in the name of the sacrifice of the cross that relieves us of having to sacrifice. The *insipiens* reminds us that the foolishness of God is also a stumbling block. A stumbling block to the Jews, sure, but just as we are all Greeks, since we are all foolish, especially when we believe we are Christians, we Christians are all Jews, because we are always prone to rest in the law, that is, in the church in its historical shape.

Here is the foolishness and the stumbling block: that Truth may be revealed to us through what the *insipiens* says about it. But then, how could theology be more than a *"mondaine philosophie"*? Barth identifies two signs in Anselm's writings, two visible signs that tend to distinguish those writings from philosophical writings: Anselm's concern for the beauty (*pulchritudo*) of his arguments, and Anselm's humor, which Barth often contrasts with Gaunilo's tragic tone.[19] Just as the foolishness cannot be considered independently from the fact that it is a stumbling block, beauty and humor are to be understood jointly. Beauty, which makes the apologetic argument a liturgical act, needs humor not to be satisfied in the contemplation of itself. But humor—without humor no theology would be possible, since the tragedy of its impossibility would reduce us to silence, and we cannot speak as long as we take seriously the unbelief of the unbeliever as well as our own unbelief—the humor that specifies theology, needs beauty not to sink into ironic detachment. Scholars often stress the beauty in Paul's letters. What about his humor? That might be, one more time, the fools, the wise men *par excellence*, those Athenian philosophers before whom Paul proclaimed the resurrection of the dead (Acts 17), who reveal, against their will, the human truth of his discourse: they laughed at him. . . .

19. Barth, *Anselm: Fides Quaerens Intellectum*, 15–16 (*pulchritudo*), and 71 (humor).

9

The Wisdom in God's Foolishness: Karl Barth's Exegesis of 1 Corinthians 1–2

Andrew R. Hay

The significance of Karl Barth's exposition of 1 Corinthians in *The Resurrection of the Dead* (*Die Auferstehung der Toten*; hereafter *AT*)[1] cannot be overlooked. The lectures comprising *AT* were given in the summer semester of 1923, alongside those on *Die Theologie der reformierten Bekenntnisschriften* (*The Theology of the Reformed Confessions*).[2] As usual, however, Barth overextended himself for the

---

1. Karl Barth, *Die Auferstehung der Toten. Eine akademische Vorlesung über I. Kor. 15*, 4th ed. (Zollikon-Zürich: EVZ, 1953 [c. 1924]) (hereafter *AT*); ET, *The Resurrection of the Dead*, trans. H. J. Stenning, reprint (Eugene, OR: Wipf & Stock, 2003) (hereafter *RD*). The quotations herein try to follow *AT* rather than *RD* for clarification. *RD* is provided where noted.
2. Karl Barth, *Die Theologie der reformierten Bekenntnisschriften 1923*, in *Karl Barth Gesamtausgabe* (hereafter *GA*), II.30: Akademische Werke, ed. Eberhard Busch (Zürich: TVZ, 1998); ET, *The*

183

series on the Reformed confessions, and found himself short of time in his 1 Corinthians lectures. But Barth still considered that what he had discovered over the hurried course of the lectures merited broader distribution, and they were published the year after their delivery. And yet, while *AT* has been in print for ninety years, the work is often ignored, even in readings of Barth's theology of the resurrection.[3] When it happens to be examined, *AT* is often handled as merely a subsidiary text, emphasizing an interpretation of Barth that is guided by the theological results of the second edition of *Römerbrief* (*The Epistle to the Romans*). In most examinations, there has been little (if any) thought on the exegetical and theological substance of Barth's reading of 1 Corinthians.[4] Weight is instead placed on more formal topics, particularly the historicity of the resurrection of Jesus Christ. N.T. Wright, for instance, parodies Barth's position on the historical-critical approach to the resurrection: "Historical work is fine, necessary even, as long as it comes up with sceptical results, but dangerous and damaging . . . if it tries to do anything else."[5] Or, perhaps closer to the point, Gerald O'Collins

---

Theology of the Reformed Confessions, trans. Darrell L. Guder and Judith J. Guder (Louisville: Westminster John Knox, 2005).

3. See, e.g., David L. Mueller, *Foundation of Karl Barth's Doctrine of Reconciliation: Jesus Christ Crucified and Risen* (Lewiston, NY: Edwin Mellen, 1990), 74–116; Otto Merk, "Karl Barths Beitrag zur Erforschung des Neuen Testaments," in *Wissenschaftsgeschichte und Exegese. Gesammelte Aufsätze zum 65. Geburtstag*, BZNW 95 (Berlin: Walter de Gruyter, 1998), esp. 202–204; Richard E. Burnett, *Karl Barth's Theological Exegesis: The Hermeneutical Principles of the* Römerbrief *Period* (Grand Rapids: Eerdmans, 2004), 26; Paul D. Molnar, *Incarnation and Resurrection: Toward a Contemporary Understanding* (Grand Rapids: Eerdmans, 2007), 5–43.

4. Of course, the seminal exception is Rudolf Bultmann's "Karl Barth, 'Die Auferstehung der Toten'," in *Glauben und Verstehen* (Tübingen: Mohr Siebeck, 1961), 1:38–64 (originally in *ThBl* 5 [1926]: 1–14; ET, "Karl Barth, *The Resurrection of the Dead*," in *Faith and Understanding* (Philadelphia: Fortress Press, 1987), 66–94. Nevertheless, there have been recent studies with fruitful results, for instance, R. Dale Dawson, *The Resurrection in Karl Barth* (Aldershot, UK: Ashgate, 2007), 33–64; and Yo Fukushima, *Aus dem Tode das Leben. Eine Untersuchung zu Karl Barths Todes- und Lebensverständnis* (Zürich: TVZ, 2009), esp. §2.4.3.

5. N. T. Wright, *The Resurrection of the Son of God* (Minneapolis: Fortress Press, 2003), 5. Barth is here subsumed under Wright's interaction with the views of Peter Carnley regarding the historical-critical method. However, for Wright's part, Barth is doing in *AT* what is now

protests that Barth claims a "historical reality for the resurrection" and yet denies "historians the right to pronounce on the matter."[6]

If we are to shift this reading of *AT* onto a more effective route, then it must come about by the practice of a close, detailed analysis of Barth's work. Such a dutiful examination of the work must not merely seek to extract from the text a theory about Barth; rather, it must try to make sense of the particular intellectual task that Barth is undertaking. Only when this condition is met can we hope to address the questions raised in Barth's comments on 1 Corinthians 1–2. In seeking to fulfill the above condition, this essay will begin by offering (1) a brief overview of Barth's exegetical and interpretive practices in *AT*, before moving (2) to examine Barth's particular eschatological, ethical, and epistemological findings in the dialectical "wisdom" and "foolishness" section of chapters 1 and 2 of 1 Corinthians.

Exegetical and Interpretive Practices in *AT*

Few presentations of Barth's exegetical routine match its erudition, and most are vague in their description of how he approaches the biblical text. Barth's exegetical readings are often represented in an intangible manner: frequently in terms of a universalized "norm" of his exegesis, so that remarks about his use of biblical narrative, for instance, in the doctrine of the Word of God in the *Church Dogmatics*,[7] are thought to stretch across the various periods of Barth's work.[8] In order to understand Barth's exegesis, a rather more precise account is needed, one that is aware of how at any particular point

fashionable in NT studies. For more on the possible agreement between Wright and Barth regarding the resurrection, see Dawson, *Resurrection in Karl Barth*, 43.

6. Gerald O'Collins, "Karl Barth on Christ's Resurrection," *SJT* 26, no. 1 (1973): 90.

7. I am pleased to see several papers in this collection that have dedicated themselves to questions brought about in *Church Dogmatics*. See, e.g., contributions by Christophe Chalamet, Edwin Chr. van Driel, and Matthias Wüthrich.

8. Often, such critical generalizations come from a place where much of Barth's work has had positive theological impact, namely, evangelical positions. For multiple engagements with these

in his thinking Barth grasps the nature of the biblical texts. Before looking directly at *AT* itself, therefore, our primary question must be concerned with what type of text Barth considers himself to be exegeting.

Apostolicity and Historicity

As Barth lectured on the Reformed confessions alongside 1 Corinthians, he began to articulate an understanding of the Reformed *Schriftprinzip* ("scriptural principle") as a way of speaking about the authority of the divine act of self-revelation: theological discourse about Holy Scripture is an instance of theological discourse about divine revelation. As the word of God, Scripture is "the witness of the *revelation* of God, of the *new* relation with humans created by God, special, direct, unique, actual, overcoming the chasm of the fall."[9] And so the *Schriftprinzip*, which Barth had come to regard as an indispensable piece of the Reformed puzzle, is not chiefly an endorsement of the biblical text per se so much as a gesture toward the event of God's self-pronouncement. "God is not indirectly but directly known only through God himself," Barth relays. "The expression for that immediacy, for the absolute *facticity*, for the paradox of revelation, is the *Schriftprinzip* precisely *by virtue* of its offensiveness."[10]

While Barth does not supplement his discussion in *AT* with such dogmatic proclamations about the nature of Holy Scripture, his manner of reading the Pauline text nevertheless indicates that he

aversions, see *Karl Barth and Evangelical Theology: Convergences and Divergences*, ed. Sung Wook Chung (Grand Rapids: Baker Academic, 2008).

9. Barth, *Theologie der reformierten Bekenntnisschriften*, 75: "Das Wort Gottes ist ja das Zeugnis von der *Offenbarung* Gottes, von dem besonderen, direkten, einmaligen, aktuellen, die Kluft des Sündenfalls überwindenden, von Gott geschaffenen *neuen* Verhältnis von Gott und Mensch, nicht von der Unendlichkeitsbeziehung des menschlichen Bewußtseins, sondern von dem Endlichwerden der Gedanken Gottes, von Jesus Christus."

10. Ibid., 79.

believes 1 Corinthians to be an element in the divine economy and not merely a religious text that can be trivialized for the purposes of historical inquiry. Rather, Barth reads Paul's letter as being apostolic in nature, namely as a religious text that is grounded in the kerygmatic mission of its author and which is, moreover, the occurrence of present divine revelation.[11] The backcloth of the text is God's radiant presence, before which both Paul and the modern reader bow. This present revelatory power of the text does not imply, however, that what Barth is aiming at in *AT* can be condensed into a *"dialectical method of argument."* Such an abridgement makes the revelatory power of the text *hic et nunc* an instance of the modern reader's work rather than of God's majestic presence. It is more correct to say that Barth's exegesis assumes that the reading of *this* text is an occurrence which demands that the reader adopt a particular position before the matter as to whose radiant presence the text testifies—a *"dialectical method of witness."*[12] Barth clarifies this particular position of the reader in two ways.

First, a theological reading of the text must be aware of the rhetoric of the text. This rhetoric is not to be studied as a subordinate literary item of this text that is to be explained through historical scrutiny of Paul's surroundings, and then converted into something more conceptual. Rather, the task of the reader entails attending to the text's address. More precisely: "Paul is . . . showing how we necessarily have to think from the standpoint of Christ, by the revealed truth."[13] Theological reading is, according to Barth, not a transcendent event; it is an example of obedience to the duty of thinking "from the standpoint of Christ."

---

11. For this thought in connection with Barth's "Hermeneutik theologischer Exegese," particularly in the *Römerbrief* period, see Eberhard Jüngel's study "Die theologischen Anfänge. Beobachtungen," *Barth-Studien* (Zürich-Köln-Gütersloh: Benziger-Mohn, 1982), esp. 83–98.
12. Dawson, *Resurrection in Karl Barth*, 34 (emphasis original).
13. *AT*, 109–10; *RD*, 184.

Second, an honest reading of the text will be aware of the inadequacy of its interpretation of the material of the text, because the material of this text is an eschatological reality of God. The reader may not suppose to "finalize" an exposition of the text. Rather, the reader is to display, as John Calvin reminds us, that humble position of being *modestus ac docilis*,[14] which is a more fitting response to the text than historical-philological expertise.

From here, Barth's approach to historical-critical method comes to light, and there is considerable evidence in *AT* to agree with Bultmann that Barth's "commentary of 1 Cor. does not stand opposed to historical-philological interpretation, but uses it or supplements it."[15] Barth sees the text as arising from a specific series of historical circumstances, and proposes a reading of Paul's "ideas in general,"[16] and more specifically of such themes as the "*veiling of women*"[17] and "Charismen."[18] *AT* is a rather good sketch of what a year earlier, in his incomplete lectures on Calvin, Barth termed the "living relationship to the Bible," that is, the reality that "the Bible receives objective study" which readers are advised to commence.[19] The specific "living" freedom that is at work in *AT* is the freedom to make use of what Barth noticed in Calvin's exegesis, in which the *fructifera doctrina* was structured "straight *from* the *proprietas* of the words, and straight from the context of history."[20] Such a structuring—not only by Calvin, but by the modern reader—Barth regarded in his first

---

14. John Calvin, *Institutionis Christianae religionis*, 1559, 1.7.5, in *Joannis Calvini opera selecta*, ed. Peter Barth and Wilhelm Niesel, reprint (Eugene, OR: Wipf & Stock, 2010), 3:71 (hereafter *OS*).

15. Bultmann, "Karl Barth," in *Faith and Understanding*, 68.

16. See *AT*, 1f.

17. Ibid., 30–33.

18. Ibid., 40–44.

19. Karl Barth, *Die Theologie Calvins 1922*, ed. Hans Scholl (Zürich: TVZ, 1993), 525: "Das Verhältnis zur Bibel ist ein bewegtes Verhältnis. . . . Die Bibel bekommt gegenständliches Interesse."

20. Ibid., 526.

dogmatic lectures as "an act we have to carry out . . . if we are to have the knowledge of Scripture . . . [because] nobody can absolutely evade the act of historical inquiry."[21] Therefore, Barth has no desire in *AT* to label such inquiry unsuitable; he simply wants to be clear that historical examination cannot pretend to make the word of God veridical, as though the "speaking of God's Word in Scripture took place in the mere conception of such a historical picture per se."[22]

AT is, as Bultmann accurately stated, a claim that "the exegesis of 1 Cor. . . . must not remain stuck in the reconstruction of an interesting contemporary phenomenon."[23] Yet, at the same time, Bultmann worried that Barth gives historical inquiry the cold shoulder, and fails to offer in 1 Corinthians 1–2 "a more accurate exegesis that starts out from the determination of the contemporary setting of the text."[24] Bultmann's point is that Barth makes theological interpretation seemingly effortless, by determining the theological *Sache* ("the subject matter") of the text from its contingent historical form. Bultmann dealt with this problem by *Sachkritik*, mining a core theological element from the text and discarding the mythological tailings.[25] Barth, on the other hand, held to the notion that the *Sache* of the text is not one textual element among many, but an act of divine revelation, to which the text is a witness and which is present both to the text's initial context and to the modern theological reader. It is in this sense that for Barth the reading of the text is the reading of the *Sache*.[26]

---

21. Karl Barth, *"Unterricht in der christlichen Religion." Erster Band. Prolegomena 1924*, ed. Hannelotte Reiffen (Zürich: TVZ, 1985), 1:312–13. ET, *The Göttingen Dogmatics: Instruction in the Christian Religion*, trans. Geoffrey W. Bromiley (Grand Rapids: Eerdmans, 1991), 1:256.
22. Ibid., 1:313–14; ET, 1:257.
23. Bultmann, "Karl Barth," in *Glauben und Verstehen*, 52; ET, in *Faith and Understanding*, 81.
24. Ibid., 44; ET, in *Faith and Undertanding*, 72.
25. Cf. ibid.: "Und dazu gehört, daß ich meinesteils nicht auf die Sachkritik verzichten kann, die aus dem Texte selbst erwächst."
26. This is certainly the case in *AT*. However, Jüngel notes that some biblical books might not

Following Paul and *Cantus Firmus*

AT is to be seen at base as an effort to echo Paul's text, to allow the *Sache* of the text to arise. Barth does not want to guide the reader through the text's historical narrative. Rather, *AT* seeks to follow the outline of what Paul has already penned, in order to usher his readers to the object of Paul's testimony. Paul's letter is thus witness, exhibiting the gospel to its hearers, the Baptist's outstretched finger pointing to the Lamb of God. And if the task of the apostle is to bear witness, the task of the reader is to follow the apostolic witness. "Upon this everything depends," Barth states, "to *follow* the movement of [Paul's] thoughts from afar and to hear with more or less clarity the most vital things which he intended to say and nowhere can say."[27]

Barth seeks to maintain this "following" of Paul's text by a combination of summary and conceptual inquiry— something that Bultmann noticed when he spoke of Barth's "ingenious reinterpretations."[28] Hence, in his reading Barth goes to great lengths to remain in line with Paul; and several cases in his comments on 1 Corinthians 1–2 demonstrate this task.

First, we might look at his comments on 1 Cor. 1:25: "The *foolishness* of God—the only thing that we ourselves can grasp about God: that in him our thoughts are confounded and become foolishness (and not only because of our incapacity, but also through God's will and ordinance)—*that* is wiser than man, God's *weakness* (that unknown void into which God transfers us when the cross really becomes the criterion of knowledge of God), *that* is stronger than man."[29]

yield to such an interpretation and, thus, "Barth knows . . . something like a *Sachkritik* of . . . biblical writings" ("Die theologischen Anfänge," 89).

27. *AT*, 64.

28. Bultmann, "Karl Barth," in *Glauben und verstehen*, 1:57; ET, in *Faith and Understanding*, 86.

At first glance, what Barth is doing here seems to be merely a thin gloss on Paul's statements. That is, Barth's parenthetical asides, at least at first sight, appear to take the text where it does not aim to go. Certainly, the wording and concepts that Barth uses are not Paul's. The apostle's "For the foolishness of God is wiser than men" couches Barth's first aside, "in him our thoughts . . . become foolishness"; and Paul's "the weakness of God is stronger than men" becomes Barth's second, the "unknown void into which God transfers us when the cross really becomes the criterion of knowledge of God." But these parenthetical assertions are augmentations that intend to highlight the meaning and power of Paul's words. Likewise, the concepts that Barth uses in his parenthetical asides—that is, "void," "transfer," and the epistemological criterion of the cross—are not amendments of Paul's words, but ways of indicating the range of Paul's language. All this to say that it would be rather rash to assume from such statements that in *AT* Barth comes to the text armed with a conceptuality of his own design. Speaking in such terms suggests that in Barth's own hands the text becomes the occurrence for an exposition of his own ideas.

Second, in the midst of his comments throughout 1 Corinthians, Barth seeks to situate himself within his overall perception of the substance of the letter. That is, in his mind, 1 Corinthians contains topical agreement. This understanding is revealed throughout *AT*; but for our purposes, it is clearly posed as a question at the end of Barth's exposition of 1 Corinthians 1–2: "Are not position and counter-position in the dispute over the resurrection, which 1 Cor.

29. *AT*, 8: "Die *Torheit* Gottes—das Einzige, was wir von uns aus von Gott zu fassen bekommen: das an ihm unsere Gedanken zuschanden, zu Torheit werden (und das liegt nicht nur an unserem Unvermögen, sondern auch an Gottes Willen und Anordnung)—*das* ist weiser als die Menschen, Gottes *Schwachheit* (jene unheimliche Leere, in die uns Gott entrückt, wenn wirklich das Kreuz zum Kriterium der Gotteserkenntnis wird), *das* ist stärker als die Menschen." Barth, by using the verb *entrückt*, may also be playing on the Pauline ἁρπαγησόμεθα of 1 Thess. 4:17 (i.e., to be "caught up," "transferred," "translated," etc.).

15 will express, already visible here in outline?"[30] In the light of this "visible" unity, Barth can present the material in chapters 1–2 not simply as a "great conglomerate of exhortations, charges, and doctrinal teachings,"[31] but as an examination of the Corinthian congregation from the viewpoint of the decisive reality of the resurrection, "the single point" from which the letter proceeds and continually "harks back again."[32] This is why Barth can speak of the *cantus firmus* of chapters 1–2: as Paul treats the various problems to be found in Corinth, he is, in Barth's view, continually looking ahead to the melody of the fifteenth chapter, in which their resolution will be presented in a grand polyphonic composition.[33]

Thus, Barth presents chapters 1–2 as "really a whole," in that they treat what is in essence a specific problem to which a specific answer is found in chapter 15. The problem in chapters 1–2 is that the Corinthian church suffers from unbridled "religious vitality," resulting in the creation of "religious σχίσματα," which threatens to obscure the sovereignty of God's grace.[34] Barth paraphrases Paul's "remarkable harangue" against the Corinthians this way: "Come back to the cause, to *God's* cause now, to the origin of your Christianity, to your generation in Christ. . . . Come down from your wisdom, from your overindulgence, from your wealth, from the kingly consciousness . . . come down into the foolishness and shame of

---

30. *AT*, 11: "Sollten Position und Gegenposition im Streit um die Auferstehung, den 1 Kor. 15 bringen wird, nicht schon hier in den Umrissen sichtbar werden?"

31. Ibid., 1; cf. *RD*, 6.

32. *RD*, 107. That this thought was on Barth's mind early on is evident in a sermon from 1920. See Karl Barth, "*April (Ostern): 1. Korinther 15,50-58,*" in *Predigten 1920*, ed. Hermann Schmidt (Zürich: TVZ, 2005), 126–34.

33. Barth is emphatic in stating that one may be lost in the seeming "Dunkelheit" of Paul's topics if one does not stop and ask, "von was ist eigentlich die Rede?" in which "den cantus firmus zu hören." *AT*, 55.

34. *AT*, 3: "religiösen . . . σχίσματα." See Bultmann's criticism of Barth's interpretation of the Corinthian "party divisions," which he says Barth adds a "falsche Nuance" by his comparing these Corinthian "Partiewesen" to "modernen Persönlichkeitskult" ("Karl Barth," 40; ET, in *Faith and Understanding*, 68–69).

Christ, where the truth is, where no man, not even the Christian man, but God is great; there I, Paul, your father in Christ, am to be found."[35]

The tone of this passage provides Barth with an overall exegetical melody as he approaches the issues found in chapters 1–2. More specifically, factional disagreements in the church arise because the antagonists fail to comprehend that the testimony of Christ should not be made "an object of religious power and feats" but, rather, "simply the relationship of wisdom to μωρία, foolishness to σοφία. It is the Σοφία of *God*, rather than the wisdom of any man."[36]

"Wisdom" and "Foolishness"

As we come to where Barth reviews the topics of "wisdom" and "foolishness," it is important to note that he sees part of his interpretive duty as trying to hear the *cantus firmus*. The conceptual apparatus for highlighting this unity is constant reference to the expression ἀπὸ τοῦ θεοῦ, *von Gott*, which he declares in a comment on chapters 1–2 "is obviously the secret nerve of this entire . . . section."[37] This *von Gott* encapsulates the critical matter of which the letter speaks, namely the conflict between "the swollen self-consciousness and power of *homo religiosus*," on the one hand, and the gospel reality that is "under the sun of Christian grace," on the other.[38]

Within what Bultmann deems "an excellent exegetical

---

35. Ibid., 6: "Umkehr zur Sache, aber zur Sache *Gottes* jetzt, zu dem Ursprung ihrer Christlichkeit, zu ihrer Erzeugung *in Christus* . . . Steigt herunter von der Weisheit, der Sattheit, dem Reichtum, dem königlichen Bewußtsein, das euch als Christen jetzt erfüllt . . . herunter in die Torheit und Schande Christi, wo die Wahrheit ist, wo nicht der Mensch, auch nicht der christliche Mensch, sondern Gott groß ist, dort bin ich, Paulus, euer Vater in Christus zu finden."

36. Ibid.; cf. *RD*, 19–20.

37. Ibid., 4; cf. *RD*, 16.

38. Ibid., 5.

overview,"[39] Barth turns to engage Paul's exposition of the gospel's antithesis to the Corinthian desertion of ἀπὸ τοῦ θεοῦ. The outline of Barth's reading of Paul's division of wisdom and foolishness can be shown rather succinctly. "Paul speaks in [chs. 1–2] that the word of the cross is to be made against the religious vitality of the Corinthians in its ruthless negativity as the indissoluble paradox," Barth says, "as the angel with the flaming sword in front of the sealed gates of paradise."[40] Because of its assertive religious vitality, the Corinthian congregation lacked a sufficient "knowledge of God" and a sufficient eschatology. This dearth spawned a damaging misperception of the situation of the believers, by failing to see Christian faith, practice, and knowledge in the light of their position before God, that is, one of dependence on what Paul calls the λόγος τοῦ σταυροῦ: that power and wisdom of God against "ruthless negativity." On Barth's reading, therefore, Paul's notion of the "word of the cross" is not simply the conceptually clumsy *entweder-oder*, but the very heart of the testimony ἀπὸ τοῦ θεοῦ, namely, "salvation . . . that can only come to us from God, and ever and always from God alone."[41] And this word of the cross is "foolishness, only foolishness to the lost,"[42] because it is God's good pleasure to save those who believe through the μωρία τοῦ κηρύγματος, "which to non-believers can only appear absurd."[43] Thus, through preaching "Christ crucified," some will come to believe, which means that some will, in Barth's dialectical tone, "believe this absurdity [*Verkehrtheit*]" of the cross: *die*

---

39. Bultmann, "Karl Barth," 40: ". . . enthält einen ausgezeichneten exegetischen Überblick"; ET, in *Faith and Understanding*, 68.

40. *AT*, 7: "Paulus redet in diesem Abschnitt. . . . Das Wort vom Kreuz soll hier der religiösen Vitalität der Korinther gegenüber geltend gemacht werden in seiner erbarmungslosen Negativität als das unauflösbare Paradoxon, als der Engel mit dem blitzenden Schwert vor der Pforte des *verschlossenen* Paradieses."

41. Ibid.

42. *RD*, 21.

43. *AT*, 8.

Weisheit in Gottes Torheit, the wisdom within the seeming absurdity and foolishness of the word of the cross.[44]

Eschatology, Epistemology, and Ethics

There is, of course, a great deal more happening in this section comprising chapters 1–2 in *AT*: an attempt to make sense of Paul's use of σοφίας juxtaposed to ἀποδείξει πνεύματος in 2:4;[45] an exposition of the "wisdom of the mature" of 2:6;[46] and the fascinating dialectical oscillation in Barth's treatment of the μωρία τοῦ κηρύγματος in 1:21. Any of these routes would make interesting inroads toward the conclusion of this essay; however, encompassing Barth's succinct yet complex presentation is an amalgamated theme that might easily be overlooked, but which is of no little importance for understanding *AT*, namely the themes of eschatology, epistemology, and ethics.

Bultmann implied that Barth's readings of "wisdom," "knowledge," and "ethics" throughout his exposition of chapters 1–2 should "be made conceptually more explicit."[47] Of course, for Bultmann this meant that Barth was not explicit enough in his exegetical approach to the text, especially in his "untenable" use of the noun σοφία of chapter 1 to interpret the σοφία of chapter 2.[48] Yet, if Bultmann's criticism is that Barth is irritatingly unclear about the philological connectors of "wisdom," "knowledge," and "ethics" between chapters 1 and 2, then one might note that his restraint mirrors the text he is reading. Then again, if the accusation is that Barth overemphasizes

---

44. Ibid.
45. Cf. ibid., 9.
46. Cf. ibid. (i.e., Σοφίαν ἐν τοῖς τελείοις).
47. Bultmann, "Karl Barth," 44; ET, in *Faith and Understanding*, 73. Bultmann praises Barth's exegesis on other occasions, saying in many places "daß B[arth] recht hat"—particularly when it comes to Barth's insistence that Paul's view is "eschatological" throughout 1 Corinthians" (cf. ibid., 42; ET, 70).
48. Cf. ibid., 42–44; ET, 70–72.

God as the subject of knowledge so that human knowers subsequently fade from view, then a more basic misreading of these sections in *AT* looms. On Barth's interpretation of Paul, it is precisely because "God himself is the subject of the knowledge of God" that the telos of humankind, as well as the anticipation of that telos in present action, is ingredient within the "capacity" to understand that "Christianity is particularly concerned about Christian knowledge; not about this and that, not about things, though they may be the last things, but about the Either-Or, the understanding or the failure to understand the three words ἀπὸ τοῦ θεοῦ."[49]

That is, Barth rejects the thought that natural knowledge is a way to God over and over again by the ἀπὸ τοῦ θεοῦ to ensure that no relation to God is given in knowledge as a human *qualitas*. Yet the grand truth of ἀπὸ τοῦ θεοῦ, *von Gott her*, does not annihilate human actuality but "reschematizes" it in light of this "Either-Or." This "reschematization" is regeneration, the obliteration of anarchic human understanding and its replacement by the "fullness of revelation" in the crucified Christ. And the actuality that replaces the old life is, indeed, wholly regenerative, because it is a creaturely repetition of ἀπὸ τοῦ θεοῦ given by the Holy Spirit. "As those who had received the *Spirit* of *God*," Barth comments on 2:10-11, "we know what is sent us from God in Christ the crucified. . . . The prerequisite of all speaking and listening in the Christian community is the πνεῦμα, the divine Holy Spirit, which opens here the mouth, there the ears."[50]

Identifying these passages outside the context of *AT* is to miss the positive ontological strength of Barth's thoughts on epistemology, ethics, and eschatology. The all-determining actuality of the crucified *and* resurrected Jesus Christ is rich in "reschematizing" power; and, in

---

49. *AT*, 10–11.
50. Ibid., 10.

light of this power, the human condition has undergone a complete, gracious change and illumination. After Good Friday and Easter Day, and in prospect of the παρουσία, that which we are not (both wise and risen) can be said to correspond to that which we are, namely, the *foolish* ones believing the wisdom and power of God. This creaturely repetition, though it is imperceptible, is central to our moral and noetic situation, that is, to the kinds of agents we are and the kinds of circumstances in which we are called upon to know and act. This is the dual "promise under which the church is placed," says Barth, to both "keep the feast . . . of the slain lamb" and to "awake [for] Easter Day is here."[51] Thus Barth can note, "chapters [1–2] are *also* to be understood in an ethical sense . . . [and] *also* [negatively as] a lack of knowledge."[52]

But in what sense is this eschatological position a moral and epistemological position? Barth's mind is distant from the visionary exhibition of such topics in the final, fragmentary paragraphs of the doctrine of reconciliation in the *Church Dogmatics*.[53] However, in his exegesis of 2:6–7 ("Yet among the mature we do impart wisdom. . . . But we impart a secret and hidden wisdom of God"), Barth resists making Paul's statement a mere moral- or epistemic-based command, and prefers to note—perhaps with Calvin's *modulo nostro attemperat* in mind[54]—that humanity "does not attain to this wisdom through the

---

51. Ibid., 12. Cf. 1 Cor. 5:8.
52. Ibid., 11.
53. See, e.g., Karl Barth, *CD* IV/4, trans. G. W. Bromiley and T. F. Torrance (London: T&T Clark, 2010), 2 (§75, Leitsatz): "A man's turning to faithfulness to God, and consequently to calling upon Him, is the work of this faithful God which, perfectly accomplished in the history of Jesus Christ, in virtue of the awakening, quickening and illuminating power of this history, becomes a new beginning of life as his baptism with the Holy Spirit" (2). My thanks are due to several comments by Christophe Chalamet regarding the possible differences between Barth's points here and his earlier exposition in *AT*. I direct the reader to Chalamet's chapter in this collection.
54. John Calvin, *Commentarius in epistolam Pauli ad Corinthios I*, in *Ioannis Calvini opera quae supersunt Omnia*, ed. J.-W. Baum, É. Cunitz and E. W. E. Ruess (Brunswick: C. A. Schwetschke, 1892), 48:337: ". . . se enim modulo nostro attemperat, quum nobis loquitur."

pursuit of some esoteric knowledge and the like." In place of this, Barth again regards the believer's moral and noetic situation as one balanced on the "scales of the cross," with both human death and the death of Christ, on the one hand, and, on the other, life eternal that God alone fully grants by "his revelation in the resurrection" and the giving of the Holy Spirit "from God in Christ the crucified."[55]

We might perhaps say that what Barth is moving toward is a notion of the human moral and noetic situation as being poised on the "scales of the cross," as somehow balancing between an event of transition into the new reality indicated both by the foolishness of Good Friday in chapters 1–2 and by the wisdom of Easter Day in chapter 15. Jesus' death and resurrection, we might say with Barth, thus creates a particular kind of human history, not as the depiction of an unwavering identity, but as the "life that we are not living and yet that is our life." Indeed, one way of understanding what Barth has found in Paul's *cantus firmus* is an application of apostolic moral and epistemological teaching—not in the sense of a virtue ethic or virtue epistemology, but of an attempt to highlight the importance of the eschatological condition of the church for such issues as life in fellowship, integrity in knowledge, and godly conduct; and, moreover, to keep the congregation from transforming the "σοφία ἀπὸ θεοῦ, which was offered unto them, the wisdom of God, into *human* wisdom."[56]

Conclusion

A portion of what Barth tries to show in the sections detailing 1 Corinthians 1–2 in *AT* is a view of the moral and noetic situation of the church balanced on the "scales of the cross of Christ"; between

---

55. Cf. *AT* 7, 10.

56. Ibid., 10: "Ihr Unvermögen . . . verwandelte die ihnen gebotene σοφία ἀπὸ θεοῦ, in Menschenweisheit."

the wisdom of God and the seeming foolishness of believing the "word of the cross"; between the reality of death and the life to come. The *Inschrift* of *AT* contains a relevant quotation from Calvin: "Although, therefore, Christ offers us in the gospel a present fullness of spiritual benefits, the enjoyment thereof ever lies hidden under the guardianship of hope, until having put off corruptible flesh, we be transfigured in the glory of him who has gone before us. Meanwhile, the Holy Spirit bids us rely on the promises. . . . We enjoy Christ only as we embrace Christ clad in his own promises."[57] Calvin's emphasis on the mysterious, promissory character of revelation in light of the *eschaton* pinpoints exactly what Barth finds in Paul, even here in chapters 1–2.

Yet what restrains Barth from conducting a more immediate discussion of eschatology, ethics, and epistemology per se in these initial pages of *AT* is probably the fact that he limits himself to the current exegetical task. In several lectures from his series on the *reformierten Bekenntnisschriften*, Barth hints at his increasing appreciation of early Reformed theology: "The early Reformed . . . shared the very unsentimental scholastic view that virtue, or in this case, religion, Christianity, was *teachable*. [That is,] what we can know on the basis of revelation, Christianity, the refraction of the divine light in the prism of human consciousness, which is not itself the light but can perhaps bear witness to that light."[58] That is, provided that the "human consciousness" remains a "refraction of

---

57. John Calvin, *Inst.* 2.9.3 (*OS* 3:400–401): "Quanvis ergo praesentem spiritualium bonorum plenitudinem nobis in Evangelio Christus offerat, fruitio tamen sub custodia spei semper latet, donec corruptibili carne exuti, transfiguremur in eius qui nos praecedit gloriam. Interea in promissiones recumbere nos iubet Spiritus sanctus. . . . Nec vero aliter Christo fruimur, nisi quatenus eum amplectimur promissionibus suis vestitum."

58. "Sie teilten die sehr unsentimentale scholastische Ansicht, daß die Tugend oder in diesem Fall die Religion, das Christentum *lehrbar* sei . . . das, was wir auf Grund der Offenbarung wissen können, das Christentum, die Brechung des göttlichen Lichtes im Prisma des menschlichen Bewußtseins, die dann nicht das Licht ist, aber vielleicht zeugen kann von dem Licht." Barth, *Theologie der reformierten Bekenntnisschriften*, 130; *Theology of the Reformed Confessions*, 82.

the divine light" and "not itself the light"—so long as the distance between the wisdom in God's foolishness and the wisdom of the age are not collapsed—then the Reformed tradition has the freedom to "reason, moralize, and historicize."[59] And this is the case when the Reformed tradition takes its guidance from the catechetic Calvin, for whom "life . . . is about *questions* [that] are raised," in which the "*answer* for human *knowing*" is found only in "*one* kind of knowledge," namely, "that we may *know* the *majesty* of our Creator."[60]

In light of this, *AT* is an example of this in action, where Barth interprets Paul's notion of "wisdom" and "foolishness" as precisely the way in which those questions about the moral-epistemic task are raised and, indeed, answered in the "one kind of knowledge": knowing the majesty of the crucified Christ. That the *loci* raised by the notions of "wisdom" and "foolishness" in chapters 1–2—namely, knowledge, morality, and eschatology—could provoke unique insights is something that captivated Barth as he contemplated Paul's First Letter to the Corinthians.

---

59. Ibid.; ET, 83.
60. Ibid., 131–33; ET, 93–94, 97.

10

The Word of the Cross in the Conflict of Interpretive Power: On the Genealogy of Theology Deriving from the Spirit of Pauline Rhetoric

Philipp Stoellger

To begin: whenever "Paul" is mentioned hereafter, a distinction is being made between the *historical* Paul, who can be reconstructed by historians, the *biblical* Paul of the canonical texts of the New Testament, and the *imaginary* Paul, who is being constituted in interpretations as well as in religious and institutional use, as the saint, cult figure, official and theological *norma normans*. Therefore, the differentiation of Paul is threefold, and it is impossible to ascribe a unity of being to these three figures. What follows is thus *not* concerned with the presentation of results derived from the textual sources, but merely with systematic questions and their discussion—in particular with the problematization of the imaginary Paul's momentum in his interpretive power (*Deutungsmacht*) and his potential impact.

Faith in the Word's Power of Interpretation

One of the most astonishing common ways of thinking is to believe that the mere naked word possesses power and efficacy—theologically speaking, to argue, believe, hope, and love "*solo verbo*." That is the case, first and foremost, of the Word of God, derived from Christ as *the* Word incarnate, but it is also true of the word of the cross as a basic formulation of Pauline theology—and so on. For the genealogy of theology it simply means: In the beginning was the word—namely in every moment of the beginning, when someone begins to speak, opens his mouth, and dares to say something. The long chain of the *logos* runs from the beginning of the world via incarnation, cross, and resurrection past Pentecost up to the "*hic et nunc.*" This (apparently) uninterrupted continuity of "the" *logos* serves as genealogy of interpretive power, which lays claim to a word "in the name of God." Whoever dares to speak truly, worthily, and fittingly in the name of God places oneself in this continuity, claims it as an authorization in order to say something, to let it be heard and seen in the manner it is said. But *who* is then speaking is far from obvious. Ultimately, the one who should be speaking is the one who is brought to speech; but this one can only speak through the voice of others, the voice that is being lent to the one who dares to speak in his name. Without such a seemingly absurd audaciousness there would be no *verbum praesens*.

Christianity, therefore, is not a scripture- or book-religion but a *word*-religion that trusts in and relies on the interpretive power of the "*viva vox.*" Thus, the rule "*sine vi humana, sed verbo,*" or more precisely, in English, "not by *human* force, but *only* by the Word of *God*" (*Augsburg Confession*, art. 28), applies to the Christian proclamation. Within Protestantism this has become the normative creedal statement and theologically a critical principle: to rely, without any force or power, on the Word, in faith, love, and hope that it will be efficient *ubi et quando visum est Deo*, "where and when it pleases God." The ecclesiastical as well as the theological renunciation of force is based on the belief in the power of the word (*Wortmacht*).

Christianity, therefore, is the rhetorical religion *par excellence*, insofar as it puts its trust in the word alone—and thus not "only" in Christ alone but in every word that someone dares to speak in his name. It can only depend on the word's interpretive power.[1] Therefore, it should not be overlooked that from Scripture through confession (*Bekenntnis*) to proclamation and sacrament, the power of the word (*Wortmacht*), the interpretive power of the word, meaning this *medium*, is relied upon without ceasing. What this means, and how it is to be understood, remains to be seen—despite any hermeneutics of suspicion targeting rhetoric or religion. In order to clarify that, a hermeneutic of rhetoric—here, more precisely, of Pauline rhetoric—is needed. *In the beginning was the word, and the word became flesh and became word of the cross and proclamation and theology—in sum: rhetoric.* What else does it become? Theology, including Paul's theology, forms itself from the start using the wisdom of the world; more precisely, using the word-wisdom (*Wortweisheit*) called rhetoric. The same is true of Jesus' words, as the parables indicate. But Jesus as rhetorician would be a different topic.

---

1. Images and visual aspects would deserve to be studied as well.

"Interpretive Power": Towards a Definition

Faith in the word relies on its *interpretive power*. That is my opening thesis. A clarification, even a provisional one, of what I mean by "interpretive power" or "power of interpretation" (*Deutungsmacht*) is in order. As a first approximation, I will say this: interpretive power means letting something be seen through speaking and showing, letting it be seen in *such* a way that the addressees see it in the same way as it was said and shown. It ultimately aims to *make* them see so that they, too, may act, feel, think, and live accordingly. The unfathomable question is then: Can interpretive power go as far as enabling belief or even producing faith?

In a second step, let me express things differently, moving toward a definition: interpretive power is, on a *personal* level, the *capacity* to interpret and, in addition, to wield power through interpretation; at a *nonpersonal* level, it is the power or the possibility to interpret or to gain power through interpretation, furthermore it is, *medially*, the *possibility* and the *potential efficacy* of an interpretation and, *structurally* (or modally), the power to *enact or realize an interpretation* (or the power to negate it, in analogy with the concept of power). From the standpoint of the originator of the interpretation, it embraces everything from the power to present all the way to getting the point across. From the standpoint of the addressee, it is the power to recognize (interpretive power is here understood using the *genetivus obiectivus*). The power *to* interpret does not clarify how an interpretation can *itself* become powerful (going *against* already recognized ones). And so this needs to be added: interpretive power is also the power of an interpretation in the *genetivus subiectivus*—it may depend on the addressee's attention or recognition, on the media and technologies (speech, picture), or on how convincing arguments are. The power to interpret usually depends on a recognized institution or order (i.e., a church, science, a constitutional court). But an interpretation can also, exceptionally, have extraordinary effects that go against recognized institutions, disturbing, expanding, reforming, or revolutionizing them (to the point of a genesis of a new order: e.g., the New Testament, the Reformation).

Interpretive power, specifically, has the capacity to enable and realize (or to negate) through interpretation, not through enforcement, domination, and force. Interpretation may at times occur using enforcement, violence, and for the sake of domination, of course, and it may render necessary the *critique* of interpretive power. Furthermore, we may note that interpretive power may also have weakening effects; it may open things up or seem powerless, which may call for support, encouragement, and promotion of interpretive power. Because of that intrinsic ambiguity, a decision can only take place in specific social, cultural, historical, and other similar situations.

Faith in the word trusts in its *interpretive power*, that is, faith relies on the coherence of the chain of logos—beginning with God via Christ in the Spirit on to Paul, Luther, and in all eternity. Certainly, not everybody bets on this, but all those who work with and subsist on words do. Even God did not wish, or was not able, to act in any other way than to create the world through God's Word, to reveal God's will in the words of the law, to let God's Word become flesh and to let us be justified "*solo verbo*," by the word alone.

Thereby enters the *power* of the word, which hermeneutically is usually kept latent—its interpretive power is where interpretation and power intersect. In this light, the conflict in Corinth appears as a conflict over interpretive power (*Deutungsmachtkonflikt*). This places a heavy burden on hermeneutics: the chiasm between the power of the word (*Macht des Wortes*) and the word of power (*Wort der Macht*) needs to be addressed, as does the power of semantics and the semantics of power. Like power, God is not readily, immediately accessible, otherwise God would be unable to act, speechless, or ineffective. Therefore, neither God nor cross nor Paul can relinquish the word—with the consequence that they each have to rely on the power of the word. But does this mean that whoever has the word has the power (and vice versa)?

The Source of the Word's Power

That raises a curious question: Who or *what empowers "the word,"* originally the Word of God? The classical answer, following the logic of the origin, is: it is empowered by its originator, God, thus also, eventually, by the king, the pope, the president, and the preacher. The wager on the word is then: *the word became spirit, and the charisma became ministry.* "Strictly speaking," it should be always the origin or originator whose power becomes effective in the word, as long as the continuity of this chain is not being disrupted, be it Roman in the form of the ministry, or Protestant in the form of doctrine. But such a chain of interpretive legitimation (*Deutungsermächtigung*) does not provide lasting reassurance. It presumes that everything is in order and that whoever adheres to this order will be all right. Whoever speaks *rite ordinatus,* ordained ritually, must speak rightly and truthfully. Here there can be no simple talk of the origin, since there is a derivation and dissipation of power coming out of the *order* or *institution.* This is so prevalent and powerful, even as a dissipation and derivation. As the questions become more specific, the power of the word (as well as of the other media) becomes more noticeable. It should be unsettling that in the power of the word that has been given by God (or, as the case may be, that has been attributed to God), the power that is *intrinsic* to the word as well as to language is always simultaneously at work.

It is by no means certain that "God" and "word" always work together peacefully, as the usage of the "Word of God" shows. Part of the intrinsic dynamic of the medium "word" has to do with its *how*, considering how "available" it is (in rhetoric, performance, staging) and how unavailable it also is (contingency, interpretation by others, other interpretations). Thus the "Word of God," to which some refer as a charismatic, "powerful word" (*Wortmacht*), is understood by others only as a spiritless "word of power" (*Machtwort*) that must be criticized accordingly.

The Inescapability of Rhetoric

Nevertheless, in a conflict, and in a conflict over *interpretive power*, referring to the long chain of *logos* going from God to the current word is of little help because *everyone* can refer to it, for good or for ill. Therefore, all that remains is to trust in the power of the word (*Wortmacht*), instead of claiming a divine word of power (*Machtwort*). Whoever expects "signs and wonders" will be disappointed and will find *sola verba*, only words. But the *power* of the word is mostly preserved in a latent way from too many inquiries. For whoever is asking questions here raises questions about the crucial basic trust of faith, that is, about the Word of God *as word*. A hermeneutics of rhetoric therefore cannot allow the *rhetorical* form of the power of the word (*Wortmacht*) to remain latent; it needs to make manifest and explicit what is supposed to remain hidden. The medium known as rhetoric has to make its own mediality invisible in order not to crash. Here hermeneutics becomes critical: it allows something, which otherwise would be stable, to become unstable.

This should not to be confused with a hermeneutic of suspicion, as if rhetoric were an indecent matter *per se* and whoever talks of Paul's rhetoric would declare the apostle to be a sophistic libertine.

Such fallacies have been spread by the Enlightenment as well as by dialectical theology—and, surprisingly, in their suspicion toward rhetoric, cultural-protestants as well as dialectical theologians and certain Lutherans are strikingly similar. Whoever distances oneself (using rhetoric) from rhetoric can confidently place it under a general suspicion. However, such misconceptions are not shared anymore among exegetes, church historians, practical theologians, or people interested in religious pedagogy. And yet systematic theologians often continue to hold on to it. One reason for this could be the presupposition that whoever speaks of rhetoric loses sight of the truth-question, as if one were bound to follow a (half-understood) Nietzsche and let sophism triumph in the end, perhaps even in its revenant form of deconstruction. *Res, non verba!*, "the thing itself, not words!," is the battle cry, the "power of truth" or "of love" is the other, instead of mere power of word (*Wortmacht*), which smacks of rhetoric. The simple answer to this would be: *rhetoric shows what is the matter* ("*was Sache ist, zeigt die Rhetorik*"). Therefore, it is unavoidable to rely on the power of words—theologically, this is perfectly legitimate if the *word of the cross* is being discussed.

Eberhard Jüngel writes: "The merciful God who justifies godless man is a *speaking God.*"[2] The background metaphor of this thesis (a thesis related to creation as well as soteriology) is thus as discreet as it is sure to be heard: God as rhetor—just as in the forensic word of justification the sinner is declared righteous. Jüngel's way of grounding this thesis (a thesis that is anything but self-evident) and that theological *hyperbolè* is remarkably profane: "Speech is the original unity of sensation and spirit."[3] Does this mean God is a

---

2. Eberhard Jüngel, *Das Evangelium von der Rechtfertigung des Gottlosen als Zentrum des christlichen Glaubens* (Tübingen: Mohr, 1999), 169; ET, *Justification: The Heart of the Christian Faith*, trans. Jeffrey Cayzer (Edinburgh: T&T Clark, 2001).
3. Ibid., 173.

rhetor because God's spirit cannot be without the body of the Word? Or that, were there no spirit, God would be without senses? Is the power of God originally the power of the sense-related Word? Did God become Word because, without it, God could not be God? Did God become Word because God had to be such in order to be discerned, effective, and powerful among us? Would a wordless God not be God—and would a godless word not be word? God and word become disturbingly indistinguishable.

The Powerlessness of the Cross and the Power of the "Word of the Cross"

In any case, what sort of power is at work here becomes ambiguous and is in need of clarification. The first answer was: interpretive power, and so a chiasm between power and semantics as well as between word and power. But *whose* interpretive power is at work here? The power of the "word alone," meaning the power of this medium? If this is already problematic with regard to God and the word—that is, knowing whether that power is possibly derived, a loan from the power of the word—then it is no less important to ask the same question about the relationship between the cross and the word. If the cross was the climax of powerlessness, it became powerful in the *word* of the cross, so that in the judgment (the justification judgment) it would become powerfully effective. Is thus the apostolic word of the cross a word of power, an overpowering of the powerless cross, or is it the empowerment, authorized "by God himself," of the cross as event of salvation? If this were the case, would the word of the cross not be contradicting the event of revelation in powerlessness? Is what became apparent *sub contrario*, in all powerlessness, to be attested *sub contradictione*, with all the power of the apostolic word of power? Or is any competing between powerlessness and power sublimated in the medium of the word's interpretive power?

This should be the crucial hope, namely, that in the word of the cross the claim to power vanishes for the sake of the crucified one. But whoever says "word" is already entangled in the agon of the powers. The conflict in Corinth is the paradigmatic manifestation of that fact. To envision power as the medium of the "princes" and powers of this world would be an unfortunate simplification. The question is more complex: How is, and which, power is used by whom, and for what purpose—and who, by following them and their pretension, empowers those claiming power? Put simply: whether the word of the cross occurs as word of power or just as the power of word that is genuinely open to being contradicted, remains exposed to the objection: *Ecce verbum*, "here is the word." Whoever seeks, using words of power, to eliminate the possibility of contradiction and the semantic fragility misses the main point.

In Paul's conflict with his opponents it becomes clear how not only God and the crucified one, but also theology, lives from the power of the word—with a latent deeper meaning where it leans on the power of God's Word, if not more. And that can lead to deceit. As Gerhard Ebeling put it: "Talking about God, something from which a particular measure of power should be expected due to the object one is talking about, is on the one hand uncommonly susceptible of distorsion, which can be endowed with the fascination for domination, or on the other hand with a defencelessness and weakness in which the specific power of speaking about God is hidden. How difficult it is, however, to trust in this hidden power!"[4] With that the problem concerning what renders a religious or theological interpretation "in the name of God" powerful is by no

4. Gerhard Ebeling, *Dogmatik des christlichen Glaubens* (Tübingen: Mohr, 1987), 1:163.

means resolved, but it has been discerned and named (without being subsequently banned). The contours of an aspect that belongs to Christology appear: since the Pauline rhetoric, "defenselessness and weakness" are a special form of religious as well as theological speech that *can* be accompanied by an immediate accreditation *sub contrario*.

The Temptation of Claiming Divine Validity for One's Word

The model of a rhetorical *mimesis* or *imitatio Christi* has been defining for the Christian rhetoric, albeit in an ambivalent way and thus never without *sic et non*. The authorization of preferably "simple" speech operates with the criterion of the conformity with its "object," which in accordance with its lowliness is represented as "poor," and only thus is it actually adequate. From there lies, concealed under the guise of *humilitas*, a claim to interpretive power on the basis of the proposition that (only) this form conforms to the content, so that the subject is really present (in the Spirit) in the speech. The tradition of contempt for rhetoric manifests itself in a rhetoric of obedience in which the will to power manifests itself in powerlessness. One's own claim to interpretive power is being delegated ("*propter Christum*") and at the same time derives from the (self-made) delegation. That is a precarious ambivalence. We find it in Luther's theology as well as in the Word-of-God theology. Even Ebeling's invitation to "trust in this hidden power," meaning Christ's power under its opposite (*sub contrario*), that is, the cross, appears to be pointing in this direction: that with this the always–still–greater power of God remains involved in the interpretive game.

The more difficult task would be *not* to trust in this power, so as to not claim it for one's own speech—be it ever so indirectly. For it is necessary to resist the theological temptation to present one's own interpretation as that of God or as "authorized by God." For that would mean gaining theological capital out of what has been and is strictly withheld from theology. No validity can be derived from God. It can only be claimed for oneself, without proxy and argumentatively. In questions of validity each one is responsible for oneself.[5] Not even a God can help here.

Talking about Powerlessness While Claiming Power

Ebeling continues: "That way the focus is put on the shocking discrepancy between the claim and the success of the speaking about God."[6] This discrepancy is part of the fundamental experiences of religious and theological discourse: talking about the power of the word, about God's Word as word of the cross, and yet remaining largely powerless—and at the same time in the midst of conflict claiming all the more power, as Paul did facing his Corinthian adversaries in the conflict over interpretive power. This leads to a *rhetorical split*: however great the powerlessness, one makes an even greater claim to power. This split becomes even wider as, for theology, the almighty God's real presence is intended or implied. Against this we need a reticence or reserve with regard to interpretive power and a *capacity to differentiate*, which does *not* "entrust" itself to God's power, claiming the power of the one to whom one is entrusting oneself, but which sees and exposes oneself as responsible for one's own interpretation. The Corinthian conflict over

---

5. "The summons of death comes to us all, and no one can die for another. Everyone must fight his own battle with death by himself, alone. We can shout into another's ears, but everyone must himself be prepared for the time of death, for I will not be with you then, nor you with me." Martin Luther, "Eight Sermons at Wittenberg (1522)," in *Sermons I*, ed. John Doberstein and Helmut T. Lehman, *Luther's Works*, vol. 51 (Philadelphia: Fortress Press, 1959), 70; WA 10,3;1,7-2,2 (1522) and Gerhard Ebeling, *Lutherstudien* (Tübingen: Mohr, 1989), II/3:463.

6. Gerhard Ebeling, *Dogmatik des christlichen Glaubens*, 163.

interpretive power shows how difficult it is to do that during a conflict.

The Conflict of Interpretive Power in Corinth

First Corinthians is the document of a conflict of interpretation that developed into a conflict of interpretive *power*. The dimension of power in this conflict is not to be grasped merely semantically, particularly at a theological-semantic level, for the social groups involved and certain individuals also had an impact on it. But since, with regard to the subject matter, it is "only" the conflict of power that is thematized, the focus remains directed toward it. *What* is being argued about is in turn a question that has to do with conflicts of interpretive power in the exegetical debate.[7] Apart from the older theories concerning a supposed Antinomianism, Judaism, Gnosis, or *Proto-Gnosis* on the various topics at hand (Lord's Supper, resurrection, ethics, etc.), the reasons for the theological divergences remain debatable. Here I assume it was a matter of:

- *wisdom*, which is evidently contested between Paul and his "opponents," that is, its interpretation and relevance, and, connected to that, pneumatology;

- *eschatology*, as far as there is an indication in 1 Cor. 4:8, that the opponents are concerned with a realized eschatology, which Paul is criticizing;

- *Christology and soteriology*, insofar as the interpretation of the resurrection (Christ and "all") is being debated;

- the *relation* between the cross and the resurrection points to the

---

7. Cf. on this Wolfgang Schrage, *Der erste Brief an die Korinther*, EKK VII/1 (Zürich: Benzinger-Neukirchener, 1992), 1:38–63.

quaestio; this relation was severed in the reception history (*Wirkungsgeschichte*).

What became important in the history of interpretation was whether the cross or the resurrection was the true salvific event, and, concomitantly, whether faith is faith in the crucified one or in the risen one. This makes sense, since it is obviously "the word of the cross" that was being debated, and so the interpretation of the crucified one and the claims to interpretive power by various interpretations. We see that again in the later questions about theology: whether it is *theologia crucis* or *theologia gloriae*. Thus becomes patent what was already contentious between Paul and his opponents: the controversy over the interpretive power of the Word or, more precisely, the apostolate as authorization, or, rather, as ground for the legitimation, of Pauline theology.

The claim to interpretive power, in Paul's argument, seeks to assert the "word of the cross" *as foolishness in the medium of wisdom* or, to put it differently, to express it *in* rhetoric *against* rhetoric. Paul's problem was already known since Plato: to engage the sophists sophistically in order to win the contest and be the better sophist—in the name of truth and wisdom. It is thus a matter of *interpretation,* not "merely" of exegesis (of Scripture) or of (methodical) interpretation; it is a matter of the prescientific, concrete, basically *sapiential* way of seeing and speaking "*quod res est*" – that is how the crucified one is painted before people's eyes so that people see him as shown and believe as indicated. Here we see the limit, for is it the case that the apostolic speech can lead to faith and make its listeners believe?

We may speak here of "interpretation" (*Deutung*), because in the conflict over the "word of the cross" it is not "only" a matter of methodical, disciplined interpretation, or of professional scriptural interpretation. "Painting Jesus before their eyes" or the christological way of creating a paradox out of wisdom and foolishness—all of that is not "simply" scriptural interpretation, methodical interpretation, or exegesis, but a rhetorical practice with all its *enargeia* and *energeia*. It is a speaking and a showing, a speaking that shows and a showing that speaks, which cannot retreat to what has been said and its methodical interpretation. In such speaking and showing something singular and infinitely complex is being expressed in utter conciseness: "Christ has risen," or the "word of the cross." But in the debate with the opponents, such dense formulae are no longer irenic expressions of consensus but polemic, conflictual ones. Had they been undisputed, these formulae would have been *topoi* and shared viewpoints on the basis of which consensus could be found. But once they themselves have become the object of conflict, their status changes; they become battlegrounds on which the conflict of interpretive power about Christ, faith, the cross, and the apostolate is being played out.

In this conflict, the word of the cross is being asserted with a claim to power, the crucified one is entangled in a conflict of power—in which the right or true word of the cross is being invoked against a *different* Christology (at least according to the Pauline construct, in which the opponents' Christology centers on the glory of resurrection as the salvific event).[8] The performative sense and purpose of such daring conflictual speech is to say and reveal what one sees and how one sees it and how it is seen in the right way. In the present case: to let the listeners see Jesus as the crucified one; to let him be seen in *the way* Paul shows him; to *make* them see in such a way—in order to *let* them *believe* and *make* them *believe* that salvation can only be found in the crucified one. Rhetorically speaking, this is persuasion technique. Put more broadly, the point is to interpret something as something so that those who hear it

---

8. Cf., by contrast, Hansjürgen Verweyen, *Gottes letztes Wort. Grundriss der Fundamentaltheologie* (Regensburg: Pustet, 2000), 338ff.

will follow, share, and pass it on. When its impact is maximal, it means that they interpret everything else—that is, God, self, world, and life—in the light of *that* interpretation.

In the Corinthian debate it is about "all or nothing": about the interpretation of Christ as the crucified one, about the cross as God's wisdom—and therefore about the master of the interpretation of that "master interpretation," of that interpretation of all interpretations, whereby the experience with all experience will begin to be "made." Paul's claim concerns no less than the normative master interpretation—with the corresponding will to interpretive power: the conflict of interpretation about the word of the cross, so that a conflict of power is taking place over interpretation, a conflict that is manifest as a conflict of interpretive *power* with others who interpret differently. The apostolic pretense lies in this: the one who is interpreted actually is the one who interprets because Christ revealed himself as a crucified one, the wisdom of God is revealed in the cross. And yet the apostolic rhetoric cannot but interpret in such a way that the crucified one interprets himself; all it can do is show him and let him be seen in such a way that belief in Christ as the crucified becomes reality. That is the deep paradox of the master interpretation which seeks to master this conflict of interpretation.

Making Paul's Claim to Power Visible

Paul thus develops, in connection with interpretive power, a theorem that has become "canonical." He operates with the long chain of the logos, where the continuity with God's power is claimed as origin and authorization of his own interpretive power, while simultaneously making his *own* (claims to) power invisible, in order not to have to decide the question of power by himself; the idea being to let God decide, God who actually has already decided.[9] Thus, what

Paul states in 2 Cor. 12:11 becomes clear: "I am being very foolish, but it was you who drove me to it." Paul's word claims for itself the full power of the apostolic ministry, in christomorphic mimesis, from the word of the cross and finally from God's Word itself. The apostolate therefore functions, unwittingly, as legitimation through God, so that the apostle is the only legitimate interpreter (speaker, preacher) as God's *delegate*. In the word of the cross, God himself interprets the cross—and so there can be no more contradiction. Whoever still contradicts this "foolishness of the impossible" (*folie de l'impossible*) would only end up in hell, in definitive exclusion.

The problem is that Paul, too, can interpret *solo verbo*, only through the word. Between divine power at the origin and the claim to power in the word of power (*Machtwort*) of the apostle, there is a third player, namely the powerful word (*Wortmacht*), that is, the word's own intrinsic dynamic—whose power of conveying and convincing is bet upon: on the word's interpretive power. The critical question for any theology is, therefore: Does one stay with the powerful word's weakness, or does one claim more in order to secure it further, be it with words of power or on the basis of an original power (with a final explanation seemingly free from interpretation)?

Paul's Use of Paradoxes

The exegetic as well as dogmatic analyses of semantics and philology are very helpful to the hermeneutical perspective on this conflict of interpretive power. They follow simultaneously the strategy of rendering things invisible as well as the paradoxes present in Paul's text. Its claim to interpretive power and, with it, its connection of

---

9. Cf., however, 1 Cor. 7:40: "But she is better off as she is; that is my opinion, and I believe that I too have the Spirit of God"; 1 Cor. 10:15: "I appeal to you as sensible people; form your own judgement on what I say"; 1 Cor. 11:13: "Judge for yourselves: is it fitting for a woman to pray to God bareheaded?"

power and semantics operates in a structure that needs to be clarified and which becomes manifest in the *creation of various paradoxes*. The structure of Paul's argument is a transvaluation of all values—with a considerable amount of "will to power." (It thus becomes noticeable that Nietzsche basically competed with Paul when it comes to God, and also when it comes to the word's power, of which Nietzsche made such virtuosic use.)

Paul operates with the following paradoxes:

- with power he asserts the *opposite* of power, that is: powerlessness mediated by power;

- with the "word of the cross" he expresses the powerlessness of Christ as the highest power as well as, in a precarious analogy, the powerlessness of the apostle as the superior power over his opponents;

- using rhetoric, he brings to expression the opposite of rhetoric—he asserts in his interpretation the opposite of interpretation, namely what is "not just an interpretation";

- with wisdom he represents foolishness, so as to refute wisdom by means of that foolishness.

The paradox centers on the question: How can the foolishness of the cross be brought to expression in the medium of the wisdom of this world? Or: How can the Christian pathos be expressed in the medium of the Greek logos? Without letting the license to foolishness (*genus humile*) get out of hand; without simply asserting it (with a gesture of superiority) as the higher wisdom; without bearing witness to it in the absence of any argument for it, so that all that is left is faith in the witness; without transforming the upending with an adversarial attitude, using dualism and exclusion; without asserting a claim to power, which puts the word of power (*Machtwort*) in the place of the powerful word (*Wortmacht*)? How to express it in such a way that, by way of the opposite, what is by no means one's own, what is other with regard to everything, comes to expression? One *could* get the impression that Paul is stumbling between the word of power and the powerful word—with the ever-recurring temptation to ultimately make recourse to a word of power, instead of relying on the weak powerful word—even though he knows that would be "foolish."

Powerful Word Versus Paul's Word of Power

The power of the word means that it lets *see* and *makes* seeing possible; it regulates, orientates, and enlightens; it opens up horizons, new realities, and possibilities, and sometimes lets even impossibilities become real; it brings into motion, stirring up affects and motivation; it converts through confession; it frees through encouragement; it claims; it fosters peace; and in the beginning, first of all, it declares free or righteous, as if the word were not only the most dangerous possession but above all the most powerful one. A word can let see, it can let see something in a *specific* way, enabling the addressees to see it in such a way that it makes them believe. This is the interpretive power of the word: saying something in such a way in order to show it in that way, and as a consequence letting us see and making us believe in that way. Even if it sounds hyperbolical, that was precisely Paul's goal, namely that the listeners not only believe in Christ, but believe in him in the *same way* as *he*, Paul. In order to achieve that he has to *let and make them believe in the same way* in which *he* interprets Christ—with the claim that this is God's interpretation (which was opened up to him, in analogy with the prophets).

To let and make see means to "adjust" what has been shown, to turn it into what it is being shown as: therefore, to "adjust" the crucified one, to "adjust" Jesus into Christ, the cross into the word of the cross, the foolishness into wisdom, and the like. This triggers the critical impulse versus religion and versus rhetoric. But this would, once again, be too quick. For "adjusting" him in a particular way means presenting him in *such a way* that others may also see, hear, and imagine, and believe him in that way. Such possibility becomes real in speech and imaginative hearing—that is, the wager on the interpretive power of rhetoric, on its power in the weakness of the word, on its revelatory potential in letting Jesus appear as the Christ, in letting the cross become, in the word of the cross, the salvific event that awakens faith, in enabling listeners to believe, in letting them take part in suffering, death, and resurrection, and by making them "eyewitnesses" who pass on what they have seen.

The word of the cross as a rhetorically produced image[10] of the cross seeks to enable faith and to make the listeners or readers believe *in that way*. Contradiction comes up against such a claim in the name of unavailability. The transition from letting and making see to making believe (it is as it is shown) is easily said, but impossible to grasp and to produce—it is an "impossible." To show something in a particular way and to make it into something that is believed, those are hyperbolical formulations. Those things might be said and are at times said of God's Word: what God says happens and is as it is spoken (Ps. 33:9), so that God may be believed. But such a transition from word to faith is a tremendous pretense. As from the side of the addressees, *understanding* can at best only be made possible and easier, something is *given* to be seen and understood, nothing more. It is impossible for the word to also make the addressees take it: it

---

10. The word *image* is polysemic here. It is an image in the mind of the speaker, an abstract image in the medium of the word, and it affects a self-created image in the listeners' imagination. The identity or at least convergence of these various meanings is by no means assured.

cannot "produce" comprehension, and even less faith. But doesn't the rhetorical production of evidence bet precisely on that (and isn't that one of the reasons for the phobia with regard to rhetoric)? When it succeeds, it *makes* us believe, *nolens volens*, better: it meets us, it "speaks to us" in a way which is prior to all knowing, willing, and choosing. The affirmation of the word always precedes our choosing. And that also means: in power and efficience the word is irresistible—*when it succeeds*.

But that only applies to the *powerful word*, not to the *word of power*.[11] Both are as different as saying something and *really* having to say something.[12] Whoever "has the say," through one's office or position, is one thing. The question remains, always: Does that person *really* have something to say? Max Weber would have spoken about office and charisma. Paul claimed both simultaneously, as we see in the debate with the Corinthians. Jesus, on the other hand, was more modest: to trust only in the word and the act, without any apostolic mandate—and thus to fail before the eyes of the world. The more astonishing it is, then, when his interpretations are being recognized retrospectively, *without* having been authorized through any mandate, for instance, when a parable, such as the "good Samaritan," is so convincing that it becomes an interpretive framework in a given culture. When it goes well, the person who has the interpretive power indeed has something to say and to show. The original gesture of interpretive power is: "But I say unto you . . ." It seems as if interpretive power has something to do with the illusion of being, and the illusion lets the world appear in *this or that* way—or it lets Christ appear *this or that* way, as the crucified one.

11. As an analogy, one could distinguish between image of power (*Machtbild*) and the image's power (*Bildmacht*), or the body of power (*Machtkörper*) and the body's power (*Körpermacht*).
12. This (calculated) shortening to a "who" is owed to conciseness and not without problems. It does evoke the fact that interpretive power is related to people's capacity to act.

When a powerful person speaks, that person speaks a *word of power* (*Machtwort*),[13] in which the power of the powerful is present and effective in the word, as with God's Word, in the judge's sentence, in the speech of a president or a pope. The power of the agent or the institution is present and effective in the "representative" word. This model reaches its limits when the representative loses credibility or speaks nonsense. The extreme case "*Roma locuta, causa finita*" with the claim to infallibility of certain papal words (*ex cathedra*) shows, in its extreme dimension, that such things do not usually apply, but that even the word of power remains dependent on recognition (or agreement).

The *powerful word* (*Wortmacht*), on the other hand, is not the power of the agent, the office, or the institution, but of the medium, for instance, the speech (or the image). Nietzsche said: "I fear we can't get rid of God because we still believe in Grammar . . ."[14] Wittgenstein's model of language games and also the speech-act theory assume that speech has its *own* power, of which we make use (or by which we are being dominated) every time we speak: "That's just how we speak." Speech makes many things possible and other things impossible, so that in speaking those parameters are inevitably used. In the actual act of speaking, another power manifests itself, the power of speech, which is effective by virtue of the way of speaking (the rhetorical tradition knows that particularly well): as they are performed, the saying or speaking, in contrast to what has been said, reveal a different power than language or the system of signs.[15] This

---

13. For a good example, see *Angela Merkel—Machtworte. Die Standpunkte der Kanzlerin*, ed. Robin Mishra (Freiburg im Br.: Herder, 2010).

14. Friedrich Nietzsche, *Götzen-Dämmerung oder Wie man mit dem Hammer philosophirt*, Kritische Studienausgabe, ed. Giorgio Colli and Mazzimo Montinari (Münich: W. de Gruyter, 1988), 6:78.

15. In media science, the power of the medium (over its "users") is the guiding model; the same is true in the history of science and of technology; we find similar methods in discourse theory and system theory.

is why declarations of love as well as insults have been taken as (precarious) analogies for the *verbum efficax* and *visible*.

The Cost of Paul's Recourse to Words of Power

What becomes visible in this discrepancy is a precarious *ambivalence* in Paul's argumentation against his Corinthian adversaries. Naturally, he wishes to have something to say (the word of the cross), he wishes to deploy a powerful word (*Wortmacht*); but as he says this he intimates that he has the say (as apostle and founder of communities), and so with words of power (*Machtworten*). This is precarious; it undermines what he *really* has to say. In the urgency of the conflict, the powerful word reaches for the word of power. The word of power's claim is supposed to strengthen the powerful word, but it does the opposite. The problem becomes even more acute as the word of power claims one singular, exclusive authorization, namely apostolicity. Then the gesture of the word of power is reinforced by the claim that God himself is authorizing this—and whoever stands against Paul stands against God, and God against that person.

This reveals a sad powerlessness: the word looks for power, for *more* power than it has on its own, but it gets lost in gestures of power that lead to an escalating self-authorization. The unconditional "will to power" as the form of the "will to truth" leads astray, so that all that remains is an escape into a hyperbole of authorization. Whoever wishes to let the word of the cross, as God's Word, come to expression in such a way that, from first to last, the word of power prevails, would let power have the final say.

Consequently, the *ultima ratio* is the exclusion of those who do not bow to this claim to power. The genealogy of the process of "hereticizing" (*Häretisierung*) or anathematizing in the name of orthodoxy is thus only too understandable—and in vain, or should one say: "for nothing"? Under the banner of the "Word of God," we can arrive very quickly at a word or power, when the powerful word, the word's power, does not yield by itself the desired recognition. One of the things we may see in the conflict in Corinth is a pathology of theology—without insinuating that such pathology was already present *with Paul*.

Real Impossibility: Paul's *"folie de l'impossible"*

Jacques Derrida wrote, with regard to the desire for forgiveness: "Pure and unconditional forgiveness, to name its most proper meaning, must not have a 'meaning,' it does not require any finality or any intelligibility. It is a folly of the impossible."[16] John Caputo followed him with his "desire to *experience the impossible*" and his "apology for the impossible."[17] The *"folie de l'impossible"*: that is wonderfully thought up and wisely said. But what makes one trust and be sure that this is not an *impossible folie*, an impossible foolishness?

Paul's transvaluation of all values of wisdom and foolishness seems, at first sight, to be paradoxical: the wisdom of this world is mere foolishness before God, and God's wisdom is mere foolishness to the world. But this is not yet a paradox, it is simply a contrast, which goes back to a difference of perspectives: what some consider wise is foolish to others—and vice versa. This is a normal disagreement, more precisely, a contrasting opposition which does not rule out that there might be a third or fourth possibility.

The contrast that is decisive is rendered more acute by Paul: the world's wisdom is blind to God, since God has made it "foolish"

---

16. "Le pardon pur et inconditionnel, pour avoir son sens propre, doit n'avoir aucun 'sens', aucune finalité, aucune intelligibilité même. C'est une folie de l'impossible." Cf. Jacques Derrida, "Le siècle et le pardon," *Le Monde des débats* 12 (1999): 10–17.
17. Cf. John D. Caputo and Michael J. Scanlon, eds., *God, the Gift, and Postmodernism* (Bloomington: Indiana University Press, 1999), 3.

(does that mean that God has made it, or that God has shown it to be inferior and useless compared to God's wisdom?). Paul continues the contest with a *comparative* that *sounds* paradoxical: the foolishness of God is *wiser* and his weakness *stronger* (1 Cor. 1:25). Just as the cross inscription INRI, the polemical exonym for Christ (foolishness) is taken up polemically and recast, *this* foolishness (if "you" choose to call it that) is the *true* wisdom. And, as in Anselm's ontological argument (*quo maius*), we find here a comparative ("wiser," "stronger"), not a superlative. This suggests a wisdom that is "always greater, higher, wider" than the entire world.

The basic paradox of a foolish wisdom and a wise foolishness falls apart into a contrasting opposition. The Pauline use of language is thus spoken clearly in a partisan and "one-sided" way, *coram Deo*. It is clear that he has already removed the paradoxical dimension of the paradox: what is true wisdom and true foolishness needs no explanation but has always been clear and unambiguous. The unfortunate side effect of that is that "foolishness of God" and "weakness of God" are no "absolute paradoxes" (as well as no absolute metaphors); they only appear to be paradoxes. The polemic of the adversaries is taken up and, once recast, surpassed. A *genuine* foolishness of *God* does not exist in the flow of this rhetoric. As a consequence, the "weakness of God" that has been built up in a parallel move is in fact not a weakness at all, either.

And so, with the use of the comparative, a simple contrast is presented: there is a wiser wisdom (and a more foolish foolishness). Foolishness has three meanings:

1. What the wisdom of the world considers as foolish;
2. what God considers as foolish;
3. what Paul proclaims as the *wiser* wisdom: the *more foolish* foolishness according to the wisdom of the world, thus an even

more *impossible folie* which, by virtue of the powerful word, framed christologically, is smarter than the wisdom of the world. What appears to be even more impossible is the most impossible "*folie*," namely that of the crucified one. And so Paul's speech of wisdom about the *wiser wisdom* becomes the figure of the third party, the "mediator" in the conflict between God's foolishness and the wisdom of the world. It is *he* who, with *his* powerful word, shows a wiser wisdom to the world, who shows the foolish wisdom of the world to God. He represents one before the other—and vice versa, whereby both see differently and can see each other differently than before. It is not God's power or the apostolic word of power but the Pauline powerful word that effects the transvaluation of *all* values: God's wiser wisdom appeared initially as a *more impossible* "*folie*"; but as the speech continues it shows itself as suffering and passion of the one who is more than impossible: the crucified one.[18]

Paul's Rhetoric: Wisdom or Foolishness?

The resulting query is this: Is Paul's rhetoric a wisdom or a foolishness before God? And is it a foolishness before the world, or a wisdom—until it becomes debatable whether the *wiser* wisdom exists

---

18. It is therefore understandable that Otfried Hofius and Cilliers Breytenbach disagreed on whether the word of the cross has reconciled the world once and for all or if it continues to reconcile (see 2 Cor. 5:19a), that is, if *katallassein* (in the *coniugatio periphrastica*) presently continues and will continue to do so in the future, or if it has taken place and is completed. Grammatically, it is located in the past. Rhetorically, it continues. *Paul* does not become the (self-appointed) mediator. Cf. Cilliers Breytenbach, *Versöhnung. Eine Studie zur paulinischen Soteriologie* (Neukirchen-Vluyn: Neukirchener Verlag, 1989); Otfried Hofius, "Rezension von Breytenbach, Versöhnung," *ThLZ* 115 (1990): 741–45; Cilliers Breytenbach, "Abgeschlossenes Imperfekt? Einige notwendig gewordene Anmerkungen zum Gebrauch des griechischen Imperfekts in neutestamentlichen Zeiten," *ThLZ* 118 (1993): 85–91; Otfried Hofius, "2Kor 5,19a und das Imperfekt," *ThLZ* 118 (1993): 790–95; Ferdinand Hahn, "Streit um 'Versöhnung': Zur Besprechung des Buches von Cilliers Breytenbach durch Otfried Hofius," *VerFor* 36 (1991): 55–64.

by the grace of Paul's rhetoric—hoping to be grounded in the crucified one, rather than merely be something invented in the midst of the difficult conflict of interpretive power. The risky wager in this powerful word is that in Paul's rhetoric of the cross both perspectives are being conveyed in such a way that the wisdom of the world is not only excluded and defamed, but also sublated and pushed beyond its boundaries, attracted by the wiser wisdom, which comes to expression in the form of rhetoric. The price for such risky speech is that it becomes a constitutively ambivalent figure. Nothing is easier to understand than the fact that opinions differ on Paul. To that extent, he carries the burdens of the world *and* of God. The sad powerlessness and escalation of power gestures, which I analyzed above, is the price of the wiser wisdom, a price he cannot avoid. What he bears witness to must appear to be preposterous—and in this very preposterousness a calculation can be seen.

On first hearing one might get a spell of dialectical dizziness, which might return during the first closer reading. But that does not last long, because it only appears to be dialectical. Paul is trying very hard with his rhetoric, but everything is and remains clear and unambiguous. There is nothing doubtful or really controversial. Toward Greeks and Jews alike the transvaluation of all values is being made unambiguously clear. This fosters and encourages consent among the Christian addressees of the rhetorical argumentation. With regard to the inner-Christian opponents, it creates a serious debate concerning the correct understanding of the wise foolishness and the foolish wisdom. *About that*, namely about the wiser wisdom, there is a real contest—with an open ending. Distinguishing himself from Greeks and Jews, Paul creates (topically and inventively) approval in the Christian community in order to attack his adversaries (those who are too wise, always wiser) and to place them before an alternative: going with him, or being excluded. Once the contest about wisdom has been opened up toward the Greeks and the Jews (with an indisputable winner, thus a rigged contest), the inner-Christian contest can be treated.

The higher, greater, broader wisdom was probably claimed first and foremost by the opponents, who have contradicted Paul and sought to "overtake" his theology. We are not only of Paul, we are not of the devil; we are of Christ! We are wiser than Jews, Greeks, and Paul put together! Paul takes up this comparative and plays along with it, so that he must bear the consequences. The race against the opponents cannot be won anymore by further appeals to wisdom. How then?

The contest in the *dromos* (the running race) is transvaluated by Paul, through a surprising change of direction. *The dromos becomes a palindrome*: on the open road of the race in the theological arena, Paul suddenly makes a U-turn, from wisdom to foolishness, and then from foolishness back to wisdom. If that were to happen at the Olympic Games, it would be something truly astonishing. As mediator he must go back and forth between God and the world and between the world and God, between wisdom and foolishness, between foolishness and wisdom, so that, in this rhetorical contest, the wiser wisdom appears in Paul's speech of wisdom.

From *dromos* to *palindrome*, back and forth, and to and fro, he walks back and forth in an always-smaller circle, finally turning on one spot. Is this the point where he unhinges the wisdom of the world, or is he revolving around himself?

For outsiders it must look more than absurd. Paul "staggers" back and forth, as I put it provisionally above. "He has lost it," would be the expected reaction. Has he become totally insane? "Not at all," Paul would answer. On the contrary, for, according to the presupposition he might have in mind, his opponents got off to a false start, or as we might put it nowadays, they are doped. In all their wisdom, they have, somehow, forgotten the foolishness, bypassing the cross in order to go straight to the resurrection. They lack the burden of God's life on earth, Christ's powerlessness and the embodied dimension of Christian existence. One could call this kind of bypassing of the old for the sake of the new a sort of soteriological impatience. The desire of completion bypasses work on what is old. They are not just wise, they are "far too wise."

Wolfgang Schrage named the position of the opponents a "hypertrophy of wisdom."[19] The opponents are not being excluded along with the Jews and the Greeks, but "reeled in and caught," their parole taken up but paradoxically upended: wisdom yes, as well as wiser wisdom. But the comparative of wisdom is grounded in the *christological* accent—and that cannot be won with pneuma and resurrection, but only with the cross. Whoever bypasses it or loses it in the race for wisdom has missed the proper start.

What Paul is doing here, by all available means of the powerful word, *can* be called, with Derrida, "*folie de l'impossible*," or, with Erasmus, a praise of folly. *But* Derrida does not know a crucified Messiah, and Erasmus does not know a dead God or a mortal soul. The actual difficulty remains unthinkable or impossible, for both of them. *From that perspective,* even Derrida's "*folie de l'impossible*" appears still soft-footed and a little bit too (worldly) wise. Most would agree that these characteristics apply to Erasmus. Ultimately, they are both "easily digestible," and therefore harmless. Paul's point is *la folie la plus impossible* ("the most impossible foolishness"), the impossible reality of the crucified one.

If even Derrida's *folie* can appear almost harmless, when "seen from that perspective," then in that other way of seeing the interpretive power of Paul's argumentation shows itself: it lets and makes see,

19. Wolfgang Schrage, *Der erste Brief an die Korinther*, 1:150.

in a particular way and differently than before, and in such a way that not only the showing, but also what is being shown, involve interpretive power, namely the crucified one in the mode of the powerful word of the word of the cross. It is not self-evident at all, it is in fact unintelligible, that the crucified one is understood and ultimately recognized as the norm-setting thrust reverser, as sapiential palindrome. In his speech of wisdom, Paul wagers on the real presence of the proclaimed in the proclamation. Thus it is understandable that *his speech*, solidified as text, later came to be construed sacramentally. But, just as with God's powerful word, the power of the word can only be interpretive power (*Deutungsmacht*), which must be attributed and handed over to what is being interpreted and at the same remain a simple word.

Handing over this word to the one who is being interpreted is a paradoxical gift: Paul interpretatively bestows interpretive power on what has been interpreted, and from which he believes to have received it, so that the listeners can see the wiser wisdom at work in Paul's speech of wisdom. This wager on the *Christus praesens* is and remains *open* and can only be won through the readers or listeners—but not on the basis of their strength or reason. It is a wager "*à fond perdu*," or "in the open." Because whoever would wish to decide the outcome of the wager with a word of power would already have lost.

If the interpreted one were to become really present in the interpretation as interpretation, it would "in-deed" (or more precisely "im-passionately") be a persistent paradox. It is vexing to say it, but as Paul brings up "foolishness" more and more forcefully, this "word-event" (*Wortereignis*) is threatened, more than it is presented, by Paul in the race for the wiser wisdom. He switches directions, back and forth, and must show the others, who continue to run, that *they*, not him, are running in the wrong direction. To do that, only a word of power can help, namely an apostolic rhetoric of authorization *pro domo*, and at the same time a polemical rhetoric of disempowerment that targets the opponents. The economy of this rhetoric is well known: universalization of inclusion (cf. Badiou), accompanied simultaneously by the production of the absolute remnant (cf. Agamben). To put it more simply: inclusion through exclusion, and exclusion through inclusion, carrying the dangerous outcome of an apocalyptic dualization, in which whoever is not with us is against us. God and world stand *against* each other, just as the apostle and his opponents until the world becomes dualized as inimical. John is known to have chosen a path of that kind, until the proto-Gnostics in the Johannine community took it too far. Such *dualizing* is not very wise, theologically as well as rhetorically, for it not only produces more problems than it seems to solve. It also undermines the role of apostolic rhetoric, which amounts to being a mediator, not an inquisitor.

Seizure of Interpretive Power: Escape Into the Apostolic Office

One consequence of this rhetorical escalation is the subsequent institutional policy of the apostolic office: the hardening of the powerful word as word of power and furthermore as institutional power, which can do without any semantic. The office serves to secure the charisma all the way until the extreme, late-Augustinian thesis according to which the institution as well as the office guarantee salvation without the need of charisma. The risk of such a development is that form may exist without spirit.

But Paul is still far from that. What is being "invented" here is only the basic contours of the later development (it functions at

231

least retrospectively as etiology of the office). Phenomenologically, it would be called the "primal foundation" (*Urstiftung*). At the powerful word's limit, the word of power appears reasonable to the apostle. At the crossroads between the powerful word and the word of power, the "interpretive community" could obviously not resist the temptation to ground the power of the word on a "higher authority," with an absolute, ultimate justification: apostolicity. The "apostle Paul" thus became a "fictional character" (*Kunstfigur*), a product of rhetorical technique, in order to produce always-more interpretive power through what appears as a self-interpretation of power.

The person of "the apostle" is thus portrayed as the "chosen one," miraculously "called" to his office—and who since then pursues an independent existence with regard to interpretive power. To be clear: first, this does not concern the historical Saul named Paul; second, it concerns the biblical, canonical Paul, who is taken as rule of the symbolic order of the canon in the canon—and who thus becomes the "center of Scripture." Third, as a consequence of all that, a "more" is made out to be Scripture, namely an imaginary Paul, the apostle as meta-historical fictional character who, in the historical reception, evolved from proclaimer to proclaimed: from missional preacher to *norma normans (non normata?)* of all preaching, and so not only to the object of preaching but, fourth, *per impossibile*, to the apostolic deployment of any preaching that may appear as wisdom of God.

How did it come to this? And which "textual signposts" (*Textsignale*) provide that possibility? The preacher in the midst of a crisis claims a charisma that obviously has *not* been recognized self-evidently and indisputably. And so his interpretive power is *not* established; in the midst of conflict it is available to others who seek to grasp it. That, in itself, is a precarious position: *Ecce apostolos*. The interpretive power, which is not being accrued "from below," has to be *built up*. In the case of a conflict, the assertion of this claim *may* use the opposite of charisma, namely total power of one's office through an external commissioning as a pneumatological para-theory for the sake of seizing interpretive power. The claim with regard to the powerful word shifts to the word of power; it shifts to the office as a function of the charisma, with the exclusiveness and singularity of the office.

Later on, in 2 Corinthians, in the rhetorical contest with the opponents, the argumentation goes down a slippery slope, as the claims for recognition escalate: "my credentials should have come from you. In nothing did I prove inferior to those super-apostles, even if I am a nobody. The signs of an apostle were there in the work I did among you, marked by unfailing endurance, by signs, portents, and miracles" (2 Cor. 12:11b-12, REB). This sounds like the apostolic Olympic games: higher, faster, stronger—more whole, complete, and wiser. This should perhaps not be heard without a certain irony. As it sounds like a competition of salvation, which always yearns for more—and therefore produces its own shortage.

Is it really still *God's* foolishness, *God's* wiser wisdom, which is expressed and asserted? What happens in such a competition of interpretive power? To be able to produce power from words, just like sparks and fire from stones, is a wondrous dimension of interpretive power. That pretension characterizes each word. But that it also "ignites," this is only conceivable with the kindling of the listeners. And in order not to leave it to them alone, a pneumatological reserve occurs here. Interpretive power that really ignites is effectively "*acheiropoietic*"; it is never made by hands of man: it is due to God's Word, not to any human word.

But this claim to interpretive power, too, can only be rendered effective through ratification on the side of the addressees. And apparently Paul failed to achieve this in Corinth. In the course of time the community disappeared, as if it had been shattered and been destroyed. The decisive ratification happened later, and all the more powerfully. The imaginary fictional character of the apostle became—not without imaginary exuberance—the canonical model for validity beyond its historical and rhetorical genesis. The rhetorical production of the apostolic word had to be erased from memory so that its validity, detached from its genesis, would always endure. The divine genesis of the apostolate as ground of validity of the institutional word of power replaced the rhetorical genesis of his powerful word.

Interpretive Power as Power of Truth?

Paul—here, the apostolically authorized text—finds himself in an *aporia* that can be explicated with the theory of interpretive power: with the simple difference between "saying something" and "really having something to say," thus between a word of power and a powerful word.

Whoever has something to say wishes also to have the say but should not wish to have it, because by so doing that person undermines what she has to say. Whoever claims more than really having something to say ruins everything. Conversely, whoever has the say *qua* office does not really have something to say, exactly *because* he has the say. There is relief and reassurance in that but also, at the same time, an escalation and a capitulation in the contest over interpretive power.

The official constitution of the office in the third century might have occurred against Gnosticism, but the model was invented with Paul's apostolic office in the first century, an "institution" that was named as such only by the subsequent institution. What remains appears as constitution theory of the office by virtue of the authorization theory. The Protestant thesis, as is well known, is *not* defined via the institution and the office as a historical succession in the office; apostolic succession is a succession of "teaching," thus the argumentatively plausible powerful word. And so "what is apostolic" must be identifiable without participating in the authorization theory and claiming it "for oneself."

The text's interpretive power (in the sense of its own momentum of interpretation, of what it really has to say) has reasons relating to the history of effects and the history of reception: in the institutionalization of the office with its etiology via the apostolic office, in the reception of Paul by Augustine, and in Luther's way of emphasizing the *theologia crucis*. Thus, the "incorporation" of the text by the ecclesial institutions (tradition, hierarchy, teaching office, theology) is an empowerment *ex post*. A question that creeps up in this history of empowerment would be the one regarding the inherent power of Paul's interpretation—in other words, regarding its argumentative power, textual form, rhetorical plausibility, performance, and, not least, its truth.

The biggest temptation, however, would be to treat the question of interpretive power as a Gordian knot, attempting to deny interpretation and power, and considering the question of truth without taking into account interpretive power. Then the incredibly simple answer would be: it is the truth that authorizes the text. It is powerful (it became and remained so) because the text is true. But who determines that? Is this being claimed or attested? And when, where, for whom? Had this to be claimed for all times and places, one would be dealing with an analytically *necessary* truth, true in all possible worlds and at all times. This is certainly not the case, and it would mistake the word of the cross for a plus and minus. It would also not correspond to the contingency of the cross (which is neither "randomness," nor "necessity," nor "even more than necessity").[20]

To decide the question of interpretive power in such a "Gordian" fashion would let "truth" (in the place of science and exegesis or dogmatics) to take the place of God and function as God's pseudonym (or as metonymy). One would follow the same (?) model of empowerment. God's power creates the apostle—God's truth verifies his interpretation—and the power of his truth legitimizes this interpretation: a powerful word legitimized by a word of power. Similarly, this would mean *etsi Deus non daretur*: the power of truth authorizes the interpretation. That is as beautiful as it is plain, and reassuringly simple.

What is complicated and disconcerting is that all these aspects can only be *relationally* (perspectively and diachronically) determined: as strength for, as power over, as truth for, and so forth. Power is continuously late in its effect; it is effective power *ex post*. A similar thing applies to truth. If power is not understood from its logic of origin and of operation as someone's (or as God's or the apostle's) attribute but *modally*, then the question has to do with what *enables and establishes* this power.

What would have to be called true is the kind of interpretive power (or powerful word) that enables what is *per se* impossible; that includes what could not be included; that forgives what cannot be forgiven, and the like. Truth *is a "folie de l'impossible."* To consider truth as "ready at hand" or as "real possibility" would leave truth underdetermined. Paul's wager has to do with truth being a real and effective impossibility, meaning that it establishes a new heaven and a new earth. But this claim is not simply "true or false," it is true when it becomes *effective* truth. This, however, cannot happen

---

20. Cf. Philipp Stoellger, "Die Vernunft der Kontingenz und die Kontingenz der Vernunft. Leibniz' theologische Kontingenzwahrung und Kontingenzsteigerung," in *Vernunft, Kontingenz und Gott. Konstellationen eines offenen Problems*, ed. Ingolf U. Dalferth and Philipp Stoellger (Tübingen: Mohr, 2000), 73–116.

independently of any interpretation. And so the shortcut about the question of truth leads back into the complexities of interpretation and the entanglement in questions of power. It is thus necessary to distinguish and see that interpretation is not all there is, even though everything is given only in, with and under interpretations. Analogously: even if truth is given and accessible only in, with and under interpretations. In order to orientate oneself in the conflicts over interpretive power, truth is a critical regulative. But to trace the power of an interpretation simply back to its truth would be phenomenally blind. And so the *question* of truth does not resolve the complexities that exist between interpretation and power (power with its conflicts).

11

On Justification and Beyond—An Attempt

Matthias D. Wüthrich

"To be justified—that used to be the most important thing."[1]

"What remains is having to be right. Being right has become the accepted substitute for being justified."[2]

These words appear in a slim 2012 volume by Martin Walser, titled *On Justification, a Temptation.* Walser deplores the anesthetization of our desire, our "ancient longing,"[3] for justification. We have forgotten, he claims, that justification used to be our existential need.

It is hardly surprising that Walser's clarion call has fallen on sympathetic ears among theologians.[4] I want to take Walser's literary

---

1. Martin Walser, *Über Rechtfertigung, eine Versuchung* (Reinbek: Rowohlt, 2012), 1.
2. Ibid., 29.
3. Ibid., 27.

intuition as a starting point for thinking about "justification." My thinking is guided by a question that does not concern Walser much but that is crucial in theological terms: the question regarding the status of justification's doctrinal articulation in Protestant theology. In recent dogmatic compendia, the doctrine of justification has been called nothing less than the "center" or "core" of Protestant theology.[5] But is it, actually?

In what follows, I want to examine whether and to what extent the doctrine of justification can still be considered the "center" and "core" of Protestant theology. This will occur in five steps: I will start with (1) a discussion of the contemporariness of the doctrine of justification, followed by (2) an analysis of its problems of adaptation, (3) its loss of relevance and (4) the semantic reductions of the concept of justification in the modern era, and conclude (5) with the question of whether and to what extent the doctrine of justification really is the article on which the church stands or falls.

On the Contemporariness of the Doctrine of Justification

The contemporariness of the doctrine of justification has been called into question time and again, mostly because of its ostensibly outmoded *juridical-penal categories and images*. I think it would be unwise, however, to agree with this blanket accusation too rashly. It is precisely those juridical-penal categories and images that contain a potential of application to the present that should not be underestimated. The doctrine of justification can very well be applied to that which Odo Marquard has called the "tribunalization of the

---

4. Cf., for instance, Ulrich H. J. Körtner's comment in *Die Furche* magazine, http://www.theologie-und-kirche.de/koertner-walser-furche.pdf.

5. See, for instance, Wilfried Joest-Johannes von Lüpke, *Dogmatik II: Die Wirklichkeit Gottes* (Göttingen: Vandenhoeck & Ruprecht, 2010), 102, 118. Joest and Lüpke relate the concepts to Reformation theology, but then expand them in a way that internalizes them in the process of reasoning.

reality of modern life."[6] He uses this term to describe a ubiquitous demand for justification. Everything needs to be justified: the family, the state, politics, gender, education, work, leisure, or, even much more banal, organic vegetables, child care, and—to use Marquard's own example—bathing suits.[7] There is nothing that does not need to be legitimized, and nothing that cannot lead to a crisis of legitimation. The late modern and postmodern person bears the "total burden of proof for its right to exist and its right to be as it is."[8] Marquard wryly suggests that this merciless burden of justification may well be "the revenge, against its proscription, of the 'justification by works' that the Reformation proscribed."[9] Today, everyone is culprit, prosecutor, and judge—or more precisely: a culpable prosecutor and judge.

The burden of justification mentioned above is not objectionable in general. In the context of science and academia, for example, it contributes to improving the quality of research. Things take a destructive turn, however, once the pressure of legitimation subtly begins to seep into even the smallest cracks of a person scratched raw, bullying one into constantly justifying oneself to oneself and everyone else for everything. It is hardly necessary to present examples, for instance from the world of the media, because we see every day how every person can be put on trial as long as it boosts ratings. Ultimately, the burden of justification leads to one overwhelming question: "By what right are you at all, rather than not being?"[10]

---

6. Odo Marquard, "Unburdenings: Theodicy Motives in Modern Philosophy," in Marquard, *In Defense of the Accidental: Philosophical Studies*, trans. Robert M. Wallace (Oxford: Oxford University Press, 1991), 9. See also Marquard's concept of "overtribunalization" in his article "Indicted and Unburdened Man in Eighteenth-Century Philosophy," in Marquard, *Farewell to Matters of Principle: Philosophical Studies*, trans. Robert M. Wallace, et al. (Oxford: Oxford University Press, 1989), 41.

7. Marquard, "Unburdenings," 8.

8. Ibid., 9.

9. Ibid.

A contemporary interpretation of the doctrine of justification would have substantial counter-arguments, from a theological point of view, against the many varieties of current tribunalizations. The claim that human beings are not justified based on their merits and works but by faith alone amounts to a fundamental criticism of all destructive tribunalizations.

Problems of Adaptation

I wrote, above, that the doctrine of justification *would have* substantial counter-arguments against the many tribunalizations we witness. It *would have* a lot of potential to be meaningful—if it could be made even remotely accessible to people today in all of its depth! It is true that there are numerous contemporary attempts to interpret the doctrine of justification. For example, it can be interpreted through the concept of love. In that case, the idea is that "God loves human beings despite their sins." Or maybe the terminology of affirmation and acceptance is employed—in this case, faith in justification is interpreted to mean: "The acceptance of being accepted by God." Or the paradigm of application is the distinction between the person and her works, emphasizing that God says yes to the person, regardless of her works or merits.[11]

These are all respectable, practical-minded attempts of adaptation. However, they often transport a certain vagueness and have the tendency to gloss over the fundamental difficulties associated with

---

10. Ibid., 8. See also Ulrich H. J. Körtner, *Reformatorische Theologie im 21. Jahrhundert* (Zürich: TVZ, 2010), 35.

11. These examples can be found in Wilfried Härle, "Zur Gegenwartsbedeutung der 'Rechtfertigungs'-Lehre. Eine Problemskizze," in Härle, *Menschsein in Beziehungen. Studien zur Rechtfertigungslehre und Anthropologie* (Tübingen: Mohr Siebeck, 2005), 81. Michael Beintker outlines a wide spectrum of other areas of application of the doctrine of justification, stating that there is no area in the life-world of human beings that cannot become relevant for justification theology. Beintker, *Rechtfertigung in der neuzeitlichen Lebenswelt. Theologische Erkundungen* (Tübingen: Mohr Siebeck, 1998), 6–7.

the theological term of justification.[12] These smooth attempts at adaptation and reformulation indirectly reveal the fundamental difficulties of raising the question of the theological meaning of "justification" today. I will state some of these difficulties:

First, we must remember that even the term *justification* is quite out of tune with our everyday usage: (1) Generally, we use this term today in the sense of self-justification and thus precisely not with the idea in mind that we are justified by *someone else*. (2) We use the term *justification* when we think we are in the right, while the theological tradition relates it to a fundamental situation in which the human being's guilt and sin is considered a proven fact. In the logic of our everyday linguistic usage, God's judgment of justification of the sinner can only be considered a misjudgment—God does not acquit those who are in the right, but those who are not.[13]

These semantic difficulties are joined by much more fundamental problems: apart from the questionability and determination of the idea of God, the doctrine of justification also presupposes a Christology, an anthropology, and thus a hamartiology that cannot readily be conciliated with the modern understanding of freedom and autonomy.[14] And this is just as true for its underlying biblical concept of justice.

All the above-mentioned difficulties taken together result in neverending lament about the lack of contemporary relevance of the doctrine of justification. This lament first and foremost focuses on the difficulty of communicating the concept to people who want to have little or nothing to do with the church. But the impression cannot be

---

12. In contrast, a study by Christiane Tietz operates at a sophisticated theological level: *Freiheit zu sich selbst. Entfaltung eines christlichen Begriffs von Selbstannahme* (Göttingen: Vandenhoek & Ruprecht, 2005). Critically expanding on Tillich and in dialogue with Kierkegaard, she develops a concept of self-acceptance that is plausible in the context of justification theology.
13. Regarding this difficulty see Härle, "Zur Gegenwartsbedeutung," 74 and 85.
14. Conversely, see Tietz, *Freiheit zu sich selbst.*

avoided that it also encompasses those circles of the churches that are more fluent in theological matters, and even theology itself.

Loss of Relevance

The nadir in this matter is widely considered to be the general assembly of the Lutheran World Federation in Helsinki in 1963, where the embarrassment regarding the contemporary relevance of the doctrine of justification became obvious.[15] Arguably, the doctrine of justification once more returned to the focus of differentiated attention in the course of the ecumenical dialogue with the Roman Catholic Church and the resulting "Joint Declaration on the Doctrine of Justification" (JDDJ) and the "Official Common Statement" (OCS). However, critical voices suggest that the doctrine of justification has lost its schismatic effect only due to its advanced *loss of relevance*.[16] In the face of the quite moderate ecumenical efficacy of these documents, it is safe to assume that not much has changed since then.

There is also the fact that the doctrine of justification prominently features mainly in those forms of Christianity that tend to be on the decrease. At any rate, it seems obvious that the relevance the doctrine of justification enjoys in Protestant circles is echoed neither in the rapidly growing evangelical-charismatic, partly postdenominational forms of Christianity nor in the global Roman Catholic Church, and least of all in the Orthodox Church.[17] Moreover, in many regions of the world it is met by the headwind of liberation theology,[18] just as

---

15. For accounts of this event, see Körtner, *Reformatorische Theologie*, 27; and Härle, "Zur Gegenwartsbedeutung," 67–68.
16. See Körtner, *Reformatorische Theologie*, 28 (with reference to R. Schenk).
17. Orthodox theology never developed a complete and unified soteriology, and juridical terms are rarely found in it. On this see Karl Christian Felmy, *Einführung in die orthodoxe Theologie der Gegenwart*, Lehr- und Studienbücher zur Theologie 5 (Münster: LIT Verlag, 2011), 159–90.
18. Gerhard Sauter, "Art. Rechtfertigung VI," in *TRE* (1997), 28:348.

the "new perspective on Paul" is cracking open old reading habits.[19] Thus, Gerhard Sauter is probably right when he observes: "In today's ecumenical situation, the doctrine of justification seems to carve out a special kind of existence. Its domain is steadily dwindling: to the realm of European and Northern American Protestantism, and even here more and more to its theology, as far as theology has retained any awareness of its denominational tradition."[20]

Semantic Reductions in Contemporary Modern Thought

In the face of the above-mentioned problems of adaptation and loss of relevance, should we nevertheless, counterfactually, insist that the doctrine of justification is the "center" and "core" of Protestant theology? As long as this assumption is plausible, at least from the internal view of European and North American Protestant theology, there is not much to say against holding on to it. But is this internal plausibility still a given? Finding an answer to this question is not all that easy. The imagery of "center" and "core," for one, is in need of more precision. A positive answer—it could be assumed—may be possible if the entire, difficult-to-define field of soteriology, with its traditional assignations of the terms *salvation* (*Heil*) and/or *redemption* (*Erlösung*), could be articulated through the doctrine of justification in a *central* and *sufficient* manner.[21]

However, precisely this possibility has been put into question with reference to the Bible. Again and again, the question has been raised whether the biblical message of redemption is not diminished by

---

19. See Ivana Bendik, *Paulus in neuer Sicht? Eine kritische Einführung in die New Perspective on Paul* (Stuttgart: Kohlhammer, 2010).
20. Sauter, "Art. Rechtfertigung VI," 28:346.
21. Of course, it cannot be overlooked that the terms *salvation* and *redemption* are also unable to express the intended soteriological subject matter without certain constrictions. I will, for reasons of readability, only talk about "redemption" in the following pages. However, this is always intended to refer to the entire soteriological field encompassed by "salvation" and/or "redemption" in a broader sense.

defining it solely in terms of justification. The problem can be clearly seen in a passage discussed in the present volume: in the first two chapters of 1 Corinthians, justification is only mentioned *once*. In 1 Cor. 1:30, Paul writes: "By God's act you are in Christ Jesus; God has made him our wisdom, and in him we have our righteousness, our holiness, our liberation." Here, Paul uses various terms for the redemption that has occurred in Christ. He mentions not only righteousness, but also holiness and liberation. All three of these terms illustrate the soteriological quality of that which is to be understood as "wisdom." Here, righteousness, holiness and liberation mean the redemption from foolishness toward the wisdom of Jesus Christ.[22]

It is certainly correct to interpret the "doctrine of justification" as the "center of Pauline theology" and as the "explication of the 'word from the cross'."[23] And it is quite appropriate to read the theology of the cross retrospectively in the light of the doctrine of justification, which was developed later. However, it is just as correct to state that the terminology of justification does not yet play a central role in the correspondence with the Corinthians,[24] since at the beginning of the letter the redemptive event is primarily described in categories of wisdom. Moreover, the hypothesis of the doctrine of justification as the center of Pauline theology must be qualified: viewed across his entire epistolary correspondence, Paul uses several semantic and metaphorical fields to express the redemption that has occurred in Christ's cross. Jürgen Becker identifies five partially overlapping fields: reconciliation, liberation, various forms of representation, atonement/expiatory sacrifice, and justification.[25]

---

22. For similar readings: Helmut Merklein, *Der erste Brief an die Korinther, Kapitel 1-4*, ÖTK 7/1 (Gütersloh-Würzburg: Gütersloher Verlagshaus, 1992), 202; and Wolfgang Schrage, *Der erste Brief an die Korinther (1 Kor 1,1-6,11)*, EKK VII/1 (Zürich: Patmos, 1991), 214–15.
23. Thus Walter Klaiber, "Art. Rechtfertigung II," *RGG* (2004), 7:102.
24. See Jürgen Becker, *Paulus. Der Apostel der Völker* (Tübingen: Mohr Siebeck, 1998), 294–95.
25. Ibid., 432–37.

From these observations, we can conclude: not only with reference to the New Testament, but even in Paul's own writings, it becomes obvious that redemption encompasses more than that which can be expressed in the terminology of justification. The discourse of redemption comprises several "language games" within itself. The observation that the semantics of redemption cannot be reduced to the semantics of justification is not new in itself, neither regarding the Bible nor classical dogmatics. With respect to the latter, this stands to reason just looking at the fact that the *locus* of soteriology is usually not limited to the subject of justification alone, but also extends to other *topoi* that cannot be reduced to justification, such as sanctification, vocation, rebirth, or election.

Now, my hypothesis is *that the problem of the semantics of redemption being reduced to the semantics of justification has been aggravated by the conditions of the modern era, for the semantic field of "justification" has been reductively reshaped compared to Pauline and Reformation theology.* A short excursus will serve to elucidate this: anyone talking about "justification" in theological terms also always makes a statement about one's understanding of sin. Sin represents the human area of deficiency to which justification is related; sin is the main doctrinal concept vis-à-vis the term *justification*. And thus, conversely, it is also true that if the understanding of sin changes, so must the understanding of justification. The Christian concept of sin, however, has undergone various transformations in modern thought. Among other things, there are several instances of *decoupling*, which I would like to call to mind.

1. *Satanology has been decoupled from hamartiology due to the elimination of the devil.* Satan, the great tempter, liar, and master of confusion between good and evil, who literally got under people's skin and cast his spell over them, has been buried in

modern times in the West. With him vanished a power prevenient to sin, one that not only evokes sin, but at the same time prevents its recognition, thereby stabilizing it. The devil has vanished from Western modern thought; today, he might at best be in the details. For the most part, this is also true for theology. Schleiermacher's following statement can be taken as representative of this modern tendency: "The idea of the Devil, as developed among us, is so unstable that we cannot expect anyone to be convinced of its truth. . . ."[26] Even though twentieth-century theology saw a strange revival of demonology, it rarely repristinated all the classical characteristics of the old Satanology.

2. *Sin has been decoupled from its biologically relayed heritage and understood as irreducible original sin.* This process already emerges in Reformation theology. Maybe it shows itself most clearly—though little known—in Zwingli: he disputes that original sin is guilt and punishment for Adam's guilt (as Augustine did), because that would mean to understate the guilt character of sin. Instead, he suggests, at least in his 1525 work on baptism, we should understand original sin (*Erbsünde*) as a hereditary "defect" and distinguish it from sin or guilt. Zwingli's decision was heavily criticized, especially by Martin Luther. Later, Zwingli largely retracted this due to reasons immanent to his theology. However, Zwingli never saw his concept of sin as being outside of Reformation theology. Zwingli's differentiation of 1525 marks a provisional turning point that shows usually more subtle decoupling in Reformation theology with great clarity.[27] Of course, the decoupling from "heritage" later was somewhat compensated with a more profound understanding

---

26. F. D. E. Schleiermacher, *The Christian Faith* (London: Continuum, 1999), 161 (§44).

27. See Matthias D. Wüthrich, "'Der präst kann ye nit sünd sin.' Zwinglis Kritik an der

of the social and societal dimension of sin, as can be seen in Schleiermacher and later in Ritschl.[28]

3. *Sin has been decoupled from suffering, illness, and death.* It is true that the *malum morale*[29] and the *malum physicum* or *naturale* are not completely separated in the modern era. *Malum physicum* can still be understood as a consequence of *malum morale*. But this consequential relation was thought of as immanent to the world. Illness is not God's punishment conveyed from above, but an effect of evil resulting from the well-arranged structures of the world. The Lisbon earthquake of 1755, of course, also showed that there is a *malum physicum* that cannot be directly integrated into such world-immanent causal relations. There is a reality of natural disaster that cannot be accounted for and tied back to moral categories. Jewish philosopher Susan Neiman has elevated the decoupling of *malum morale* and *malum physicum* emerging here to be the mark of the history of modern philosophy.[30]

This decoupling, too, can be observed paradigmatically in Schleiermacher: for him, social evil indeed is a direct, *immediate* consequence of sin. Natural evil, in contrast—such as pain and death—is only *indirectly* related to sin. Objectively speaking, natural evil does not emerge from sin; that is only the case subjectively: the sinful person understands natural evil as punishment for her sins.[31] Schleiermacher's verdict is quite

---

traditionellen Erbsünde und ihre Barth'sche Rezeption," in Eva Harasta, ed., *Erbsünde* (Neukirchen-Vluyn: Neukirchener Theologie, 2012), 29–46.

28. Cf. Schleiermacher's reformulation of original sin as "the corporate act and the corporate guilt of the human race," in *The Christian Faith*, 285 (§71).

29. For simplicity's sake here I equate sin and *malum morale*. Of course, from a theological perspective, it must be emphasized that at least original sin in Reformation theology—in contrast to the sins (plural) resulting from it—precisely is not a moral, but a transmoral factor.

30. Susan Neiman, *Evil in Modern Thought: An Alternative History of Philosophy* (Princeton: Princeton University Press, 2002), 39, etc.

31. Schleiermacher, *The Christian Faith*, particularly 319–20 (§76.2).

remarkable: the traditional concept of death as a consequence of sin itself now appears to be the expression of sinful self-interpretation.[32] Twentieth-century theology largely followed Schleiermacher in the distinction between a natural death and a subjectively interpreted death due to sin, thereby factually ratifying this decoupling as well. The same can be said about illness, suffering, and pain, with death being only the most extreme of these conditions.

What is the result of all these decouplings (and eliminations)? It would be appropriate to speak of an *isolation* of sin from the figures of evil preceding and following it. This isolation results in *semantic reductions* and in the concept of sin being recoded in a more anthropocentric vein. In my view, these reductions concern the embedding of the concept of sin in creation theology, and they especially concern aspects of its bodily, cosmic manifestation. For example, the devil—traditionally a creature himself—stood for the bodily tribulations of human beings just as well as the overall cosmos. He represents an aspect in creation taking on a destructive existence of its own. For Paul it was still clear in Romans 8 that sin evokes the nothingness of all creation and its groaning. Sin, sins, the consequences of sin, death, and the law form a network.

The Reformers still considered it obvious that justification is related to a wider horizon of redemption integrating not only sin, but with it also death and the devil[33]—without wanting to naturalize sin in

---

32. That and how the connection between sin and death is a prerequisite in Reformation theology is shown for instance in question 42 of the Heidelberg Catechism.

33. Thus Luther, for example, repeatedly talks about evil by defining it as a network, a mesh of sin, death, and the devil—he talks of redemption "from sin, death and the devil." Ewald M. Plass, *What Luther Says* (St. Louis: Concordia, 2006), 343; and WA 35,477,6-9 or in *The Small Catechism* ("from all sins, from death and from the power of the devil," http://bookofconcord.org/smallcatechism.php). Thus, it is hardly surprising that in Luther's *Small Catechism*, justification also gains a dimension of creation theology. Especially his first

any way. This mythical network of evil and its immanent logic definitely breaks apart in the modern era. What remains are strange blank spaces in the discourse on evil (in a wider sense). Particularly in the twentieth century, these blank spaces caused theology to be somewhat lost for words. Of course, there were also creative efforts to refill these blank spaces in the twentieth century, for example, Karl Barth's doctrine of nothingness and Paul Tillich's concept of the demonic.

It is not my intention to use this deconstruction of the concept of evil in modern thought to record a history of decline from the good origins. I do not want to go back before Schleiermacher. I am merely trying to *point out a problem*. It must be assumed that the above-described semantic reductions in the field of hamartiology also led to semantic reductions in the term of justification. And I think I have made plausible, in this indirect way via the concept of sin, my *hypothesis* that the problem of reducing the semantics of redemption to the semantics of justification has intensified in the modern era.

If this hypothesis is correct, the question is all the more urgent: Can the term *justification* today still claim to comprise all that can be said about the redemption of the human being as a whole, including her bodily-creaturely aspects, including also the sometimes tragic aspects of her life?[34] Have we succeeded in capturing the dimensions of redemption of the *word of the cross* just by explicating it with the terminology of justification? Is that really the be-all and end-all, the height of wisdom?

That is doubtful. If we want to describe the redemption of human beings in theological terms, we must, I think, *not only think about*

article strikingly uses justification terminology. This is pointed out by, among others, Oswald Bayer, *Aus Glauben leben. Über Rechtfertigung und Heiligung* (Stuttgart: Calwer, 1990), 85.

34. Oswald Bayer has made remarkable attempts in this direction by trying to develop the creation theology dimensions and implications of Luther's concept of justification for the present day; see the preceding footnote.

justification, but also beyond it. Beyond it, and not only because of the problems of adaptation and the loss of relevance of the doctrine of justification. Beyond it mainly because even the Bible uses various semantic and metaphoric fields to talk about redemption, and because Christ's cross does not only refer to sin alone. Beyond it, also, because the semantic field of the term of justification has been reductively recoded in the modern era.

But if the soteriological reach of the semantics of justification is so precarious, can it still be appropriate to understand the *doctrine* of justification as the "center" and "core" of Protestant theology? Is the doctrine of justification really still the *articulus stantis et cadentis ecclesiae,* the article on which the church stands and falls—as expressed particularly in the Lutheran tradition?[35] Is it still the central article in the sense that it can be made the *criterion of all theological doctrinal statements of Protestant theology?*[36]

The Article on Which the Church Stands and Falls?

As I see it, there are three ways to respond to this question: (*a*) categorical denial, (*b*) affirmation subject to formal conditions, or (*c*)

---

35. Here, as earlier, the term *doctrine* is interpreted in a very wide sense. It includes the Pauline concept of justification just as that of the reformers, even though it is clear that what they called doctrine or article differs in character, regarding its proximity to the "Holy Scripture," its claim to validity and its degree of explication, from that which is called "doctrine" in systematic theology today. On the historical background: Theodor Mahlmann, "Zur Geschichte der Formel 'Articulus stantis et cadentis ecclesiae,'" *Lutherische Theologie und Kirche* 17 (1993): 187–94. In this specific form, the expression is probably first found in the works of the (Reformed) Genevan Francis Turretini in 1682; it is undisputed, that in substance it can be traced back to Martin Luther himself (see Theodor Mahlmann, Art. "Articulus stantis et (vel) cadentis ecclesiae," *RGG* (1998), 1:799–80.

36. This formula was and usually still is being related (also regarding the 18th article of the "Joint Declaration on the Doctrine of Justification") to its function as a doctrinal criterion for the sum total of dogmatic doctrinal statements (see, for instance, Härle, *Zur Gegenwartsbedeutung*, 69), while the ecclesial aspect, which is contained in the formula itself, is often presented as only secondary.

affirmation subject to the condition of a specific differentiation of content.

Without claiming to represent the current state of the discussion in all of its aspects, I want to comment briefly on these three possible responses. Special attention will be paid to Reformed theology (*a* and *c*, above). Its decisions are interesting insofar as it—despite extensive overlap with Lutheran theology regarding the definition of the doctrine of justification's content—often has determined the doctrine's function in a different way.[37]

a. With regard to the strong emphasis on the doctrine of sanctification in Reformed theology, it is hardly surprising that the definition of the doctrine of justification as the central article is at times categorically denied. Of course, this rejection is not based solely on the doctrine of sanctification, but also concerns the orientation—we might say, the "grammar"—of theology as a whole. Thus, Karl Barth states programmatically: "The *articulus stantis et cadentis ecclesiae* is not the doctrine of justification as such, but its basis and culmination: the confession of Jesus Christ. . . . The problem of justification does not need artificially to be absolutised and given a monopoly."[38]

Without losing sight of this christological access, John Webster goes one step further and votes against giving the doctrine of justification the status of *articulus stantis et cadentis ecclesiae*: "the only Christian doctrine that may legitimately claim to exercise a magisterial and judicial role in the corpus of Christian teaching is the doctrine of Trinity, since in that doctrine alone all other doctrines have their ultimate basis."[39] Accordingly, he considers it necessary

---

37. Cf. Michael Weinrich and John P. Burgess's "Preface" to their edited volume *What Is Justification About? Reformed Contributions to an Ecumenical Theme* (Grand Rapids: Eerdmans, 2009), x.
38. Karl Barth, *CD* IV/1, trans. G. W. Bromiley (London: T&T Clark, 2010), 15.

to locate the doctrine of justification in a "comprehensive trinitarian soteriology," and to develop "a quite different trinitarian model of justification."[40]

Whatever one may think about these two theologians' counterproposals, their criticism of the doctrinal status of the doctrine of justification is hard to disagree with—at least if one considers it necessary to make the doctrine of justification the central article *according to its scope of content and its material body of doctrine.*

b. The second possible response takes precisely this condition as its starting point. It tries to evade the dilemma between a validity claim aiming at the doctrinal whole and the materially restricted scope of the doctrine of justification by suggesting a formal principalization in addition to the material determinations. This tendency toward principalization, which emerged in the nineteenth century, can take several forms.[41] As an example, let us look at Paul Tillich. Regarding the doctrine of justification as the *articulus stantis et cadentis ecclesiae,* he states:

> I call it not only a doctrine and an article among others but also a principle, because it is the first and basic expression of the Protestant principle itself. It is only for unavoidable reasons of expediency a particular doctrine and should, at the same time, be regarded as the principle which permeates every single assertion of the theological system. It should be regarded as the Protestant principle that, in relation to God, God alone can act and that no human claim, especially no religious claim, no intellectual or moral or devotional "work," can reunite us with him.[42]

Tillich talks about the *Protestant* principle, but he does not see it

---

39. John Webster, *"Rector et iudex super omnia genera doctrinarum?* The Place of the Doctrine of Justification," in Weinrich and Burgess, eds., *What Is Justification About?*, 38; see also 47.

40. Ibid., 42 and 55.

41. Gerhard Sauter sees it implemented in the twentieth century in various ways by Paul Tillich, Rudolf Bultmann, and Gerhard Ebeling. Sauter, "Art. Rechtfertigung V," 28:329–30.

42. Paul Tillich, *Systematic Theology* (Chicago: University of Chicago Press, 1963), 3:223.

as limited to either the churches of the Reformation or any other church. "[I]t transcends every particular church, being an expression of the Spiritual Community."[43] Moreover, it must be complemented with the "Catholic substance" as the concrete embodiment of the presence of the divine spirit.[44] Quite understandably, Gerhard Sauter thinks that principalizations such as this threaten to erode the doctrine of justification.[45] At least, Tillich wants to retain the doctrine of justification in its material body, too, instead of understanding it solely in the sense of a formal principle of the relationship between God and human being. Of course, it cannot be overlooked that in other works, Tillich not only reinterprets the doctrine of justification regarding the question of its meaning, but significantly relativizes it in the process.[46]

Regarding the question of the doctrine of justification's centrality, Tillich's solution thus is to posit that it is the central article not due to its material provisions, its contents, or its juridical terminology, but solely based on its formal definition as the Protestant principle. Only in this version, solely based on principle and emptied of most of its content, does the doctrine of justification form the *articulus stantis et cadentis ecclesiae.*

However, it remains questionable whether (1) the material and formal-theoretical definitions of the doctrine of justification can be distinguished as neatly as Tillich's solution suggests, and, if that is the case, whether (2) the doctrine of justification in its form as a principle can still be called the doctrine of justification in the full sense.

A certain affinity to Tillich's way of addressing the issue of the

---

43. Ibid., 3:245.
44. Ibid.
45. Sauter, however, refers to Tillich's work *The Protestant Era* (Chicago: University of Chicago Press, 1948), in "Art. Rechtfertigung V," 28:329–30.
46. For example, think of Tillich's book *The Courage to Be* (New Haven: Yale University Press, 1952).

doctrine of justification's centrality can also be found in more recent approaches. Gunther Wenz, for example, assigns the doctrine of justification the function of a "regulative idea, as it were" to the overall context of dogmatics as a whole.[47] Of course, Wenz operates on the basis of a different concept of justification, but he, too, develops a formalization (if not principalization) of the doctrine of justification regarding its role as the *articulus stantis et cadentis ecclesiae*.

c. A third option remains—an option that is probably the most popular in current Protestant theology (at times with a certain overlap with the second option). The variations in which it can be observed have in common that they differentiate the term of justification in a specific way, with a corresponding effect on the understanding of the doctrine of justification. To illustrate this third

---

47. Gunther Wenz, *Grundfragen ökumenischer Theologie. Gesammelte Aufsätze* (Göttingen: Vandenhoek & Ruprecht, 1999), 1:78.

option, I once again choose two examples of Reformed theology[48] to show the scope of Reformed interpretations:

Even though Michael Weinrich and John P. Burgess emphasize that the doctrine of justification is "arguably the interpretive key to all other doctrines," they hasten to add: "even as it is conditioned by each of them."[49] This conditional relationship particularly seems to apply to the doctrine of the covenant and the doctrine of the Trinity: "Together, covenant and Trinity underlie the doctrine of justification and help to account for its critical place in the overall theological, confessional system."[50] Thus, according to Weinrich and Burgess, it would be wrong to elevate the doctrine of justification to the level of a "super-doctrine that determines the meaning of all other doctrines."[51]

---

48. Of course, there are also significant variations in theology informed by Lutheran thought: for example, think of Eberhard Jüngel who, together with Gerhard Gloege, turns the doctrine of justification into a category that determines all of our thoughts, words, and actions before God and that is to be understood as the "hermeneutical category" of theology. According to Jüngel, the doctrine of justification becomes such a category "because it brings all of theology into the dimension of a legal dispute: that is, the legal dispute of God about His honour, which is at the same time a legal dispute about the worth of human beings." Jüngel, *Justification: The Heart of the Christian Faith*, trans. Jeffrey F. Cayzer (Edinburgh: T&T Clark, 2001), 48. Here the horizon of the doctrine of justification is defined so widely that it scales the whole of theology. However, the question must be asked whether the concept of theology is not constricted by this. I am citing two other examples: Wilfried Härle assumes that the doctrine of justification can only be understood as the *articulus stantis et cadentis ecclesiae* to the extent that, on principle, it represents the *"comprehensive* self-interpretation of the Christian faith" (Härle, *Zur Gegenwartsbedeutung*, 78; see also Wilfried Härle and Eilert Herms, *Rechtfertigung. Das Wirklichkeitsverständnis des christlichen Glaubens* [Göttingen: Vandenhoek & Ruprecht, 1980], 10). However, it must first be reclaimed as such. According to Härle, the existential contemporary relevance can only be uncovered by means of significant hermeneutical efforts and requires the overcoming of juridical-penal semantics (*Zur Gegenwartsbedeutung*, 104). A similar point is made by Pierre Bühler, a Reformed theologian influenced by Luther who proposes to interpret the message intended by the term *justification* in such a way that it can be translated into several linguistic games that are comprehensible today. Pierre Bühler, *Ablass oder Rechtfertigung. Was brauchen wir zum Jubiläumsjahr 2000?*, trans. Esther Schweizer (Zürich: Pano Verlag, 2000), 57–67.

49. Michael Weinrich and John P. Burgess, "Introduction: Justification in a Reformed Perspective—Key Theses," in Weinrich and Burgess, eds., *What Is Justification About?*, 3.

50. Ibid., 2.

51. Ibid., 3.

Against this background, it is hardly possible to call the doctrine of justification the *articulus stantis et cadentis ecclesiae* in the traditional sense. Accordingly, Weinrich and Burgess take another approach: they propose to differentiate between the "message (or proclamation) of justification" and the "doctrine of justification."[52] The former is understood in a very wide sense, so that Weinrich can state later on: "justification may be envisaged as a key theme in the Bible as a whole, even where the Bible does not speak explicitly about justification and the juridical side of God's justice. There is a non-juridical use of justification that functions as the yeast in the whole of God's history with Israel and all humanity."[53] Maybe we can put it this way: for Weinrich and Burgess it is the word of justification on which church and theology stand and fall, but not the doctrine of justification.

For Jürgen Moltmann, the traditional Lutheran and Tridentine doctrine of justification is too caught up in the context of the medieval sacrament of penance. He proposes, against the background of the controversies surrounding the "Joint Declaration on the Doctrine of Justification," to reinterpret the doctrine of justification in the context of a fundamental "doctrine of the justification of God and human." Based on the biblical discourse of justice, he unfolds God's justice as a justice that both justifies the perpetrator and brings him to justice, and that also gives justice to the victim: a justice in which God comes into God's right concerning the human being as a whole. At the same time, the human being—in the course of these demonstrations of justice—in turn justifies God and proves God right.[54]

---

52. Ibid. See also "Preface," ix, as well as the distinction of a wide and a narrow concept of justification in Martien Brinkman and Michael Weinrich, "Justification as Reconciliation," in *Reformed World* 54 (2004): 69–70.

53. Michael Weinrich, "Justified for Covenant Fellowship: A Key Biblical Theme for the Whole of Theology," in Weinrich and Burgess, eds., *What Is Justification About?*, 10–11.

54. Jürgen Moltmann, "Die Rechtfertigung Gottes," in *Das Kreuz Jesu. Gewalt–Opfer–Sühne*, ed. Rudolf Weth (Neukirchen-Vluyn: Neukirchener, 2001), 120–39.

With the help of a more comprehensive, biblically determined understanding of justice and law, Moltmann expands the concept of justification and integrates it into a more broadly defined doctrine of the justification of God and human beings. In his article, Moltmann does not explicitly refer to the question of whether and to what extent the doctrine of justification is to be considered the *articulus stantis et cadentis ecclesiae*. Factually and indirectly, however, his modified doctrine of justification gives a clear answer: as it is traditionally understood, the doctrine of justification is not the central article.

I asked above whether and to what extent the doctrine of justification forms the central article of theology. We have seen that Protestant theology has responded to this question in widely different ways. Some may consider this question to be a relic of controversial theology and early Protestant self-delineation, an issue that is no longer in need of thought and effort. However, I think that further and more fundamental discussion is indeed advisable. For one, regarding the question 1 Cor. 1:30 provokes of how *a theology of the wisdom and foolishness of God* relates to the doctrine of justification. And second, regarding the fundamental question of the *organizational principle of theological logic* that always accompanies the question of the central article. Third, I think the question of why the doctrine of justification should be that one article on which, not theological systematics, but the *church* stands and falls, is far from obsolete. This last question should be particularly controversial with regard to the upcoming Reformation jubilees of 1517 and 1519.

12

———

The Foolishness and Wisdom of All God's Ways: The Case of Creation *Ex Nihilo*

Kathryn Tanner

God violates the norms and expectations of those who take themselves to be wise and in that way appears foolish in the eyes of the world.[1] The cross of Christ is the most startling, scandalous, and in that sense paradigmatic instance of this. But I believe Christian theologians soon generalize from it. In all God's activity *ad extra* God violates the expectations of the wise by being intimately connected

1. A slightly different version of this article was first published under the title "Creation *ex nihilo* as Mixed Metaphor" in *Modern Theology* 29, no. 2 (2013): 138–55. The editors wish to thank John Wiley & Sons for permission to publish it.

to a world of loss, suffering, and conflict. God for us is simply a God who breaks down the wisdom of the wise: a God of radical transcendence who always and everywhere violates the usual canons of good sense, common standards of sense making. And yet—again as a generalization of 1 Corinthians 1–2—this foolishness on God's part brings its own deeper wisdom. Intelligibility arises out of the violation of standards of good sense. God's ways with respect to the world—on the cross and elsewhere—begin to make sense just to the extent one is willing to let one's standards of sense making be compromised.

Divine Transcendence

Divine transcendence in this sense is not a doctrinal affirmation of any ordinary sort but a grammatical remark about the failings of all theological language: it signals a general linguistic disturbance, the violation of commonsense standards of predicative attribution, in language about God. Following one common way of making this point about divine transcendence, one could say that God is not a kind of thing: God is beyond every genus. God's transcendence means that God is not one instance among others of a general sort of thing, distinguished from (and ranked hierarchically with respect to) those others by the supreme degree to which it exhibits the designated quality. Divinity is not a class term; and therefore things within the world cannot be differentiated and ordered by the degree to which they exhibit such a (non-)predicate. For this reason talk about God systematically violates the usual canons of sense making.

The Implications of Divine Transcendence for Theology

Since God is in this way incapable of absorption into a general category, God has a nonpredicative identity, one could say. God is identified, in other words, by this very failure to mean. God becomes the paradigmatic unassimilable Other, the (paradoxically nonpredicatively grounded) paradigm for all that remains indigestible to sense-making practices that insist on the exhaustive, homogenizing subsumption of particulars under general concepts. What it means to say that God is transcendent cannot, as a result, be captured semantically in the particular statements that affirm it—such statements as, "God is beyond identity and difference." Such statements do not, in other words, effectively convey a meaning for the term *transcendence*. That "meaning" is instead merely displayed or shown in the nonsemantic surplus of theological language itself, in the failure to mean that haunts all theological claims, in the unclosable gap between the recognition *that* theological claims signify and the inability to specify exactly *what* it is, conceptually, that they convey.

This account of transcendence has the following implications for theology. The first is that no set of concepts or images is proper to it. A theology that abides by these apophatic commitments makes do with whatever categories are at hand, twisting and violating them according to its own fundamentally nonsemantic purposes. Theological discourse is therefore always a hybrid discourse, in two senses. First, theology is always haunted by the resonances of the categories and images proper to other fields of discourse, resonances that it draws upon and disturbs in the process of its own discursive self-constitution. It always contains what it is working discursively to set itself against; borrowed language always carries the undertones appropriate to that language's more usual field of application, no matter how perverse its new theological employment. Theological discourse is therefore never simply itself—never simply religious in sharp distinction from the secular, or Christian in simple opposition to what is pagan or Jewish. It arises as an internal modification of that over against which it comes to define itself. Second, this sort of theology makes do with almost anything to hand, in an apparently indiscriminately profligate raiding of multiple fields of discourse. It borrows from all sides to produce a seemingly anarchic bricolage, fundamentally "disciplined" by only a thoroughgoing refusal of sense, by the systematic repudiation of all ordinary canons of sense making.

Theology of this apophatic sort does not, moreover, respect the proper boundaries of the particular concepts or images it deploys. This is an important subsidiary form of linguistic disturbance beyond the basic forms mentioned earlier: basic canons of sense making are violated, but so, too, are particular linguistic habits about what follows from what, habits based on established boundaries of the meanings of particular terms. This sort of semantic violation—of particular categories and images—means, first of all, that affirmations about God do not imply corresponding denials. Talk about God violates the Spinozistic dictum, maintained in ordinary language about things, that all determination is negation; and the reverse. In other words, language about God contravenes the way in ordinary speech that the affirmation of certain qualities implies the denial of others, and the denial of certain properties implies the affirmation of others. For example, when one denies that God is a body it does not follow that God is spiritual (or whatever is ordinarily incompatible with materiality). And the reverse holds as well: when one affirms that God is immaterial, one is not denying that God has bodily existence. Similarly, when one denies that God can be rendered by images, one is not implying that God is an abstractly definable concept; and the reverse. In sum, God transcends the application of all ordinarily contrastive terms. As a result, mutually exclusive categories (for example, categories of both intentional agency and natural causation) can be used to the same end. Second, the "same" categories, conversely, are susceptible to widely disparate uses. Links of presupposition and implications among statements that follow a category's ordinary sense are often disrupted in different ways, by different theologians or by the same theologian, depending on the purpose to be served. Moreover, any new links of presupposition and implication formed by such theological disruption are highly fragile and far more susceptible to breakage than is the case, for example, with the more firmly established habits of everyday speech that theologians are often reworking. This fragility holds for discursive links in the broad sense of both language and action. There are no necessary—and in that sense proper—consequences of theological claims. Theological claims can easily be made to do an uncommonly wide variety of things.

Divine Transcendence and Creation *Ex Nihilo*

This sort of account of divine transcendence arises in tandem with an account of creation *ex nihilo* by way of an internal modification of a widely held Greco-Roman problematic or dilemma surrounding the question of how a God different from the world can be intimately involved with it (or, perhaps better stated, directly responsible for it and for the qualities it displays). The dilemma is this: God is either like some of the things one finds in the world and then there is no problem saying that God is intimately involved with the world. God is intimately involved with just those things that are most like the world. Or, God is radically different from the world—not like anything in it—but then God cannot have anything very directly to do with it. What makes no sense is what Christians come to affirm: that a radically transcendent God is directly productive of the entirety of the world, as the doctrine of creation *ex nihilo* implies.

The philosophical principle—the wisdom of the wise—that lies behind the dilemma would seem to be "like is involved with like." But supporting such a principle is simply the commonsensical idea that, were unlike things to be intimately involved with one another, their natures would be compromised. Some things, one could say, are essentially defined by not being like other things and were these different kinds of things to be too intimately associated with one another they would corrupt one another's natures. The boundaries that essentially define a kind of thing have to be guarded against those things that it is defined as not being.

Christians resist either pole of the dilemma (and therefore the principle upon which it rests) to the extent they want to hold that nothing in the world is like God (a version of monotheism), and yet affirm that God is intimately involved with the world as its creator and redeemer. Certain distinctively Christian preoccupations with Jesus would, moreover, make such resistance imperative. There is a growing desire, in at least some Christian quarters in the first few centuries CE, to affirm a peculiarly heightened intimacy between God and Jesus, which nevertheless does not compromise the difference between God and humanity: God in the highest (and not merely some lesser, mediating deity) is to be identified with Jesus, who is a human being like any other in respect of his humanity (and therefore not some superman, some quasi-divine human, mediating between divinity and ordinary humans).

A way out of the dilemma is found when accounts of both God's transcendence and God's involvement in the world as creator are radicalized. The result is a consistently apophatic view of divine transcendence and a doctrine of creation *ex nihilo*. In such a fashion, sense is made from the nonsensical; the two affirmations that seem in conflict with one another now appear compatible.

Because this Christian position is produced as an internal modification of the Greco-Roman problematic, that problematic has to be explored with some thoroughness. Consider the first horn of the dilemma, where God is like the world and directly involved in it. One finds a supposition of that sort in popular Greco-Roman polytheism. Greek and Roman gods and goddesses are very much like human beings, the chief differences being their immortality and superhuman powers. Humans can indeed become gods after death: emperors are deified; heroes are, too. The flip side of this similarity to humans is that gods are quite integral to the normal run of human events. The gods are the source of those things that regularly and normally occur in human life. They have very particular domains corresponding to their characters. For instance, the belligerent Ares is the God of war. As a whole they represent all the things that commonly befall a person and that he or she must take into account and adjust to if things are to go well, and all those things that one can go against only at one's peril.

In the rational theologies that follow Greco-Roman criticism of this popular polytheism—for example, the rational theologies of Plato and his followers, Stoicism, Aristotle and his followers—one finds a similar dynamic in more sophisticated form. Divinity is generally still a class name, a sortal term, specifying those principles within the world responsible for order, pattern, and regularity. The characteristics of divinity, how divinity is defined, follow from those functions: what is divine is eternal, stable, unchanging, simple, and rational. Any number of things can therefore be called divine: (a) The cosmos as a whole can be called divine insofar as it is thought to be eternal and harmonized by proportion among its parts. (b) Heavenly bodies can be called divine in that they are thought to be eternal (because immaterial) and in that they move in regular circular motions. (c) Principles of mathematics—numbers, geometrical figures, proportions—can be considered divine in that they seem to be ordering principles par excellence, to be eternal truths and to capture a kind of ideal perfection never instantiated in fact. (d) Forms or ideas in a Platonic or Aristotelian sense can also be called divine insofar as they provide intelligibility, enable one to generalize about the nature of things, and appear to have a stability, permanence, and ideal quality not found in the multiple, changing, and impermanent things to which they give shape. (e) Finally, soul can be considered divine as a self-propelling source of motion that is assumed to be regular in accord with intelligible ideas. All these instances of divinity can be ranked by degrees; some are more divine than others. Soul, for example, usually has a lower rank than forms or ideas since as a principle of movement it is part of the world of time and change and may work only in tandem with, and therefore is inextricably bound up with, changeable, impermanent material bodies.

If divinity is one principle among others that are necessary to explain the way the world is, then there is obviously no problem in saying that divinity is intimately involved with the workings of the world. Divinity is simply one of the world's essential factors or components. Divinity is primarily responsible for a particular aspect of the world as we know it: its ordered, regular aspects; just those aspects of the world that are most like divinity.

But often no sharp distinction is drawn between nondivine and divine aspects of the world in order to make the integration of diverse principles within the world seem plausible. In Stoicism, for instance, the divine world soul is itself material along with the world it pervades and arranges—soul is just a more ethereal or fiery form of matter. That similarity of nature seems to be why the two—soul and body—can be so well integrated. In Plato, too, material things, despite their impermanence and mutability, can share or participate in the eternal forms. The form of Life can therefore have something directly to do with living things because changing and impermanent embodied things can be like the form Life; they can share in its qualities.

The second horn of the dilemma is found where more dualistic accounts of divinity are offered in Greco-Roman thought, accounts in which divinity is opposed to everything in the world. Consider Plato's distinction between a world of being and becoming, between an intelligible world and a material world. According to this more dualistic way of characterizing divinity, divinity does not seem to be a principle in the world but a principle quite distinct from *any* in it. The intelligible world is simply opposed to the world of time, change, and motion, as a whole; the whole world—with all its components—is simply not divine. This more dualistic account of divinity comes out in Plato's more dualistic treatment of the forms in portions of the *Parmenides*, according to which things of this world do not participate in the divine forms but are merely pale imitations of them. As pale imitations of the forms, things of this world have a kind of internal sense but no intelligibility or order that is in any active way bestowed upon them by the forms. A more radically transcendent and less this-worldly notion of divinity is also suggested by Plato's account of the idea of the Good in the *Republic*, an idea that seems beyond all the forms as some sort of ineffable principle or source of their unity.

Aristotle's unmoved mover can also be interpreted as a similar propulsion of divinity outside the world of change and impermanence, although Aristotle, unlike Plato, would reject any claim of transcendent forms and therefore reject *that* Platonic way of making the point about divinity in opposition to the world of becoming. The unmoved mover of Aristotle seems to be setting the whole eternal cycle of motion in the heavens into motion from beyond it. The unmoved mover does not seem to be a principle in the world but outside it in some sort of sovereign indifference to the whole of what is going on there.

Beyond Transcendence as Distance

Some of these examples—Plato's dualistic rendering of the forms, Aristotle's unmoved mover—already suggest how the more transcendent God becomes in these Hellenistic world-pictures, the less God seems to have much to do very directly with the world as we know it. But that sort of implication is especially evident in many of the religious cosmologies of a mixed Platonic, Aristotelian, and Stoic character in the second and third centuries CE—for example, in Middle Platonism. Here a high God, a supremely transcendent God, is set into the mix of fundamental principles or components of the cosmos (matter, forms, or ideas, active intelligence, and soul) as they figure in Plato's myth of world construction in the *Timaeus*. The new supreme, transcendent divine principle typically combines Aristotle's unmoved mover thinking itself with Plato's discussion of the idea of the Good in the *Republic* and some metaphysical suggestions about a supreme principle of unity in Plato's *Parmenides*. (Plato himself does not make the latter connection in the *Timaeus*, though there is some mysterious reference to the father of all as an additional principle to the ones I mentioned.) This high God or first God or supremely transcendent God seems to set off a multiplication of divine principles that are all more or less designed to explain the same thing: order and rationality in the cosmos. Divine principles are multiplied to produce a kind of buffer zone between the first God and the material world that is rationally ordered. For example, in the Middle Platonist Albinus, there is a *prime intelligence* (thought thinking itself, the source of thought), then a *secondary intelligence* (an actualized intellect, perhaps thought thinking the forms), a *potential intellect* (thought capable of thinking and perhaps brought to think by an already actualized intellect), then a *world soul* (a living thing possessed of intellect), and then *lesser divine souls or intellects* with more restricted spheres of operation. The high God, consequently, is not directly concerned with ordering the world of time and change; instead these intermediary divine principles are. These lesser deities are less divine, more like what is not divine—matter—and therefore the more appropriate ordering principles for it. They can order matter in a way that will allow it to be what it is: something characterized by impermanence and change. The first God is only responsible for ordering the intellect of the second divine principle most like itself. So, not only is the supreme God responsible for only what is like itself—rationality, order, pattern, proportion—but the first God is not even directly responsible for those things (at least insofar as they make up ingredient features of the world as we know it).

The transcendence of God is imaged here as distance; transcendence is understood spatially, as a distance or spatial interval occupied by intermediary divinities. And one finds much the same thing in a more straightforwardly Aristotelian cosmology that talks about the first God as simply the unmoved mover. There is the same spatialized understanding of transcendence as distance and the same multiplication of divinities to explain order in the world. The unmoved mover directly influences only what is most like itself—the single, eternal circular motions of the heavenly bodies—and it is these heavenly bodies that are themselves responsible, in turn, for the multiple and linear movements of generation and becoming on earth (for example, the growth of plants).

One also of course finds much the same thing in Gnosticism. Because they often denigrate the material world more than simple Platonists or Aristotelians would, Gnostics tend to multiple divine principles almost *ad infinitum* to produce a buffer zone between the high God and this world (while also including a moment of disruption and disorder within the descending scale of divine beings). Only at the end of this scale of divine beings is there a divinity dumb and disordered enough to produce the deformed and disintegrated components of the world as we know it: matter, active world-forming souls, and sparks of divinity.

Yet it is the very emanationist principles found in Gnosticism, and maintained more consistently in neo-Platonism (that is, without a Gnostic moment of disruption and disorder and a personalistically conceived demiurge), that suggest a way beyond the dilemma. In the emanationist scheme the typical Hellenistic characterization of the first God begins to enable God's involvement in the world to be deepened in both scope and manner. There are no longer a number of independent cosmological principles (as there are in Plato or Albinus or Aristotle) but all the factors that go into the world as we know it are the ultimate productions of the first God. The first God is therefore ultimately responsible for matter as well as form or ideas; matter is also ultimately traceable back to the first God through a number of intermediary deities. And divinity is involved in the world not just as an ordering principle but as a productive principle: everything comes out of or emanates from the first God. Although clearer in a neo-Platonist such as Plotinus, one finds the same thing in Gnosticism, despite the break in emanations with the deformed products of the last divinity (out of which the world is constructed by art): everything in the world in some way unfolds out of the divine realm. In sum, we find here a wider scope for the indirect involvement of the first God—including matter—and a deeper manner of involvement, a productive involvement.

The neo-Platonism of Plotinus begins to reveal what it is about the characterization of the first God that suggests this widening of scope and deeper involvement. First of all, Plotinus suggests that there is something about the way the first God is characterized that breaks the like-is-involved-with-like principle. Plotinus foregrounds the very common Hellenistic idea that the first God is formless or beyond form—neither a this or a that, not any particular kind of thing. The same thing is indicated by saying that the first God is beyond being—meaning that God is beyond *finite* being, which is itself only by being a definite something, a particular sort of thing in contrast to other sorts of things. If the forms of things—intelligible ideas—come from the first God (these are usually in Hellenistic cosmologies the primary and immediate product of the first God), then, Plotinus points out, like is not coming from like but forms are grounded in what they are not—the formless—and the principle "like from like" does not hold. More importantly, Plotinus suggests that it is just *because* the first God is not a kind of thing that it can be responsible for more than what it is like. "The cause . . . of all existing things cannot be any one of these things."[2] Because God is not any particular kind of thing, God is able to produce any sort of thing and therefore all of them. What Plotinus seems to be suggesting here is that what limits the scope of God's involvement to a particular kind of thing—intelligibles, forms—is the characterization of God as a particular kind of thing. Talking about God as beyond kinds removes the limitation. One must avoid characterizing God in terms of one side of a contrast that applies to things in the world, because doing so makes it hard to see how God can be responsible for the contrast *as a whole*, how God can produce both sorts of thing that constitute the contrast.

Plotinus also suggests that something about the usual characterization of the first principle conflicts with the idea that transcendence means distance. Distance in space, separation, is not what the difference between the first God and everything else implies. The first principle is not, in other words, located at a distance from everything else in space as the spatial models of cosmic

---

2. Plotinus, *The Enneads* 6.9, section 6, trans. Joseph Katz, in *The Philosophy of Plotinus* (New York: Appleton-Century-Crofts, 1950), 149–50.

principles so common in Greco-Roman thought suggest. Even though Plotinus uses a spatial model, one should not take the model literally. Why not? Because God is different from everything else by containing no difference. That sort of characterization of the first principle—that it contains no multiplicity—is quite common in Hellenistic philosophy. Given such a characterization, Plotinus argues, the One—the first principle—cannot be absent from or far from anything, since the first principle contains no difference in itself with which to be separate from it. The One has to be perfectly present everywhere—to every sort of the thing—because it is just that one which excludes difference and exteriority. "As the One does not contain difference, it is always present (to everything)."[3]

In sum, the more transcendent God is, the more intimately involved God is with everything. The two go together. And the dilemma is thereby resolved.

Plotinus, however, fails to follow through on this insight consistently. First of all, he commonly falls back on the idea that like is directly involved only with like. The first principle produces directly only what is most like itself—*Nous*—the intelligible, the eternal, what is as unified as anything can be short of the One. The direct operation of the One still seems restricted by kind. Second, talk of the unity of the One, rather than suggesting what is beyond all contrasts between kinds, seems to involve a simple contrast with what is multiple. The One is not also beyond the contrast between the one and the multiple, but becomes a kind of thing among others, that kind of thing which is one rather than internally divided. This means that beings which include difference and multiplicity are not really present to the One as the beings they are—multiple and internally differentiated beings. To be one with the One, present to it, one must

3. Ibid., 152.

leave multiplicity and difference behind. One must become like the One to be present to it, one with it. "We are present to the One insofar as we contain no difference."[4] "The One is not absent from anything though in another sense it is absent from all things. It is present only to those who are able to receive it . . . by virtue of their similarity to it" (and that means by virtue of their leaving difference and multiplicity behind).[5]

With Irenaeus, we see something like what I have suggested could be gotten out of Plotinus, the sense, that is, that Hellenistic ideas about God's radical transcendence suggest something that most Hellenistic philosophers do not realize: God is intimately involved with everything. Particularly in Book 2 of his *Against Heresies*, Irenaeus takes Gnostic ideas about divinity as a pleroma—a fullness without limit, the all, what contains everything without itself being contained (very common Hellenistic ideas about God)—and argues that they do not suggest what the Gnostics assert: that the first God has nothing very directly to do with this world, that the first God is far off at a distance and that we must escape this world, leave it in spirit and in flesh, in order to return to that first principle. The argument here is rather simple. If God is this unlimited fullness then nothing really exists outside its direct field of influence and concern, as the Gnostics assume. When the Gnostics say that the material world is produced by and under the control of a defective principle—the demiurge—who exists and exerts his influence outside the fullness of God, then they put a limit around God, they suggest that God is contained by something else, and therefore they imply that God is not really God. If God is what the Gnostics say God is—fullness without limit—then God's presence and influence are unrestricted in their range; there is nothing that exists apart from God

---

4. Ibid.
5. *Enneads* 6.9, section 4, 145.

and nothing that is not subject to God's direct influence. God is the measureless context and source for everything; everything is in God's territory, as Irenaeus puts it.

The conclusions of this argument are also used by Irenaeus to dispute the idea of divinity as a generic category and to affirm monotheism in that sense. If God is not at a distance from the world, then there is no need for, no place for, intervening divine principles to relate God to the world outside God. There is instead only one God, and all the intermediary deities that Gnostics talk about are really only names for what exists all together and at once in that one God. Irenaeus is really replaying here the same sort of argument he used to dispute a limited scope for the first God's influence. If there are many deities at a remove from the first God and those deities appear sequentially, temporally, out of the first God by a process of emanation, then the first God again appears to be a limited being, something contained, a being circumscribed in time and place. These various deities must therefore exist in the first God—the only God there is, is that one God—and because they are in God they are all equally God and bear no relations of before and after with respect to one another.

Again, the solution to the dilemma is to show that what makes God different from what is not God is exactly what ensures that God is directly and intimately related to everything. And in order to show that, one must develop in very particular ways both the claim about God's transcendence and the claim about God's involvement in the world. First, God's transcendence has to be talked about in such a way that the difference between God and the world is not like any of the differences among things within the world. And that basically means that the difference between God and the world is not to be discussed as a simple difference between kinds, the sort of difference that distinguishes sorts of beings within the world. God is neither like the world nor simply unlike it. God is beyond the difference between like and unlike, beyond simple identifications or simple contrasts. That is just what makes God different from anything else.

Second, God's involvement in the world—particularly as a productive principle—should have an unlimited scope and be utterly direct in manner. That, I take it, is the point of creation *ex nihilo*. To say that God creates by working on anything (for example, uncreated prime matter) or with (or through) anything (for example, with the help of, or by means of, other creative principles) would be to restrict the scope of God's creative activity and/or to make that activity less than immediate in its relations with at least some features of the world. Saying either one would also run counter to the radicalized account of divine transcendence, by suggesting that God is a sort of being alongside others. To claim that the world is created out of God—the other alternative to a creation *ex nihilo* position—would also run counter to this radicalized account of divine transcendence if the claim were taken to mean the quasi-divinity of the world, the world's difference from God in degree of divinity. Emanationist imagery, as I will show in a moment, is often retained in creation *ex nihilo* accounts (for obvious reasons given its importance to the move beyond what I have been calling the Greco-Roman problematic), but with significant warping.

The practical resonances of these radicalized claims about God's transcendence and creative agency need have very little to do, therefore, with support for a principle of coercive domination or for dualistic hierarchies among creatures. When seen as a modification of the Greco-Roman problematic, radicalized transcendence seems designed to prevent the divinizing of any this-worldly status quo, while relativizing the significance of differences among creatures: none of those differences makes any difference with reference to intimacy to God. (I leave out of account here the difference between good and evil, which is often a serious complicating feature of these sorts of accounts.) In contrast to views typical of the first horn of the Greco-Roman problematic, the given order and reason of things in this world (both natural and sociopolitical) are not likened to the divine and due respect as such. Nor are qualities associated with rationality and order privileged over against the messy realities of embodied existence.

Creation *ex nihilo* means that there is nothing outside the direct reach of God's beneficent working as creator, nothing that in its obstructing power might mean the world is fated to remain only as good as it now appears or has been up until now (as in the first horn of the Greco-Roman problematic), nothing that must simply be escaped or left behind in the search for the greater good (as in the second horn of that dilemma). One need not (as in the first horn of the dilemma) simply resign or accommodate oneself to how the world works on the supposition that this is the best that the divine cosmic principles can do given the other recalcitrant cosmological materials with which they must work. Nor (as in the second horn) does a pessimism about the messy material features of this world prompt one to pin one's hopes on extrication from those features, on refusal of them, purification from them. Instead, one can entertain extravagant hopes for a genuinely novel future good for the world as a whole, pinning one's hopes on the unconstrained productive powers of a God who gives rise to the whole world without being it, rather than on the unrealistically optimistic belief that the world is really (at least potentially) much better than it has so far appeared to be.[6]

---

6. Tertullian's "Against Hermogenes" can be read to be making these practical points.

Mixed Metaphors

Creation *ex nihilo*, as I have suggested above, constitutes itself as the rejection of both creation from or through something, and creation out of God. But since this relation with what it rejects is constitutive of creation *ex nihilo*, neither rejection is total. Typically, creation *ex nihilo* positions include the imagery and concepts of both these rejected viewpoints—on the one hand, personalistic images and concepts appropriate for artifactual production, and, on the other, the naturalistic images and concepts associated with emanation—while violating their proper bounds. It is the mixing of these two seemingly incompatible sets of images and concepts to discuss the very same divine productive process that, one might say, distinguishes the creation *ex nihilo* position. It is the other typical way that creation *ex nihilo* generates sense out of the violation of common sense.

Divine Transcendence in the Creative Act: The Case of Thomas Aquinas

Usually, one or the other set of images and concepts takes primacy. For example, in the medieval period Thomas Aquinas makes the idea of God's intentional agency in creating the world primary: God conceives the world to be created, intellectually, and brings it about through an act of free will. Bonaventure is influenced more by the Dionysian emanationist language of self-diffusion: God radiates out into the world like light or flows out into the world like water from its source. Similarly, in the modern period Friedrich Schleiermacher is more inclined to talk of the necessity of God's operations in ways that might suggest natural causality and Karl Barth to talk of God's loving freedom in highly personalistic terms. These divergent emphases approximate one another, however—by way of the mixing of the two sets of images and concepts, and through the severity of the modifications made to even the preferred imagery.

Aquinas, for example, resists making emanationist categories his primary ones for a number of reasons. First, natural production (which is the model for creation out of God) suggests that what is produced is of the same kind as its producer. For instance, the effects of heat are hot; offspring are the same kind of animals as their mothers; and so on. The radical account of transcendence forbids divinity to be in this way a kind shared with the world. Second, natural causes are restricted in their effects; they tend to produce only a single sort of effect or instance. Fire only heats; mares give birth only to other horses. Used to talk about God's creation of the world, such language would therefore restrict the scope of what God is responsible for as creator. Aquinas associates this restriction of effects with the necessary character of natural causes' productivity: they must be productive to the extent their natural capacities are actualized; they therefore do not act by free choice. Acting on intention, on the other hand, makes possible (in principle) an infinitely extensible diversity of productions. For example, a free agent can choose to make a house, or go to the store, or write a book, and so on. Third, natural causes already include in themselves, in a higher form, what they give rise to. When applied to God and the world, this might slight the value and dignity of created things outside God; the world, it seems, would be better off remaining as it exists within God (where it exists *as* God).

He favors personalistic imagery, then, by default, by a kind of process of elimination, but also because he thinks such imagery helps show the all-inclusive scope of God's activity as creator—and (as I now suggest) the transcendence of God. Language of intentionality—language of knowing, believing, thinking, willing, intending—has a peculiar grammatical structure: verbs of intention have clauses for their grammatical objects ("I think *that* such and such"). The terms in those clauses therefore have what is called in modern logical parlance referential opacity, that is, the terms only refer to their objects under a particular description of them; and therefore the truth of a statement concerning intentions does not necessarily carry over when terms with a different meaning but the same reference are substituted in the object clause. (For example, if it is true that I think Barack Obama is handsome, that does not imply that it is true that I think the current president of the United States is handsome, because I may not know who the current president is.) Referential opacity means that what characterizes the willing, thinking, intending, and so on, of the subject need not also characterize the referents of the terms in the object clause. Nothing, indeed, is implied one way or another. For example, my thinking ill of others may be necessary (because I am an inveterately nasty person) without that ill will or the necessity of it implying anything about the referents of my scorn. They may not be as bad as I think they are (who knows?) and if they are, they are not necessarily so because I need to think they are. If one talks about God's creating the world using intentional language (for example, if one says God creates the world by the very process of intellection and will) then one's language about God will display the idea of God's transcendence: the world need not be like or unlike God; what is said about the character of God's knowing and willing will imply nothing either way about the character of the world.

Despite this preference for personalistic language, Aquinas modifies it so severely that emanationist language is rehabilitated. God produces the world like a human being might freely choose to build a house of which she has a mental conception. That is the preferred imagery. But in God's case there are no materials; God's creation of the world presupposes nothing prior to it, upon which

God works. And there are no tools, no means. Indeed, God creates the world without any intervening process at all, immediately. The rejection of creation on or by way of anything requires all such modifications.

The last modification of personalistic agency, in particular (that is, the denial of any intervening process), was already intimated in saying above that God creates in the very process of thinking and willing. God, unlike a human agent, does not have to take any additional action to bring about what God intends. What would be intransitive acts in human beings—acts of reasoned willing that remain in the agent—are therefore transitive acts (like my picking up a hammer to build a house frame) in God, that is, acts with external effects. The closest analogues here are the favorite images of the emanationist scheme. For instance, fire and sunlight produce their effects immediately, without doing anything, without any intervening process, just by being themselves. (Images of bodily reproduction are unsuitable for this purpose.)

Aquinas also severely modifies the usual presuppositions and implications of the language of free choice, so that again emanationist language resurfaces. God's free choice of the world involves no deliberation; God never begins to so choose after a time of not doing so; God's choice involves no successive acts; and so on. The idea that God does not have to do anything in order to create the world extends, in short, even to having to make a decision. God creates the world simply by being what God always is; God creates the world insofar as God is always already in act. Everything God needs to create the world is already prepared. God does not come to decide to create the world; if that is God's intention, then God always intends to create the world. Again, the sun illuminating the air, fire heating things up, would seem the closest analogues. Fire does not need to do anything that it is not already doing to heat up what is brought near it; it is already throwing off heat. That is all just part of what it means to be fire.

Ultimately, all that is left of the idea of free choice for Aquinas is the idea of a non-necessary logical relation between God's being and nature, on the one hand, and God's intention to create the world, on the other. From God's existence and nature one cannot infer with any logical necessity that God wills the world—this one or any one at all. The latter does not follow from the former by any necessary logical implication. Aquinas thinks that personalistic imagery is better able to display this point since natural causes (that work immediately) are necessarily productive (unless hindered or defective). Fire, or example, has no choice but to heat up the surrounding air; it would not be itself without doing so.

Theologians who favor emanationist imagery are generally more wary of untoward anthropomorphic connotations of personalistic language: "God as a fussy, arbitrary little deity who, after aeons of inertia, suddenly decided to create a world."[7] To insist on God's free choice in creating (especially while reserving language of emanation for intra-trinitarian processions) is to suggest a simple contrast with agents who do not act by free choice, in violation of a radical view of divine transcendence. Repudiating language of free choice (without refusing personalistic imagery), Schleiermacher, for example, suggests that, if anything, God should be talked about as the perfect artist "who in a state of inspired discovery thinks of nothing else, to whom nothing else offers itself, save what he [sic] actually produces."[8] "[To] suppose that God also decides and produces by choice and deliberation [is] a view which from of old every form of teaching in any degree consistent has repudiated."[9] It is better simply to say that

7. Arthur Hilary Armstrong, "Platonic *Eros* and Christian *Agape*," *Downside Review* 79 (1961): 111.
8. Friedrich Schleiermacher, *The Christian Faith*, ed. H. R. MackIntosh and J. S. Stewart, Fortress Texts in Modern Theology (Philadelphia: Fortress Press, 1976), §55, 225.
9. Ibid.

God creates the world necessarily in the way fire and light necessarily produce their effects while denying that in the case of God necessity excludes freedom. "We must . . . think of nothing in God as necessary without at the same time positing it as free, nor as free unless at the same time necessary."[10]

Indeed, theologians such as Bonaventure who favor emanationist imagery do not just assert that in God's case necessity and freedom are not at odds; they have a way of explaining the freedom of this God's necessary creation, the freedom of God who would not be God without diffusing God's own goodness outward to the creature. God is good and the good must diffuse itself, but this diffusion of the good is already perfectly achieved in God's own trinitarian life: perfect self-diffusion results in exact equality with the one who diffuses and this is only possible if the effects of such diffusion are themselves perfectly divine. There is no need, therefore, for God to diffuse the good in creating; the God whose trinitarian life is already constituted by self-diffusion would be perfectly fecund even if there were no world. God does not need to create as if in not doing so God would suffer a lack; God creates instead because of the superfluity, the excess, of God's already achieved goodness. The imagery is now no longer simply of water but of an overflowing spring; not simply of light but of superabundant effulgence.

Creating the world can for these reasons be thought of as an act of generosity, an unforced demonstration of regard for what is other than God. (The point of God's already achieved perfection is not therefore to stress the isolated self-sufficiency of God.) Self-communication of the good, an impersonal cosmological principle maintaining that what is good naturally brings forth the good, becomes a gracious concern for the good of others. Personalistic language returns in the language of love now applied to the primarily

10. Ibid., §54, 217.

impersonal imagery of natural causation, fire heating and light illuminating.

This argument for God's freedom in creating is, indeed, not far from Aquinas's own support for a non-necessary relation between God's existence and nature, on the one hand, and God's willing of the world, on the other.

> God wills things apart from himself [sic] in so far as they are ordered to his own goodness as their end. Now in willing an end we do not necessarily will the things that conduce to it, unless they are such that the end cannot be attained without them. . . . But we do not necessarily will things without which the end can be attained. . . . Hence, since the goodness of God is perfect, and can exist without other things inasmuch as no perfection can accrue to him from them, it follows that his willing things apart from himself is not absolutely necessary.[11]

In short, here, too, it is the already achieved fullness of divinity that suggests the beneficent gratuity of what God does in sharing the good with creatures.

From the primary standpoint of emanationist imagery, Bonaventure is also able to counter the great majority of Aquinas's other worries about it. First of all, natural causes need not be limited in their effects, anymore than intentional agents are. "Just as you notice that a ray of light coming in through a window is colored according to the shades of the different panes, so the divine ray shines differently in each creature."[12] Something like this argument is found as far back as Gregory of Nyssa: "The energy of fire is always one and the same; it consists in heating: but what sort of agreement do its results show? Bronze melts in it; mud hardens; wax vanishes; . . . asbestos is washed by the flames as if by water;

11. Thomas Aquinas, *Summa Theologiae*, 1a, Q19, art. 3, trans. Fathers of the English Dominican Province (Westminster, MD: Christian Classics, 1981), 1:105.
12. Bonaventure, "Collations on the Six Days," Twelfth Collation, section 14, trans. Jose de Vinck, in *The Works of Bonaventure* (Paterson, NJ: St. Anthony Guild Press, 1970), 5:179.

[etc]."[13] Moreover, as Aquinas himself well knows, thinking of God in terms of a self-diffusive, perfect good is enough to make the point about the universal range of God's creative production, without any help from intentional language. The perfect good will extend its causality as much as possible to as many things as possible.[14] And the divine goodness, because it is perfect, requires an indefinitely extended multiplicity of finite goods to approximate its own goodness in finite form.[15]

In the second place, the emanationist model need not run counter to radical transcendence by suggesting that God's substance is parceled out to created things, or somehow thinned out to make them, like a narrow stream from a fulsome pool of water or like a wave of heat from something much hotter. Instead (with the usual theological freedom to violate the proper boundaries of particular images/concepts), one could say that God's creation of the world is a kind of duplication of what God is in the form of something that is not God. It is not an exact duplication. There would be no point to that; creation would not be creation but God all over again. Instead, creation is a duplicate in the form of an image. God does not share God's nature or substance (since it is not a kind of thing susceptible of sharing in that sense); what God produces is an image of God. The world is the image of God (or more exactly, for Bonaventure, the image of the proper Image who perfectly shares the divine substance, Christ) that God throws off simply by being God. Like the projection of a shadow or the aura or glow of a brilliant object, like the halo surrounding the sun, this after-image of creation is not what God is, it is not part of God's own being. It is the spontaneous effect that God throws off in virtue of so intense a superabundance.

13. Gregory of Nyssa, "Against Eunomius," Book 1, ch. 27, trans. H. A. Wilson, in *Nicene and Post-Nicene Fathers*, Second Series (Peabody, MA: Hendrickson, 1994), 5:71.
14. See his *Summa Contra Gentiles*, Book 1, ch. 75, section 6.
15. Ibid., Book 2, ch. 45, section 2.

Conclusion

Talked about as *both* a natural principle and a personal agent, God must be neither in a proper sense. This is a particular version of the Dionysian principle that all things can be affirmed of God (a cataphatic version of transcendence) where this is taken to suggest, more fundamentally, that all things must be denied of God (apophasis). All theological categories become tropes; all categories taken up by theology, from out of their proper fields of application, are troped or twisted. It is in this fashion that theology gains whatever sense it has.

13

Witnessing to the Cross, Forgetting Human Sin: A Systematic-Theological Inquiry in the "Word of the Cross" (1 Cor. 1:18)

Henning Theissen

The Difference between Word and Name

Words are not the same thing as concepts. While concepts make things accessible to reason and thought, words make them accessible to speech (*parole*). In ordinary language there may not be much need to differentiate neatly between the two, especially since speech and thought are closely interrelated, perhaps even closer than language (*langue*) and thought. But, at least in part, their interrelatedness is due to their common opposition to what in ordinary language is called reality. Speech and thought are among the most important devices of the human soul for conceptualizing reality. It may be naïve to identify reality with a world outside ourselves to which we refer in speech and thought. But it can hardly be denied that for the human soul there is an opposition between an inner and an outer world, and this opposition is mirrored in the difference between speech and thought, on the one hand, and things, on the other.

If we follow these distinctions, the Pauline expression λόγος τοῦ σταυροῦ or "Word of the Cross," which we encounter in 1 Cor. 1:18, is not the *concept* called cross but literally the *Word* of the Cross. This means that the expression does not sufficiently contain features to categorize certain things or phenomena as specimen of a logical class called λόγος τοῦ σταυροῦ, which would amount to a concept "cross." This deserves particular notice because it implies that it would be mistaking categories to consider the cross itself a specimen of the Pauline Word of the Cross. In Paul's thought, there is a categorical difference between the cross and the Word of the Cross, the latter being that which enables us to call the former cross. Apparently, this difference is the same for the relationship between any given thing and the word used to make it accessible to speech. However, the Pauline Word of the Cross is not just a test case to the general rule of what words do—particularly because the Word of the Cross cannot be generalized. (This is also why I spell both "Word" and "Cross" with a capital "W" and "C.") There is only one cross made accessible through this word, and that's the cross on which Jesus of Nazareth was crucified. Correspondingly, there aren't any other such words like the Word of the Cross in Paul's thought. (I will turn to the Word of Reconciliation, 2 Cor. 5:19, which constitutes an analogy to the Word of the Cross, in the final section of this essay.)

It is with respect to this lack of generalization that the difference between word and concept, speech and thought comes into play. In ordinary language, to make a given thing accessible to speech is to denote it using words. These words may be individual terms like names, for instance, if a particular human being is to be denoted. They may also be general terms if the thing to be denoted allows subsumption under logical categories. Whether individual or general terms are required depends on the nature of the given thing, if it is an individual or a specimen of a logical class. However, the reason why Jesus' cross would be inaccessible to speech without the Word of the Cross has nothing to do with the difference between individual and general terms. Even though Jesus is clearly an individual, his cross is not. There have been thousands of crosses like his. Even the Gospels mention two further individuals crucified next to him on Golgotha, and the fact that these are different individuals does not cause their crosses to differ logically from his.

In sum, the reason why the cross would be inaccessible to speech without the Word of the Cross is not logical but soteriological. As Ingolf U. Dalferth puts it, "the cross is soteriologically mute";[1] it is literally "deadly silent." In other words, the cross itself could not start any soteriological discourse; the Word of the Cross is required for that, and it is even the very start of any soteriological discourse.

If we look at the Pauline Word of the Cross from this point of view, its categorical difference from the cross becomes very clear. Soteriology does not start from the cross, it starts from the Word of the Cross. Of course, this statement requires a hermeneutical change of perspective from logic to soteriology. But this does not mean to dismiss logic altogether, since there is a logic of soteriology at work in the Pauline Word of the Cross. The basic intention of my present

---

1. Cf. I. U. Dalferth, "Das Wort vom Kreuz in der offenen Gesellschaft," in Dalferth, *Gedeutete Gegenwart. Zur Wahrnehmung Gottes in den Erfahrungen der Zeit* (Tübingen: Mohr Siebeck, 1997), 62.

paper is to unfold this soteriological logic of the Word of the Cross. (To that end, several sections of my essay will include records of Paul's Corinthian correspondence.)

Given the categorical difference between the soteriologically inaccessible cross and the Word of the Cross, which is at the beginning of the soteriological discourse, the language of this discourse does not, as semantic theories might suggest, refer to a reality distinct from it. Correspondingly, by making the cross accessible to speech, the Word of the Cross does not semantically refer to a thing outside of language called cross and is therefore not a significative phonetic unit (*vox significativa*). Rather, as starting point of the soteriological discourse, the Word of the Cross is pragmatically part of a larger speech unit (*pars orationis*), and whatever its significance may be, it must be detected within that larger unit.[2] As Paul's Corinthian correspondence shows, this larger unit, as set forth by the Word of the Cross, is the apostolic tradition.

To consider the *Word* (not concept) of the Cross in terms of the philosophy of language as part of a larger speech unit and not as a significative phonetic unit[3] implies a fundamental shift in understanding the *cross* theologically. While it is widely agreed *that* the Word of the Cross is the starting point of soteriology and even of Christian theology in the broadest sense of the term,[4] it is disputable *how* it starts theology.

If it is the nature of words to make things accessible to speech, then it would seem natural that the Word of the Cross *represents* the

---

2. As Günter Bader indicated to me, my understanding of the term *vox significativa* is narrower here than the usual (denoting any semantically laden sound), whereas that of *pars orationis* is wider than the technical use, which denotes the rhetoric unit of the sentence.

3. I am here relying on a number of contributions that Stephan Meier-Oeser has made to the *Historisches Wörterbuch der Philosophie* (*HWP*); cf. his articles on "Symbol" (*HWP*, 1998, 10:710–23), "Wort" (*HWP*, 2004, 12:1023–30), and "Zeichen" (*HWP*, 2004, 12:1155–71).

4. So, with reference to Paul Ricoeur, e.g., Heinrich Assel, art. "Zeugnis," in *RGG*, 2005, 8:1852–54.

cross. Representation here means to make something present that is literally absent so the result will not be physical presence, but presence in speech. It is obvious how far-reaching the consequences will be that this concept of representation has, say, for the doctrine of the last supper and the words of institution. But before turning to any of these dogmatic problems it is advisable to dwell a bit over the underlying hermeneutics. For instance, in terms of the philosophy of language, this sort of representation is not what words but, rather, what *names* will do. The function of words is weaker, since by making things accessible to speech, they needn't do more than denote them so that what is being talked about becomes clear, but without any further effect on that which is denoted except that it becomes the *object* of speech. In contrast to this, by using the name of a particular person, we make that person present in discourse while that person is physically absent, and thus that person's name represents the very person as a possible *subject*, not just as an object of speech. The reason why we do this is that we consider persons to be individual subjects who cannot be categorized under logical concepts. Given this difference between possible subjects (names) and objects (words) of speech, the seemingly natural statement that the Word of the Cross represents the cross becomes doubtful.

Obviously the cross is not a possible *subject* of soteriological discourse, since it cannot initiate that discourse. But (as has been stated earlier) it is not its possible *object,* either, since it cannot be categorized under logical concepts due to its soteriological muteness and inaccessibility to speech. This is why the access to the cross in speech is neither through concept nor through name, but through word. This implies that the Word of the Cross doesn't categorize the cross (like a concept would do) or represent it (like a name would do).

Record of Paul's Corinthian Correspondence

The debate in 1 Corinthians 1–4 is about the nature of the apostolic office and ministry. Paul has been struggling ever since Damascus to be recognized as an apostle, for he was no witness of Jesus in his earthly days. Moreover, his struggle has been twofold: he has struggled with the "columns" of Jerusalem over the issue of the uncircumcised believing in Jesus, and he has struggled with other early Christian missionaries, particularly of Corinth, who, like him, have never physically encountered the Messiah they proclaimed. Claiming himself an apostle despite the fact that he was no eyewitness of Jesus, Paul could hardly deny Apollos or any other of the Corinthian missionaries the same honor. Given this general state of affairs, Paul makes a surprising distinction when introducing the Word of the Cross. Apostolicity, he states, is only that sort of missionary practice which proclaims the Word of the Cross, that is, which preaches Jesus as the crucified one. This criterion is double-edged in that it follows the Jerusalem line of argument requesting faithfulness to the earthly Jesus while simultaneously taking the Corinthian stance in abandoning the eyewitness criterion: "I decided [ἔκρινα, from the same root as 'criterion'] to know nothing among you except Jesus Christ [with Jerusalem], and him crucified [with Corinth]" (1 Cor. 2:2).

This double criterion enables Paul to argue on *apostolic grounds* for his mission to the Corinthian community—while at the same time differentiating these apostolic grounds of the Christian community from its exclusively *christological fundamentals:* "no one can lay any foundation other than the one that has been laid; that foundation is Jesus Christ" (1 Cor. 3:11).

Here Paul clearly makes a distinction between that which is *christological* and that which is *apostolic,* thus founding the church on christological, not on apostolic, grounds. Considering the categorical difference between the cross and the Word of the Cross, it would seem natural if this difference was equivalent to the one Paul makes between the crucified Christ and the apostles who proclaim him. But that is not the case. Since it is not the cross, but the Word of the Cross, that initiates the soteriological discourse, and since it is this discourse that makes the church, we must conclude that both Christ and the apostles belong with the Word of the Cross. For Paul, there is obviously a difference between the cross and the one who is on the cross. Although Christ is the one *on* the cross, he does not belong *with* the cross, but with the Word of the Cross. This is to say that, according to Paul, the crucified Christ himself is the first to make the cross accessible to the Christian community. Christ himself is the one who starts the soteriological discourse, he is the primordial Word of the Cross. The apostolic Word of the Cross is to be distinguished from its primordial form, the christological Word of the Cross.

With respect to the double distinction between the cross and the Word of the Cross as well as between the two forms (christological and apostolic) of the Word of the Cross, my reflections will proceed in three steps dealing with (1) the cross, (2) the christological, and (3) the apostolic or ecclesiological Word of the Cross.

The Cross as Divine Name

Inaccessible to speech without the Word of the Cross, the cross is "soteriologically mute" (Dalferth), a wordless sign of death. However, the Pauline Word of the Cross proclaims it as a symbol of life that opens a future beyond the Lord's death (see, for instance, 1 Cor. 11:26). How is that shift from sign of death to symbol of life possible?

Following a general theoretical distinction, a symbol is a sort of sign whose signifying function is embedded in a community of interpretation. Exploring the hermeneutical relationship between the sign and its community of interpretation, we come across the concept of *witness*. For, according to Paul Ricoeur, any witness has a "dialogical structure," between the act of giving the sign (*témoignage-acte*) and its interpretation as sign (*témoignage-récit*): "Someone gives a sign of the absolute without willing or knowing so, and someone else interprets it as sign."[5]

If we apply this theoretical model to the Word of the Cross, the result will be to consider the cross as sign of the absolute. Revelational theology has regularly argued in this fashion that the act of crucifying Christ, more than a mere historical incident, was also an act which revealed God's grace. However, the epistemological problem with this type of theology is that the parameters of the revelational act must not be confused with those of the historical act, for otherwise the theological idea of God revealing Godself in the cross of Jesus would amount to identifying the subjects of the historical act of crucifixion with the subject of the revelational acts of God. Against this problem, Ricoeur's concept of witness is an excellent remedy, for he unmistakably states that the one who gives a sign of the absolute does so unwillingly. Therefore, to consider the crucifixion of Christ as God's *revelation* paradoxically implies that this revelation is *concealed* from those who crucify Jesus.

On Pauline terms this means that the absolute of which the cross is a sign will be God's *name*, for according to Paul's letter to the Philippians it is not by his death alone, but especially his "death on the cross" (θανάτου δὲ σταυροῦ, Phil. 2:8c, is probably Paul's

---

5. My translation of the French original: Paul Ricoeur, "Emmanuel Lévinas—penseur du témoignage" [1989], in Ricoeur, *Lectures 3. Aux frontières de la philosophie* (Paris: Seuil, 1994), 92: "Une structure dialogique du témoignage s'esquisse ici entre le témoignage-acte et le témoignage-récit. Quelqu'un donne un signe de l'absolu, sans le vouloir ni le savoir; un autre l'interprète comme signe." ET, Paul Ricoeur, "Emmanuel Lévinas: Thinker of Testimony," in *Figuring the Sacred: Religion, Narrative, and Imagination*, ed. Mark J. Wallace (Minneapolis: Fortress Press, 1995), 115–35.

addition to an older christological hymn) that Christ is given the absolute name (so to speak) or "the name that is above every name" (Phil. 2:9)—that is, the tetragrammatic name. As can be seen from the biblical traditions of the burning bush, the tetragrammatic name reveals God by simultaneously concealing God. The reason for this is the diversity of subjects which is symbolized in the bush that burns but is not consumed (Exod. 3:2) or in the various invocations of the God who reveals/conceals Godself in the bush (Exod. 6:3). As traditional Jewish exegesis of these passages has argued, it is God who gives the divine name as sign of the absolute (God's uniqueness), but it is Israel who is called to sanctify God's name and thus attest to God's uniqueness.[6] It seems to me that this is in perfect accordance with Ricoeur's model of witness. And what is even more, the burning-bush tradition links this model with the distinctions from the first section of my essay.

The *name* conveyed to Moses in Exod. 3:14 represents God in the strict sense of making God present when God's name is invoked. At least in part, its power to represent God accounts for the fact that this name is not pronounced in traditional Judaism. Hence, to sanctify God's name cannot amount to representing God; rather, it makes the otherwise inexplicable name accessible to speech. Using terms from the first section of my essay, to sanctify God's name is to transfer it from name to *word*—and again, in Judaism God's word, which makes God's name accessible to sanctification, is of course God's Torah, by which Israel is supposed to live.

From the viewpoint of Reformation theology, a similar thing can be said of the cross as sign of the absolute. To consider it a revelation of God amounts to categorizing it as a *name* representing that which it names. That is partly why Luther thought that Jesus' cross was

---

6. Corresponding Talmudic sayings are the motto, of and back the monotheistic argument, of Hermann Cohen's *Religion der Vernunft aus den Quellen des Judentums* (1919).

functionally equivalent to the tetragrammatic name of God. There is evidence that he considered the cross a divine name.[7] The point behind this is probably that, for Luther, God's presence unmasked any alleged human perfection as sinful.

It may seem odd to contemporary Christianity and its theological awareness of Israel to find the cross equivalent to the tetragrammatic name of God. A possible explanation for this is the biblical mention of the inscription on Jesus' cross (*Iesus Nazarenus Rex Iudaeorum*), which in religious art is rendered with four capital letters as INRI—on Luther's terms this could be considered to communicate christologically the tetragrammatic name of God, JHWH.[8] However unhistorical this combination of the cross and the name of God may be, it is clear in its theological meaning. The cross represents God in the sense of literally making God present on earth—the consequence of this being that, for a Lutheran understanding of revelation (*finitum capax infiniti*), the Lord himself (in the divine nature of Jesus Christ) dies on the cross. This is in accordance with New Testament writings such as 1 Cor. 11:26, where it is stated that the celebration of the Lord's Supper is a proclamation of "the Lord's death until he comes." However, the Lord's death can only be proclaimed to open his future ("until he comes") if it is accessed through the word, that is, if it is

---

7. On what follows, see Heinrich Assel, "Der Name Gottes bei Martin Luther. Trinität und Tetragramm—ausgehend von Luthers Auslegung des Fünften Psalms," in *EvTh* 64 (2004): 363–78. Assel, who in this article prolongs his postdoctoral research on the divine name, focuses primarily on Luther's distinction between ineffable and communicative forms of the divine name (*nomen proprium vs. nomen praedicatum*), on which I will draw in my next section. But in addition to this, Assel (364n7) alludes to Luther's thesis "CRUX sola est nostra theologia" (AWA 2,319,3), which is presented as Luther's "true theology of the divine name" ("wahre Namenstheologie"; ibid.). That the Latin *crux* for "cross" contains four letters, like the *tetragrammaton*, seems important in this respect.

8. For Luther's combination of the tetragrammatic and the christological name in general, see the preceding footnote. Moreover, in his 1543–45 lectures on Genesis, Luther interprets the INRI inscription as dissolving the commandment to obey earthly authorities, because as *rex Iudaeorum* Jesus requested of the Jews their obedience not to the second, but to the first table of the Decalogue, that is, to God's name (WA 44, 19,14-24).

clear that God who thus dies is no other than Jesus Christ or God born as man. In other words, the cross will remain a sign of death unless it is interpreted by the word which states that the name of the God who is made present in the cross is no other than the name of Jesus Christ.

If we thus reconstruct the intuitions of Luther's seemingly speculative doctrine of the cross as a divine name, it seems fairly compatible with our distinctions made in the first section of this essay. The only (but important) incompatibility is that Luther considered the christological interpretation of the tetragrammatic name also a name. Following our distinctions, the INRI is not a name, but a word that makes the ineffable tetragrammatic name accessible to speech.

The Christological Word of the Cross as God's Wisdom

Let me stop here to briefly summarize my argument so far. Applying Ricoeur's theory of witness to Luther's understanding of the cross, we have made a hermeneutical distinction between the cross as a sign that reveals God's tetragrammatic name and the INRI inscription that offers a christological interpretation (not elimination) of this name. What remains noteworthy about this hermeneutical distinction is that its two components cannot be separated on theological terms, since for a trinitarian theology the cross as sign of God's tetragrammatic name and its christological interpretation in the INRI inscription are interrelated. This means that what we encounter in the christological Word of the Cross is an unfolding of the inner-trinitarian relations of the triune God. To put it more boldly, what God does in Christ is also what God does in Godself. Here the focus of our reflections moves from Christology (cross and Word of the Cross) to the doctrine of God (immanent and economic Trinity), but we are still within the scope of 1 Corinthians, since Paul himself develops the Word of the Cross out of reflections on God's wisdom and foolishness. Hence, a few remarks are in order on these features of the doctrine of God.

Dogmatically speaking, the Pauline reflection on God's move from wisdom to foolishness (1 Cor. 1:20-25) is usually dealt with in terms of the relationship between God's freedom and God's grace. Influential contemporary theologies such as Karl Barth's (in *CD* II/1) have stressed that God's freedom is God's grace. Although this identification appears perfectly appropriate on dogmatic terms, it does not tell us much about the nature of either freedom or grace. Two features, I think, deserve particular notice if we state that freedom is gracious and grace is free.

First, if God shows Godself to be gracious toward humanity, God is merely driven to do so by God's own decision. There is no obligation whatsoever for God to be gracious. This implies that God is not only free to be gracious but, second, that God also remains free in God's grace. Just as God cannot be forced to be gracious, grace itself, far from being an irresistible force inflicted on human beings, requests them to freely believe in it. While the latter is widely agreed—belief cannot originate in force but only in freedom—the former seems much more disputable. If the "triumph of grace" (to borrow a book title from G. C. Berkouwer) is free, isn't then freedom over grace and thus freedom finally reserved to God? I think that the point of Barth's (and others') identification of freedom and grace is not meant to deny the difference between divine and human freedom, but to deny any divine retention between freedom and grace. This implies that the nature of God's freedom is grace. In other words, God's grace isn't revealed in the incarnation alone, but is also at work in the internal relations of the Trinity. That is why God's freedom isn't altered by God's grace or vice versa.

Freedom here cannot mean sovereignty in the sense of unlimited authority, but the opposite. Divine freedom always reckons with the limits and obstacles it comes across, but masters them by ministering to them. This is obviously the case in the life and death of Jesus who is God's grace incarnate, but the doctrine of God states that the same applies to God's deity. This doctrine is by no means speculative, but draws on numerous strands of the biblical tradition which tell us that God actuates God's freedom in decisions that seem to violate God's deity because they turn wisdom into foolishness (to put it in the Pauline terms used in 1 Corinthians 1–2). Among the most impressive examples of this are the frequent mentions of a repenting God who does not carry out a verdict God has already sentenced because that would injure God internally and thus violate God's deity (see, for instance, Hos. 11:8-9).[9] What makes these examples of God's repentance so impressive is that the characteristic traits of grace or mercy which God shows in these instances apparently amount to altering deity to humanity, but still they cannot be explained on any other ground than the divine freedom to do so.

Record of Paul's Corinthian Correspondence

The motif of a divine repentance seems particularly suitable to account for the identification of freedom and grace we encounter in contemporary doctrines of God. God's move from wisdom to foolishness, as expressed in 1 Corinthians 1–2, follows just the same motif. Both God's freedom in repentance and God's move from wisdom to foolishness teach Bible readers new words to make God's ways with humanity accessible to human speech. Let me explain.

It seems foolish to proclaim the cross as God's promise for future (as Paul does in 1 Cor. 11:26), and it would be nothing but foolish

---

9. On the whole issue of divine repentance, cf. the masterly monograph by Joachim Jeremias, *Die Reue Gottes. Aspekte alttestamentlicher Gottesvorstellung*. BThSt 33. (Neukirchener: Neukirchen-Vluyn, 1997). It seems that the more recent study by Jan-Dirk Döhling, *Der bewegliche Gott. Eine Untersuchung des Motivs der Reue Gottes in der Hebräischen Bibel*. HBS 61 (Freiburg-im-Br.: Herder, 2009), largely confirms the main lines of Jeremias's argument.

if that were the wisdom of that proclamation itself, that is, if that wisdom originated in the Word of the Cross and not in the cross itself. But as has been stated, the Word of the Cross initiates the soteriological discourse by bearing witness to what God himself does on the cross. In other words, the wisdom of the cross teaches those who bear witness to it new understandings of God's wisdom and makes them forget the old ones. For instance, freedom is no longer to be thought of as unlimited sovereignty but as readiness for repentance and mercy. The recipients of the Pauline proclamation gain wisdom in terms of this new wording for freedom, while they become fools with respect to the old way of understanding freedom. This is what Paul stresses in another passage of his Corinthian correspondence: "From now on, therefore, we regard no one from a human point of view [Greek: "according to the flesh"] even though we once knew Christ from a human point of view [Greek: "according to the flesh"], we know him no longer in that way" (2 Cor. 5:16, NRSV).

Turning to the distinctions from the first section of my essay, this wisdom in new and foolishness in old wordings is why the Word of the Cross is to be considered a word, that which makes the cross accessible to human speech. For if the cross represents God's new way of freedom as grace, then the Word of the Cross teaches us wisdom about this new freedom, while we are supposed to forget the old way of freedom as unlimited sovereignty.

It seems that there is a more general rule behind this. By bearing witness to the cross, the Word of the Cross demarcates that which cannot be forgotten and distinguishes it from that which can be forgotten. Oblivion here is not just the opposite of remembrance; rather, remembrance inplies a new kind of oblivion that might be called active oblivion. It means that to witness to God's new way of freedom as grace and repentance amounts to forgetting the old way of freedom. For if in God's repentance God is gracious and does not carry out a verdict that has already been sentenced, it means that God no longer remembers, but forgets that on which the verdict has been returned. In other words, God's grace means actively *forgetting* human sin, which amounts to *forgiving* it. It seems, therefore, that learning wisdom in God's new way of freedom is the same thing as becoming a fool in the old way of freedom.

However, this proves true only for the christological Word of the Cross. Just as freedom that is identical with grace, active oblivion is reserved to God. In human relations things turn out differently. Human repentance does not erase the remembrance of the falterings that require repentance but, rather, deepens it. It seems, therefore, that there is a difference between divine and human wisdom and foolishness, and this difference also affects the Word of the Cross that proclaims God's move from wisdom to foolishness. That is why the present reflections would be incomplete without considering the apostolic Word of the Cross.

The Apostolic Word of the Cross as the Church's Witness

The result of my observations up to this point has been that the Word of the Cross teaches wisdom in God's new ways of freedom and grace as active oblivion of sin while making fools of human sovereigns and authorities and their old way of freedom. What does that mean for human witness to the God who exercises this new way of freedom? If the freedom actuated on the cross is exclusively a merely divine name, as Martin Luther stated, and if active oblivion of sin is reserved to God, does that not mean, then, that in human relations freedom will continue to be the exercise of authority? In other words, won't human witness of the cross—even if it was apostolic—have to be totally different from the witness that the crucified Christ bears to his own cross?

We encounter here a variety of meanings which the term *witness* can adopt if we limit ourselves to Ricoeur's hermeneutical understanding that witness is the interpretation of a sign given by someone else as sign. On this hermeneutical basis, the missionary propagation of the gospel is witness, but such is also the readiness to martyrdom for the sake of that which is witnessed. In other words, both a more dogmatic and a more ethical sense of witness fit in with Ricoeur's hermeneutical concept. The crucial point in both the dogmatic and the ethical cases is that the witness is not the person who first gave the sign to be interpreted in witness, but that by interpreting it as sign the person who interprets it gets existentially involved in the issue. If we apply these basic hermeneutics of witness to the Word of the Cross, it seems consistent that the apostles who bear witness to Christ's cross should undergo the same kind of personal involvement in the cross that Christ has suffered. This would lead to the narrowest possible relationship between the missionary and the martyrological sense of witness, but would it not, on the other hand, completely level the difference between the christological and the apostolic Word of the Cross?

Record of Paul's Corinthian Correspondence

There is no simple answer to that question. That there is a difference between the christological and the apostolic Word of the Cross, it can, once again, be learned from Paul's Corinthian correspondence. In 2 Cor. 5:18–19, Paul makes a distinction between the Word of Reconciliation, which is an equivalent of the Word of the Cross, and the ministry of reconciliation. As Otfried Hofius has argued in a number of insightful essays, they are not to be confused, although they both convey God's grace to humankind and can thus be categorized as Word of the Cross in the sense that they both open an access to the cross which reveals God's grace. But while the former is a christological term synonymous to the gospel itself, the latter is an ecclesiological one denoting the obligation to spread the gospel.[10] I think that Hofius's differentiation between the two terms is extremely helpful if we keep in mind that neither of them is *word* in the sense of the distinctions introduced in the first section of this essay.

Drawing on this concept of word, it can be stated that both the christological and the apostolic Word of the Cross make the cross accessible to human speech, but they do not render accessible the same aspects of the cross. Wisdom in active oblivion of sins is something only Christ can bear witness to, while the apostles are fools at this new way of freedom, although their witness is not detached from it, either. For if the new way of freedom as grace means forgiving sins by actively forgetting them, this does not only imply a new understanding of oblivion as something active instead of passive, but it also entails a new understanding of that which is forgotten, namely sin.

The apostolic Word of the Cross is *word* in that it addresses things as sin and thus makes them accessible to God's forgiveness even if they are in themselves no sins in the sense of transgressions "before God" but, rather, some mischief in human relations. By so doing, the apostolic witness opens up new ways for coping with such mischief beyond the old (that is, either moral or juridical) ways of categorizing "sin." It deserves to be noticed that such renewed speech about sin is also witness in the sense of Ricoeur's understanding. For if "sin" is not defined as this or that sort of thing but as addressing certain things "before God," as Ricoeur points out in his *Symbolism of Evil*,[11] this

---

10. Otfried Hofius, "Erwägungen zur Gestalt und Herkunft des paulinischen Versöhnungsgedankens" [1980], in Hofius, *Paulusstudien* [I], WUNT 51 (Tübingen: Mohr, 1994), 6–7.

11. Paul Ricoeur, *Symbolik des Bösen (Phänomenologie der Schuld II)* (Münich: Karl Alber, 1988), 60–61, on the significance of "before God." ET, *The Symbolism of Evil*, trans. Emerson Buchanan (Boston: Beacon, 1969), 50.

address will always be someone else's interpretation of a given sign as si(g)n. A good example of this is the intercessory prayer, for unlike other forms of prayer, it prays for someone else and on their behalf. In the apostolic Word of the Cross, the "church" speaks accordingly on behalf of the "world" and thus addresses the world's concerns "before God," making them accessible to the wisdom witnessed by the christological Word of the Cross. In sum, the christological and the apostolic Word of the Cross collaborate in opening up new ways of addressing worldly and human concerns "before God." Thus the two forms of the Word of the Cross bridge the gap between wisdom and foolishness, witnessing to the cross of Jesus in which God actuates God's wisdom for the salvation of humanity.

14

The Cross of Christ and God's Power

Marc Vial

In 1 Cor. 1:23–24, Paul writes: "we proclaim Christ nailed to the cross; . . . he is the power of God and the wisdom of God," before adding, in v. 25, that "the weakness of God is stronger than human strength" (REB). The link between the cross of Christ and the power of God is thus explicitly made by Paul. Consequently, one must ask whether it is possible, in a Christian theological perspective, to think about something we may call God's "almightiness" from the event of the cross and, first, from the "word of the cross" around which the second half of 1 Corinthians 1 centers.[1]

---

1. The words 'omnipotence' and 'almightiness' are here taken as synonyms. Both correspond to the French term 'toute-puissance.'

Contemporary Critical Approaches to
God's Omnipotence

Before considering the *de jure* question (Is it possible to think about divine almightiness from the *locus* of the cross?), let us briefly consider the *de facto* question: How is the problem of omnipotence treated nowadays? That question seems misplaced, since often in contemporary theology the "word of the cross" either does not play any role in the construction of a discourse on divine omnipotence, or it leads to a disqualification, in principle, of such a discourse.

Hans Jonas's *The Concept of God after Auschwitz* is a good example of the first approach. Jonas's short text, as is well known, constitutes one of the most spectacular critiques of divine omnipotence. His thesis can be briefly summarized: God did not intervene at Auschwitz "not because he chose not to, but because he *could* not . . ."[2] There is no need here to study Jonas's argument, since it is well known and since it has been analyzed several times, in more or less critical manners.[3] For our present purpose, it is more interesting to consider briefly two aspects of Jonas's interpretation of omnipotence (these two aspects are good examples of the way the theme of omnipotence is often dealt with nowadays): the question of the starting point of a reflection on this topic, and the question of the definition of omnipotence. With regard to the first aspect, as the reference to Auschwitz makes very clear, the starting point of Jonas's discourse on omnipotence is the experience of evil, of which the Holocaust represents the apex. That is what led Jonas to eliminate omnipotence

2. Hans Jonas, *Der Gottesbegriff nach Auschwitz. Eine jüdische Stimme* (Berlin: Suhrkamp, 1987), 41; idem, "The Concept of God After Auschwitz: A Jewish Voice," in *The Journal of Religion* 67 (1987): 10.
3. See, for instance, Marie-Geneviève Pinsart, *Hans Jonas et la liberté. Dimensions théologiques, ontologiques, éthiques et politiques* (Paris: Vrin, 2002), 17–77. For a critical analysis, see, among others, Paul Clavier, *L'Énigme du mal ou Le tremblement de Jupiter* (Paris: Desclée de Brouwer, 2010).

from the list of divine attributes. His way of focusing on the problem of evil, in his text, is such that his reflection ends in a theodicy. Not a traditional theodicy, to be sure, since Jonas combines the goodness of God and the presence of evil not with, as usual, God's omnipotence, but the negative proposition "God is *not* omnipotent." But this is a theodicy nevertheless.[4] Indeed, the negation of omnipotence explicitly seeks to defend God's innocence: God is not responsible for evil in the world; how could God be since God cannot stop it?

We turn to the second aspect: defining omnipotence. As it appears, the notion of omnipotence signifies nothing else than the capacity to do anything, here the capacity to intervene in history in order to change its course. It is because omnipotence is defined in such a way that, given the presence of evil, the notion needs to be erased from the list of divine attributes.

A similar conclusion has been reached by a good number of Christian theologians who take the event of the cross into consideration when thinking about divine omnipotence. In an article bearing the telling title "From the Pantocrator to the Crucified One," Canadian theologian Jean Richard has retraced the steps which lead them to that conclusion.[5] In their reflections, the "word of the cross," far from sustaining a theological reflection about omnipotence, becomes its condition of impossibility. At times, this move is legitimized, perhaps not so fairly, with a quote from one of Bonhoeffer's letters from prison:

> God lets himself be pushed out of the world on to the cross. He is weak and powerless in the world, and that is precisely the way, the only way, in which he is with us and helps us. Matt. 8:17 makes it quite clear that Christ helps us, not by virtue of his omnipotence, but by virtue of his weakness and suffering. Man's religiosity makes him look in his distress

---

4. See Jean-Daniel Causse, "Le mal, la faute et le péché," in *Introduction à l'éthique. Penser, croire, agir*, ed. Causse and Denis Müller (Geneva: Labor et Fides, 2009), 277.

5. Jean Richard, "Du pantocrator au crucifié," *Théologiques* 8, no. 2 (2000), 49–75.

to the power of God in the world: God is the *deus ex machina*. The Bible directs man to God's powerlessness and suffering; only the suffering God can help.[6]

On the basis of that quote, some have seen in the kenosis revealed on the cross no less than the deliberate renunciation of omnipotence.[7] The motif of the *deus ex machina* shows this well, however: that position, however different it is from Jonas's, has in common with it an important aspect, namely the interpretation of divine omnipotence as a capacity to intervene within history in order to modify its course. Being omnipotent is reduced here to the capacity to eradicate evil. As a consequence, the cross is understood as the most obvious contradiction to divine omnipotence.

The question thus arises: Is it not the case that such critiques of omnipotence, regardless of their reliance (or lack thereof) on the cross, betray a lack of criticism in that they forfeit a critique of the very concept of omnipotence? Especially concerning the critique in the name of kenosis and the cross, isn't that critique neglecting, despite its own claim to the contrary, the "word of the cross," in the sense that it does not allow the notion of omnipotence to be defined by that word? Is it not the case that its negation of omnipotence presupposes an abstract notion of omnipotence, that is a concept which is not developed in relation with the "word of the cross," or in relation with how God reveals the way in which God is God, before reaching the conclusion, down the line, that the notion of omnipotence does not adequately express what is manifested in the event of the cross? But, if that is the case, what value does such a

---

6. Dietrich Bonhoeffer, letter from July 16, 1944, in *Letters and Papers from Prison*, trans. Christian Gremmels, et al., *Dietrich Bonhoeffers Works*, vol. 8, ed. John W. de Gruchy (Minneapolis: Fortress Press, 2010), 479–80.

7. I was unable to read Jean-Marie Glé's article "Penser Dieu créateur. Une démarche difficile," *Christus* 185 (2000): 38–45, an article which, according to Jean Richard, is a good example of what I am describing here. I rely on the summary Richard gives in "Du pantocrator au crucifié," 53.

negation have, if not the (rather unimportant) value of a tautology that negates God's omnipotence if omnipotence is conceived in a way which does not befit God?

Omnipotence and the Word of the Cross

It may be objected that these formal considerations only have weight insofar as it is indeed possible to ground discourse on the word of the cross; to that objection a second one may be voiced: Is it really the case that the word of the cross has something to do with divine omnipotence?

Certainly, it may be conceded that the word of the cross does not represent the final word on the question of divine omnipotence. To begin with, terminologically speaking it must be noted that nowhere in 1 Cor. 1:18-25 do we find the term that was put to use in the theology of omnipotence and in the first Christian creeds, be it the Apostles' Creed or the Athanasian Creed: I of course have in mind the word *pantocrator*. Paul is interested in divine *dunamis*, not *pantocratoria*. And if we move from the words to the substance, we must acknowledge that this particular chapter in 1 Corinthians does not portray the theology of *pantocratoria* that Jean-Pierre Batut analyzes in his dissertation on divine omnipotence in pre-Nicene theology.[8] It is a different text from that epistle, 1 Cor. 15:24-26, which provided one of the biblical foundations for the pre-Nicene theology of reality that we call "omnipotence." There we read: "Then comes the end, when he delivers up the kingdom to God the Father, after deposing every sovereignty, authority, and power. For he is destined to reign until God has put all enemies under his feet; and the last enemy to be deposed is death" (REB). On the basis of these words,

8. Jean-Pierre Batut, *Pantocrator. 'Dieu le Père tout-puissant' dans la théologie prénicéenne* (Paris: Institut d'études augustiniennes, 2009).

according to Batut, some of the fathers interpreted the *pantocratoria* as the divine lordship that will become manifest when history will come to an end, when God's last enemies will be subdued by Christ. But we must note that this lordship is partly linked to the work accomplished in and by the Son, and that Origen relates it to the cross. For this lordship is nothing else, concretely, than the effectiveness of God's paternity, an effectiveness through which human beings are made sons and daughters in the Son, an effectiveness of which the cross is the proleptic manifestation insofar as "it anticipates the end of death's rule and the new creation."[9] Origen writes about this lordship in the following excerpt from his *On First Principles*: "And here is how 'the last enemy [death, the devil] is destroyed' must be understood: its being, which was made by God, does not perish: what perishes is its intention and adversary will, which do not proceed from God but from the enemy itself. It will be 'destroyed', therefore, not in such a way that it no longer is, but in such a way that it no longer is 'enemy' and 'death.' For 'nothing is impossible to the Almighty, and nobody is incurable for its creator."[10] Clearly, we are very far, with that interpretation of omnipotence, from the one that is commonly accepted nowadays, which reduces it to the capacity to intervene in history.[11] And so the common interpretation of omnipotence, which seems self-evident to us, was in fact preceded by a prior interpretation, which ended up being replaced, if not by medieval notions of *omnipotentia*, at least by some of them: I have in mind the specifically Scotist notion of *potentia absoluta*.[12] More importantly, it

---

9. Ibid., 433.

10. Origen, *Traité des principes* III,6,5, ed. Henri Crouzel and Manlio Simonetti, SC 268 (Paris: Cerf, 1980), 244–45, rev. trans. by Batut, *Pantocrator*, 420.

11. According to Batut (*Pantocrator*, 420n294), there is here an implicit quotation of Job 42:2, and so *omnipotens* is not an adequate translation of *pantocrator*, insofar as Job claims that "God can do anything." Batut reaches this conclusion because, in his mind, *pantocrator* does not mean "being able to do anything" (that would be *pantodunastès* or *pantodunamos*). But it is not clear, despite the implicit reference to Job, why what Origen is writing has nothing to do with *pantocratoria*.

is Paul's interpretation, which links the question of God's power with the event of the cross, which was largely forgotten.

We now turn to this interpretation, in 1 Corinthians. In the first occurrence of the word δύναμις, in v. 18, it is the *logos* of the cross itself that is the δύναμις τοῦ θεοῦ: "The message of the cross is sheer folly to those on the way to destruction, but to us, who are on the way to salvation, it is the power of God" (REB). As Daniel Gerber has noted, power is not opposed to weakness here, but to absurdity.[13] Already in the preceding sentence (v. 17), Paul asserts that Christ sent him "to proclaim the gospel, and to do it without recourse to the skills of rhetoric, lest the cross of Christ be robbed of its effect [literally: lest it be emptied]" (REB). The word of the cross or, which is the same for Paul, the gospel can be identified with God's power at least insofar as that word is a logos which, despite the fact that it does not conform to the world's logic, is nevertheless a logic.[14] As such, it does have a signifying power. But more can be said. In the first volume of his commentary on 1 Corinthians, Wolfgang Schrage sees a link between the aspect of the "word of the cross's" power with its salvific effect. He considers it a *Heilsmacht* or a *Heilswirkung*: it is God's power because it creates faith, because it effects salvation.[15]

But 1 Corinthians goes even further, since God's power is not only related to the "word of the cross," but also to Christ himself:

12. See Olivier Boulnois, "Ce que Dieu ne peut pas," in *La Puissance et son ombre. De Pierre Lombard à Luther*, ed. O. Boulnois (Paris: Aubier, 1994), 56–57.

13. Daniel Gerber, "La Croix. Représentations théologiques et symboliques," in *La Croix. Représentations théologiques et symboliques. Journée d'étude du jeudi 19 septembre 2002, organisée à Strasbourg par le Centre d'Analyse et de Documentation Patristiques*, ed. Jean-Marc Prieur (Geneva: Labor et Fides, 2004), 18.

14. Jean-Luc Marion, *Le croire pour le voir. Réflexions diverses sur la rationalité de la révélation et l'irrationalité de quelques croyants* (Paris: Parole et Silence, 2010), 18: "Même le paradoxe de [l]a crucifixion, qui contredit 'la sagesse du monde', reste encore un *logos*, 'le *logos* de la croix', qui oppose à la sagesse du monde encore une autre *sophia*, la 'sagesse de Dieu'."

15. Wolfgang Schrage, *Der erste Brief an die Korinther*, EKK VII/1 (Neukirchen: Neukirchener-Patmos, 1991), 1:171–74.

in v. 24 we see the motif of the crucified Christ as "the power of God." Two things can be said here. First, with regard to Paul's way of identifying Christ with God's power: How is Christ God's power? Paul does not say it explicitly but, if some of the most recent commentators are correct, it seems that God's power must be understood insofar as Christ effects God's salvific power. Wolfgang Schrage and Joseph Fitzmyer concur on this point.[16] Insofar as the cross is the manifestation of the salvation of the foolish and the weak, the one who dies on it represents what we can call God's power in action, insofar as he does not manifest that power in any other way than in the act through which he accomplishes it.[17] Here, too, the motif of power is cast in soteriological terms, and it is probably not unreasonable to think that it is because of this fundamentally soteriological dimension of power that God's weakness is said to be "stronger than human strength" (v. 25), more powerful than what is commonly thought to be powerful.

This theme of weakness leads us to the second remark about v. 24. Briefly stated: what God's weakness, the passion, puts into question, is not God's power as such, but a certain understanding of divine power. Clearly, Paul affirms *simultaneously* God's weakness and power, just as he affirms *together* God's foolishness and wisdom. And just as God's foolishness is not the opposite of wisdom, but a wisdom that differs from human wisdom and is superior to it, in the same manner God's weakness is not the opposite of God's power, but a power that is "stronger" than human power, even as it puts into question what is commonly thought to be powerful. In a way, it is

16. Ibid., 1:190. Joseph A. Fitzmyer, *First Corinthians: A New Translation with Introduction and Commentary* (New Haven: Yale University Press, 2008), 155: "The Gospel of the message of the cross is the power of God, because in that message the Crucified Jesus is proclaimed as the one who brings God's power to deliver human beings from the evil of sin and moral destruction. Thus the cross of Christ is not emptied of its meaning (1:17)."

17. Schrage, *Der erste Brief*, 188: "Christ is not merely a paradigm of the manifestation of God's strength and wisdom. He truly embodies them."

not absurd to say that Paul objects, even before having heard them, to the claims that play God's weakness against God's power. He rejects them in particular by distinguishing between God's power and the "miracles" or "signs" that, according to him, Jews demand. The fact that the cross puts into question any conception of omnipotence which reduces it to a capacity to intervene at any moment in history, that fact does not cancel out a theology of power, nor, if I am not mistaken, a theology of divine almightiness. Certainly, God's foolishness is *real*, just as God's weakness is *real*: the crucified one has *really* suffered and died. There can be no Docetism here, a mere semblence of weakness. And yet, it is *this particular death*, that is, the death *of the crucified*, which constitutes what we could call the "matrix" of God's power, which *really* unfolded itself in this *real* death. As Schrage puts it when commenting on 1 Cor. 1:25, weakness is the "mode" through which God overcomes,[18] and God does not overcome in any other way than by taking part in human beings's weakness in the person of the crucified, of whom Paul writes elsewhere that God "made him into sin for us" (2 Cor. 5:21). God's weakness is thus *nothing else* than God's power; it is *another kind* of power, a power that differs from our usual understanding of power.

On that basis, may we talk about the power that exceeds any worldly power as an omnipotence? I think we may, on two conditions: first, that we acknowledge the fact that, even though we build on Paul, such an affirmation goes beyond the Pauline texts; and, second, that we clarify the way in which God's power, as I interpret it, exceeds any power *in* or *of* this world. The last part of my text will focus on this second point, in conversation with Eberhard Jüngel,

---

18. Ibid., 189: "Precisely at the point where God reveals Godself in the mode of foolishness and weakness, God is, because God is God, the one who overcomes. . . . God participates in this foolishness and weakness in order to save on the cross—the cross being itself weak and foolish—the fools and the weak."

who has sought to think about Paul's theology of the cross as well as about divine omnipotence, interpreting the latter within the context of the former.

Jüngel's Doctrine of God's Almightiness

Jüngel's theology of divine omnipotence is framed by two claims: God is omnipotent, first of all, insofar as God's self-identification with the crucified marks the event through which death and sin no longer have the power to separate from God; and, second, God can enter death and sin without ceasing to be God, or, more pointedly: it is precisely by entering death and sin that God *is* God.[19] Let us take a closer look at these two claims.

1. The first thesis, which interprets God's omnipotent act as the act through which God rids death and sin of their power to separate from God, is founded on an analysis of the event of the cross. The deep influence of Paul's thought on Jüngel is obvious when he argues for the centrality of the "word of the cross," but also when he claims that

---

19. Eberhard Jüngel, *God as the Mystery of the World: On the Foundation of the Theology of the Crucified One in the Dispute between Theism and Atheism*, trans. Darrell L. Guder (Grand Rapids: Eerdmans, 1983), 219–20: "Talk about the death of God implies then, in its true theological meaning, that God is the one who involves himself in nothingness. This is not contradicted by belief in the resurrection from the dead. On the contrary, the proclamation of the resurrection of Jesus reveals the sense in which God involves himself in nothingness. He does not do so in order to destroy nothingness but rather so that nothingness will be drawn into God's history. God battles nothingness by not leaving it to itself. . . . Talk about the death of God means, accordingly, in its interpretation through the proclamation of the resurrection of Jesus: (a) that God has involved himself with nothingness; (b) that God has involved himself with nothingness in the form of a struggle; (c) that God struggles against nothingness by showing it where its place is; (d) that God gives nothingness a place within being by taking it on himself. In that God identified himself with the dead Jesus, he located nothingness *within* the divine life. . . . In bearing annihilation in himself, God proves himself to be the victor over nothingness, and he ends the negative attraction of 'hell, death, and the devil.' By proving himself to be this victor, God reveals what he truly and ultimately is. God is that one who can bear and does bear, can suffer and does suffer, in his being the annihilating power of nothingness, even the negation of death, without being annihilated by it. In God nothingness loses its negative attraction and thus its annihilating effect." The rest of my paper can be seen as an interpretation of this passage. For the original version: *Gott als Geheimnis der Welt. Zur Begründung der Theologie des Gekreuzigten im Streit zwischen Theismus und Atheismus* (Tübingen: Mohr, 2010), 297–98.

the cross should not be considered independently of the resurrection (or vice versa). The central motif is thus the resurrection of the crucified one. Analyzing both of these terms is the key to a proper interpretation of divine omnipotence.

If the notion of resurrection enables to think *that* God is almighty, it does not, however, by itself allow us to give an account of *the way in which* God is almighty. For in simply saying that God overcomes death in raising the one the Christian faith confesses as God's Son, we remain stuck in an ordinary, pious assertion that, with its triumphalistic accents, does not say anything at all about the way in which, concretely, God is almighty. It is only by considering that the resurrection is the resurrection *of the crucified one* that discourse on almightiness loses its triviality and becomes precise. But to speak of the crucified's resurrection means, for Jüngel, speaking of God's identification with the crucified. We will eventually have to take into consideration the trinitarian overtones that are present in this notion of identification. For now, we can note that such an identification means that God fully sides with the one who is subjected to death on the cross. The one who endured *this death* endured it for something, and God is fully consonant with that "something," with Jesus' "cause." But what this "cause" is, and what *this death*, the death on the cross, means, needs to be specified. Right from his first works on the "death of God," Jüngel has claimed that we cannot really understand the death of the crucified one if we do not take into consideration what underlies the biblical (especially the Old Testament) conception of death. To put it briefly, the place of death, the *sheol* is, in Jüngel's interpretation, the wilderness of all wildernesses, since it is a place that is void of God's presence. It is the place of God's absence insofar as it is the place where there is no relation with God.[20] In this

---

20. Eberhard Jüngel, *Tod* (Stuttgart: Kreuz-Verlag, 1977), 98–101.

context, death is interpreted as an alienating power (*Fremdmacht*), as it alienates those it touches from God.[21] In Jüngel's view, it is precisely in relation to the idea that God is external to death, to the point where God is of no help to those who endure it, that the New Testament and especially the Pauline motif of Christ's passion responds. More to the point: it is to this idea of death that the motif of God's identification with the crucified one responds. Identifying Godself with the crucified one means here, for God, exposing Godself to death, taking upon Godself the alienating power that the crucified endured.

It is in this way, according to Jüngel, that God exercises God's omnipotence: in confronting death. It is by manifesting how God is not foreign to death that God deprives death of its *alienating* power. God truly overcomes death precisely by not avoiding it for Godself or for God's Son. The specificity of divine omnipotence lies in the fact that, far from excluding the Son's impotence, it manifests itself precisely in the crucified's impotence. In addition, insofar as it leads to the overcoming of death, this omnipotence does not consist in death's annihilation. Rather than putting an end to death, Easter expresses the fact that this death no longer has any separating power. (The similitude with the quotation from Origen, above, may be involuntary, but it is remarkable.) Death no longer has separating power, for God, in identifying Godself with the crucified, has, so to speak, taken it up within Godself. And so Jüngel writes, in one of his earliest publications on the death of God:

> It is in the Son of God's impotence [*Ohnmacht*] that death was deprived of its power [*entmächtig worden*]. . . . [The resurrection] means that the death of God, insofar as it determines God's being, changes death. In the event of the death of God, God *lets* death determine God's being, and,

---

21. Eberhard Jüngel, "Das dunkle Wort vom 'Tode Gottes'" (1968), in Jüngel, *Von Zeit zu Zeit. Betrachtung zu den Festzeiten im Kirchenjahr* (Munich: Kaiser, 1976), 45.

therefore, has already determined death. In the event of God's death, death is *determined* in such a way as to *become* a divine phenomenon [*Gottesphänomenon*]. . . . We will still die. But neither death nor life will be able to separate believers from God's love, a love which has become event in the death of God.[22]

The allusion to Rom. 8:38–39 is clear: "there is nothing that can separate us from the love of God in Christ Jesus our Lord" (REB). In *God as the Mystery of the World*, Jüngel sees in Rom. 8:31 ("If God is on our side, who is against us?," REB) the summary of Scripture.[23] Personally, I would take the final verses of Romans 8 as the basis of any Christian theology of divine omnipotence: if God is omnipotent, it is because no worldly power is capable of disrupting the relation God maintains with us, despite everything and even despite us.

2. But if God is omnipotent, it is also because God is the one who can endure death and its annihilating power without being annihilated by it, that is, without ceasing to be, without ceasing to be God. This is the second basic thesis, if I am not mistaken, in Jüngel's theology of omnipotence. The first thesis had to do with God's omnipotent *act*; the second one, to which we now briefly turn, concerns God's omnipotent *being*. Here is the main claim: the act by which God integrates, so to speak, death within Godself corresponds to God's being, insofar as God determined Godself to be Godself (that is, God) by taking upon Godself the annihilating power of nothingness. This claim touches on trinitarian theology. Two brief remarks are in order.

I have mentioned several times the idea of God's identification with the crucified one, and I have stated, as a first point, that God is fully consonant with Jesus' "cause." But to say that God *recognizes* Godself

22. Eberhard Jüngel, "Vom Tod des lebendigen Gottes. Ein Plakat" (1968), in Jüngel, *Unterwegs zur Sache. Theologische Erörterungen I* (Tübingen: Mohr Siebeck, 2000), 121, and 123–24.
23. Jüngel, *God as the Mystery*, 221 (*Gott als Geheimnis*, 300).

in the crucified one means, according to Jüngel, that the crucified
one is one of God's mode of being: the mode through which God
endures the annihilating power of sin and death. But enduring such
an annihilating power means nothing else than enduring separation
from God. At this juncture, the theology of the cross appears as
a trinitarian theology, since it involves reflecting on more than a
distinction: it involves reflecting on an opposition between two
divine modes of being, or, to use classical terms, it involves a
separation between the persons of the Father and the Son. The fact is
that it is not possible to think such an opposition or separation, and
to think this matter in such a way that these two modes of being do
not end up contradicting each other, without involving a third divine
mode of being that links the other two: in classical terms, the person
of the Holy Spirit, here understood in an Augustinian fashion as
vinculum caritatis. The Holy Spirit is *vinculum caritatis* in two ways: (1)
insofar as it guarantees the unity of the Father and the Son *in the midst
of their extreme separation*; and (2) insofar as it guarantees the human
being's communion with the Father, in the Son, despite sin which
separates the human being from God.[24] In sum, trinitarian theology

---

24. God "as the one who loves and who separates himself from his beloved, not only loves himself
but (in the midst of such great self-relatedness still more selfless) loves another one and *thus* is
and remains himself. . . . Again with John, we speak of *God as Spirit* when we have to interpret
the death-accepting separation of loving one and beloved one so that the loving one and the
beloved have to *let each one participate* in their mutual love. And we are also speaking of *God as
Spirit* when we have to interpret the death-accepting separation of loving one and beloved one
in such a way that God in the midst of this most painful separation does not cease to be the *one
and living* God, but rather is supremely God as such. God is the one and living God *in that he* as
the loving Father gives up his beloved Son and thus turns to those others, those people who are
marked by death, and draws the death of these people into his eternal life. Thus, in the midst of
his separation from him, the loving Father remains in relationship to his beloved Son. Pointedly
and yet expressing the heart of the matter, the Johannine Christ says, 'For this reason the Father
loves me, because I lay down my life, that I may take it again.' And thus he is the beloved Son
who, in the midst of his separation from the Father, relates to him. In that way God is Spirit,
establishing the link between Father and Son in such a way that man is drawn into this love
relationship. And in that sense the perfected identification of God with the crucified man Jesus
is the mutual work of the Father, the Son, and the Holy Spirit." Jüngel, *God as the Mystery*,
327–29 (*Gott als Gehemnis*, 449–50).

represents the endpoint of the theology of the cross, insofar as it enables us to think about the death of the crucified one as a "divine phenomenon," that is, as the taking up (the assumption), *within God himself*, of death and sin's annihilating power. It enables us to think that God can integrate death within Godself without ceasing to be God.

This leads to us think that it is precisely by assuming this annihilating power that God *is* God. This is my second remark, which has to do with Jüngel's trinitarian theology, and more specifically with his view on the immanent Trinity. Briefly stated, if God remains God until the event in which God integrates death within Godself, it is because that act corresponds to God's being, exactly as, according to Jüngel in his "paraphrase" of Barth in *Gottes Sein ist im werden*, it is from all eternity that God determined Godself to identify Godself with the *lost* Son of man.[25] The word *lost* is important here. It is by keeping God's eye, from all eternity, on the lost human that God determines Godself, in God's second mode of being, to join humans in their perdition, in order to integrate them within God's communion. It is in relation to this properly soteriological dimension of God's self-determination in or toward God's second mode of being that Jüngel criticizes Rahner's interpretation of the immanent Trinity: it is not enough (if I see correctly) to replace the distinction between the *logos asarkos* and the *logos ensarkos* with the distinction between the *Verbum incarnandum* and the *Verbum incarnatum*, that is, as Rahner does, to shed light on a prior disposition to incarnation; such prior disposition must

---

25. Eberhard Jüngel, *God's Being Is in Becoming: The Trinitarian Being of God in the Theology of Karl Barth: A Paraphrase*, trans. John Webster (Edinburgh: T&T Clark, 2001), 93: "'In God's eternal purpose it is God Himself who is rejected in his Son.' But since in the *historia praeveniens* the Son of God is already in covenant with the *lost* son of man, God in his eternal being takes seriously the 'threat of negation.' In precisely this way God maintains to the end his *Yes* to himself as his *Yes* to humanity. And precisely in this, God's being *remains* in *becoming*."

be understood not only as predisposition to become *embodied* (*Menschwerdung*), but also and above all as predisposition to become *flesh* (*Fleischwerdung*).[26] Such free predisposition, then, means the predisposition to joining the midst of sinners, to integrating nothingness. In other words, the power of nothingness is all the more powerless with regard to God's being that God is, so to speak, already open to it. Far from ceasing to be, far from ceasing to be God, God is in conformity with the way in which God is eternally, when God integrates death and sin in order to disintegrate, in our favor, their separating power. That is *how* God is omnipotent, *how* God is God.

What precedes obviously does not exhaust the theme of divine omnipotence. For even if we agree that reflection on divine omnipotence must begin with the act—manifested in the event of the cross—through which God expresses Godself as God by integrating in God's communion those that are separated from God, even if we confer a fundamentally soteriological orientation to divine omnipotence, the questions of God's governance of history, of God's providence and its relation to omnipotence, remain. And these questions require that we risk a discourse on God in relation to evil. This is not the place for this, and it is not possible here to give a detailed account of Jüngel's proposal on this topic. We can limit outselves to saying that in Jüngel's opinion theological discourse on this theme ends up in an inevitable aporia, which consists in the contradiction between God's being as fully revealed (*esse revelatum Dei*), which implies that God's omnipotence can only be the

---

26. Eberhard Jüngel, "Das Verhältnis von 'ökonomischer' und 'immanenter' Trinität. Erwägungen über eine biblische Begründung der Trinitätslehre—im Anschluß an und in Auseinandersetzung mit Karl Rahners Lehre vom dreifaltigen Gott als transzendentem Urgrund der Heilsgeschichte" (1975), in Jüngel, *Entsprechungen: Gott–Wahrheit–Mensch. Theologische Erörterungen II* (Tübingen: Mohr Siebeck, 2002), 272. For an English translation, see "The Relationship Between 'Economic' and 'Immanent' Trinity," *Theology Digest* 24 (1976): 179–84.

omnipotence of love, and the hiddenness of this fundamentally loving omnipotence as it operates in our present history (*opus absconditum Dei*), since, according to Jüngel, we cannot exclude that God may be using evil as God governs the world.[27]

We may, or we may not, agree with this conclusion. As such, it reminds us that theology should not be in the business of solving every single riddle, and that, on the topic of evil, it should not veer too quickly toward theodicy. More generally, Jüngel's thought is among the proposals which, while taking into consideration the problem of evil, enable us to call into question the reflex that consists in addressing the theme of omnipotence on the basis of theodicy or on the basis of the problem of evil. For if we agree that it is not wise to *reduce* omnipotence to the idea of a divine capacity to intervene in history in order to rectify its course, the main "location" of the theology of almightiness is not the problem of evil, but trinitarian theology, which is itself called for by a theology of the cross. If Jüngel's theology does not provide us with a ready-made, comprehensive doctrine of omnipotence, it does give us something like its prolegomena, by pointing in the direction of the place (namely, the cross) from which it is possible to think about it in a new way, even if that means thinking about it differently from the ways

---

27. Eberhard Jüngel, "'My Theology'—A Short Summary," in *Theological Essays II*, ed. John Webster (Edinburgh: T&T Clark, 1995), 18 ("'Meine Theologie'—kurz gefaßt" (1985), in *Wertlose Warheit. Zur Identität und Relevanz des christlichen Glaubens. Theologische Erörterungen III* [Tübingen: Mohr Siebeck, 2003], 14): "How is the miserable reality of life compatible with the glorious truth that God is love? How can God be a joyful word when his creatures experience his omnipotent action in such a way that it conceals itself in terrible world experiences? Faith suffers in this discrepancy. . . . between the being of God which has been revealed and his deeply concealed action, between the revealed God and his hidden work." See also idem, "Gottes ursprüngliches Anfangen als schöpferische Selbstbegrenzung. Ein Beitrag zum Gespräch mit Hans Jonas über den 'Gottesbegriff nach Auschwitz'" (1986), in *Wertlose Wahrheit*, 151–62 (esp. 161–62) and, for a theological grounding of the theme of God's hidden work: "The Revelation of the Hiddenness of God. A Contribution to the Protestant Understanding of the Hiddenness of Divine Action" (1984), in *Theological Essays II*, 120–44 (*Wertlose Wahrheit*, 163–82).

that seem obvious to us, and thus considering God's almightiness as the divine attribute thanks to which no worldly power can compel God not to be God, not to be God *for us*. By inviting theologians to begin with the event of the cross, Jüngel's proposal calls on them to reflect on the fact that God's omnipotence is not just any omnipotence, since it is not the power of just anybody.

15

God's Weakness and Power

Christophe Chalamet

Several well-known contemporary philosophers have been struck in recent years by the apostle Paul and, in at least one case, by the theme of "universalism."[1] But Paul is, of course, not only the author of the famous sentence of Gal. 3:28: "There is no such thing as Jew and Greek, slave and freeman, male and female; for you all are one person in Christ Jesus" (NEB). He is also the one who, like no other, concentrated Christian thought and life on the figure of Christ crucified—"I resolved that while I was with you I would not claim to know anything but Jesus Christ—Christ nailed to the cross" (1 Cor. 2:2, REB)—and who, from there, spoke of God's "weakness" and

---

1. Alain Badiou, *Saint Paul. La fondation de l'universalisme* (Paris: Presses universitaires de France, 1997); ET, *Saint Paul: The Foundation of Universalism*, trans. Ray Brassier (Stanford: Stanford University Press, 2003).

"foolishness," which are a "scandal" to the eyes of the "wise" of this world.

In his book *The Weakness of God*, John D. Caputo invites and calls theologians to think differently about God and to keep in mind, in that effort, the theme of God's "weakness."[2] He is, of course, referring to 1 Cor. 1:25: "The folly of God is wiser than human wisdom, and the weakness of God stronger than human strength" (REB). Among the questions Caputo asks is the following: Have Christianity and Christian theology adequately interpreted Paul's provocative sentences from 1 Corinthians? Caputo raises some of the basic questions of any theo-logy. He writes: "let us have the heart to ask, What is being called for when we call out, when we say and pray the name of God? What are we calling up when we call for the coming of God's kingdom?"[3]

Caputo has a keen sense for the immense reversal Jesus' message represents: the first will be last, the powerful will be brought down from their thrones, the lowly will be raised on high, enemies must be loved, and so forth.[4] That is indeed a fascinating aspect of the gospel. But he goes further and wonders whether all the revolutionary language whereby God chooses weakness to the point of identifying Godself with the figure of the crucified Jesus, is not at the end of the day at the service of a project which is in fact about power. Is "weakness" something God relates to only for a time, after which divine power will be manifested in all its glory and strength? Paul's "brilliant discourse," this "revelatory document," is it not in the service of power, ultimately?[5] Here is the important question Caputo raises. Contemporary constructive theology should not evade it.

2. John D. Caputo, *The Weakness of God: A Theology of the Event* (Bloomington: Indiana University Press, 2006).
3. Caputo, *The Weakness of God*, 20.
4. Ibid., 13–15.
5. Ibid., 17, 26.

In several places, Caputo has a good time making fun of "the police of orthodoxy" that might descend on him because of the radicality of his claims.[6] But, seriously, recent and contemporary theology have not been waiting on the North American philosopher to raise anew the question of the relation between God's love and God's power. Caputo writes as if Christian theologians had not tried, since Luther and up to our day, to *overcome* a philosophical theology or metaphysics of omnipotence. Is his book as original as he thinks?

> Suppose we dare to think about God otherwise than metaphysics and metaphysical theology allow? Suppose we say there is at least this much to the death of God: that the God of metaphysical theology is a God well lost and that the task of thinking about God radically otherwise has been inescapably imposed upon us? Suppose we say that metaphysical theology has been given enough time to prove its case and that the time has come to think about God in some other way? What then?[7]

What, then? Well, there are already a number of important proposals that have been made in the last century, not to mention earlier ones.[8] Still, Caputo's book deals with these issues with such acuity and radicality that it deserves our attention. For it could well be that our contemporary theological reflection is still bound by presuppositions that are foreign to the gospel, and that the long process of "evangelizing" God, that is, thinking about God starting with the gospel, which was triggered (or triggered anew) by Protestant

---

6. Ibid., 12.

7. Ibid., 23.

8. Caputo quotes Moltmann three times, each time favorably. Luther is mentioned twice, but never in relation to his theology of the cross. Bonhoeffer's name appears twice, but without any allusion to his talk of God's suffering and weakness. On the other hand, Caputo is grateful to William Placher for his book *Narratives of a Vulnerable God* (306n35, and 3; as a "postliberal" theologian, Placher prolonged Barth and the early Moltmann, roughly speaking). Is Caputo's book conceivable without an entire theological tradition that has sought to overcome metaphysics? Protestant theology, especially, has sought, since Luther and to this day (Ritschl, Herrmann, the entire dialectical school, all the way to Moltmann and Jüngel), to overcome philosophical theology, metaphysics, and all forms of what certain Lutheran theologians sometime like to call (a bit too hastily) "*theologia gloriae*."

theology in the sixteenth century, may need a "reboot." Christian reflection about God must always be reformed anew.

Calvin as Obstacle?

Luther's early theology of the cross represents a decisive stage in the reception of Paul's text. In the last century, Walter von Loewenich's book, *Luthers theologia crucis* (1929), led to a rediscovery of Luther's insights on the topic of the cross, which had not been at the forefront of the "Luther renaissance" in the 1910s and early 1920s. But what about this other important reformer of the sixteenth century: John Calvin? How did he conceive of divine power and weakness?

Isn't Calvin *the* thinker of God's "majesty" and "sovereignty," much more than God's "humility"? Isn't Calvin an "obstacle" when it comes to thinking about divine humility and weakness? Everything seems to confirm that. It is "God's authority which is the starting point of Calvin's doctrine of God," writes the eminent Calvin scholar François Wendel. But what does that mean? What is the meaning of the word *authority* here? "Authority, in Calvin, means power and domination. He uses the term indifferently in relation to God, the princes and the magistrate."[9] Certainly, one should add that God's authority goes hand in hand with God's love and fatherly care, but there seems to be a reciprocity in the way one informs the other. It is a two-way street in which God's love is determined by God's majesty *and vice versa*. And so "humility," not to mention weakness, is above all a *human* feature, of which divine majesty seems to be pure. But, of course, that is not the entire story, since the Christian faith confesses Christ the mediator, who brought together the divine majesty and the human misery, who took upon himself "the humility of the cross."[10] God

---

9. François Wendel, *Calvin et l'humanisme* (Paris: Presses universitaires de France, 1976), 88–89.
10. This expression is a recurring one as Calvin comments on 1 Corinthians 1–2. See, for instance,

thus does not simply "humble" human beings when God encounters them. God humbles *Godself.*

The theme of accommodation, as is well known, is a key theme in Calvin's thought, which combines a certain theocentrism with a certain christocentrism, without the latter having too much of an impact on the former, so as not to talk about God in a manner too unworthy of God. "For who even of slight intelligence does not understand that, as nurses commonly do with infants, God is wont in a measure to 'lisp' in speaking to us? Thus such forms of speaking do not so much express clearly what God is like in Godself as accommodate the knowledge of him to our slight capacity. To do this he must descend far beneath his loftiness."[11] In keeping with the theological principle of divine accommodation, which Calvin shares with several patristic thinkers, one may guess that Paul's claims about divine weakness and foolishness will have less to do with Godself, in a realistic sense, than with the way in which God appears to and is portrayed for us. And there might not be a full correspondence between the way in which God encounters us and God's very being. In this interpretation, a gap will remain between God and the manner in which God decides to come to the world.

Here is how Calvin interprets 1 Cor. 1:21–22 ("As God in his wisdom ordained, the world failed to find him by its wisdom, and he chose by the folly of the gospel to save those who have faith. Jews demand signs, Greeks look for wisdom," REB) in his 1546 commentary[12] of Paul's epistle:

John Calvin, *The First Epistle of Paul the Apostle to the Corinthians*, trans. John W. Fraser (Grand Rapids/Carlisle: Eerdmans/Paternoster, 1960), 33 (on 1 Cor. 1:17).

11. *Institutes of the Christian Religion* 1,13,1, ed. John T. McNeill and Ford Lewis Battles (Philadelphia: Westminster, 1960), 1:121. See also 2,12,1 (465), as well as his fourth sermon on Job (*Calvini opera* 33:57).

12. Calvin wrote the preface to the volume on January 24, 1556, ten years after writing the commentary.

Paul makes a concession when he calls the Gospel the *foolishness of preaching*, for that is precisely the light in which it is regarded by those 'foolish wise men'. . . , who, intoxicated by a false confidence, have no fears about subjecting the inviolable truth of God to their own feeble censorship. And besides, there is no doubt that human reason finds nothing more absurd than the news that God became a mortal man, that life is submissive to death, that righteousness has been concealed under the likeness of sin, that the source of blessing has been subjected to the curse. . . . All the same, we know that the Gospel is, in the meantime, hidden wisdom, which surpasses the heavens in its height, and at which even the angels are astonished.[13]

A little bit later, Calvin goes on to write this:

When the Lord deals with us in such a way that He seems to act in an absurd way because He does not make His wisdom plain to see, nevertheless what appears to be foolishness surpasses in wisdom all the shrewdness of men. Further, when God hides His power and seems to act in a weak way, what is imagined to be weakness is nevertheless stronger than any power of men. But we must take note, in looking at these words, that there is a concession, as I noted a little earlier. For anyone can see quite clearly how improper it is to ascribe either foolishness or weakness to God, but it was necessary to use such ironic expressions in rebutting the insane arrogance of the flesh which does not hesitate to strip God of all His glory.[14]

When Paul speaks of the "foolishness of preaching," he "makes a concession," for God "seems to act in a weak way," hiding God's power, but in reality this weakness is "stronger than any power of men." Purposefully, Calvin repeats himself twice on the theme of "concession," revealing its importance to him. For it is obvious "how improper it is to ascribe either foolishness or weakness to God." These can only be "ironic expressions," whose goal is to bind and humble us. "Foolishness" and "weakness" are much more adequately

13. Calvin, *The First Epistle*, 40.
14. Ibid., 42. See also 54, on 1 Cor. 2:7: "for when He speaks to us He accomodates Himself to our capacity."

predicated of human beings than of God; "whatever by ourselves we think concerning him is foolish, and whatever we speak, absurd."[15] Calvin's main concern, in his commentary of 1 Corinthians 1–2, is to avoid "strip[ping] God of all His glory." This is not surprising at all, from a theologian who gave birth to a tradition whose motto became *soli Deo gloria!* Calvin's concern runs throughout his works, and his doctrine of the last supper is a clear example of it: circumscribing the presence of Christ in the elements of the bread and the wine, or enclosing Christ in them, "detract[s] from his heavenly glory."[16] This concern against "enclosing" Christ in material, bodily elements is a basic concern in Calvin's Christology. The French reformer maintains that the Word fills the universe even as it becomes flesh in Jesus. This distinctive aspect of Calvin's Christology, which in fact is already a patristic and medieval theme, has been labeled *extra calvinisticum* by its seventeenth-century Lutheran critics. Its Nestorian tendencies are clear.[17]

God "seems" to act in weakness, but in truth God has simply "hidden" or "veiled" God's power. Is Calvin betraying a certain

---

15. *Institutes* 1,13,3 (1:124).

16. *Institutes* 4,17,19 (2:1381).

17. See, for instance: ". . . the very same Christ, who, according to the flesh, dwelt as Son of man on earth, was God in heaven. In this manner, he is said to have descended to that place according to his divinity, not because divinity left heaven to hide itself in the prison house [French: "loge"] of the body, but because even though it filled all things, still in Christ's very humanity it dwelt bodily [...], that is, by nature, and in a certain ineffable way," IV.xvii.30 (2:1402–403). For Heinrich Büllinger's concern about Calvin's Nestorian tendencies, see his *Decades*, ed. Thomas Harding (Cambridge: University Press, 1851), 267–68, as well as Bruce L. McCormack, "'With Loud Cries and Tears': The Humanity of the Son in the Epistle to the Hebrews," in Richard Bauckham, et al., eds., *The Epistle to the Hebrews and Christian Theology* (Grand Rapids: Eerdmans, 2009), 44n13. Karl Barth considered the "*extra calvinisticum*" a "theological disaster." Karl Barth, *Learning Jesus Christ through the Heidelberg Catechism*, trans. Shirley C. Guthrie Jr. (Grand Rapids: Eerdmans, 1981), 77. For a not-fully-convincing attempt at rehabilitating what should be called the "*extra carnem*" (rather than the "*extra calvinisticum*"), see Christopher R. J. Holmes, "Bonhoeffer and Reformed Christology: Towards a Trinitarian Supplement," *Theology Today* 71 (2014): 28–42. For a much more adequate treatment, see Darren O. Sumner, "The Twofold Life of the Word: Karl Barth's Critical Reception of the *Extra Calvinisticum*," *IJST* 15, no. 1 (2013): 49–57.

Docetic tendency here? Jürgen Moltmann thinks so.[18] But the matter may be a little bit more complex, for Calvin was convinced that faith will never be firm and stable unless it bases itself on Christ's weakness.[19] Christ's "infirmity" or weakness was in no way *only* a "seeming" infirmity. It was very real. There, not in the majesty of the divine Logos, lies faith's "support." Calvin echoes Luther in his *Heidelberg Disputation* when he writes: ". . . all the wisdom of believers is concentrated in the Cross of Christ."[20]

Calvin's anti-Docetic points need thus to be noted. What he does *not* do is to inscribe the weakness of Christ in his theo-logy, in his thinking and speaking about God. The Son's descent is essentially directed toward us, it does not have major incidences on God, who remains a glorious, majestic God. In no way should the word of the cross detract from the events of the resurrection and the ascension, according to Calvin. Even when considering God's very being, love does not seem to be the most basic character of God's being, for "nothing is more characteristic of God than eternity and self-existence ['autousia']—that is, existence of Godself, so to speak."[21] Are these remnants of a more philosophical view of God in the midst of a theology that sought (without fully realizing its intention) to be "simply" docile to the Word of God?

18. Jürgen Moltmann, *The Crucified God: The Cross of Christ as the Foundation and Criticism of Christian Theology*, trans. Margaret Kohl (Minneapolis: Fortress Press, 1993 [1991]), 259 ("a rather docetic christology").

19. "Ainsi il advient que nostre foy cherchant Dieu en sa gloire céleste, et en sa lumière inaccessible, s'esvanouit, et la chair sans estre esmeue d'ailleurs, suggère mille imaginations et brouilleries, pour nous destourner du droit regard de Dieu. . . . Les Théologiens de la Papauté quand ils disputent, ou (pour mieux dire) gazouillent de l'object de la foy, font seulement mention de Dieu, et laissent là derrière Jésus-Christ. . . . Ces bestes orgueilleuses ont honte de l'humilité et abjection de Christ: et pourtant ils veulent voler jusques à la Divinité incompréhensible de Dieu. Mais quoy? la foy ne parviendra jamais jusques au ciel, si elle ne se soumet humblement à Jésus-Christ, qui semble par apparence estre un Dieu petit et abject: et ne sera jamais ferme et stable, si elle ne cherche son appuy en l'infirmité de Christ." Commentary on John 14,1, in *Commentaires de Jehan Calvin sur le Nouveau Testament* (Paris: Meyrueis, 1854), 2:292.

20. Calvin, *The First Epistle*, 32 (on 1 Cor. 1:17).

21. *Institutes* 1,14,3; I:163.

Power Manifested in Weakness

Christian theology, it seems to me, cannot give up the theme of God's power (δύναμις). Eberhard Jüngel was correct to maintain it in his important conversation with Hans Jonas, according to whom there is no other possibility, after Auschwitz, than renouncing it.[22] What is at stake, still today, is to let the gospel tell us what God's "power" is like. The question has mostly to do with the modalities and the nature of God's power. Christian theology has made important progress on this point in the second half of the twentieth century, when it began to interpret "power" and "divinity" not as a temporary "veiling," which allows God to encounter and redeem us but which has little to no impact on who God is (Calvin's position), but as manifested *precisely* in God's debasement and weakness. "Power" and "divinity" must be interpreted not in an abstract manner but specifically from this debasement and descent. Karl Barth, among others, interpreted Jesus' passion "as the action and, therefore, the passion of God Himself."[23]

In his doctrine of reconciliation (*Church Dogmatics*, part IV), Barth radically puts into question the idea that Jesus' "divinity" could be identical to force or power understood in all-too-human terms, whereas Jesus' "humanity" would be synonymous with weakness. If we understand the two natures in such a way, then yes, God is "veiling" Godself as God humiliates Godself, so that this descending movement does *not* correspond to God's very being. Barth's stunning

---

22. Hans Jonas, "The Concept of God After Auschwitz," in Lawrence Vogel, ed., *Morality and Mortality: The Search for the Good after Auschwitz* (Evanston, IL: Northwestern University Press, 1996), 131–43; idem, "The Concept of God After Auschwitz. A Jewish Voice," *The Journal of Religion* 67, no. 1 (1987): 8–9. Eberhard Jüngel, "Gottes ursprüngliches Anfangen als schöpferische Selbstbegrenzung. Ein Beitrag zum Gespräch mit Hans Jonas über den 'Gottesbegriff nach Auschwitz'," in Hermann Deuser, et al., eds., *Gottes Zukunft. Zukunft der Welt* (Münich: Chr. Kaiser, 1986), 265–75.

23. Karl Barth, *CD* IV/1, 245 (*KD* IV/1, 270). The English translation is revised here and there.

proposal, his *coup de force*, in *Church Dogmatics* IV/1, lies in his way of breaking with this logic. We see this very clearly when he writes:

> The problem posed is not that of a theodicy: How can God will this or permit this in the world which He has created good? It is a matter of the humiliation and dishonouring of God Himself. . . .[24]

> And it is a matter of the answer to this question: that in this humiliation God is supremely God, that in this death He is supremely alive, that He has maintained and revealed His deity in the passion of this man as His eternal Son.[25]

Barth goes much further than Calvin and other theologians who preserve a distance, a gap between Jesus' suffering and the Father. Barth was perfectly aware of the radicality of his claims:

> . . . it is not enough simply to follow the great line of theological tradition and to reject all thought of an alterability or alteration of God in His presence and action in the man Jesus. . . . it is something very bold and profoundly astonishing to presume to say without reservation or subtraction that *God* was truly and altogether ["ganz"] *in Christ*. . . . The statement of this identity . . . aims very high. In calling this man the Son or the eternal Word of God, in ascribing to this man in His unity with God a divine being and nature, it is not speaking only or even primarily of Him but of *God*.[26]

This is a theological approach that urges us to think about God by starting not with preconceived ideas about power and the like, but with Jesus' concrete existence. A theologian such as Moltmann, along with others, certainly learned much from Barth, as can be seen from Moltmann's book *The Crucified God*. And yet Moltmann went too

24. Barth, *CD* IV/1, 246. "Es geht um die Erniedrigung und Entwürdigung Gottes selbst. . . ." (*KD* IV/1, 271).

25. Barth, *CD* IV/1, 246–47. "Und es geht um *die Antwort* auf diese Frage: dass Gott vielmehr eben in solcher Erniedrigung aufs Höchste Gott, in diesem Tode aufs Höchste lebendig war, dass er seine Gottheit gerade in der Passion dieses Menschen als seines ewigen Sohnes eigentlich bewährt und offenbar gemacht hat" (*KD* IV/1, 271).

26. Barth, *CD* IV/1, 183 (*KD* IV/1, 199–200).

far, one may argue, in the direction of interpreting the meaning of the cross by focusing on God's inner trinitarian life, rather than on God's dealing with the world. Moltmann became fascinated with the purely theo-logical dimension of Jesus' passion, which at times led to a neglect of the heart of the gospel, namely the reconciling of *the world* effected by God.[27]

Here is the revolutionary thesis Barth unfolds in the first volume of his doctrine of reconciliation:

> We will mention at once the thought which will be decisive and basic in this section, that God shows himself to be the great and *true* God in the fact that God can and will let God's grace bear this cost, that God is capable and willing and ready for this condescension, this act of extravagance, this far journey. What marks out God above all false gods is that they are not capable and ready for this. In their otherworldliness and supernaturalness and transcendence, etc., the gods are a reflection of the human pride which will not unbend, which will not stoop to that which is beneath it. God is not proud but precisely in his high majesty God is humble. It is in this high humility that He speaks and acts as the God who reconciles the world to himself.[28]

If we draw the consequences of this way of thinking about God's majesty and humility to the theme of power and weakness, will we deny the (legitimate) claim that God's power manifests itself precisely in the weakness and dereliction of Jesus' cross? If we follow Barth's

---

27. See Christian Ducquoc's important critique (Ducquoc was a brilliant French Dominican theologian): "Je ne suis pas sûr que cette fascination de la croix et de l'abandon de Jésus par Dieu expriment au mieux ce dont il est question dans le messianisme original de Jésus. Elle transfert en un débat intra-divin ce qui rend paradoxale notre histoire sous la promesse." *Messianisme de Jésus et discrétion de Dieu. Essai sur la limite de la christologie* (Geneva: Labor et Fides, 1984), 248. See also Hubert Goudineau and Jean-Louis Souletie, *Jürgen Moltmann* (Paris, Cerf, 2002), 110–11, and 122. Moltmann does admit his intention was to focus on God's triune being, but he does not see any problem with it: "In *The Crucified God* I interpreted the event on Golgotha as something that happened between Jesus, the Son of God, and the God whom he called his Father, and thereby came upon an approach to the Trinitarian mystery by way of the theology of the cross." Moltmann, *A Broad Place: An Autobiography*, trans. Margaret Kohl (Minneapolis: Fortress Press, 2007), 201.

28. Barth, *CD* IV/1, 159 (*KD* IV/1, 173).

effort to bring to light all of the human, all-too-human conceptions not only of God's majesty but also of God's power, will it not become necessary to qualify God's power in such a way that the term does not mean (in God's case: unlimited) "strength" or a sort of superhuman capacity without any limitation, an infinitized "power"? Will it not lead us to talk of divine power "not as 'force' but as Christo-form 'authority'"?[29]

Barth writes:

> True divinity in the New Testament is being in the absolute freedom of love, and therefore the being of the Most High who is high and almighty and eternal and righteous and glorious not *also* but *precisely* in His lowliness. The *direct* New Testament attestation of *this* divinity of Christ is the attestation of the man Jesus himself as the Son of God become flesh and suffering and crucified and dying for us, the message of *Christ* crucified (1 Cor. 1:23; 2:2). It is clear that in the sense of the New Testament this and this alone is decisive and basic.[30]

There is no "divinity" which, abstracted from God's condescension, is "simply" or "purely" majestic in the human senses of the term. God is not majestic "alongside," independent from God's humbling in Jesus. With Barth we are undoubtedly in a strikingly different theological landscape than with Calvin's thought.

Barth himself draws the consequences of his interpretation of "divinity" for the theme of omnipotence: God's "*omnipotence* ('Allmacht') is that of a divine plenitude of power ('Machtvollkommenheit') in the fact that (as opposed to any abstract force; 'abstrakte Mächtigkeit') it can assume the form of weakness and impotence and do so as omnipotence, triumphing precisely in this form."[31] A Christian theology of divine power cannot simply be a

---

29. Sarah Coakley, *God, Sexuality, and the Self: An Essay 'On the Trinity'* (Cambridge: Cambridge University Press, 2013), 343.

30. Barth, *CD* IV/1, 191–92 (*KD* IV/1, 209).

theology of mere "power" (or of mere "weakness," for that matter, unlike what Caputo suggests), just as the subject matter of theology is not simply "God" but, rather, God's being in act (centrally: God's act *ad extra*). At every step, in Christian theology, the crucial point is to qualify everything one is saying through the gospel, and the biblical witness read through the gospel.

Beyond Divine Weakness as a "Principle"

It is no less problematic, it seems to me, to envision divine "omnipotence" in abstraction from the cross and what the cross manifests (about ourselves, religion, and God), than to imagine a divine "weakness" that loses sight of God's δύναμις or power. To make "power" or "weakness" into a single hermeneutical principle that serves as a key to think about God risks missing the living God.[32] When dealing with divine power and weakness, it is never about an "either/or," it is not an alternative. We should also avoid simply juxtaposing the two. The goal is, rather, to think one through and with the other. If we interpret divine power through God's love as manifested in the condescension and humiliation of Jesus, then notions such as vulnerability and weakness will of necessity be a part

---

31. Barth, *CD* IV/1, 187 (*KD* IV/1, 205). Barth (unfortunately) does not dwell on this revised notion of "omnipotence" on that page.

32. New Testament scholar Jean Zumstein puts it well: "Aussi faut-il bien se garder d'ériger un nouveau système qui verrait désormais Dieu se manifester exclusivement dans les valeurs inverses à celles que les Juifs et les Grecs associaient au divin. Argumenter de cette façon, ce serait à nouveau nier l'altérité de Dieu, méconnaître sa liberté et vouloir mettre la main sur lui. Ce serait succomber au danger de la contre-dépendance. Ce serait induire que Dieu renonce à toute sagesse, à toute force, à toute vie." Zumstein, "Paul et la théologie de la croix," *ETR* 76, no. 4 (2001): 491–92. Zumstein is of the opinion that both Jürgen Becker (*Paulus. Der Apostel der Völker* [Stuttgart: UTB, 1998], 221) and Wolfgang Schrage (in his commentary of 1 Corinthians, *Der erste Brief an die Korinther*, EKK VII/1 [Neukirchen-Vluyn: Neukirchener, 2013], 189) fall "for a good part" into that error (492n25). Zumstein continues: "Le Crucifié ne se laisse pas mettre en système, il ne peut jamais faire l'objet d'une explication définitivement satisfaisante ou apaisante. Ou alors il a cessé d'être le Crucifié. Le Crucifié reste à jamais facteur de trouble, un facteur de crise, un écueil insurmontable pour l'intelligence, la sensibilité et la piété." Ibid., 495.

of our theological reflection. God acts freely, but in that free act God "does something unnecessary and extravagant, binding and limiting and compromising and offering Himself in relation to man by having dealings with him and making himself his God. In the fact that God is gracious to man, all the limitations of man are God's limitations, all his weaknesses, and more, all his perversities are his."[33] If we wish not to project *our* notions of God's weakness (not just our notions of divine power!), we might want to think God's weakness as the expression of a δύναμις which, itself, is the δύναμις of God's very being as love.

Christian theology will do well not to speak "simply" of divine power, that is, without reflecting on divine power as an expression of divine love, and so as a power that is not invulnerable. This is a problem in the Nicene Creed (but a creed is not a theological treatise), which does not qualify "omnipotence" when it simply asserts "*credo in unum Deum, patrem omnipotentem.*"[34] If Jesus' suffering says something of God, as Barth and others believe it does, then that suffering is not accidental or temporary, it is not about to be simply left behind in a glorious ulterior moment or, worse, in a revenge that lets divine "power" reveal its fullness and glory. Weakness is not the last word in Christian theology, but neither are conceptions of power or glory that are "unbroken" and void of suffering. The marks of Jesus' wounds do not disappear. Suffering is assumed, "taken up" in God's life.[35]

> . . . the New Testament describes the Son of God as the servant, indeed as the *suffering* servant of God. Not by chance ("zufällig") and temporarily ("beiläufig"). Not merely to prove and show his mind and disposition. Not merely to win through by conflict to a concrete goal.

33. Barth, *CD* IV/1, 158 (*KD* IV/1, 172–73).
34. Étienne Babut, *Le Dieu puissamment faible de la Bible* (Paris: Cerf, 1999), 17–19.
35. For a different, indeed antithetical opinion on this matter, see Edwin Chr. van Driel's thought-provoking contribution to the present volume.

He is not *also* suffering, his suffering is not a foil meant to emphasize what is otherwise his glory. No, he suffers necessarily and, as it were, essentially, and so far as can be seen without meaning or purpose. He is a suffering servant who *wills* this profoundly unsatisfactory state, who *cannot* will anything other in the obedience in which he shows himself the Son of God.[36]

Jesus' suffering qualifies his being, as well as God's, forever and not just for a time, according to Barth. One may wish to exercise caution, with regard to such statements, for suffering should not be "divinized" (otherwise human suffering may soon be sought out or praised), it should not become something "positive," as if God did not oppose it while assuming it. Assumption of it does not cancel opposition to it. The dangers of perverted versions of Christian theology on the topic of suffering, dangers that have been rightly denounced by the "masters of suspicion" in the last two centuries, need to be kept in mind. What should be shown is how God's power finds its fulfillment, its finality, but not its "end" in the sense of "cancellation," in weakness and nowhere else (ἡ γὰρ δύναμις ἐν ἀσθενείᾳ τελεῖται; 2 Cor. 12:9b). There, divine δύναμις finds its completion, revealing what it is truly capable of.

36. Barth, *CD* IV/1, 164 (*KD* IV/1, 179–80).

16

The Paradox of Faith

Hans-Christoph Askani

Either/Or: A Surprising Alternative

There are only two possibilities: either one understands 1 Corinthians 1–2—that is, to put it in a concentrated way: the word of the cross (1 Cor. 1:18)—as the center of the Christian faith, or one does not understand 1 Corinthians 1–2 as the center of it.[1] Such a claim may seem trivial, as if one were saying: there are only two possibilities, either 1+2=3 or 1+2≠3. How can one claim that the mathematical example or, to give another example, the statement "either it is raining or it is not," are claims which are self-evident, whereas the above thesis ("either one understands 1 Corinthians 1–2 as the center

---

1. I focus on 1 Corinthians 1–2 knowing full well that the first four chapters of the epistle wrestle with the "theme" which interests us (e.g., 3:18ff.; 4:9-13), a theme which is present in other parts of the Corinthian correspondence (2 Cor. 2:14-16; 4:7-12; 6:3-10).

of the Christian faith, or one does not") expresses something that goes beyond evidence? In both cases, we find an alternative, an either/or. Might it be possible that an expression which has the form of such an alternative (an *exclusive* alternative: either/or) could nevertheless surprise us? Indeed, it might, if both options that are in play, or at least one of the two, had *unforeseen*, perhaps even *unmeasurable*, implications; if advocating *for* or *against* 1 Corinthians 1–2 as the center of the Christian faith had deeply significant consequences. "If you claim that 1 Corinthians 1–2 must *not* be interpreted as the center of the Christian faith, do you really know what you are saying? Would you be able to express the distinguishing feature of the Christian faith without referring to what is expressed in these chapters?"

Or, alternatively: "You claim that the whole specificity of the Christian faith is concentrated and expressed in such paradoxes? Are you thus saying, in effect, that the Christian faith cannot be understood in another way, that it cannot be conceived apart from a fundamental, irresolvable opposition between human and divine wisdom? And if you do so, how will you be able to give an account of it?" With these ways of putting things, the alternative I suggested at the very beginning is far from being self-evident, far from being fully grasped in all its implications.

There is, or there may be, something bold on both sides. On the one side: Who would dare *deny* that 1 Corinthians 1–2 is at the center of the Christian faith? On the other: Who would make a positive, rigorous case *in support* of that claim? Such questions bother us,[2] not

---

2. An image may be of use here: the image of the path. Some paths are bordered with grass. If one leaves the path for a while, there is no problem: one finds oneself amidst grass and flowers. (Reflecting about the alternative between 2+2=4 and 2+2≠4 is similar to such a path: on both sides one is in the realm of correct or incorrect statements.) Then there are ridges, with the abyss on either side. The alternative I began with (about 1 Corinthians 1–2 being or not being the center of the Christian faith) seems to me to be of the sort that whatever one's position about it, one is always at risk of falling into the abyss.

only because we don't immediately know the answer, but because behind these questions lies the restlessness of these two chapters' content, and especially of some specific sentences:[3]

- "The message of the cross is sheer folly to those on the way to perdition, but to us, who are on the way to salvation, it is the power of God." (1 Cor. 1:18)

- "God has made the wisdom of this world look foolish!" (1 Cor. 1:20b)

- "As God in his wisdom ordained, the world failed to find him by its wisdom, and he chose by the folly of the gospel to save those who have faith." (1 Cor. 1:21)

- "The folly of God is wiser than human wisdom, and the weakness of God stronger than human strength." (1 Cor. 1:25)

- "I resolved that while I was with you I would not claim to know anything but Jesus Christ—Christ nailed to the cross." (1 Cor. 2:2)[4]

In all of this we find a concentration of paradoxical formulations to which we have gotten used through almost two millennia of Christian history, but which, to "fresh," "unsuspecting" eyes, contains unexpected twists. It is because of such twists in the message about Christ—in the middle of the "evangelical" message (!)[5]—that the "either . . . or" in my introduction is anything but trivial. Positioning oneself in relation to such twists is never trivial. At the bottom of such nontriviality, we find questions such as: Can we, as Christians (that is, as those who claim for ourselves Christ's name) really consider the

---

3. Unless otherwise noted, all biblical quotations come from the Oxford Study Bible (NRSV).

4. We may also quote 1 Cor. 2:7a: "I speak God's hidden wisdom, his secret purpose." Rudolf Bultmann notes—rightly, in my opinion—that σοφία in 2:6—3:2 has a different meaning than in the first chapter; cf. his article "Karl Barth, *The Resurrection of the Dead*," in *Faith and Understanding* (Philadelphia: Fortress Press, 1987), 70–71.

5. 1 Cor. 1:17; cf. 1:23!

cross, and the crucified one, as the reality on which everything hinges for our faith? And how can we *think* that?

That last question, namely "how can we *think* that?," can be interpreted in several ways. (*a*) There is a problem: How do we think about it in order to find the solution? That is the way we deal with things in our daily lives. Technical problems, however complex they may be, belong here. They are, in principle, resolvable. Many scientific problems of all kinds, even many human problems, can be—sometimes after great efforts—*resolved*. Here what "thinking" is, what it means, is already presupposed and appears to be clear. Thinking means identifying and resolving a problem through our intelligence. (*b*) And yet there is another *kind* of problem. For instance, I carry on me, with me, and within me the weight of a past that is too heavy for me. Or: as someone who believes in God I do not understand why there is evil in the world. These realities disturb my thinking, they are a source of unceasing restlessness for my thinking. Here the question that arises not only has to do with the way in which I can find a solution, but with the way in which *I think*: How can I think, if no solution is to be found? In such cases, what "thinking" means is not immediately self-evident. What is to become of "thought" in the face of irresolvable problems? What does "thinking" mean *here*?

It is exactly this type of question that we face when dealing with 1 Corinthians 1–2: What does "thinking" mean if the point is to think our faith through and if—at the same time—this faith is led into a tension where God's wisdom and foolishness meet, where, to be more precise, God's wisdom turns out to be foolish . . . ? What happens to thought as it undergoes such an aggression?

The Logic of 1 Corinthians 1

Let us turn now to the text itself!

"As I re-read 1 Corinthians 1–2"—it was with these words that I wanted to introduce this second section, but as I was about to write them I became hesitant, as a question came to me: "As I re-read . . ." Have I really re-read? Is it possible to *read* 1 Corinthians 1–2?

I will begin by answering very subjectively. I can say, in a twofold sense, that I have *not* read it. First, when we begin to read a text, we usually have, at least initially, the *desire* to do so; we have a certain *curiosity*. . . . Turning to the first two chapters of 1 Corinthians, I had no desire, no curiosity—as if the text, far from attracting me, was pushing me away. Second, when we read, we usually go from one sentence to the next, as if we were guided by a movement, a logic, a dynamism that is intrinsic to the lines our eyes and our mind follow (the lines are, it may be added, the symbol and promise of the possibility of this continuing movement of understanding). But is there a logical continuity in and between the lines of 1 Corinthians 1? My impression is that the opposite is the case. Instead of continuity, rupture; instead of linear logic, paradoxical tensions. We don't feel guided from one sentence to the other. There is no place for ordinary curiosity; no continuity, no time for understanding.

Let us take a look at certain verses and at their mutual coherence and interrelation. At the beginning of his epistle, Paul is worried about division within the Corinthian community. Some claim for themselves a certain apostle who baptized them, others claim another one. Thus Paul states: "Thank God, I never baptized any of you, except . . ." (1:14), and a little bit further: "For Christ did not send me to baptize, but to proclaim the gospel . . ." (1:17)—this is the first surprising twist: as if baptism and preaching stood in competition with one another!⁶ Even if this opposition is astonishing for us, it would perhaps have made sense in the tense situation in Corinth. But the second part of the sentence introduces a second formulation, or, better, takes us in a *wholly different direction*: "Christ [sent me] to proclaim the gospel; and to do it *without recourse to the wisdom of speech ...*"—if until then Paul's letter was determined by the situation in Corinth, now it is suddenly turning to a substantive reflection.[7]

Before turning to the content, let us observe what is going on rhetorically: until then Paul has calmly unfolded his thought, but now a thought comes up that is steering him in a different direction. This thought, which he cannot master, disrupts *the course* he had set for his letter. It is as if the apostle was saying, suddenly, to the Corinthian community and to himself: "but enough of this chatter, let's talk seriously now!" But it is not the author who is taking the initiative to switch subjects, it is the subject (the "theme") that introduces itself

6. Hans Conzelmann pointed out the element of surprise in this passage: "we ask ourselves what the rejection of the σοφία λόγου, 'wisdom of words', has to do with baptism." *1 Corinthians: A Commentary on the First Epistle to the Corinthians*, trans. James W. Leitch (Philadelphia: Fortress Press, 1975), 37. Other commentators have also remarked on the abrupt transition. See, for instance, H. Lietzmann and W. G. Kümmel, *An die Korinther I-II*, HNT 9 (Tübingen: Mohr, 1949), quoted in ibid.

7. Johannes Weiss mentions the sudden introducing of the theme (the foolishness of the word of the cross) in 1:17: "Paul introduces, suddenly and without preparation, with οὐκ ἐν σοφίᾳ λόγου, a keyword (*Stichwort*) which he had not used up to that point, and thus obtains the theme of the following paragraph. This way of introducing, 'silently' but nevertheless rather abruptly, the theme of what follows, is a stylistic trick Paul regularly uses." *Der erste Korintherbrief* (Göttingen: Vandenhoeck & Ruprecht, 1910), 23. The meaning of the expression "οὐκ ἐν σοφίᾳ λόγου" is not easy to determine, according to Conzelmann. Even if he takes into consideration the possibility that Paul may be alluding to a "slogan" used in the Corinthian context, Conzelmann underscores (here he refers to Bultmann) the "dialectic" which is at play here: "Paul, too, must pursue wisdom." *1 Corinthians*, 37. Herbert Braun's terminological comments in relation to "the σοφία τοῦ λόγου in 1 Cor. 1,17" are very helpful. He points out the proximity that exists between the terms νόμος and σοφία λόγου, particularly in Paul's eschatological perspective. See his *Gesammelte Studien zum Neuen Testament und seiner Umwelt* (Tübingen: Mohr, 1962), 178–81. Compare with Weiss, *Der erste Korintherbrief*, 24. Against an overly restrictive interpretation of "wisdom" (a certain group in Corinth which had a special fondess for it), Ulrich Wilckens states "that the cross and the wisdom of the world are mutually exclusive, and *principally so*" ("daß *grundsätzlich* Kreuz und Weltweisheit sich ausschließen"). Wilckens, *Weisheit und Torheit. Eine exegetisch-religionsgeschichtliche Untersuchung zu I. Kor 1 und 2* (Tübingen: Mohr, 1959), 24 (my italics).

as switch in the discourse. The topic was "who has baptized whom," and *suddenly* Paul speaks of something else. Of what? Of a, of *the*, of the *main*, perhaps of the *only* true distinguishing feature of the gospel: the "cross of Christ," which must not be "emptied" or "annihilated." In just a few words, the turn in Paul's evolving thought has taken place.

The Logic and Rhetoric of 1 Corinthians 1:14-18

If one reads, without any prior knowledge of it, what we call v. 17 of that chapter, it is as if one is leisurely walking one's favorite Sunday walk, and then, from one step to the next, one falls into a bottomless abyss. Is what we are reading here a text? Is it possible to *read* this? As if that were not enough, the following sentence adds another layer, to such a high point that nothing more can seemingly be added: "The message of the cross is sheer folly to those on the way to perdition, but to us, who are on the way to salvation, it is the power of God." (1:18). Let's try to reconstruct the logic of what ties together vv. 14–18:

- Thank God, I never baptized any of you (otherwise you would have used that, too, as a pretext for your divisions!)

- truth be said, I did baptize (but not much)

- anyway, that was not the most important thing

- the most important thing was something different. What was it? "My" message.

[and now the punch line:]

- concerning the message, by the way: it did not fit in with the coherence, the logic of speech (σοφία λόγου), the rules of thought as you or, rather, as all of us know them. It was sense-less

- not just that: it *could* not fit with that logic, it *had* to be sense-less, incomprehensible

- why? Because of its content: the cross of Christ. For (this is implied) the cross of Christ is not logical or coherent.

The turning point is in v. 17! What, then, does "verse" 18 do? It explains why, in the middle of v. 17, there needed to be a collapse, a catastrophe with regard to logic. Usually an explanation makes something difficult to understand more intelligible. Is it the case here?

"The message of the cross is sheer folly to those on the way to perdition, but to us, who are on the way to salvation, it is the power of God" (1:18). What is happening in this claim? What we have already sensed finds its explicit expression: in this realm, in what is at stake here—in the cross of Christ—there is something incomprehensible. "You've seen correctly: we are dealing with a foolishness!" As if that were reassuring! "Where there is faith, there is foolishness!" Is that a good apology of faith?

But that's not all Paul says here. He adds: "The message of the cross is sheer folly to those on the way to perdition." What does that mean? Who are these people? According to the translation of the Oxford Study Bible which I cited, they could be those who have lost their way, they no longer follow the right path. Thus everything would fit into place: for those who have lost the right path, the message of the faith is foolishness. That's logical or normal, since they have lost the right path! There is nothing surprising in the fact that to them God's wisdom is "foolishness." But is that the meaning of Paul's sentence? Paul's reference to Isa. 29:14 in the very next sentence suggests a much less conciliatory interpretation: "Scripture says, 'I will destroy the wisdom of the wise, and bring to nothing the cleverness of the clever." Far from being reassuring, this is unbearable, unacceptable. And indeed, the sense of the Greek word ἀπολλυμένοις (the parallel with σῳζομένοις shows it) is not active but passive. It is not those who took a wrong way, it is those who are designated to be lost. We will come back to this problem.

If we wish to get a sense of Paul's *boldness* or, more precisely, if we wish to "*measure*" Paul's boldness—or the boldness of what is talking through and almost despite Paul[8]—all we need to do is look at the *toning down* that several translations and commentaries have judged necessary to offer in order to purify the text of everything which is disturbing. Let us take a quick look at some of them. "In this entire section, Paul does not condemn authentic human wisdom, gift of God and capable of knowing God . . . , but only a prideful, boasting wisdom" (*Bible de Jérusalem*, 1973). The official ecumenical French translation of the Bible[9] annotates the verse "God has made the wisdom of this world look foolish" (1:20b) in the following way: "In this passage as a whole, *wisdom*, an activity of human reason, is not criticized as such, since it is God's work. But the apostle denounces it because of its *pretension* to be the single and ultimate norm." The New Testament scholar and translator Ulrich Wilckens has found a different solution: he uses, in several instances, the word "Unsinn" (to translate μωρία, 1:18.21, and μωρόν, 1:25), between quotation marks, and adds: ". . . that is why the opinion according to which there is a contradiction between the Christian faith and honest,

---

8. He is "apostle," i.e., sent out, and he is that not only at the beginning of his mission, he remains that, in all he says, he is *always* sent out!

9. *Traduction œcuménique de la Bible* (Paris: Cerf-Les Bergers et les Mages, 1976).

reasonable knowledge cannot find its grounding in Saint Paul . . .[10]
More examples could be given.[11]

The Word of Salvation

Let us return to 1:18 and take into special consideration the structure
of that sentence as well as its inner balance or imbalance:

10. "Therefore the opinion according to which there is no fundamental contradiction between the
    Christian faith and honest rational knowledge cannot claim Paul for itself. It is much more
    likely that Paul had in mind specific theories of enthusiastic, reckless piety which focused
    only on one's own interest and not on the 'upbuilding' of the whole community." *Das Neue
    Testament*, trans. Ulrich Wilckens in coll. with W. Jetter, E. Lange, and R. Pesch (Zürich-
    Einsiedeln-Köln: Mohn, 1983), 564–65. Wilckens had a more nuanced approach in his doctoral
    dissertation, as we saw above.
11. Among recent studies L. L. Welborn's book *Paul, the Fool of Christ: A Study of 1 Corinthians
    1–4 in the Comic-Philosophic Tradition* (New York: T&T Clark, 2005) deserves mention. There,
    too, one finds an attempt at toning things down. Among other things, Welborn articulates
    two theses: (*a*) the conflict between the μωρία of the Word of the cross and the σοφία of
    the world has its *Sitz im Leben* in the opposition between a wealthy, educated, cultured "elite"
    and a class marked by poverty. "The term μωρία designated the attitude and behavior of a
    particular social type: the lower class moron. . . . That this is the right understanding of Paul's
    characterization of 'the word of the cross' as μωρία, is demonstrated by the way in which Paul
    continues in 1 Cor. 1.26-28: those who are 'called' by 'the word of the cross' are, for the most
    part, persons without education, wealth, or birth; they are 'the foolish, . . . the weak, . . . the
    low-born, . . . the despised, the nobodies'" (1–2; see also 3, 5, 101, 117, 166, 249–50, 253, etc.).
    (*b*) Paul's discourse uses as its "model" the comic tradition" (3, see also 101, 118, 248, etc.),
    "the language of jest and mime" (2), "the popular culture" (vii) with its "gallows humor" (2,
    etc.)—all in all a language in which something as terrible and disgusting as a death on a cross
    could only be presented in satiric form (248). My interpretation contradicts Welborn's in every
    respect. Following the options presented by Welborn, I express it in this way: (1) The salvific
    event of the cross, far from presupposing, as its background, a prior conflict, opens the horizon
    of a conflict that did not exist until then, a conflict which, consequently, cannot be reduced
    to a certain, demarcated field (whatever may be the nature of that demarcation). The conflict
    takes place between the world, its "understanding," on the one hand, and God's paradoxical
    revelation and its "understanding," on the other. (2) What is not "stupid" in the sense used by
    Welborn (see 1), what is, however, indissolubly *paradoxical*, is the link between the cross and the
    gospel: the fact that salvation is given to us in the death which God did not avert from Godself,
    and the fact that this salvation comes to us through the word—usually a word that belongs to
    the logic of the world, but in this case a word that belongs to God's logic—which springs from
    this death and which announces it. (3) In conformity to this paradoxical event, Paul does not
    talk following this or that scheme (e.g., a rhetoric or poetic scheme); on the contrary, he himself
    is searching for a language, which is not available to him and which, the more he progresses in
    formulating things, the less he is master of it. The whole challenge of interpreting 1 Corinthians
    1–2 does not consist in identifying other discourses that move in similar directions, but in
    plumbing an unfathomable discourse and an unfathomable logic, a logic which protests against
    any claims at mastery and which, in the absence of mastery (!), gives itself as a *promise*.

Ὁ λόγος γὰρ ὁ τοῦ σταυροῦ τοῖς μὲν ἀπολλυμένοις μωρία ἐστίν, τοῖς δὲ σῳζομένοις ἡμῖν δύναμις θεοῦ ἐστιν. "For the Word of the cross is foolishness to those who are lost, for those, however, who are saved—us—it is the power of God" (1:18; my trans.). The sentence consists in two parts that stand in radical opposition with one another; that opposition could actually not be more radical. The same entity is one thing to some, the very opposite to others. To some: (human) foolishness. To others: (divine) power.[12] Who belongs to these two groups? Οἱ ἀπολλύμενοι—οἱ σῳζόμενοι. Those who are lost—those who are saved. In order to understand this alternative, it is necessary to see that what is at stake here surpasses the ordinary coordinates of the world. It is not about the opposition between happiness and unhappiness, for example—these would be mundane categories; Paul speaks about something else, about the opposition between salvation and perdition, an opposition that surpasses the measures of the world.

The point of reference in relation to which the distinction, the division, is being drawn (the "entity" I alluded to above) is nothing but *a word*. "Ὁ λόγος γὰρ κτλ." Why a word? Can an answer be given just on the basis of the sentence's structure, without dealing with the content of that word? Yes, indeed: the only thing in the world (I am tempted to add: and in heaven) in relation to which the contours of the horizon of foolishness, of non-sense (μωρία) *begin to appear*, is the "word." In relation to a purely material thing, even in relation to an event, unless there is a discourse that "accompanies" it, the question of foolishness (in its dimension of "radical senselessness") does not come up. This is so because the question of senselessness (or meaninglessness) rises only when a sense (or meaning) is presupposed.

12. For the second part we would have expected not "power" but "wisdom," exactly as Paul says further on (v. 21). Here, however, the stress is on God's power. I will return to this difference.

From that observation comes a question that is among the most decisive in relation to our text: *Could it be that the event of the cross of Christ had to become* Word of the cross *in order that one may become foolish—or not—in relation to the cross?* By itself the cross would not have made that possible. It becomes possible in the link between the cross and the resurrection, in the link between the cross and the word of the cross. Only the resurrection "shows" us what the cross itself never would and could: namely, that there is a *meaning* of the cross. The cross, *this* cross is not dumb. In passing: the statement through which Bultmann interprets the meaning of the resurrection,[13] namely that "Jesus was risen in the kerygma," appears here in the sole context that confers it its pertinence. The point is not to say (as Bultmann's opponents imagined): "I don't believe he was really, bodily, risen, I can only say he was risen in the word, that is, he is proclaimed to this day, and so forth." Something else is at stake here, namely to know how the cross could have become the object of faith. How could the cross become the crucial dimension of human existence as it stretches between life and death, between life's hope and death's despair? Paul's answer, sketched in the most succinct way, is: because the cross speaks . . . (and Bultmann follows Paul).

Divine and Human Logic

Why, though, is it necessary to be able to become foolish? Why is the Christian faith not possible without that possibility, a possibility which, it must be added, does not pertain to the realm of improbable absurdities, a possibility that is not located at the margins of the reality of faith, but right at its center? We might answer by saying: because it is, after all, "crazy" that God is stronger than death; and because it

---

13. *Cf.* Rudolf Bultmann, "Das Verhältnis der urchristlichen Christusbotschaft zum historischen Jesus," in *Exegetica* (Tübingen: Mohr-Siebeck, 1967), 469. See W. Kasper, *Jesus der Christus* (Mainz: Matthias-Grünewald-Verlag, 1974), 156.

is even "crazier" that God is stronger than death *in undergoing death in his son Jesus Christ.* Such claims are so worn by our Christian heritage that their surprising and irritating dimensions have almost disappeared, have been engulfed in a correctness of which we are the managers, the masters, the specialists. Yet such correctness is precisely what is irrelevant, insufficient here, namely in the midst of the whirlwind in which even the apostle Paul is struggling with what exceeds his abilities. The point is thus not to articulate correct (or incorrect) statements, even deep ones. The point is, rather, to find out how one may reach a level where it no longer is possible to say such (correct) things without facing the possibility of falling in an abyss, that is, without exposing oneself to the reality of a word that will never become manageable. Why will it never become manageable? Because it does not simply *reflect* but also *creates* reality, a reality that would not be without it.

"Ὁ λόγος τοῦ σταυροῦ," says Paul. The question, in relation to this word, is not so much "What can we say about it, how can we form an opinion about it?" but, rather, "How does it strike us, how does it seize us?" How does it form an opinion about us? The expression "the word of the cross" points to an entanglement between reality and word that *always* surprises us. We are placed before this question: Might there be a word that never actually comes from us? Paul's text, his way of articulating his thought, a thought which he articulated and which, at the same time, escapes his mastery, comes near this reality, comes near this discourse's shift: shift not only of its content, but of its origin and ultimately of its mode of speaking.

In 1 Corinthians 1–2 this new reality, this upending of the understanding of reality, of our access to it (but who accesses to whom, here?), is indicated through a scandal. This scandal is doubly underscored: (*a*) with the statement that one and the same word can be foolishness and wisdom: human foolishness, divine wisdom;

(*b*) with the claim that salvation or perdition are related to this foolishness and this wisdom. But Paul goes even further: not only does he audaciously introduce an infinite contrast (between salvation and perdition), not only does he relate that contrast to the acceptance of the foolishness of the "word of the cross," but the human capacity to accept it or not is taken away from the human person. "For the word of the cross is foolishness to *those who are lost* . . ."[14] Are they "lost" because the word is foolishness to them, or is that word foolish to them because they are lost? The structure of the Greek sentence leaves that question open. Both options are possible. In the first-case scenario, the responsibility belongs to those who do not understand that word, whereas in the second-case scenario the responsibility would be God's. A third option is to keep this *unresolved*. The question then remains *open*. If one follows that option, according to which the open, ambiguous dimension of the sentence is deliberate, then, of course, the question arises: What is the point of that ambiguity?

The Crisis between God's Logic and Our Logic

In my opinion, the point is to express the idea that, with our presuppositions (and even with our questions), we do not grasp what is at stake in these words. If we begin with our logic, trusting in the laws of our thought, we will never find out the logic of what is happening here. The question, which originally was: What may we understand?, now becomes: Where are we being relocated? In which logic? In which place? Where is God being relocated? In which logic? Paul's text leads us into the κρίσις of this type of questions. If we wished to express their intention within the parameter of "our"

---

14. Weiss notes the difficulty to translate the Greek present passive participle in German (*Der erste Korintherbrief*, 25).

text, we probably would have to ask ourselves: Is "foolishness" really only for *other* people? In other words: Isn't it the point here to admit or guess that God's logic is not the same as ours? Didn't the author of this text want to say that?

A moment ago I argued that the point was not to formulate correct (dogmatic or exegetical) statements in relation to Christ's death and its meaning but, rather, to ask, Who may legitimately say something correct here? Who will be placed at a level where their words become something different than the ex-pression of an *opinion*: where they become the ex-position to a truth that transcends the speaker, the effect or the vehicle of an encounter which, instead of belonging to us, confronts us with a dispossession of ourselves. (That is exactly what Paul calls "foolishness.") The senselessness of which Paul talks is the flip side of that dispossession. The transformation of the question (that is, not to know which word is correct, but *from where* the word that concerns us the most is said, in *which way* this word encounters us) is expressed by the apostle through an irresolvable paradox: *in relation to the cross of Christ, which has become for faith (and only for faith) Word of the cross, foolishness as a human option is unavoidable.* In that way, and only in that way, the "divine option" manifests itself: that foolishness is wisdom, or, to use another term, "power" (i.e., a reality that creates reality).

That power and that wisdom, however, do not belong to us. Are we ready to enter into that logic? Which logic? The logic according to which God's logic (or order) is not ours? If we are ready, we are saved (this at least is how I understand Paul).

The Whirlwind in Which Wisdom and Foolishness Meet as the Condition of Salvation

We have tried to read the text of 1 Corinthians 1–2, especially the few verses in its center. As we did, it became almost impossible to us to read them in the usual way. The paradoxical character of these sentences which, instead of finding resolution at one point, becomes stronger and stronger, leads any reading, any interpretation, astray. We're ready to allow for the presence of a paradox in a text, as long as it is punctual. But when the paradox is spread out, as it were, reinforced and underlined, then we face a dilemma—an unresolved dilemma.

It seems to me that such a dilemma, that configuration, is Paul's message. It is thus unnecessary and even impossible to jump directly to the content of the text ("What does it say?"). The structure of the text, its rhetoric—not in the sense of the art of the rhetorician, but in the sense of what the message actually *does* with the text, what it does *of* the text—conveys the gist of it.[15] It takes us up in a movement, a highly specific movement, for where we would like to move on, "it" goes slower, and where we would like to stop, "it" explodes. That movement comes from the message, it *is*—strictly speaking—the message. The noncoincidence between the logic of the world and God's logic.

Most commentators have thought that such noncoincidence could not be the final word. I have suggested these interpretations seek to *attenuate* things. One of the most acute commentators of the epistle, Johannes Weiss, is himself an example of this tendency. Considering in a focused manner one short passage (1:17-18), Weiss points out the unresolved tension.[16] But he is unable to let the tension take

15. I understand "rhetoric" very differently from Margaret M. Mitchell in her book *Paul and the Rhetoric of Reconciliation: An Exegetical Investigation of the Language and Compositon of 1 Corinthians*, HUTh 28 (Tübingen: Mohr, 1991). Mitchell sees in Paul's rhetoric a "strategy" (35, 214, etc.) whose goal is to fight divisions within the Corinthian community, for the sake of "unity" (210, 213, etc.). In contrast with such an instrumental understanding of rhetoric, I conceive of it as a form of speech that the message gives to itself (rather than the author giving that form to his message).

16. Consequently, Weiss underlines the fundamental character of the opposition between faith

up the whole space: Paul's developing thought tends, according to Weiss, toward a solution. As is clear in the end of Paul's reasoning, the idea that the gospel is μωρία turns out to be his opponents' idea (40), and Paul's discovery can be summarized with the following doctrinal statement: "'Human wisdom' is an unstable ground for a living religion; faith in the fully religious sense of the term can only be found where a revelation, a divine self-communication, takes place."[17] Would Paul have developed all these ideas, all of these contradictions, to reach that idea, that dogmatic truth?

According to me, not only the meaning of the text, but also whatever is working itself out *within* the text, what bothers and torments it, is passed over in that interpretation. It is "wisdom" as the world's principle that provokes and—at the same time—irritates Paul's reflection; what he is talking about is the *shaking* of that wisdom, in that shaking lies the ground of faith. There is no reconciling of these two principles. That fact is the "message."

Are we ready to welcome that message, which is restless and which conveys restlessness all the way until the end? Paul did not want, he probably *could* not express "his" gospel in any other way than through a whirlwind in which wisdom and foolishness meet, in which values—and not just any values, but precisely those which are absolutely not susceptible of that operation, namely understanding and its opposite—are inverted.

The "word of the cross" is thus not one example, among others, of a paradox; it is the paradox itself. The paradox not as an intellectual

and wisdom, specifying that "Paul principally refuses to ground the faith of the community in a human way. The cross of Christ would be emptied . . . if one sought to demonstrate the reasonableness of *what is essentially irrational*." Weiss, *Der erste Korintherbrief*, 23, see also 24, 27; my italics.

17. And Weiss concludes: "Here we finally find the final explanation of the astonishing sentence in 1:17—and in that way the passage concludes harmoniously." *Der erste Korintherbrief*, 51, see also 25.

or rhetoric twist, but the paradox of a situation, the situation of the encounter between the living God and human beings.

Are there, in the history of theology, moments or reference points that reflect the light of such original paradoxes? In what we call his *Pensées*, Pascal wrote: "'Ne timeas pusillus grex.'[18] 'Timor et tremore.'[19]—Quid ergo? Ne timeas, [modo] timeas: Fear not, provided you fear; but if you fear not, then fear."[20]

These remarks don't say anything else but this: God's order is not ours, and our order is not God's. In that lies salvation. Or, to put it differently, looking at human beings: it is only when you are a fool that you are not a fool *before God*; and if you are not a fool, you are being foolish (before God).

---

18. Luke 12:32: "Fear not, little flock . . ."
19. Phil. 2:12: ". . . with fear and trembling."
20. Blaise Pascal, *Pensées*, trans. W. F. Trotter (New York: Dutton, 1931), CreateSpace Independent Publishing Platform, 2011, fr. 775.

17

"To Know Nothing Except Jesus Christ, and Him Crucified": Supralapsarian Christology and a Theology of the Cross

Edwin Chr. van Driel

Supralapsarian Christology vs. a Theology of the Cross

"Supralapsarian Christology" is an account of the divine motives for the incarnation on which the incarnation is not contingent upon sin. Proponents of supralapsarian Christology do not deny that God deals with the sin problem through the incarnate Christ, but they hold that there are deeper and more important reasons for the incarnation than reconciliation and redemption. In this christological model the goal of creation is a love relationship with human beings, and in this relationship God comes as close to God's creatures as God can—in becoming human. Hence, the name "supra-lapsarian"—in the ordering of divine intentions, even before (*supra*) God willed to allow for sin (*lapsus*, fall), God intended to become incarnate. As such, "supralapsarian Christology" is to be contrasted with "infra-lapsarian" Christology, the notion that the sole motivation for the incarnation is to deal with the problem of sin.

Supralapsarian Christology thus seems to decenter the cross. Although it acknowledges the cross as God's means of dealing with sin, the dynamic of sin, reconciliation, and redemption is not considered to be the sole or even deepest motivation for the incarnation. Therefore, the cross is not the central moment in the story of God and humanity. How, then, does such a christological approach sit with a *theologia crucis*, which suggests the cross as the lens through which the relationship between God and human beings is to be seen? That is the question I raise in this essay.

Exploring this issue is complicated for at least two reasons. First, like "infralapsarianism," "supralapsarianism" is a family name. It does not stand for a particular theory, but for a family of ideas. Just as many theologians agree that the sin problem is the sole motivation for the incarnation, while disagreeing on how the incarnate one deals with sin, so, too, do supralapsarian theologians differ among each other in the argumentative strategies used to support their christological position. Rather than exploring a variety of supralapsarian Christologies, I take my starting point in this essay in a particular supralapsarian account, one that I developed several years ago in a book entitled *Incarnation Anyway*.[1] I will therefore begin with a

---

1. Edwin Chr. van Driel, *Incarnation Anyway: Arguments for Supralapsarian Christology* (New York: Oxford University Press, 2008). In this book I analyze different versions of supralapsarian Christology, arguing that each of the three ways in which, according to the biblical narrative, God relates to what is not God—in creation, in eschatological consummation, and in reconciliation—can be used as the basis for a supralapsarian argument. My own arguments,

section in which I summarize the supralapsarian argumentative strategy I propose in that book.

The second complication is that "theology of the cross" does not stand for one particular christological theory either, but for a number of different theological arguments. For this essay I choose three prominent types of crucicentric arguments and explore whether or not these interfere with supralapsarian lines of thought.[2] The first crucicentric argument I will discuss is *soteriological*. The cross, so the argument goes, negates all anthropocentric methods for achieving salvation. It shows that there is no soteriological advancing from humans to the divine; salvation is not a divine perfecting of a promising human beginning but, rather, brings all human efforts to an end—salvation comes through the creature's death, and resurrection. An example of such soteriological argument is the *Urtext* of cross theology: Martin Luther's *Heidelberg Disputation*. Next I engage an *epistemological* crucicentric argument, the soteriological argument's epistemic parallel: just as the cross negates all anthropocentric methods for achieving salvation, it likewise puts an end to all suggestions that human beings can access God through their own devices.[3] As an example of such argument I refer to the doctrine of revelation Karl Barth developed in the first volume of

---

developed at the end of the book, are based on God's drawing creation into eschatological consummation. One reviewer, evaluating these arguments, commented that for me "supralapsarianism is opposed to a *theologia crucis*" (David W. Congdon, "Review of *Incarnation Anyway*," http://www.ptsem.edu/library/barth). This seemed to me a rather premature, but also intriguing, comment. Premature, because in my discussion I had not mentioned a *theologia crucis* at all. Intriguing, because I do share Congdon's intuition that at least some arguments used in *theologiae crucis* seem inconsistent with some forms of supralapsarianism. This essay is meant to create some conceptual clarity about these relationships.

2. I follow Rosalene Bradbury's use of the adjective "crucicentric" as meaning "pertaining to the theology of the cross," whereas "cruciform" recalls the cross itself; see Bradbury, *Cross Theology: The Classical Theologia Crucis and Karl Barth's Modern Theology of the Cross* (Eugene, OR: Pickwick, 2011), 1n4.

3. In distinguishing between the soteriological and epistemological argument I was helped by the discussion in ibid.

his *Church Dogmatics.* Third, I look at an hermeneutical argument, which holds that the very narrative about the relationship between God and human beings should be cruciform. Here I delve into the work of the New Testament scholar J. Louis Martyn. While I do not claim that these three arguments exhaust the range of *theologiae crucis*, I believe this exploration will begin to map the territory and lead to greater clarity as to the nature of both supralapsarian Christology and theologies of the cross.

As to the relationship among these three crucicentric arguments themselves: the first two are formal, since they want to shape the rules for what counts as valid theological strategies. The last one is material, suggesting a particular shape to the actual narrative of the relationship between God and God's creatures. The three arguments could all be held simultaneously but do not necessarily need to be, as will be illustrated by my contention that one could hold the first two in conjunction with my version of supralapsarian Christology, but not the last one. As a matter of fact, in a final section to this essay I argue that the first two crucicentric arguments are driven by intuitions very similar to the ones that shape supralapsarian Christology, and that holding these arguments while simultaneously embracing a supralapsarian position is not only possible, but even fitting.

Finally, before I embark on my discussion, it may be good to explicitly delineate the topic of this paper from a different one: the relationship between supralapsarian Christology and doctrines of atonement. This in itself is a fascinating topic. As I noted above, while supralapsarian Christology posits that the incarnation is not contingent upon sin, it does not deny that once sin has entered the picture, God takes care of the sin problem through the incarnate one. Supralapsarian Christology does not deny the atonement; it simply places it in the context of a larger story. As such, supralapsarian Christology could be combined with a multitude of atonement theories. It may be, however, that the particular kind of supralapsarian arguments with which one operates limits the kind of atonement theories to which one consistently can adhere. This is a topic that will have to wait for another day.[4]

Incarnation Anyway

In *Incarnation Anyway*, I offer three arguments to support a supralapsarian Christology. The first of these is what I call an argument from eschatological superabundance. It starts from an observation that has been made by supralapsarians and infralapsarians alike: that the *eschaton*, the final goal of creation, is better than the *proton*, the beginning of creation. The *eschaton* is not simply the restoration of the *proton*. There is in the *eschaton* an abundance, a richness in intimacy with God and in human transformation that the *proton* did not know. Traditionally, theology describes this intimacy with God as the *visio Dei*: in the *eschaton* we are so close to God that we will see God face-to-face. The gain of human transformation is usually described with the words of Augustine: while in the *proton* human beings were able not to sin (*posse non peccare*), in the *eschaton* they will be unable to sin (*non posse peccare*).[5]

What is at stake for the supralapsarian in all of this is that in the Scriptures this eschatological extra is intimately bound up with the person of Christ. We will change for the better because we are

---

4. For a first exploration, see my entry on "Supra/infra Lapsarianism" in *T & T Clark Companion to the Atonement*, ed. Adam J. Johnson, forthcoming. A different way to express this delineation is that whereas I concentrate in this essay on the place of the cross in the wider narrative of the relationship between God and God's creatures, I forgo a discussion of what exactly happened on the cross. For this reason I will also not engage Jürgen Moltmann's *The Crucified God: The Cross of Christ as the Foundation and Criticism of Christian Theology*, trans. Margaret Kohl (Minneapolis: Fortress Press, 1993 [1991]). Even while this book is often seen as a prime example of a twentieth-century *theologia crucis*, the heart of the book is a reinterpretation of what happened on the cross.

5. Augustine, *De civitate dei* 20,30.

modeled after Christ, both in body—in the resurrection, this body of humiliation will be conformed to the body of his glory, as Paul so poetically says (Phil. 3:21)—and in spirit, in that in our minds and hearts we will be like him (cf. Rom. 8:28; Phil. 3:10; 2 Cor. 3:18). We will be modeled after Christ, the closer we are to Christ—"we will be like him, for we will see him as he is" (1 John 3:2).

Well, says the supralapsarian, if the *eschaton* is thus a gain over the *proton*, and this gain is thus given to us in Christ, after whose incarnate presence we are modeled and in whose incarnate presence we are made to see the Father, then do we receive this eschatological extra, all this gain, because of sin? Because that is what one would have to say if Christ's coming is contingent upon sin. Without sin, no incarnation; without incarnation, no *eschaton*. And that cannot be true. Sin is powerful, but not that powerful. Sin does not bring us closer to God. We would therefore do better to understand all this in a supralapsarian way. The abundance of the eschatological life cannot be contingent upon sin. And since Christ is the embodiment of this abundance, neither is the incarnation contingent upon sin.

My second argument zooms in on one particular aspect of the eschatological consummation: the promised *visio Dei,* the vision of God. On the traditional understanding of this notion, the vision of God will fully wrap human beings in the enjoyment of God. For bodily, sensory beings this includes sensory contact. And eschatological humans will be bodily, sensory beings, since the resurrected Christ is a bodily, sensory being, and he is the model for what will happen with us in our eschatological resurrection. Therefore, if the eschatological goal of humanity is to enjoy God fully in the beatific vision, this vision should not be understood purely in terms of intellectual cognition, but should also imply sensory perception. To fully enjoy God means that we should be able to hear, see, touch, and embrace God. However, this can only take place if God makes Godself present in bodily form.[6]

My third argument for supralapsarianism hinges on the notion of divine friendship. There is a small but discernible line in the biblical narrative that conceives of the relationship between God and God's people as a form of friendship. Abraham and Moses are called God's friends (Exod. 33:11; Isa. 41:8; see 2 Chron. 20:7; James 2:23). Christ uses friendship language and says to his disciples: "I do not call you servants any longer . . . but I have called you friends" (John 15:15).

The theologically important point about conceiving of God's relating to humanity as a form of friendship is friendship's motivational structure. Friendship is motivated by a delight in and a love for the other. It enjoys the other's goodness and the goodness the relationship with the other embodies. Of course, friendship can be disrupted, disregarded, betrayed. All of these can motivate friends to seek forgiveness, reconciliation, healing of their relationship. Yet the friendship itself is not based on the episodes of disruption and reconciliation, but on a deeper sense of love and delight. Therefore, when God calls Abraham and Moses, and when Jesus addresses his disciples as friends, not slaves, these relationships are defined not by human sin and need for reconciliation, but by a deeper, preordinate sense of love. It is true, all of these relationships are also tainted by human failure and betrayal. The narratives of Abraham and Moses tell

---

6. Of course, understanding the eschatological vision in this way, as the enjoyment of God both with the intellect and with our senses is to go against the standard understanding of the *visio Dei*, which is almost exclusively intellectual. I am aware of only two prominent exceptions: the medieval theologian Robert Grosseteste (see his *De Cessatione Legalium*, ed. Richard C. Dales and Edward B. King [London: Oxford University Press, 1986], 128), and the Puritan theologian John Owen (see Suzanne McDonald, "Beholding the Glory of God in the Face of Jesus Christ: John Owen and the 'Reforming' of the Beatific Vision," in Kelly M. Kapic and Mark Jones, eds., *The Ashgate Research Companion to John Owen's Theology* [Surrey, UK: Ashgate, 2012], 141–58). But I actually think such departure from the standard theological understanding receives strong support from the biblical material on which the theological notion of the beatific vision is based. See *Incarnation Anyway*, 157–59.

us about distrust, disobedience, and unbelief. Jesus calls his disciples friends in the context of a conversation about his imminent death: "No one has greater love than this, to lay down one's life for one's friends" (John 15:13). But while the death is motivated by the friendship, the friendship is not motivated by death. Jesus becomes his disciples' savior because he is their friend; not the other way around.

If this is true, it would be an impoverishment to read all Jesus' actions, all his words, and finally, his very presence as motivated by human sin and the need for reconciliation. To do so would be to lose sight of other feelings and emotions, of a deeper layer of motivations that might be at play in the relationship between God and human beings. One of these motivations, I suggest, is laid bare in a fascinating story about Moses. God and Moses just have had a lover's quarrel; the issue being resolved, Moses wants to reconcile, and he, the friend of God, therefore asks to see God's face (Exod. 33:18). Moses wants to make sure things are right again between God and himself, and therefore he longs for the visible, tangible presence of the Lord. For embodied human beings, when it comes to crucial moments of our friendship, it is not enough to hear a voice going to us from a pillar of clouds; it is physical presence that we want. And the Lord, understanding the longing of God's friend, makes Godself available to Moses, as much as God can (Exod. 33:21-23). I suggest we should read the incarnation as God's final and permanent answer to humanity's longing, the ultimate availability of the Lord, no longer in a pillar of cloud, no longer in a momentary appearance of dazzling glory, but in a human form, with a human face, visible, tangible, audible.[7]

For the sake of a comparison with a theology of the cross, it is important, before we move on, to point out one central feature of

---

7. In other words: what the supralapsarian is after is the intrinsic importance of the "play of the Word," which, as Andrew Louth explains, is missing in Maximus the Confessor (above, 95-97).

these arguments. These three have a common starting point: the story as we have it, the incarnation event as it happened; and they press whether an infralapsarian account can fully make sense of this scriptural narrative. In that sense, these arguments thus follow a very different strategy than traditional supralapsarian arguments, which usually conceive of the supralapsarian case in terms of a counterfactual—"Would God have become incarnate if we had not sinned?"—to which the supralapsarian then answers affirmatively. The downside of this traditional strategy is that it leaves the supralapsarian open to the objection of "speculation." As John Calvin, an infralapsarian, put it pointedly: in speculating about a counterfactual situation in which we had not sinned, the supralapsarian can be accused of trying to get away from the fact that she actually did sin and, according to Calvin, it only shows that she is not "content with this very Christ who was given to us as the price of our redemption."[8] But my arguments are not open to such critique. I do not ask what would have happened if we had not sinned; I ask about the incarnation as it happened, about the Christ as we have him; and my point is that the incarnation as it happened gives us so much, and is so rich in terms of divine friendship and intimacy that it cannot be explained as only a divine countermeasure against sin. Granted: the biblical narrative does not carry supralapsarianism on its sleeves, and so the case has to be made in terms of inferences and arguments. But this is not different from, let us say, the notion of a divine Trinity or the doctrine of the two natures of Christ. In that sense, supralapsarian Christology is thus in good company.

Theologia Crucis: The Soteriological Argument

How does such an approach to supralapsarian Christology relate

8. John Calvin, *Institutes of the Christian Religion* 2,12,5, ed. John T. McNeill, trans. Ford Lewis Battles (Philadelphia: Westminster, 1960), 1:469.

to a theology of the cross? A first line of argument that underlies important *theologiae crucis* is soteriological in nature. The cross, so the argument goes, negates all anthropocentric methodologies for achieving salvation. It shows that there is no soteriological advancing from humans to the divine; salvation is not a divine perfecting of a promising human beginning but, rather, brings all human efforts to an end—salvation comes through the creature's death, and resurrection.

An example of such soteriological argument is the *Urtext* of cross theology: Martin Luther's *Heidelberg Disputation*. It may be surprising to see Luther's text advanced as a soteriological argument; after all, the central theses in which Luther coins the terms "theologian of the cross" and "theologian of glory" are cast in epistemological terms:

> 19. That person does not deserve to be called a theologian who looks upon the invisible things of God as though they were clearly perceptible in those things which have actually happened (Rom. 1:20).

> 20. He deserves to be called a theologian, however, who comprehends the visible and manifest things of God seen through suffering and the cross.

> 21. A theologian of glory calls evil good and good evil. A theologian of the cross calls the thing what it actually is.[9]

However, a purely epistemological reading of these theses misses that they come at the conclusion of a soteriological train of thought.[10] In the preceding theses Luther has dealt with humans' desire to offer building blocks for their salvation, "to advance on their way to righteousness" (thesis 1). The first twelve theses deal with the

---

9. Martin Luther, *Heidelberg Disputation*, theses 19–21, in *Career of the Reformer I*, ed. Harold J. Grimm, *Luther's Works*, vol. 31 (Philadelphia: Fortress Press, 1957), 40.
10. Cf. the comments by Gerhard O. Forde, *On Being a Theologian of the Cross: Reflections on Luther's Heidelberg Disputation, 1518* (Grand Rapids, Eerdmans, 1997), 69–70.

notion of good works, the following six with the idea of good willing. Luther rejects both. Our good works actually make matters worse, because they feed our religious aspirations and thereby seal us off from the gift of free grace. Our will is bound to evil and therefore even imagining that doing our best will prepare us for grace would "add haughty arrogance" to our misery and thereby double our sin.[11] The theologian of glory now begins to cry out of despair: she finds that there is nothing she can do, there is nothing to hold on to, nothing that can help her to make progress toward salvation. This is exactly where one needs to be in order to receive grace, Luther believes: "it is certain that man must utterly despair of his own ability before he is prepared to receive the grace of Christ," as thesis 18 reads.[12] The cross is not a moment in a larger train of advancing toward righteousness, but is the negation of any human salvific striving. In the face of the death of one's own abilities, one now is able to receive forensic grace: "He is not righteous who does much, but he who, without work, believes much in Christ" (thesis 25).[13] It is in this context that Luther formulates his theses about the theologian of glory and the theologian of cross. They should thus be read as reflections on the soteriological argument Luther just advanced. The theologian of glory believes she can make sense of the cross in a larger story of human advancing toward God, and she believes that cruciform grace is nothing more but the keystone of human works and willing. As such, she "calls evil good and good evil." She does not realize that exactly our seemingly good acts and good desires only lead us away from grace. What she thought she knew about God only works against her: it blinds her to the grace of a God who is willing to die for her. In other words, her theological

---

11. *Heidelberg Disputation*, commentary on thesis 16, *Luther's Works*, 31:50.
12. Ibid., 40.
13. Ibid., 41.

epistemology is wrong because it leads to soteriological disasters. By contrast, the theologian of the cross lets herself be exposed by the "suffering and the cross." This is what all our own striving leads to: death. As such, the theologian of the cross "calls the thing what it actually is."

How does this line of argument sit with a supralapsarian Christology? Three observations need to be made. First, the kind of soteriology implied by the *Heidelberg Disputation* and my supralapsarian arguments converge rather than clash in that both emphasize the unconditional nature of God's gracious relating to humanity. My argument suggests neither a soteriological advancing from the human to the divine nor a human conditioning of the salvific will of God. As in Luther's soteriology, there is, rather, the opposite move: a God who freely condescends to become the friend of God's creatures.

This first point helps us to negotiate the next observation: that supralapsarian Christology and a theology of glory nonetheless seem to coincide in that both want to place the cross in the context of a larger story—something a *theologia crucis* is set against. The difference is, however, that a theology of glory sets the cross in a larger narrative of nature, whereas my supralapsarian approach places the cross in a larger narrative of grace. A theology of glory reduces the cross to the divine keystone in humans' growth on the path to righteousness. By contrast, the story told by supralapsarian Christology is one about a God who from the beginning of creation intends to condescend graciously in an incarnate form—a narrative that thereby shapes humanity, rather than being shaped by it.

This notion of a larger supralapsarian narrative of grace is of importance for a third observation. Because of this larger narrative, there is one point of divergence between supralapsarianism and the soteriological argument for a *theologia crucis*: the notion that one "must utterly despair of his own ability before he is prepared to receive the grace of Christ" (thesis 18). This part of the argument reflects an infralapsarian logic: if the incarnation is solely contingent upon sin, then indeed one needs to be convinced of one's sin before one can welcome the incarnate one. After all, it is only because of sin that one is in need of Christ. In a supralapsarian logic, however, Christ is not just welcome because of our sin; he is welcome because he is the one for whom we were created.

In engaging this difference between supralapsarian Christology and a theology of the cross, the supralapsarian believes there are important theological and spiritual advantages to her position. First, according to the logic of the *theologia crucis*, the preacher has to preach sin before she can preach Christ: she has to lead the hearers to despair before they can embrace the good news. It is for this reason that a Lutheran hermeneutic is shaped by the dynamic of law and gospel, sin and forgiveness. But a preaching that centers the narrative of Christ on the dynamic of sin and forgiveness leaves the preacher open to the misunderstanding that the most important thing the Christian faith has to say about human beings is that they are sinners. But, of course, that is not the case—the most important thing the Christian faith has to say about human beings is that they are beloved children of God. The supralapsarian may preach exactly that. On her narrative, she does not have to preach sin in order to preach Christ; she can preach Christ as the offer of love and friendship with God; and it is thereafter, in the light of that offer of friendship and love, that human beings discover themselves as sinners.

And second, since according to the infralapsarian logic our relationship to Christ is triggered by a problem, namely sin, this relationship is in its origin therapeutic: Christ is the troubleshooter. The relationship can therefore be said to be functional. The believer needs Christ for something: she has a problem. But what happens when the problem is solved and the believer's need is met? What basis is there for a continuing relationship? There seems to be none. The believer may grow in her understanding of herself and her relationship with God. She may come to see herself as a forgiven creature, destined for an eschatological future in which the stain of sin is permanently removed, sin's guilt and shame permanently cast behind God's back (Isa. 38:17). But it is not clear how Christ could be part of such a future. Since, according to the infralapsarian logic, the believer's relationship to him is purely functional, it is a relationship permanently defined in terms of sinner and Savior, problem and solution, sickness and medicine; and, once the problem of sin is removed, the basis for the relationship is removed as well. For a faith so centered on the person of Christ as Christianity is, this is a serious theological, spiritual, and psychological problem. But with a supralapsarian understanding of Christ we do not need sin in order to benefit from the incarnation; we do not need sin in order to relate to Christ. If the intimate presence of God in Christ is the goal of all things, then all aspects of our lives are related to him. It is here, I believe, that supralapsarianism has an important contribution to make.

Theologia Crucis: The Epistemological Argument

The epistemological argument for a *theologia crucis* suggests an epistemic parallel to the soteriological argument laid out in the previous section. Just as the cross negates all anthropocentric methodologies for achieving salvation, it likewise puts an end to any suggestion that human beings can access God through their own devices. The cross, one could say, is an expression of the absolute otherness of God; of a God whose wisdom and strength are not located "on a scale extending *beyond* the human, as if the wisdom of God were continuous with, just considerably further along, the spectrum of human wisdom," but, rather, "separated entirely from the human scale of norms."[14] In combination with some epistemological principles, this otherness of God leads to the conclusion that such God can only be known by those to whom God makes Godself known in particular events of revelation.

An example of such epistemological stance is the doctrine of revelation Karl Barth develops in his *Church Dogmatics*. Barth's doctrine of revelation is based on two correlated arguments concerning our inability to know God. Both arguments combine the notion of the otherness of God with an epistemological premise. In the first argument it is the epistemological premise that "like is only known by like."[15] The conclusion is that divine revelation can only happen mediately. Humans cannot know God directly, since God is completely unlike creatures. Only a medium that is alike to creatures can reveal God. The second argument combines the notion of God's otherness with the epistemological premise that knowledge of an object equals power over the object.[16] This combination leads to the conclusion that God can only be known if Godself gives God to be known. God, as the complete other, falls outside the scope of creaturely power. Only God is master over Godself.

Barth himself suggests that these two epistemological premises amount to the same content.[17] This is where Barth is mistaken, as is clear simply from the different results of these two arguments. The first argument amounts to a need for incarnation. If only a creature can reveal God, divine self-revelation calls for God to assume creaturely form. Such form would unveil God, but also veil God.

---

14. John M. G. Barclay, above, 12.
15. In Barth's terms: "we resemble what we can apprehend." *CD* II/1 (Edinburgh: T&T Clark, 1957), 188.
16. In Barth's terms: "to apprehend certainly means to possess." Ibid., 189.
17. Ibid., 188–89.

It would unveil, because God makes Godself an object of human knowledge; it would veil, because it would reveal God mediately, "under the sign and veil of other objects different from himself."[18] The second argument amounts to a need for the Holy Spirit. Only God has power over who will hear God's revelation. "The Lord of speech is also the Lord of our hearing."[19]

If that is what a theology of the cross wants to say, there is no conflict with the particular kind of supralapsarian Christology I put forward. As I have emphasized, my supralapsarian arguments are not rooted in speculation. Because they reflect solely on the story as we have it, the event of God's revelation, they do not try to access God on their own devices. They argue, rather, that the event as it happened cannot be understood differently than as a supralapsarian story.

However, the ontological and epistemological arguments that are at work in Barth's thought do not turn on what is a result of sin, but on what is given with the nature of the Creator and creation. And this means that if divine self-disclosure is part of the goal of creation, and this self-disclosure can only take place through incarnation, then the incarnation has to be supralapsarian in intent. But, of course, if the epistemological argument for a *theologia crucis* looks anything like Barth's position, and Barth's position implies supralapsarian Christology, then the same has to be said about this form of crucicentric theology.[20]

Theologia Crucis: The Apocalyptic Argument

The previous two arguments for a *theologia crucis* seek to help shape the rules for what may count as valid theological thinking: the cross

---

18. Ibid., 16.
19. Karl Barth, *CD* I/1 (Edinburgh: T&T Clark, 1956), 182.
20. For Barth's own development on this score see *Incarnation Anyway*, 77n67.

negates all soteriological and epistemological advancing from humans to the divine. The crucicentric argument I discuss in this section is oriented differently. It is focused on material content: it does not so much outline the criteria for theologizing as much as it seeks to determine the shape of the narrative about the relationship between God and humanity. Such narrative, the argument goes, needs to be cruciform. This argument is rooted in an apocalyptic reading of Paul, as advanced by the German New Testament scholar Ernst Käsemann and his American student J. Louis Martyn. Martyn's work in particular has received significant attention from theologians as of late, so I will focus on his work.[21]

According to Martyn, Paul believes he lives in a "twice-invaded world." Heaven and earth were created in such a way that the earth part of it is permeable, subject to entry from outside.[22] The first such incursion happened when sin entered the world. For Paul, Martyn argues, "sin" is not so much an individual affair caused by volitional choices, but a matter of suprahuman powers that have invaded and enslaved God's creation.[23]

This world, however, was again invaded when the earth was

21. See Douglas Harink, *Paul among the Postliberals: Pauline Theology beyond Christendom and Modernity* (Grand Rapids: Brazos, 2003); Nathan R. Kerr, *Christ, History, and Apocalyptic: The Politics of Christian Mission* (Eugene, OR: Cascade, 2009); David H. Kelsey, *Eccentric Existence: A Theological Anthropology* (Louisville: Westminster John Knox, 2009), 478–500; Douglas Harink, ed., *Paul, Philosophy, and the Theopolitical Vision: Critical Engagements with Agamben, Badiou, Žižek and Others* (Eugene, OR: Cascade, 2010); Joshua B. Davis and Douglas Harink, eds., *Apocalyptic and the Future of Theology: With and Beyond J. Louis Martyn* (Eugene, OR: Cascade, 2012). The following analysis of Martyn goes back to my "Christ in Paul's Narrative: Salvation History, Apocalyptic Invasion, and Supralapsarian Theology," in Mark W. Elliott, et al., eds., *Galatians and Christian Theology: Justification, the Gospel, and Ethics in Paul's Letter* (Grand Rapids: Baker Academic, 2014).
22. For a very clear sketch of Martyn's understanding of the relationship between creation (the world), fallen creation (*this* world), and new creation, see his essay "World without End or Twice-Invaded World?," in Christine Roy Yoder, et al., eds. *Shaking Heaven and Earth: Essays in Honor of Walter Brueggemann and Charles B. Cousar* (Louisville: Westminster John Knox, 2005), 117–32.
23. Ibid., 121; and J. Louis Martyn, *Galatians: A New Translation with Introduction and Commentary*, The Anchor Bible 33A (New York: Doubleday, 1997), 95–97.

climactically and determinatively entered by God in the person of Christ. Paul calls this divine invasion apocalyptic (Gal. 1:12, 2:2), not in the sense of God "unveiling something that was previously hidden, as though it had been eternally standing behind a curtain" and now finally in the present age was revealed, but, rather, as a violent divine apocalyptic incursion that brings this world, the cosmos as we know it, to an end.[24] In this context Martyn points out that when Paul describes the result of Christ's coming, he does not speak of "a new age," but of "a new creation."[25] By speaking of "a new creation," Paul signals that God's invasion results not in "merely repairing this world" but, rather, "in fundamental contrast to this world, God's new creation is *the* new."[26]

This new creation is established, Martyn holds—and this is key to the topic at hand—not in Christ's resurrection, but in Christ's crucifixion. As such, the shape of the eschatological world goes against our expectations:

> We should have preferred to hear that God has established the *new* creation by raising Jesus from the realm of those who have died. Or that God will establish the new creation at the parousia of Christ. Especially when speaking of God's new creation, can we not move *from* the odious cross *to* the glorious resurrection and the hoped-for parousia? Although Paul takes for granted the world-changing resurrection of Jesus . . . he is far from allowing that event to avert his glance from the cross. He sees the new creation in the cross.[27]

God's invasion and victory does not come in brutal power as, for instance, Caesar's army would; rather, it comes and is fundamentally shaped by the weakness of the cross. Even the resurrection does not leave the cross behind—as Martyn argues, quoting Käsemann, "'The

24. Martyn, *Galatians*, 99.
25. J. Louis Martyn, "The Apocalyptic Gospel in Galatians," *Interpretation* 54 (2000): 254.
26. Martyn, "World without End," 126.
27. Martyn, "The Apocalyptic Gospel in Galatians," 259.

theology of the resurrection is a chapter in the theology of the cross, not the excelling of it.' Seen through resurrection lenses, the cross itself remains the event of God's weak power, the event in which power is, in fact, transfigured and thus fundamentally redefined."[28] The new creation is therefore fundamentally cruciform. The bodily shape of the new creation is, Martyn claims, the church, and this church is "cross-bearing"—it is "the community of those who . . . are conformed to the crucified one for the sake of others."[29]

Of the several crucicentric arguments, this one alone does not sit well with supralapsarian Christology. The reason is that on Martyn's reading of the story, the incarnation is contingent upon God's invasion of the world, and this invasion in turn is contingent on the invasion of sin. God's entering of the world is a response to a problem. It is not part of the original design of creation; it is solely motivated by a state of affairs that is an attack on God's design, not part of it: sin invading and enslaving God's creation. Jesus is thus "plan B."

That for Martyn the incarnation is indeed solely contingent upon sin is underscored by his conceptualization of the *eschaton*. Martyn's account rightly suggests that Christ makes a twofold difference: he overcomes the power of sin and he inaugurates an eschatological reality, the new creation. A theologically important question is how these two aspects of Christ's work relate. A supralapsarian account would argue that a christocentric eschatological consummation is the essential goal of God's creation. On such understanding we are, as it were, created "for Christ" (Col. 1:16). Because Christ is central to all of creation, he is also to be the one who, when creation is overcome by the powers of sin, draws creation back to God in

---

28. Martyn, "World without End," 126; quoting from Ernst Käsemann's *Perspectives on Paul* (London: SCM Press, 1971), 59.
29. Ibid., 128.

reconciliation and redemption. This redemptive work of Christ is done for the sake of his eschatological work: we are redeemed so that we may be part of the new creation. The cross is thus a function of the eschatological difference that Christ makes. Whereas Christ's redemptive work is accidental to God's relating to creation—if sin had not invaded creation, redemption would not have been necessary—the eschatological work is, rather, essential: it is for this that we were created.

On Martyn's account, however, a christocentric eschatological future is not the essential goal of creation. The cross is not a function of the *eschaton*, but the *eschaton* is a function of the cross. Only in the cross is the new creation established, and this *eschaton* is cross-shaped. But the cross is, of course, contingent upon sin—and so is Christ's eschatological work.

At this point the supralapsarian would want to press a variation of a concern I expressed earlier. That for infralapsarians the *eschaton* is "cross-shaped" seems inevitable. If the incarnation is contingent upon sin, then our relationship with Christ is, in a strong way, based on sin. No sin, no Christ. It is therefore, in a sense, a rather functional relationship. Jesus comes because we have a problem; he comes because there is a job to do. But what happens when the job is done? What if sin no longer is a problem? Then, it seems, we no longer have need of Christ. That suggestion goes against the central and enduring place Christ both has in Christian spirituality and the biblical narrative of the *eschaton*. The only solution to that problem seems to be Martyn's: the *eschaton* is cross-shaped. The theologically less sophisticated version of that argument is the idea that in the *eschaton* till all eternity we will be singing praises to Jesus for his sacrifice.

As a supralapsarian, I press this question: if the *eschaton* is cross-shaped, then has sin not won? If until all eternity we are singing praises to Jesus for his sacrifice, then is our relationship with God, and subsequently our own identity, not permanently shaped by sin? Is sin thereby truly overcome? Supralapsarian Christology offers here another option. Because our relationship with Christ is not based on sin, we will also not have to permanently remember either our sin or Christ's sacrifice. Because the cross is not central in our relationship with God, it can at some point be forgotten. That seems to be exactly what is promised to us. As Miroslav Volf argues in his book *The End of Memory*, the *eschaton* will exactly entail the gift of forgetting.[30] "The former things shall not be remembered or come to mind," as God promises in Isaiah (Isa. 65:17). On a hermeneutical theology of the cross that is a problem. On a supralapsarian Christology, it is exactly right.[31]

A *Theologia Crucis* Argument for Supralapsarianism

In the previous sections I discussed three ways of construing a theology of the cross. The first two were formal arguments that seek to shape the rules for what counts as acceptable theological arguments. I argued that they can easily be squared with

---

30. Miroslav Volf, *The End of Memory: Remembering Rightly in a Violent World* (Grand Rapids: Eerdmans, 2006), 131–213.

31. During the oral presentation of this paper at the *Wisdom and Foolishness of God* conference it was pointed out to me that a notion of eschatological forgetting of sin and cross sits uneasily with the idea that the resurrected Christ would have the marks of his wounds even eschatologically. This is true. And so the supralapsarian will have to say that just as all memory of the cross will be erased, so will be Christ's wounds. This in turn means that while Christ was resurrected in a glorified body, his body is nonetheless not yet perfected. While this may not be the way the tradition usually conceived matters, I do not believe this is intrinsically problematic. Christ's resurrected and ascended *life* is not perfected—after all, he is still "waiting 'until his enemies would be made a footstool for his feet'" (Heb. 10:13)—so why would we say his *bodily existence* has been perfected? Of course, embedded in the thought of eschatological forgetting is another supralapsarian argument—if it is true that Christ is the essential center of the *eschaton*, and if it is true that in the *eschaton* we will receive the gift of forgetting of all evil and wrong, then the incarnation cannot be contingent upon sin, lest we forget why Christ is there in the first place: a supralapsarian argument from the eschatological loss of memory.

supralapsarian Christology. The problem lies with the third argument. For the apocalyptic *theologus crucis* the cross is the focal point of the relationship between God and humanity. The supralapsarian tells a different story. She believes the cruciform narration overestimates sin and underestimates supralapsarian divine love. The cross, therefore, will have to be decentered. While supralapsarian Christology and an apocalyptic *theologia crucis* thus part ways, in this final section I want to suggest, as a conclusion, that there is an interesting convergence of motives between the supralapsarian narrative and what drives the epistemological and soteriological crucicentric arguments.

On a *theologia crucis* as shaped by the first two formal arguments, what happens on the cross is completely contradictory to our usual religious thinking. It reveals that what we "naturally" take to be right and good about God and ourselves is actually contradictory to God's ways and truth. As the charter text of cross theology says, we expect God to act in wisdom, but God's saving act appears in foolishness. We find it more fitting for the divine to act in power, but God acts in weakness (1 Cor. 1:18-25). God's acts do not fit the mold we have designed for them. In order to see and understand God's acts for what they are, we need to be told about them. We do not recognize them on our own devices; we need revelation. In the light of this revelation we discover that our criteria for the fittingness of divine acts are skewed; that the things we think to be beneath God's dignity are actually expressions of God's very ways of dealing with us: condescension, humility, love.

This debate between a *theologia crucis* and a *theologia gloriae* about which acts are becoming of the divine has a parallel in discussions between infralapsarian and supralapsarian christological thinkers. Much infralapsarian thought is premised on the idea that the incarnation is a humiliating act which God enacts only because God's hand is forced, as it were. A prime example is Anselm's *Cur deus homo*, one of the key texts of infralapsarian christological thought. The intention of Anselm's treatise was to contribute to an ongoing debate between Jewish and Christian medieval theologians about the incarnation, in which the Jewish rabbis had argued that the incarnation was derogatory of the dignity of God.[32] As is clear from the discussion's progression, that argument had hit home. Thus, when Anselm enters the discussion he does not challenge this fundamental premise, but tries to show that given the circumstances, God could not have done otherwise—there was no other way to solve the problem of sin.[33] Supralapsarian Christology, however, challenges the basic premise. What the infralapsarian regards as embarrassment, the supralapsarian regards as the heart of God's relating to creation. That the incarnation is a humiliating act that needs justification is true only if we try to fit God's actions in a preconceived mold. The actual events tell us that the incarnation is not an emergency measure brought about by the problem of sin, but an expression of the very relationship of friendship and love for which God called us into being. Our understanding of what is fitting for divinity will need to be formulated in the light of God's actual acts, not the other way around.

The supralapsarian christological stance is thus structurally parallel to that of the soteriological and epistemological argument for a *theologia crucis*—and not only formally, but also materially. Both positions emphasize that what is becoming of God should be

32. Cf. R. W. Southern, *Saint Anselm: Portrait in a Landscape* (Cambridge: Cambridge University Press, 1992), 198–202.
33. As Anselm's conversation partner Boso frames the question: "I ask you, therefore, to reveal to me something which, as you know, many people besides me ask about, namely this: 'By what necessity or logic did God, almighty as he is, take upon himself the humble standing and weakness of human nature with a view to that nature's restoration?'" *Cur deus homo* 1,1, in Anselm of Canterbury, *The Major Works*, ed. Brian Davies and G. R. Evans (Oxford: Oxford University Press, 1998), 266.

determined not by a preconceived concept of divinity but by God's actual acts. And both positions underscore than in God's acts God reveals Godself as one who relates to creation in humility and love. If that is the case, could not these two positions be presented as causally ordered? That is, could the *theologus crucis* be persuaded that the fullest expression of God's condescending love—God's own, incarnate presence—is not just a response to sin, but that the cross should be placed in a larger, supralapsarian narrative? At the very least, given the intuitions that are undergirding the cruciform arguments, this seems to be fitting.[34]

---

34. I would like to thank my wife, Kimberly Miller van Driel, for her comments on an earlier version of this essay, and for translating many of my Dutchisms into proper English.

Contributors

Hans-Christoph Askani is professor of systematic theology at the University of Geneva. He has published monographs on translation and Franz Rosenzweig, on creation (*Schöpfung als Bekenntnis* [Tübingen: Mohr Siebeck, 2006]), and has a particular theological interest in literature.

Günter Bader is professor emeritus of systematic theology at the University of Bonn. He has written extensively on language, metaphor, the sign of the cross, and the Psalms. One of his most recent books is *Psalterspiel: Skizze einer Theologie des Psalters* (Mohr Siebeck, 2009).

John M. G. Barclay is Lightfoot Professor of Divinity at the University of Durham. He is well known internationally for his studies on Paul. He has recently published *Paul and the Gift* (Grand Rapids: Eerdmans, 2015).

John D. Caputo is emeritus professor from Syracuse University and Villanova University. His many books in hermeneutics, philosophy of religion (*The Weakness of God: A Theology of the Event* [Bloomington: Indiana University Press, 2006]; *The Insistence of God: A Theology of Perhaps* [Bloomington: Indiana University Press, 2013];

The Folly of God: A Theology of the Unconditional [Santa Rosa: Polebridge Press, 2015]), and ethics have received critical acclaim.

Christophe Chalamet is associate professor of systematic theology at the University of Geneva (formerly: Fordham University, 2003–2011). He has an ongoing interest in modern Protestant theology and is about to publish a monograph on Paul's triad of faith, hope, and love (in French).

Michael T. Dempsey is associate professor of systematic theology at St. John's University in New York City. A specialist of Thomas Aquinas's thought, he has edited the essay collection *Trinity and Election in Contemporary Thought* (Grand Rapids: Eerdmans, 2011).

Adam Eitel is visiting assistant professor of ethics at Yale Divinity School. He received his PhD from Princeton Theological Seminary.

Anthony Feneuil is a faculty member at the "Centre de recherche Écritures" of the University of Lorraine (Metz). His most recent book is titled *Plus qu'une expérience? Les enjeux épistémologiques de la notion d'expérience chez K. Barth et H. Bergson (1932)* (Paris: L'Âge d'Homme, 2015).

Andrew R. Hay recently received his doctoral degree in theology from the University of St. Andrews. His dissertation focused on the theme of divine light in a trinitarian perspective.

Andrew Louth is emeritus professor of Patristic and Byzantine studies at the University of Durham. His contributions to the study of the Greek-Eastern tradition, including the mystical theologies of Pseudo-Dionysius, Maximus the Confessor, and John Damascene, are numerous and well known.

Kellen Plaxco received a joint doctorate from the University of Leuven (Philosophy) and Marquette University (Theology), where he recently completed a dissertation on Didymus the Blind, Origen, and pro-Nicene theology."

Philipp Stoellger is professor of systematic theology, dogmatics, and philosophy of religion at the University of Heidelberg. He has edited numerous books and published, among other monographs, *Passivität aus Passion. Zur Problemgeschichte einer categoria non grata* (Tübingen: Mohr, 2010).

Kathryn Tanner is Frederick Marquand Professor of Systematic Theology at Yale University Divinity School. One of the most prominent contemporary theologians, she has recently authored *Christ the Key* (Cambridge: Cambridge University Press, 2010).

Henning Theissen, a doctor in systematic theology and a Privatdozent at the University of Greifswald, holds a Heisenberg Grant from the Deutsche Forschungsgemeinschaft (German Research Foundation). He has published *Die berufene Zeugin des Kreuzes Christi. Studien zur Grundlegung der evangelischen Theorie der Kirche* (Leipzig: Evangelische Verlagsanstalt, 2013).

Edwin Chr. van Driel is Directors' Bicentennial Associate Professor of Theology at Pittsburgh Theological Seminary. His first book is titled *Incarnation Anyway* (Oxford: Oxford University Press, 2008). He is currently working on a book offering a theological reading of contemporary Pauline exegesis.

Marc Vial teaches at the University of Strasbourg's Protestant Faculty of Theology. He has published books as well as numerous articles on medieval, Reformation, and contemporary theology. His next monograph, which he recently completed, is titled *Pour une théologie de la toute-puissance de Dieu. L'approche d'Eberhard Jüngel* (Paris: Classiques Garnier).

Matthias D. Wüthrich is a doctor in systematic theology and Privatdozent at University of Basel's Theological Faculty. He has published *Gott und das Nichtige* (Zürich: Theologische Verlag Zürich, 2006) as well as *Raum Gottes. Ein systematisch-theologischer Versuch, Raum zu denken* (Göttingen: Vandenhoeck & Ruprecht, 2015).

Index of Names

Abrissell, Robert of, 126

Aesop, 12–13

Agamben, Giorgio, 231

Albinus, 270, 272

Alston, William, 169

Ambrose of Milan, 110

Andreae, Johann Valentin, 154

Anselm of Canterbury, xvi, xvii,
    167–68, 173–80, 225, 381

Aquinas, Thomas, xv, 32, 101–37,
    279–86

Aristotle, 33, 102, 107, 157–58,
    267-72

Armstrong, Arthur Hilary, 283

Askani, Hans-Christoph, xix–xx

Assel, Heinrich, 292, 298

Athanasius of Alexandria, 71, 77,
    80, 95

Augustine of Hippo, 45, 53, 56,
    64, 110–11, 122, 124–25, 235,
    248, 363

Ayres, Lewis, 72, 76–77, 82

Babut, Étienne, 338

Bader, Günter, xvi, 154, 292

Badiou, Alain, 172–73, 231, 325

Barclay, John M. G., xii–xiv, 11,
    16, 28, 62, 68, 90, 373

Bark, Sigurd, 176

Barnes, Michel René, 71–77

Barth, Karl, xvii, 42, 167, 171,
    173–76, 179–81, 183–200, 251,
    253, 279, 300, 321, 327–39,
    343, 361, 373–74

Barton, Carlin A., 9

Basil of Caesarea, 87

Batut Jean-Pierre, 311–12

Bayer, Oswald, 251

Becker, Jürgen, 246, 337

Beeley, Christopher, 87

Bendik, Ivana, 245

Benjamin, Walter, 49

Bennett, Byard, 83

Berkouwer, Gerrit Cornelis, 300

Betz, Hans Dieter, 140–42

Bishop, Richard W., 79

Blaumeiser, Hubertus, 143

Bocur, Bogdan, 77

Boethius, 102, 107, 110

Bonaventure, 279, 284–86

Bonhoeffer, Dietrich, 49, 309–10, 327

Borsche, Tilman, 164

Boulnois, Olivier, 313

Boyle, Leonard E., 101

Bradbury, Rosalene, 361

Bradley, Denis J., 102

Brant, Sebastian, 146

Brecht, George, 149

Bredow, Gerda von, 159

Breidenbach, Johanna, 165

Breton, Stanislas, xi, 22, 30

Breytenbach, Cilliers, 226

Briggman, Anthony, 72, 75–76

Brown, Alexandra R., 4

Bucer, Martin, 144

Bühler, Pierre, 257

Bultmann, Rudolf, xvii, 23, 25, 44, 50–53, 184, 188–90, 192–95, 254, 343, 346, 352

Burgess, John P., 253, 257–58

Burnett, Richard E., 184

Calvin, John, xix, 42, 188, 197, 199–200, 328–34, 336, 367

Caputo, John D., xiv, 59–63, 68, 70, 224, 326–27, 337

Casarella, Peter J., 162

Causse, Jean-Daniel, 309

Chalamet, Christophe, xix, 22, 42, 185, 197

Chenu, Marie-Dominique, 102, 126

Chrysostom, John, xiv–xv, 90–92, 95

Cicero, 9–11, 104, 143, 146

Clavier, Paul, 308

Clement of Alexandria, xiv, 69

Coakley, Sarah, 336

Cohen, Hermann, 297

Colie, Rosalie L., 144–45, 155

Congdon, David W., 361

Conzelmann Hans, 346

Crossan, John Dominic, 28, 35

Cusa, Nicholas of, xvi, 139–40, 145–46, 155–65, 195

D'Angelo, Paolo, 147

Dalferth, Ingolf U., xviii, 291, 295

Dawson, R. Dale, 184–85, 187

Decosimo, David J., 108

DelCogliano, Mark, 87

Dempsey, Michael T., xv, 135

Derrida, Jacques, 23, 25–27, 34, 43–44, 56, 64, 173, 224, 229

Descartes, René, 173, 175

Didymus the Blind, xiv, 69–72, 76–87

Dieter, Theodor, 144

Dionysius the Areopagite (Pseudo-Dionysius), xv, 93, 95–96, 102, 110

Döhling, Jan-Dirk, 301

Doig, James C., 102

Dominic (saint), 125

Döring, Klaus, 140

Dostoevsky, Fyodor, 31

Ducquoc, Christian, 335

Ebeling, Gerhard, 210–12, 254

Eckhart (Meister), 49

Eitel, Adam, xv, 63

Elders, Leo J., 103

Erasmus, xvi, 139–40, 145–58, 161, 164–65, 229

Escher, Maurits C., 149

Euler, Walter Andreas, 155

Eunomius, 87

Felmy, Karl Christian, 244

Feneuil, Anthony, xvi–xvii, xx, 59

Fitzmyer, Jospeh, 314

Forde, Gerhard O., 368

Fossum, Jarl E., 72

Francis of Assisi, 124–26

Freud, Sigmund, 169

Gaunilo of Marmoutiers, 180

Gauthier, René-Antoine, 102–3

Gerber Daniel, 313

Gesché, Adolphe, 79

Glé, Jean-Marie, 310

Gleason, Maud W., 6

Gloege, Gerhard, 257

Gombrich, Ernst H., 149

Goudineau, Hubert, 335

Grandjean, Michel, 60

Grant, Robert, 75

Gregory of Nazianzus, 87, 94–97

Gregory of Nyssa, 87, 285–286

Gregory the Great, 134

Gross, Angelika, 148

Grosseteste, Robert, 365

Gundersheimer, Werner L., 161

Hahn, Ferdinand, 226

Hankey, Wayne J., 103

Härle, Wilfried, 242–44, 252, 257

Haubst, Rudolf, 161

Hay, Andrew R., xvii, 61

Heidegger, Martin, 23–28, 44, 46, 50

Hengel, Martin, 6

Herms, Eilert, 257

Heron, Alasdair, 78

Herrmann, Wilhelm, 327
Hilary of Poitiers, 110, 130
Hoff, Johannes, 164
Hofius, Otfried, 226, 304–5
Holmes, Christopher R. J., 331
Horbury, William, 75
Hughes, Patrick, 149
Huizinga, Johan, 98

Irenaeus (saint), 72, 75–76, 275–76

Jeremias, Joachim, 301
Joachim of Fiore, 60
John of Kyzikos, 94
John Paul II, 60
Jonas, Hans, xix, 308–10, 333
Jordan, Mark D., 102–3, 112
Josephus, Flavius, 7, 9
Jüngel, Eberhard, xix, 42, 187,
    189, 208, 257, 315–27, 333
Justin, Martyr, 7

Kaiser, Walter, 146, 148–50, 152,
    155
Kant, Immanuel, 42, 142, 173,
    175–76
Kantorowicz, Ernst, 29–30
Karlstadt, 144
Käsemann, Ernst, 18, 375–77
Kasper, Walter, 352
Kelsey, David H., 375

Kerr, Nathan R., 375
Kierkegaard, Søren, 28–30, 44, 49,
    243
Klaiber, Walter, 246
Klibansky, Raymond, 144
Korthaus, Michael, 143
Körtner, Ulrich H. J., 240, 242,
    244
Kümmel Werner Georg, 346

Lausberg, Heinrich, 147
Lebeau, Jean, 145
Lebreton, Jules, 72
Lee, Harper, 11
Lefèvre d'Étaples, Jacques, 155
Leo XIII, xv, 103
Leppin, Volker, 155
Lietzmann Hans, 368
Litfin, Duane, 4
Lobsien, Verena, 155
Logan, A. H. B., 75
Lombard, Peter, 101
Longenecker, Bruce W., 15
Louth, Andrew, xiii-xiv, 69, 71,
    89, 366
Luther, Martin, xii, xvi, xix, 22,
    26–27, 42, 50, 139–65, 205,
    211–12, 235, 248, 250–53,
    257, 297–99, 303, 327–28, 332,
    361, 368–71

MacDonald, Scott, 103

Mahlmann, Theodor, 252

Malloch, Archibald E., 145

Mann Phillips, Margaret, 150

Marion, Jean-Luc, xiii, 60–61, 313

Marquard, Odo, 240–41

Martin, Dale B., 29, 38

Martyn, J. Louis, xx, 68, 362, 375–78

Maximus the Confessor, xiv–xv, 89, 92, 94–99, 366

McCormack, Bruce L., 331

McDonald, Suzanne, 365

Meggitt, Justin J., 15

Meier-Oeser, Stephan, 155, 164, 292

Meillassoux, Quentin, 171–73

Melanchthon, 65

Menander of Laodicea, 158

Merk, Otto, 184

Merklein, Helmut, 246

Metzke, Erwin, 155

Miller, Clarence H., 146

Mitchell, Margaret M., 356

Mollat, Michel, 125

Molnar, Paul D., 184

Moltmann, Jürgen, 42, 258–59, 327, 332, 334–35, 363

Montaigne, Michel de, 170–71

Mueller, David L., 184

Müller, Denis, 64

Neiman, Susan, 249

Nero, 19

Neumeyer, Martina, 147, 158

Nietzsche, Friedrich, xii, 37, 43, 45, 65, 150, 208, 218, 222

Nilsson, Martin P., 17

Nygren, Anders, xii

O'Collins, Gerald, 184–85

O'Grady, Paul, 103

O'Rourke Boyle, Marjorie, 154

Origen, xiv, 69–79, 81, 83–84, 86–87, 312, 318

Overbeck, Franz, 177

Ovid, 56

Owen, John, 365

Owens, Joseph, 102

Pascal, Blaise, 170, 358

Paterson, Craig, 104

Pavlovskis, Zoja, 146

Pfnür, Vinzenz, 148

Pinsart, Marie-Geneviève, 308

Pitta, Antonio, 149

Placher, William C., 327

Plass, Ewald M., 250

Plato, 33, 92, 104, 110, 140–42, 144, 153–54, 214, 267–72

Plaxco, Kellen, xiv–xv

Pliny the Younger, 19

Plotinus, 272–75

Plutarch, 149
Pugh, Matthew S., 104

Radde-Gallwitz, Andrew, 75–76, 87
Rahner, Hugo, 98
Rahner, Karl, 321–22
Rebhorn, Wayne A., 146
Richard, Jean, 309–10
Ricoeur, Paul, xviii, 292, 296–97, 299, 304–5
Ritschl, Albrecht, 249, 327
Rock, John P., 129

Sauter, Gerhard, 244–45, 254–55
Schleiermacher, Friedrich D. E., 179, 248–51, 279, 283
Schoedel, William R., 75
Schrage, Wolfgang, 213, 229, 246, 313–15, 337
Segal, Alan F., 72
Socrates, 12, 32, 141, 147, 152–54, 156–57
Souletie, Jean-Louis, 335
Southern, Richard W., 381
Steinberg, Saul, 149
Stoellger, Philipp, xiv, xvii, 60, 236
Stump, Eleonore, 104
Sumner, Darren O., 331
Sylvester, Richard, 146

Tacitus, 6, 19–20
Tanner, Kathryn, xviii
Tertullian, 75, 278
Theissen, Gerd, 15
Theissen, Henning, xviii
Thompson, M. Geraldine, 145
Tietz, Christiane, 243
Tillich, Paul, 45, 243, 251, 254–55
Torrell, Jean-Pierre, 102, 114, 127
Turretini, Francis, 252

Uebinger, Johannes, 159

Valkenberg, G.B.M. Wilhelmus, 112
Van Buren, John E., 27
Van Driel, Edwin Chr., xx, 185, 338, 360
Venning, Ralph, 144
Verweyen, Hansjürgen, 215
Vial, Marc, xix
Volf, Miroslav, 379
Vollenweider, Samuel, 142
Von Lips, Hermann, 141
Von Loewenich, Walter, 328
Von Lüpke, Johannes, 240

Walser, Martin, xviii, 239–40
Walz, Angelus, 101
Webster, John, 253–54
Weinrich, Michael, 253, 257–58

Weisheipl, James A., 114

Weiss, Johannes, 346, 354, 357

Welborn, Larry L., 4, 7, 12, 350

Wendel, François, 328

Wenz, Gunther, 256

Westhelle, Vitor, 2

Wilckens, Ulrich, 346, 349–50

Williams, Rowan, 76

Wittgenstein, Ludwig, 222

Wright, N. T., 184–85

Wüthrich, Matthias, xviii, 185, 248

Zumstein, Jean, 337

Zwingli, Ulrich, 248